Preaching the Gospel of John

Preaching the Gospel of John

Proclaiming the Living Word

Lamar Williamson Jr.

Westminster John Knox Press

LOUISVILLE • LONDON

Unless otherwise indicated, Scripture quotations are from the New Revised Standard Version of the Bible, are copyright © 1989 by the Division of Christian Education of the National Council of the Churches of Christ in the U.S.A., and are used by permission.

Book design by Sharon Adams
Cover design by Kevin Darst & Jennifer K. Cox

First edition
Published by Westminster John Knox Press
Louisville, Kentucky

This book is printed on acid-free paper that meets the American National Standards Institute Z39.48 standard. ♾

PRINTED IN THE UNITED STATES OF AMERICA
04 05 06 07 08 09 10 11 12 13 14 – 10 9 8 7 6 5 4 3 2 1

Library of Congress Cataloging-in-Publication Data

Williamson, Lamar.
   Preaching the Gospel of John : proclaiming the living Word / Lamar Williamson, Jr.– 1st ed.
      p. cm.
   Includes bibliographical references.
   ISBN 0-664-22533-0 (alk. paper)
   1. Bible. N.T. John–Homiletical use.   2. Bible. N.T. John– Study and teaching.   I. Title.

BS2615.5.W54 2004
226.5'06–dc22
                                                          2003064526

*To all who are
or who will become
beloved disciples of Jesus Christ*

CONTENTS

Introduction

The Light of which the Fourth Gospel speaks has been shining in the darkness for two millennia. During these millennia innumerable commentaries upon this Gospel have been written and read. This is not because the nature of the Light changes, but because the world in which it shines is different in each time and place. The making of many books about Jesus and the Gospels goes on unabated, but no commentary has ever exhausted the meaning of the Gospel according to John. The goal of this one is primarily to help pastors and teachers to interpret the Gospel of John faithfully and so to be light-bearers in their own time and place.

Light itself is not something seen; it is something by which one sees. The interpreter's work is to enable others to see what is in the Gospel of John. The Fourth Gospel itself is given to enable the reader to see Jesus—and Jesus, the true Light, is given so that all may see God. Why read, study, preach, or teach the Gospel of John?

Some of the most memorable and important words in the Christian faith are found in the Fourth Gospel:

> God so loved the world that he gave his only Son, so that everyone who believes in him may not perish but may have eternal life. (3:16)

> If you continue in my word, you are truly my disciples; and you will know the truth, and the truth will make you free. (8:31–32)

> I am the way, and the truth, and the life. No one comes to the Father except through me. (14:6)

> This is my commandment, that you love one another as I have loved you. No one has greater love than this, to lay down one's life for one's friends. You are my friends if you do what I command you. (15:12–14)

Seekers, and anyone who wishes to guide seekers, may find an introduction to Jesus himself through John's stories of his encounters with other seekers: a highly respected religious leader, a social outcast, a royal official, a discouraged paralytic, hostile authorities and audiences, a hungry crowd, a woman caught in adultery, a blind beggar, and a grieving family. Followers of Jesus, and would-be followers, may discover themselves in Jesus' dealing with disciples who were afraid, or unfaithful, or weak, or skeptical. Many readers of different kinds will find in John words they can live by, words about the Word that have still their ancient power.

The Fourth Gospel is famous for its difference from the other three Gospels. For those who know about Jesus through the action-packed narratives of the Synoptic Gospels, John presents a more leisurely, reflective selection of signs and discourses in which the voice of Jesus, risen and alive, speaks through the words of the evangelist. In the Synoptics, Jesus speaks primarily about the kingdom of God and gives instruction about how to enter and live in it. In John, Jesus speaks primarily about himself, about God the Father, and about how disciples can, through believing and loving, grow into an intimate relationship with God and one another that he calls eternal life. It is a perspective on Jesus that offers living water for the aridity of the institutional church and bread for the hungry hearts of individual disciples.

For whom is this commentary intended? It is written for preachers and teachers. It offers exegetical notes in the part labeled "Exploring the text," while the part labeled "Preaching and teaching the Word" offers points of contact with life today that may stimulate reflection in preparing a sermon or lesson plan. The writer has been sensitive to texts that figure prominently in church lectionaries, and comments note connections with the liturgical year. All lectionary references, unless otherwise noted, are to the Common Lectionary (Revised) as it appears in the *Book of Common Worship* of the Presbyterian Church (U.S.A.) and the Cumberland Presbyterian Church.[1]

Of equal importance are the teachers, ordained or unordained, who are responsible for church school classes, women's circles, men's Bible study groups, youth fellowships, and any other context in which the Bible is studied. Literary, historical, and theological issues raised by the Fourth Gospel are highlighted for focus in such studies. The writer has attempted to avoid academic jargon and scholarly footnotes without "dumbing down" the explanation of the text. Greek terms are used sparingly in connection with their English equivalents. A select bibliography is appended for users who may wish to pursue issues in greater depth.

Individual readers of John, though not the primary target audience, may also find this book helpful as they engage the Fourth Gospel for their own spiritual nurture or intellectual satisfaction. Those who are perplexed by the seeming paradoxes of this Gospel–its love command and its bitter polemic, its inclusiveness and its exclusiveness–will find here a sensitivity to these issues. The writer's reflections on his own struggle with them appear in an afterword.

A glossary of terms and concepts central to the Gospel appears at the back of this book. In the text, such a word is printed in boldface type when it first appears in a section when reference to the glossary may be helpful. Following the glossary is a select bibliography of major commentaries referred to in notes.

Scripture references are to the New Revised Standard Version (NRSV), unless otherwise noted. Other English versions are referred to by the following abbreviation: Authorized (King James) Version (AV), New American Bible (NAB), New English Bible (NEB), New International Version (NIV), New Jerusalem Bible (NJB), Revised English Bible (REB), Revised Standard Version (RSV), and Today's English Version (Good News Bible) (TEV).

The primary guideline for this commentary is the structure and purpose of the Gospel itself. After the prologue, the notes are organized in three main parts. Part one, "Meeting the Living Word," considers Jesus' encounters with all sorts of people (John 1–12). Part two, "Words to Live by," refers to Jesus' Last Supper and farewell discourse with his disciples (John 13–17). Part three, "The Word That Does Not Die," follows Jesus from his betrayal and arrest through his death, resurrection, and post-resurrection appearances (John 18–21).

The urge to acknowledge help I have received in writing this book has made me realize that my entire life as teacher, preacher, and writer has been undergirded by a gracious, interdependent network of collegial support. My debt at the close of the present task is too great to enumerate. I cannot let the manuscript go, however, without mentioning the role of two individuals: Professor Patrick D. Miller Jr., without whose encouragement the project would have been abandoned early on, and my life partner, Ruthmary Bliss Williamson, without whose steadfast work as motivator, editor, proofreader, critic, and companion, the book could not have been completed.

The Prologue

The good news with which the Fourth Gospel begins is that humans are neither first in the world nor alone in the world. The **Word** is first, and God has come to us.

The prologue to the Fourth Gospel bears witness to what Jesus Christ meant to a group of people who had come to know him near the end of the first century C.E. Those early Christians saw in Jesus the uncreated light of God, a light that they knew as the Word. Getting to know him was like seeing the dawn break over all creation and in their life as a community. It was like being invaded by grace and truth and life. It was like coming to know God. They set down these words about the Word, to the end that the Word might also become flesh in the lives of those who read this Gospel.

Exploring the text

While most of the Fourth Gospel consists of narrative and discourse, the eighteen verses of its prologue are written in exalted, poetic prose. The poetic style that is the language of revelatory proclamation predominates. Verses 6–8 and 15, however, contain a straightforward prose narrative about the witness to Jesus by a man named John. If the rest of the prologue were removed, these verses about John would lead directly in to 1:19 and would constitute a beginning for the Fourth Gospel like that of Mark.

The prologue lifts readers above history and into mystery, the mystery of God's eternity, glory, inner nature, and saving purpose. It prepares readers to enter the narrative of Jesus' life with openness to an invasion from above. The structure of the prologue mirrors this invasion:

1–5   The Word in the beginning with God
6–9   The light coming into the world
10–13   Responses to the life of the Word in the world
14–18   The glory of God in the Word made flesh

1

This structure suggests a movement forward through time, but only two moments are clearly identified: the existence of the Word in the beginning with God, and the embodiment of the Word among his own people in the world. **Above/below** movement is central to this Gospel. The more significant movement here is downward from above, a movement that is reflected repeatedly in the Gospel and echoed by a return from below to above.[1] The life of the Word-made-flesh is lived out on the plane of history, but it is an event in eternity. At critical moments—especially Jesus' death and resurrection, referred to in this Gospel as "the hour"—the action transcends all time, for in this event time is invaded by eternity.

The main purpose of the prologue is to say who Jesus is. Its correlative purpose is to announce who readers may become through believing in him.

THE WORD IN THE BEGINNING WITH GOD (1:1–5)

The first five verses of the Gospel of John point to a mystery beyond all words. This evangelist speaks in deceptively simple language, using terms that have become basic for Christian theology. Five of them appear in these first five verses: Word, God, life, light, and darkness.

"Word" (*logos*) is almost as hard to define as is the mystery to which it points. Although it expresses a fundamental element in John's understanding of Jesus Christ, *logos* does not appear again in the Gospel of John in its weighty, theological sense. The meaning of the other four terms can best be understood by noting how they are used in the remainder of the Fourth Gospel, but their interplay is important in this hymn that sings of eternal realities.

God was in the beginning (1:1–2), created all that is through the Word that enlightens all human beings (1:3–4), sent John the witness (1:6–7), gives birth to children, namely to all who receive and believe the Word (1:12–13), and is the Father of Jesus Christ, who, in a unique way, is God's only Son (1:14, 18). The affirmation about God that matters most to the fourth evangelist is the last. Jesus' many references to God as **Father** are a key component in the evangelist's insistence on the unique relationship between Jesus and God. In John 1:1–5 "God" refers to the creator who is the source of all that exists and the origin of all life, distant from everything except the Word, but in the Gospel as a whole God is the Father who has drawn near to us in Jesus Christ and seeks a warm, intimate relationship with all who will receive, believe, and abide in him (1:12–13).

"Life" and "light," introduced in 1:3b–4, are major themes in John's account of Jesus from beginning to end. Each is used often, and both belong to the realm of God.

"Life" (*zoe*) is introduced in the prologue, stated as the goal of the Gospel at the end, and defined in the story of Jesus that lies between.

"Light" is closely linked to life and is diametrically opposed to darkness in the Fourth Gospel. These three themes are introduced in relationship to the Word in 1:4–5.

The contrast between life and light on the one hand and darkness on the other alerts readers to the dualistic worldview of this evangelist. This worldview also appears in the contrasts between above and below, truth and falsehood, life and death. Above is the realm of God, truth, life, and light, a light that is analogous to the visible manifestation of the divine presence in the Hebrew Bible or to the brightness of ultimate reality in Plato's myth of the cave.

A stylistic element typical of the Fourth Gospel appears in verse 5. The text says that the darkness did not comprehend (AV, NASB), understand (NIV) or overcome (RSV, NRSV, NAB), or master (NEB) the light. The Greek verb *katelabon* can mean either "grasp" or "overcome," so any of these translations is acceptable. This is the first example of double entendre in the Gospel of John, a form of wordplay that the fourth evangelist uses often. This verse affirms that the darkness did not comprehend the light and also that the darkness did not overcome it.

THE LIGHT COMING INTO THE WORLD (1:6–9)

These verses move from the realm of ultimate reality before all creation into the world of time, space, and human existence. The abstract ideas of verses 1–5 give way to a common noun (man) and to a proper name (John).

John is "a man sent from God" (v. 6). He is like Jesus, who often refers to himself as the one whom God has sent and to God as the sender.[2] Unlike the Synoptics, the Fourth Gospel does not call John "the baptizer," or a "messenger," nor does it describe him as a prophet.[3] Here, instead, John is a witness. God sent him "as a witness" to testify to the light when it came into the world. The Fourth Gospel prefers the language of witness (seeing and saying what one has seen) to that of prophecy (speaking for God). The verb to bear witness or to testify (*martyreo, martyroumai* from which "martyr" is derived) appears only twice in the Synoptic Gospels, but thirty-three times in John. Bearing witness is a major Johannine theme.

The argumentative tone of verse 8—with its insistence that the role of the witness is subordinate to that of the true light, repeated in 1:15 and driven home by John's own last words in 3:30–has led many scholars to believe that the fourth evangelist was addressing, among others, a sect of the followers of John the Baptist, seeking to win them to faith in Jesus. (See comments on 3:26–30 and 4:1–2, below.) These verses in the prologue insist that John is not the light but is a witness to it.

Witnesses say what they have seen and heard or attest to the truth of another's testimony. John's role is to recognize the true light when it appears, and to call attention to it so that others may recognize it and believe–that is, recognize, trust in, and commit themselves to the light. Repetition of the expression "Come and see" emphasizes the prominent Johannine theme of witness.

John appears once more in the prologue (1:15), prominently in 1:19–36, and once more in 3:22–30, after which he disappears from the stage of the Fourth Gospel. His witness, however, does not disappear. It continues to figure in Jesus' encounters with his adversaries (5:33–36) and in the coming to faith of many (10:40–42).

Verse 9 is transitional. It contrasts what is said about John, the witness, in verses 6–8 with what is said about the true light in verses 9–18.

Editors and translators of the Greek text differ in how the participial phrase "coming into the world" is related to the rest of the sentence. It may either mean that "The true light, which enlightens everyone, was coming into the world" (NRSV, text) or "He was the true light that enlightens everyone coming [=who comes] into the world" (NRSV, note b). Both possibilities affirm that the light enlightens every human being.

RESPONSES TO THE LIFE OF THE WORD
IN THE WORLD (1:10–13)

This paragraph shifts attention to two human reactions to the coming of the light. On the one hand, the world did not know him (the Word, v. 10), and his own people did not accept him (v. 11). On the other, some received him, believed in his name, and were empowered to become children of God (v. 12). The dichotomy of light and darkness, announced with cosmic dualism in verse 5, is elaborated on the level of history in verses 10–13. Verses 10–11 continue the theme of darkness, verses 12–13 the theme of light. The tension between the universality of the light (vv. 4b, 7, 9) and the duality of light and darkness (vv. 5, 10–13) pervades the entire Gospel.

All the verbs in 1:10–13 are in the past tense, yet they speak of present reality. They say that there is a blindness in the world that does not know the light when it comes.

Verse 10 alerts the reader to the varied ways in which **"world"** (*kosmos*) is used in the Fourth Gospel. It sometimes designates the inhabited world, the theater of human history (1:10a); sometimes, as a synonym for "all that is," it refers to the entire created order, to all that came into being (1:10b); and sometimes it means the realm of unbelief, those who fail to recognize Jesus Christ and therefore turn away from his light (1:10c). The last usage of "world" is introduced here for the first time.[4] The term is used more than seventy-five times in the Fourth Gospel, far more often than in all the Synoptic Gospels and all the epistles of Paul combined. It is a key term in Johannine theology, whose specific meaning can be determined only in context, as its use in three senses in 1:10 exemplifies. Interpreters should exercise discernment to avoid misunderstanding.

Verses 11 and 13b warn that it takes more than human birth to become a child of God. This warning, however, is accompanied by a marvelous promise to all who believe that they have been given "power to become children of God" (1:12) and have been born of God (1:13).

"Believe" is one of the major themes of the Fourth Gospel. For the fourth evangelist, faith is not something one has; it is something one does, closely related to doing the truth (3:21). "Believe" has a considerable semantic range: believing statements about Jesus (11:27; 20:31); acknowledging the truth of Jesus' words (2:22; 4:41; 5:46–47); a disposition of trust in Jesus and his words (6:68–69); action based on such trust (4:50; 14:12); seeing and knowing who Jesus really is (4:42; 9:38); and personal commitment to him in love and adoration, obedience and service (20:28–29).

A series of vignettes shows that faith, like birth, is a process of growing insight (for example, the Samaritan woman, 4:1–42; the royal official, 4:46–54; the beggar blind from birth, 9:1–41), crowned by the ringing affirmation of faith by Thomas with which the reader is invited to identify (20:28–29). Receiving Jesus usually occurs like the breaking of dawn in the course of a personal encounter with him. Nurtured by obedient love and service (13:1–17, 34; 14:15–17), believing issues in abiding in Christ and fruitful, joyful living (15:1–17). The purpose of this Gospel is to lead readers to believe the Word, to come to the light, and by believing to become children of God (1:12; 20:31).

THE GLORY OF GOD
IN THE WORD MADE FLESH (1:14–18)

These verses contain the revelation toward which the prologue has been building. It begins with the theologically packed affirmation of 1:14. Three key terms of Johannine theology appear here: flesh, glory, and truth.

"Flesh" (as in Paul and Platonism) usually stands for the opposite of spirit. It has just appeared in this sense in the expression "the will of the flesh" (1:13) and will appear again in opposition to the spirit in 3:6 and 6:63. It is this pejorative understanding of flesh, as much as the suggestion of cannibalism, that renders Jesus' affirmations about eating his flesh in John 6:51–56 so offensive. To affirm that the Word became flesh is a shocking contradiction of the common notion that God is pure spirit and that flesh is impure. It proclaims as fundamental to the gospel an impossible possibility: the eternal Spirit became mortal flesh at a particular time and place in human history. For John the incarnation is an incredible gift that belongs to the mystery of God's love.

"Glory" suggests "the dazzling light of the Lord's presence." In John 1:14, however, God's glory is seen not as a transcendent vision but in human flesh as the reflection of a father's character in an only son. In the first of Jesus' signs (2:11) the father's character is seen in the son's unlimited mastery of matter used in an act of unobtrusive service.

The last words in John 1:14, "grace and truth," are repeated when the identity of the incarnate Word is finally named in 1:17b. Grace also appears in 1:16 to describe the gift from God's fullness that believers in Jesus Christ have received, then is not used again in the Fourth Gospel. Grace is contrasted with law (1:17a), but in the Gospel of John (unlike Paul) grace takes second place to truth. **"Truth"** is identified with the reality of God, revealed in Jesus Christ.

In some cases truth simply denotes a statement that is accurate or that would hold up in court, but in key texts in John truth refers to ultimate reality in personal terms.[5] The repeated reference to truth in the prologue (1:14, 17b) alerts reader to the personal nature of truth and its close connection with Jesus Christ.

The identity of the one in whom the Word became flesh remains to be revealed. The suspense is sustained by insertion of another word from the herald in which John the witness testifies that the coming one is greater than he is (1:15). Then, speaking for an entire community that knows the Word, the prologue exults: "From his fullness we have all received, grace upon grace" (1:16). This one is greater than John and greater than Moses and the law (1:17a). His name is Jesus Christ (1:17). He has made God known!

The affirmation that "no one has ever seen God" (1:18a) refers to the darkness in which the light shines (1:5) and introduces a theme, seeing, that plays a prominent role in the entire Gospel. In variant forms of the Greek text, "God the only Son" (1:18b) combines two key terms (*theos,* God, and *huios,* son) and seeks by that combination to preserve the rich sense of *monogenes* (one-of-a-kind) which the King James Version expressed by "the only begotten Son." The evangelist's awestruck affirmation here is echoed by Thomas's climactic declaration of faith, "My Lord and my God!" in John 20:28. Both express the wonder of those who, in meeting Jesus Christ, found that he "exegeted" (*exegesato*)–explained, made plain–what had not been clear before. "God the only Son . . . has made [God] known" (1:18).

Preaching and teaching the Word

The prologue to the Fourth Gospel challenges preachers and teachers because it is a pin-cushion of words that are much spoken and little understood. The interpreter must work hard to understand, then speak simply and avoid trying to appear erudite. One must not allow fascination with its language to distract attention from the basic human hunger to which this passage speaks: the hunger to know God. The text contains rich food for the hungry. Its power and beauty are best realized by reading it whole, but in order to be digested it must be chewed a little at a time.

1. In Advent and at Christmas time. The prologue of John is the Gospel reading for Christmas Day and the Second Sunday after Christmas for all three years in the Roman Catholic and Revised Common Lectionaries (First instead of Second Sunday after Christmas in the Episcopal lectionary). In addition, 1:6–8, 19–28 (verses dealing with John the witness) are appointed for the Third Sunday in Advent, year B.

The verses about John the witness are of continuing significance to interpreters who may read this note. They underscore the important but subordinate role of a witness to Jesus Christ. John's witness in the prologue (1:6–8, 15) and in 1:19–28 and 3:30 is a healthy antidote to an interpreter's sense of self-importance. The ease and frequency with which cults spring up around gifted preachers and teachers reflects a common tendency to confuse witnesses with the light itself. It is, of course, easier to applaud the witness than to walk in the light.

John 1:1–18 is particularly significant at Christmas time, when Christians celebrate the Feast of the Nativity and read the infancy narratives of Matthew and Luke. They remember and relive God's coming into human history through the conception and birth of a baby. The Fourth Gospel has no birth narrative, but its prologue is appointed to be read on Christmas Day because it announces the mystery of the incarnation. Nativity says what happened; incarnation says what it means.

Preachers and teachers should read the whole passage aloud to themselves several times in order to offer to God a fit instrument to lead in worship through reading to attentive hearers this hymn to the Logos. Since the text recurs every Christmas Day, the sermon might focus on just one of the key terms in the text, taking up a different one each Christmas in a cycle of five or six years.

2. A series of lessons or sermons. The four Sundays in Advent are also a good time (but not the only good time) to preach a series of sermons on the key terms in John 1:1–18: God the Father, Word, life, light, world, believe, glory, grace, and truth. These words, discussed in context in the notes above, are treated more fully in the glossary. Preachers can decide which ones to proclaim in a given year and articulate the focus of each sermon, perhaps in a title. For instance, "In the beginning . . . God" (John 1:1//Gen. 1:1 and the God-shaped hole in our hearts); "Get a life" (John 1:3–4, "All that came to be was alive with his life" [NEB and REB note], and in Christ that life is eternal); "Living in the light" (1:5, 9, 14, 18 and related texts in John and 1 John on coming to the light, seeing life clearly, and walking in the light); and "The Word that became flesh" (John 1:14, ultimate reality revealed in speaking and hearing, in Jesus Christ, and in us); or "Glory, grace, and truth" (alternate approach to 1:14, glory instead of glitter at Christmas, and God's grace in a person who is truth itself in human form). The goal of such a series of sermons is to engage in sustained contemplation of the mystery of the Word that transcends words, to the end that believers may find their lives increasingly transformed, sustained, and directed by the Spirit of the living Christ. A similar series of Bible studies would consist of word studies, inviting participants to look up many of the references throughout the Fourth Gospel given in parentheses in the exegetical notes above and in the glossary, guided by a teacher who has already thought a lot about them. The goal of such a series would be an enriched theological understanding of Jesus Christ.

3. A hymn sing or special choir event. Some churches have a service of lessons and carols during Advent. Benjamin Britten's *Ceremony of Carols,* broadcast every Christmas Eve from Kings College Chapel, Cambridge, England, is a pattern that can readily be adapted by interspersing the reading of the prologue to the Gospel of John with appropriate hymns and carols. Many of these include lines based on the prologue: "Veiled in flesh the Godhead see; hail the incarnate Deity, pleased in flesh with us to dwell . . . Light and life to all he brings" ("Hark! the Herald Angels Sing," stanzas 2 and 3); "Word of the Father, now in flesh appearing!" ("O Come, All Ye Faithful," stanza 2); "He came down to earth from heaven who is God and Lord of all" ("Once in Royal David's City," stanza 2); "Son of God, love's pure light radiant beams from thy holy face, with the dawn of redeeming grace" ("Silent Night, Holy Night," stanza 3); "Break forth, O beauteous heavenly light" (First line, hymn of this name). The preacher and choir director can collaborate in matching appropriate music to the biblical text and in deciding what might be sung by the entire congregation and what by the choir. A liturgist who can read clearly and with understanding is essential to the achievement of worship through this service.

"O Word of God Incarnate," "O Gladsome Light," and other hymns down through the ages have expressed the mystery of the Word made flesh. The preacher or teacher can draw effectively on them in seeking to communicate the message of John's prologue.

4. For individual devotional use. The prologue, like the entire Gospel, is significant for persons who yearn to know God or to experience God's presence more often and more deeply. We do not need to search for God but only to recognize the one in whom God came to live among us and whose Spirit remains in us. Although that recognition may begin with a moment of insight, it can be sustained and deepened by intentional dialogue with Jesus. Silent meditation on the prologue is a good way to sustain that dialogue, reading a few verses at a time, reflecting on key words, responding to the Word by writing a few words in a journal. This discipline can be continued by reading on in the Fourth Gospel, looking for the grace of God in Jesus' encounters with all kinds of people and listening for the truth of God in Jesus' discourses.

The prologue also invites readers to watch for the light that enlightens everyone (1:9) in the lives of all whom they meet, recognizing Christ in sometimes unexpected places. Jesus promised to live in his disciples (14:15–17, 23), which means that the Word can in some measure become flesh in our lives, too (15:4–5, 7). Such is the fruit of a sustained, intentional dialogue with Jesus in one's life.

PART ONE

Meeting the Living Word
1:19–12:50

First Witness, First Disciples, First Encounters

John 1:19–3:36

"A man whose name was John" (1:6) initiates the action in the Fourth Gospel and, having fulfilled his role, disappears from its pages at the end of chapter 3. These three chapters introduce a number of elements that characterize this Gospel. The notes that follow treat these chapters as a block of material dealing with "firsts": the first witness, John the Baptist (1:19–34); the first disciples, Andrew, Peter, Philip, and Nathanael (1:35–51); the first sign, water into wine (2:1–12); the first hostile confrontation, Jesus and the temple authorities (2:13–22); then, after a brief transition (2:23–25), the first open-ended encounter (Jesus and Nicodemus, 3:1–21) and the first summary (Jesus and John, 3:22–36).

THE FIRST WITNESS: JOHN THE BAPTIST (1:19–34)

The events reported in chapter 1 take place on four successive days (1:19, 29, 35, 43) in Bethany on the east side of the Jordan, where John was baptizing (1:28). The exact location cannot be determined, since there are no other certain references to it in the Bible or elsewhere, but it is not to be confused with the Bethany, just across the Mount of Olives from Jerusalem, where Lazarus, Martha, and Mary lived (11:1–12:8). John is never called "the Baptist" in the Fourth Gospel, since the evangelist is less interested in the baptizing he does than in the witness he bears.

Exploring the text

John the witness is the focus of attention on the first day (1:19–28), although he tries to shift the focus away from himself. "The Jews" have sent priests and Levites from Jerusalem to ask John who he is and what he is doing. This is the first appearance of the expression "the Jews," which plays an important role in the Fourth Gospel.[1] Its meaning in this text is clear: these are the religious authorities in Jerusalem, the guardians of orthodoxy and of public order. They ask, "Who are you?" John's answer,

13

"I am not the Messiah," presumes that they want to know whether or not he claims to be the Messiah. No overt hostility is expressed here, but the emphatic quality in John's reply is significant. So is the legal terminology in John's answer to their follow-up questions: testimony (*martyria,* v. 19), confess (v. 20), interrogate (vv. 21, 25). This language foreshadows Jesus' formal trial before the high priest in chapter 18.

The follow-up questions (v. 21) concern two other figures associated with end-time expectations in sectarian Judaism of the time: Elijah (Mal. 4:5) and a prophet like Moses (Deut. 18:15–18). The eschatological expectations of the Essene community at Khirbet Qumran, located on the west side of the Dead Sea not far from where John was baptizing on the east bank of the Jordan, included a prophet, a priestly messiah, and a royal messiah. Perhaps the priests and Levites wished to know whether or not John was part of this troublesome sect. In any case, the questions raised by the Jerusalem emissaries are expressions of suspicious self-interest, a darkness that is latent in all religious movements and institutions. John's "voice crying in the wilderness" (1:23) is an expression of the light that is dawning on the plane of human events.

In the second part of John's dialogue with investigators from Jerusalem (1:24–28), the Pharisees ask why he is baptizing if he is not any of the prominent figures associated with Israel's hope for the coming kingdom of God. Who or what gives John the right to baptize?[2] In his answer, John turns attention from himself to the one to whom he will bear witness, but whom he does not yet name. John baptizes with water, but he announces another who is standing among them, unrecognized and unknown. Although this one is coming after John, his greatness so far exceeds John's that the witness is not even worthy to perform the duty of a slave; that is, to untie the thong of his sandal.

On the second day (1:29–34), John does name the greater one who is coming, though he is not yet present. His name is Jesus, and his titles are "Lamb of God," because of what he does, and "Son of God," because of who he is. John alone is on stage, but through his eyes his hearers see Jesus, coming toward John, and so do readers then and now.

The affirmation of the priority and preexistence of Jesus in 1:30 echoes 1:15 and anticipates 8:58 (see comment there). The christological title Lamb of God appears only twice in the New Testament, both times in this passage (1:29 and 36).[3] "Lamb of God" also occurs in the Agnus Dei of Christian liturgy. Overfamiliarity has for many readers dulled the wonder and mystery of recognizing in Jesus the one who is before all others and the Lamb of God who takes away the sin of the world. This title almost surely alludes to both the Passover lamb and the Suffering Servant of Isaiah 53:7 and may on the lips of John the Baptist be a kingly title, as in Jewish apocalyptic writings and the book of Revelation.[4] It is hard to grasp any of these allusions apart from early Christian understandings of the death of Jesus that blended various Old Testament images.

For John the witness, that recognition of Jesus was by no means a matter of course. Twice he affirms, "I myself [even I] did not know him" (vv. 31, 33), any more than you do (v. 26). Each of these statements is followed by a "but" and a statement about revelation. In the first of these statements John gives a delayed answer to the Pharisees' question about why he was baptizing and adds that he saw "the Spirit descending from heaven like a dove, and it remained on him." In the Fourth Gospel it is John the witness who alone sees the descent of the dove. John's statements make it clear that God gave the sign and revealed its meaning. No one can know who Jesus is, not even John the witness, unless the Holy Spirit of God reveals his identity. John can only say what he has seen, and bear witness ("testify") to what God has told him the sign means: that Jesus is the Lamb of God who takes away the sin of the world (1:29), who will baptize with the Holy Spirit (1:33), and who is the Son of God (1:34).

Preaching and teaching the Word

1. Suspense. The power of suspense is a significant element in the first chapter of John. Its significance for preachers lies more in the cultivation of a preaching style than in the preparation of a particular sermon. In 1:19–34, as in the prologue, the Gospel writer at first withholds the name of Jesus (until 1:29), just as he reveals the purpose of the entire work only at or near the end of the Gospel (20:31). Of course, he is not coy about who Jesus is. In contrast to the Gospel of Mark, in which Jesus never attributes to himself any messianic title, the Fourth Gospel has already announced to readers by the middle of the first chapter that Jesus is Word of God, Lamb of God, and Son of God. Nevertheless, this Gospel demonstrates suspense and—more than the others—expresses the mystery of Christ's person. The ideas people remember are the things they say to themselves. While careful exposition and earnest proclamation are useful, recognition of Jesus Christ rests on cumulative evidence, personal encounter, and the inner testimony of the Holy Spirit. The task of the preacher or teacher as a good witness is to say what he or she has seen and leave room for the Holy Spirit to say some things in the hearts of hearers.

2. Self-image. A sermon on John the Baptist's self-understanding as revealed in John 1:19–34 and 3:25–30 might be helpful to those who are concerned about their self-image. John knows who he is (1:23). He preaches with bold assurance and treats the messengers of the religious authorities in Jerusalem rather brusquely, though correctly. But he recognizes that he is playing second fiddle to Jesus, a part that he plays gladly and well. The only description John would accept for himself was "a voice." So faithfully did he fulfill his calling that when, two millennia later, people around the world hear the words, "Prepare the way of the Lord,"[5] the voice they hear is that of John the Baptist. A healthy self-image is one that evaluates self with reference to and with the eyes of Jesus Christ.

3. The Lamb of God. When the lectionary Gospel reading is John 1:29–42 (Second Sunday, Ordinary Time, year A), preachers might focus on verses 29 and 33, in which John assigns to Jesus the title "Lamb of God." The phrase is best known through its liturgical setting in the Agnus Dei ("O Lamb of God that takest away the sins of the world, have mercy upon us; . . . grant us thy peace") and in the repeated line of the familiar hymn "Just As I Am": "O Lamb of God, I come." An evangelistic sermon would appeal for faith in Jesus' death for our sins and commitment of our life to him. A lesson, taught by a church musician, could deal with the place of the Agnus Dei in Christian worship through the centuries and use it in worship during the lesson. Both would point to Old Testament roots of the image of the lamb and to texts in John that testify to the love of God shown in the death of Jesus on the cross (3:14–16) as well as his victory over sin (12:31–33; 19:30) and death (chap. 20).

THE FIRST DISCIPLES: ANDREW, PETER, PHILIP, AND NATHANAEL (1:35–51)

How do people come to know Jesus?

This question underlies the two paragraphs on Jesus' first disciples (1:35–42, 43–51). It also lies behind the preceding paragraphs about John the Baptist, even though the presenting question there was "Who is John?" and in the present passage is "Who is Jesus?"

Exploring the text

Verse 35 shifts the action from John and his followers to Jesus and his first disciples. The word disciple, or learner, presupposes a teacher or master with whom the disciple enjoys a relationship of respect, loyalty, and emulation. Jesus' disciples share center stage with him through chapter 12; his instructions to and prayer for his disciples occupy the bulk of chapters 13–17.

Andrew, an Unnamed Disciple, and Simon Peter (1:35–42)

Jesus' first disciples came from among the disciples of John the Baptist, who directs them to Jesus. This short scene portrays three ways of getting to know Jesus: by hearing the testimony of a preacher and acting on it, by a personal encounter with Jesus, and through being introduced by a family member.

In verses 35–37, John bears witness to who Jesus is and directs the attention of his hearers to him ("Look, here is the Lamb of God!"). John's witness is effective: two of his disciples leave him to become disciples of Jesus. Then (1:38–39) Jesus takes the initiative to make contact with Andrew and another of John's disciples by asking what they are looking for. In answer to their question, "Where are you staying?" he invites them, "Come and see," a theme which is repeated in the following scene and later by a woman in Samaria (4:29). Next (1:40–42) Andrew brings his brother, Simon, to meet Jesus.

The naming of Peter occurs earlier here than in the other Gospels, and in such a way as to underscore Jesus' clairvoyance. Jesus knows his birth name without having been introduced: "You are Simon, son of John." He also sees what Simon will become and gives him a new name, Cephas, an Aramaic word that the evangelist translates into Greek as Peter—"Rock" in English. In this Gospel, however, Peter is not the first disciple. Andrew and an unnamed disciple precede him. This anonymous disciple has been variously identified as the "other disciple" of 18:15–16; the "disciple whom Jesus loved" (13:23; 19:26; 20:2–4, 8; 21:7, 20), the evangelist himself, or all of the above rolled into one as long tradition would have it. The identity of this disciple is one of the Fourth Gospel's many historical riddles, but the important point for the evangelist is Andrew's conviction that he and his companion have found the Messiah, God's anointed one.

The verb "found" suggests that Andrew and his brother, Simon, along with many others have been looking for the appearance of the Messiah promised to Israel. The exact nature and pervasiveness of messianic expectation among Jews in the time of Jesus is a subject of debate among scholars. This expectation took revolutionary shape in two Jewish revolts within a century of the death of Jesus, and it is likely that many people in Jesus' time wondered whether prominent figures like John the Baptist and Jesus might be Messiah.

Messianic expectation was definitely important to the evangelist, who alone among the writers of the New Testament retains and transliterates the Hebrew or Aramaic term, *messias* (here and at 4:25), before giving its Greek equivalent, *christos*. He devotes the first scene in his story of Jesus to John's disclaimer of this title and the implicit suggestion—now made explicit—that the title belongs rightly to Jesus.

The Fourth Gospel presupposes several dimensions of the messianic expectations current in the Judaism of its time and emphasizes one of them: that Messiah would be the king of Israel (1:49; 12:13–15; 18:33, 37; 19:3, 14, 19). The idea that he would free Israel from the yoke of Rome and inaugurate the kingdom of God on earth is set aside, however (6:15; 18:36), and replaced by the understanding of Messiah as Son of God (1:49; 20:31), revealer of the truth of God (18:37), and the one in whom God draws near to humankind and humankind to God (1:14, 17–18; 14:7, 9; 15:5, 9–10; 17:21). When Jesus asks the first two disciples, "What are you looking for?" he asks them to articulate their own expectations regarding Messiah. When Andrew says, "We have found the Messiah," he uses a term that expresses his highest religious hopes. Something about this man leads Andrew to sense that in Jesus he has found what he is looking for. Only further contact with Jesus will clarify precisely who it is that he has found, but already he knows that in Jesus he has met God's Anointed, and he wants to share this discovery with those close to him.

Philip and Nathanael (1:43–51)

At verse 43 Jesus for the first time in this Gospel takes the initiative to call a disciple. The action is reported very briefly: "[Jesus] found Philip and said to him, 'Follow me.'" The evangelist brackets the call by a report of Jesus' decision to go to Galilee (1:43a) and an explanation that Philip's hometown (as well as that of Andrew and Peter) was Bethsaida, a small, obscure fishing village in Galilee (1:44). When these three decide to follow Jesus, they begin a journey that has put their town on the map and has made their names known throughout the world.

Although he is mentioned in the Synoptic Gospels only in lists of the twelve apostles, Philip stands out in the Gospel of John. Not only is he the first disciple whom Jesus calls and the one who brings Nathanael to Jesus (1:45–46); Jesus turns to Philip with the problem of how to feed a large crowd (6:5–7), Greeks who want to see Jesus come to Philip (12:20–22), and at the Last Supper Philip is the one who says to Jesus, "Show us the Father" (14:8–9), setting the stage for one of Jesus' major discourses. He is not to be confused, however, with Philip the evangelist, who appears frequently in the canonical Acts of the Apostles (Acts 6:5; 8:4–13, 26–40; 21:8).

In verses 45–51 the narrative continues the theme of finding: Philip finds Nathanael (1:45a) and says, with an excitement the reader can appropriately imagine, "We have found him" (1:45b). By referring to Jesus as the one "about whom Moses in the law and also the prophets wrote," Philip affirms that he is the one to whom all the Scriptures bear witness. No specific reference is given or intended, but Philip invites Nathanael to find in Jesus the fulfillment of God's promises and purpose. By speaking of Jesus as "son of Joseph from Nazareth" Philip is identifying Jesus by giving his father's name and place of origin. He commends Jesus to Nathanael as a fellow Galilean. The expression "son of Joseph" underscores the humanity of Jesus, ignoring the Synoptic witness that Jesus is Son of God, born of a virgin. Scholars have seen here an earlier tradition, more historically reliable than the virgin birth narratives of Matthew and Luke. It is doubtful that the evangelist would find this hypothesis convincing, but it is true that the Fourth Gospel grounds Jesus' deity in his preexistence rather than his birth.

Nathanael's response indicates a different kind of skepticism. Excavations in recent years at Sepphoris, a large commercial center only a few miles from Nazareth, may explain the disdain that Nathanael seems to have expressed for its smaller neighbor: "Can any good thing come out of Nazareth?" (1:46a). Besides, how could Messiah ("any good thing") come from Nazareth when Scripture has said that "the Messiah is descended from David and comes from Bethlehem" (7:42), and another tradition held that when Messiah comes no one will know where he is from (7:27)? In any case, Nathanael's initial response is not excitement but skepticism. Philip makes no appeal to reason, but invites Nathanael to experience Jesus personally: "Come and see" (1:46b).

In Jesus' dialogue with Nathanael (1:47–51) the theme of finding gives way to that of seeing (1:46, 47, 48, 50, 51). Even while Nathanael is on his way to see Jesus, Jesus sees him coming and says (translated literally), "Look! Truly an Israelite in whom is no falsehood (treachery or deceit)." Jesus sees more than the figure in the road; he sees Nathanael's heart and knows him through and through. Nathanael, amazed, asks (paraphrased), "Where did you get to know me?" Jesus' answer, "I saw you under the fig tree before Philip called you," indicates more than clairvoyance. It links seeing and knowing, a recurrent theme in the Fourth Gospel. For Nathanael it is evidence of divine omniscience. Jesus' answer completes the three-way link of seeing, knowing, and believing. The promise "You will see greater things than these" is an invitation to Nathanael to keep watching and to the reader to keep reading with a readiness to look and to see.

Jesus' final word to Nathanael (1:51) is of special significance to interpreters. "Angels of God ascending and descending upon the Son of Man" alludes to the story of Jacob at Bethel in Genesis 28, in which "he dreamed that there was a ladder set up on the earth, the top of it reaching to heaven; and the angels of God were ascending and descending on it" (Gen. 28:12)–or "on him."[1] Although the Mishnah, like Christian translations of

Genesis, prefers the interpretation according to which the angels ascended and descended upon the ladder, John 1:51 presupposes that Jacob dreamed that angels were ascending and descending upon *him*, mute messengers of the fact that though he had fled from Esau, he could not flee from God. God saw him; God was in that place.

In Jesus' reference to the story, Jacob is replaced by the Son of Man, a Hebrew expression which at root simply means "human being." Although the most important titles for Jesus in the Fourth Gospel are Messiah and Son of God, here, as in the Gospel of Mark, Son of Man is the only christological title that Jesus is reported to have used for himself. It is used in a dozen texts in John, nowhere with greater significance than here. In John it can mean either that Jesus is the archetype of the human race or that he is the revealer who comes down from heaven and returns to heaven—the man from heaven. The latter sense dominates the use of Son of Man in the Nicodemus passage of chapter 3 and in the references to Jesus' coming and going in the later chapters of the Gospel. Here, however, the Son of Man does not descend and ascend; rather, angels of God ascend and descend upon him. The allusion can only be to Jacob's dream. Jesus, as Son of Man, is the one in whom all humankind can experience Jacob's discovery that he is not alone, that God sees and knows, and that light shines in the darkness because the Word became flesh and lived among us (1:14).

The allusion to Jacob's dream at Bethel (v. 51) throws light on Jesus' reference to Nathanael as a true Israelite (v. 47). In Genesis 28 Jacob flees from his brother Esau, whom he has deceived and defrauded, but in Genesis 32 and 35 Jacob the supplanter is given a new name, Israel, to signify a new self. Jesus addresses Nathanael as a true son of Israel in whom is no Jacob.

Throughout the preceding dialogue, Jesus has addressed Nathanael in the second person singular, even in the promise, "You will see greater things than these" (1:50). But the "you" in verse 51 is plural. Jesus is no longer addressing only Nathanael; rather, through these words on the lips of Jesus, the evangelist is addressing readers. The Fourth Gospel nowhere tells of Nathanael seeing angels; indeed, the only other mention of Nathanael is in the list of seven disciples to whom Jesus showed himself by the sea after his resurrection (21:2). The promise in 1:51 is to those who, in a variety of times and places, will see Jesus and discover in him God's envoy to earth. For John's first readers, this was a daring affirmation that the locus of revelation is no holy place but is rather the person of the Son of Man, who is the human one ("Jesus son of Joseph from Nazareth," 1:45) and at the same time the man from heaven (Dan. 7:13–14).

John 1:45–51 exemplifies a well-known principle of biblical interpretation sometimes attributed to Bonhoeffer but based on Søren Kierkegaard's aphorism "Life can only be understood backwards, but it must be lived forwards."[2] The principle is that one must read the Bible forward and interpret it backward. Only on reading and understanding the conclusion of this passage in verse 51 can one understand the richness of its allusions in verse 47. And only on reading and understanding the entire Gospel of John can one fully appreciate the introduction in John 1 of a set of disciples different from the usual apostolic list, the inseparability of discipleship and witness (each one wins one in this chapter), the two-level use of seeing and knowing and their relationship to believing, the contrast between a true Israelite (used only here in the Gospel of John) and "the Jews" used so often as a cipher for those whose unbelief disqualifies them as the true people of God. Only the reader who perseveres to the end will see all the author had in mind from the beginning and, assisted by the spirit of the living Christ, may come to believe what these first witnesses saw in Jesus.

Preaching and teaching the Word

1. Seeking and finding. Jesus' first words in the Fourth Gospel are his question to the two unnamed disciples of John who followed him as he walked by, "What are you looking for?" (1:38). The question is echoed by "We have found" on the lips of Andrew (1:41) and Philip (1:45). Amid the many manifestations of the human search for meaning in a rootless, restless time, Jesus' question presupposes that anyone who notices him at all is looking for something. One precondition for finding is to identify and articulate what one is looking for. Few in our time are looking for Messiah. The interpreter may know his or her hearers and learners well enough to sense some of the things they are looking for, but the wiser way would be, like Jesus, to invite them to name their yearning. Many may discover that they share the uncertainty expressed in the counterquestion offered by the unnamed two in the text (1:38) who really do not know how to define what they want. They must first spend some time with Jesus in order to see more clearly what it is they are looking for. Augustine of Hippo (354–430 C.E.) wrote, addressing God, "You have made us for your own, and our hearts are restless until they rest in you."[3] He met Jesus three centuries after the Fourth Gospel was written and was able to say with Andrew and Philip "I have found him." For any restless searcher for meaning in this and every time, the word of the interpreter must be that of Jesus (1:39) and of Philip (1:46), "Come and see!" followed by some concrete suggestions based on personal experience about where and how seekers may meet the living Word.

2. Titles for Jesus. John 1 contains a remarkable litany of titles attributed to Jesus: the Word, Lamb of God, Messiah (Christ), the one about whom Moses in the law and also the prophets wrote, Rabbi, Son of God, king of Israel, and Son of Man. Each one was rich with meaning for Jewish Christians at the end of the first century, but to discover their meaning for believers today is a challenge. To stuff them all into a single sermon might produce a painful case of theological indigestion, but a series of lectures and discussions on these titles could be enriching. The teacher should study each term carefully, using a concordance to flush out the relevant texts in John and one or more good Bible dictionaries, then condense the findings in a brief presentation. After each presentation, participants could brainstorm on points of contact between that title and their own experience. Willingness to wait for responses is a key to good discussion.

3. Two-way communication with God. The shift from the singular to the plural "you" in verse 51 means that here the risen Lord, through the evangelist, is making a promise to those who, in a variety of times and places, come to see Jesus. They will discover in him God's envoy to earth who is constantly sending and receiving messages to and from home when all other means of communication have broken down. They will discover that the locus of revelation is no holy place but is rather a person: Jesus, the Son of Man. To realize that promise personally and to help others to experience it, the preacher or teacher needs to explore the title "Son of Man," a term foreign to Western culture in the twenty-first century. But if the text is to become a living word for hearers today, the interpreter must move beyond reasoned explanation to personal witness about prayer as two-way communication. We listen to God by hearing Jesus speak through the Gospels and in the lives of disciples today. We speak to God by a regular discipline of private prayer, each under his own figurative fig tree, and through deeds of loving service. The word about angels ascending and descending in 1:51 offers to anyone, anywhere the possibility of experiencing through Jesus Christ opened heavens and two-way communication with God.

THE FIRST SIGN: WATER INTO WINE (2:1–12)

Many people find it hard to hear the word this text addresses to us because of the static in our culture. In a society in which alcoholism cripples countless individuals and alcohol-related accidents maim and kill not a few, what's so good about changing water into wine? Besides, who believes in miracles?

To tune in clearly to the message of this narrative, one must imagine a situation in which there are no screaming headlines about highway mayhem nor any tut-tutting teetotalers, then set aside one's skepticism about the possibility of miracles and listen expectantly to the story the evangelist has to tell. Only on the surface is it a story about turning water into wine. Underneath, it is about the glory of God revealed in Jesus Christ.

Verse 11 states that this is the first of Jesus' **signs,** thus assigning its place in the context of the Fourth Gospel. The second sign, also at Cana, is also labeled (4:54), indicating that the evangelist may have viewed the intervening material as a unit. Five other signs are not numbered by the evangelist, but all are miracle stories that reveal who Jesus is. All appear before chapter 13, which leads Raymond Brown and others to refer to chapters 1–12 as "The Book of Signs."[1] In John the miracles of Jesus are not simply proofs of his supernatural power; they are symbols of his relationship to God. That is why Jesus never performs them on demand and speaks of them not as "signs" but as "works" in which he is doing the work of his Father. Others, including the evangelist, call them "signs" because they point to Jesus and can lead people to believe in him. Belief in Jesus as a miracle worker is unsatisfactory (2:23–25; 4:48; 6:26), but in some texts John uses "sign" as a favorable designation for a miracle that leads people to see Jesus for who he really is (2:11; 4:54; 20:30–31).[2] The changing of water into wine at Cana is the first of many "greater things" that Jesus promised Nathanael he would see (1:50), and the first of seven great signs through which the evangelist hopes to lead readers to life-giving faith. It is "the miracle of the epiphany," because through it Jesus for the first time in this Gospel manifests his glory.[3]

Exploring the text

In typical miracle story form, the text describes a problem (2:3–5), tells what Jesus did to solve it (2:6–8), and by means of the reaction of the steward offers proof that a miracle has occurred (vv. 9–10). The evangelist's comment in verse 11 about the reaction of Jesus' disciples states the significance of the story from his point of view.

(a) The brief setting (2:1–2). The setting follows upon Jesus' decision to go to Galilee (1:43) mentioned in connection with the call of Philip of Bethsaida and the coming to faith of Nathanael. Cana, the home town of Nathanael (21:2), was probably located some nine miles north northwest of Nazareth. It is called Cana of Galilee at the beginning and at the end of the text (vv. 1, 11), partly to distinguish it from the Cana near Tyre and partly to note that Jesus' ministry began in Galilee.

(b) The problem (2:3–5). The wine has given out, as reported in a brief dialogue between Jesus and his mother, whose name is not given here or

anywhere in the Fourth Gospel. She seems to know of his miracle-working power (though no miracle has yet been reported in this Gospel), and she suggests that he do something about the problem. Jesus' reply ("Woman, . . .") did not sound as brusque in his day as it does in ours. Then it was the normal, polite way of addressing women. Jesus also addressed as "woman" the Samaritan (4:21), Mary Magdalene (20:13), and his own mother in the tender scene at the foot of the cross (19:26).[4]

The idiomatic expression *ti emoi kai soi* (literally "What to me and to you?") is not necessarily a rebuke but a sort of declaration of independence, a distancing from his mother's implicit request. His action is governed not by Mary's intercession, but by his own understanding of the will of God. "My hour has not yet come" introduces a recurrent theme by which the Fourth Gospel points to Jesus' being lifted up on the cross as the supreme revelation of the glory of God.[5] This is one of many instances of the truth noted at John 1:45–51 that the Gospel of John, though it must be read forwards, can only be understood backwards.

His mother's reply, "Do whatever he tells you," acknowledges that Jesus is in control and indicates that she has not taken his answer as a firm "No." Her faith takes the form of persistent expectation, like that of the royal official from this same town who later begs Jesus to come see his dying son and will not be put off by Jesus' first reply (4:47–50).

(c) What Jesus did about it (2:6–8). The water jars described in verse 6 are essential to the story. They are made of stone, because their purpose is to hold the water for Jewish purification ceremonies like the ritual washing of hands before and after a meal. Stone, unlike earthenware, did not itself contract ritual uncleanness.[6] The size and number are unusually large. Translations differ in the figures used to give a contemporary equivalent for the contents of each jar, but "twenty or thirty gallons" is close enough. One jar should be abundantly sufficient for the needs of a household; six would be unheard of. Just to find the water sufficient to fill them would be difficult, and the thought of adding 120 to 180 gallons of wine late in the wedding festivities is staggering. The exaggerated figures in verse 6 are probably due to "the narrator's desire to represent a miracle of transformation of super proportions."[7]

The servants obey the mother's admonition literally and do what Jesus tells them to do, first by filling the jars up to the brim with water, then by drawing some out and taking it to the chief steward or master of the feast.

(d) The steward's reaction (2:9–10). These verses show readers that a miracle has occurred. The miraculous element is handled discretely. The steward does not realize a miracle has occurred, and the servants who do say nothing about it. The steward, assuming that the bridegroom has

replenished the supply of wine, chides him because he has "kept the good wine until now." His comment completes the account of the miracle in a way that suggests to readers that the "good wine" may have symbolic significance.

Some of the first readers of this Gospel were probably familiar with stories in which the god Dionysus was the cause of miraculous transformations of water into wine.[8] These analogies in the cultural context of the time would lead readers (as well as guests at the feast in Cana) to conclude that Jesus was a miracle worker with divine powers. The evangelist, however, immediately points to a more appropriate reaction.

(e) The evangelist's comment (2:11). In addition to situating this miracle story as the first in John, the evangelist's comment states that it revealed the glory of Jesus Christ. The meaning of **"glory"** in 2:11b is basic to the interpretation of the passage and of the Gospel of John as a whole. Here glory refers to the majesty, radiance, and substantive weight of God's essential nature. What is revealed by the turning of water into wine is not primarily the power of the miracle worker, but "the divinity of Jesus as the Revealer."[9]

This is why the Dionysian analogies are less helpful than parallels found in the writings of Philo of Alexandria, the apostle of Hellenistic Judaism. In his allegorical interpretation of Old Testament texts Philo depicts the Logos as God's cupbearer and concludes that the wine that the Priest-logos brings forth instead of water stands for God's gifts of grace, joy, virtue, wisdom, and all that characterizes the higher or spiritual life. Similarly, in this text wine is "an apt symbol for all that the fourth evangelist conceives Christ to have brought into the world."[10]

Upon reading 2:11b, the first readers of John's Gospel would surely have remembered the words of 1:14: "And the Word (Logos) became flesh and lived among us, and we have seen his glory, the glory as of a father's only son, full of grace and truth." The repetition of "glory" in 2:11 would have suggested to readers who knew Philo that the one whom disciples have already recognized as the Messiah (1:41), the one about whom Moses and the prophets wrote (1:45), the Son of God and King of Israel (1:49), may now, in light of his having turned water into wine, also be recognized as the Logos, the eternal Word.

All of these predicates (Messiah, Son of God, King of Israel, Logos) follow the conjunction "that." Verse 2:11c, however, affirms that "his disciples believed *in* him." The sign that they experienced produced in them not just an expanded creedal understanding, but the dawning of a new light about who Jesus is, and a deepening of their relationship to him as disciples. Trust and obedient commitment are not absent in John, but the main thrust of "believe" in this passage and throughout the Gospel lies elsewhere. For this evangelist believing is reverent awe combined with warm intimacy.

Verse 12 is transitional and geographical, permitting the reader to trace Jesus' movements from Bethany beyond Jordan (1:28), to Cana of Galilee (2:1), then to Capernaum on the northern shore of the Sea of Galilee. The few days Jesus spent in Capernaum with his mother, his brothers, and his disciples serve as a biographical link and a narrative spacer between the two important scenes in this chapter.

Preaching and teaching the Word

Verse 11 is the evangelist's own comment on the significance of Jesus' turning water into wine: it was the first sign through which Jesus revealed his glory, and when they saw this sign, his disciples believed in him. The text is rich with allusions to theological themes that may be pursued as the preacher or teacher seeks to explore this question on the Sunday between January 14 and 20 in Year C, as suggested in several lectionaries, or on other appropriate occasions.

1. Epiphany. In the long lectionary tradition of the church John 2:1–11 (12) is the Gospel lesson associated with Epiphany (January 6), along with Matthew 2:1–12, because the celebration of Christ's Epiphany was set on the day of the feast of Dionysus, which was also held to be the date of the wedding at Cana. This is an epiphany miracle, for epiphany comes from a verb which means "to show oneself," "to appear." This line of interpretation should be handled with care on account of its pagan associations. The Gospel is ambivalent about belief aroused by miracles but includes the story as the very first of the signs by which Andrew, Peter, Nathanael, and perhaps one other (1:37) were led to genuine belief in and deeper commitment to Jesus Christ. The evangelist wishes, by this story of Jesus' abundant provision for a joyful feast, to lead the reader also to meet Jesus in the common joys of life and find in him the glorious presence and power of God.

2. Pentecost. This text is appropriate for a sermon on Pentecost Sunday or for a lesson on the meaning of Pentecost, because in the Fourth Gospel water is a symbol of the Holy Spirit, explicitly in 1:26, 33 and 7:37–39, and implicitly in 3:5 and 4:10, 15. At Cana Jesus transforms the water of ritual purification into joyful wine. It is a paradigm of the way the living water that Jesus gives–the Holy Spirit (7:37–39)–adds sparkle and zest to the common ventures of life, like marriage, and even to religious rituals. In its exuberance and superabundance this splashy miracle at Cana typifies the way God gives the Holy Spirit without measure (3:34) and the way in which some Christians receive the Spirit today.

3. At a wedding. The occasion that gave rise to this text suggests that it might be appropriately preached at a wedding or used in premarital counseling. Jesus' first public appearance was as a guest at a wedding in which he not only shared the nuptial joy of the young couple but made an appreciable contribution to it. In doing so, he revealed to eyes of faith the glory of the eternal Word who created us male and female and declared this arrangement good. The pastor, preacher, or teacher who has stayed with this text long enough to drink deeply of its riches can be a channel through which the Holy Spirit brings a special dimension of joy to a woman and a man beginning life together.

4. At a baptism. The jars that were filled with water at Cana were "for the Jewish rites of purification" (2:6), and the discussion that arose between John's disciples and a Jew presupposed that the baptisms performed by John the witness were ritual washings for purification (3:25), like the washings (*baptismous*) of cups, pots, and kettles at Mark 7:4. At Cana, Jesus gave a new quality and a new significance to the water of purification. So can the Holy Spirit, whom the water of baptism symbolizes, give new and eternal life to the person baptized. The preacher can teach this in a communicants' class and explain it in a baptismal homily, but only the Spirit can transform the water in the font into "a spring of water gushing up to eternal life" (4:14), cleansing from sin, giving second birth, and turning the flatness of life into a "sober inebriation."[11] Prayer is therefore an essential element if the interpretation is to mean much.

5. In a communion homily. Sacramental symbolism is veiled but unmistakable at several points in the Fourth Gospel. John's account of the Last Supper in chapter 13 includes nothing about the institution of the Lord's Supper, nor does this Gospel report the baptism of Jesus. Yet references to baptism are frequent in chapters 1 and 3, and the long bread of life discourse in chapter 6 clearly refers to the Eucharist in the saying, "Very truly, I tell you, unless you eat the flesh of the Son of Man and drink his blood, you have no life in you" (6:53). Just as the latter discourse can be read as a homily on the eucharistic bread, so the wedding at Cana can be (and has been) read as an acted parable about the eucharistic wine. Raymond Brown reviews many internal indications of sacramental intent in John 2:1–12 but views them as "at most poetic allusions which do no more than make a eucharistic interpretation *possible*." Such symbolism is secondary. "The primary meaning of the wine is clearly Jesus' gift of salvation, for which light, water, and food are other Johannine symbols."[12]

6. Cautions about preaching and teaching this text. Some interpreters, focusing on the six stone water jars for the Jewish rites of purification (2:6) have seen here a story about the changing of the water of Jewish ritual into the wine of the gospel.[13] The theme of the rejection of Judaism and its replacement by Christianity (supersessionism), so common to much patristic biblical interpretation, has led to unspeakable atrocities against the Jewish people through the centuries. In the text, "this miracle is . . . neither a rejection nor a replacement of the old, but the creation of something new in the midst of Judaism."[14] In today's world, a supersessionist interpretation of the text is inappropriate, even inexcusable.[15]

It is easy to misinterpret the role of Jesus' mother in this text. A Catholic commentator has aptly written,

> The temptation of the Catholic preacher may be to over stress Mary's intercession with her Son; of the Protestant, her initial rebuke by her Son. Both will be wrong, of course, for the story is at root about neither. It tells about the disclosure in ordinary family festive circumstances of the hidden glory of Jesus the Son.[16]

Some evangelical interpreters in the Puritan tradition have been embarrassed by this story about Jesus' producing prodigious quantities of wine. Dwight L. Moody grasped the nettle firmly and stressed Jesus' power to transform, not just water but human lives. He often told about a recent convert who said, "I don't know whether or not Jesus can turn water into wine, but I know that in my house he has turned whiskey into milk and furniture!"

Faithful interpretation attends first of all to what the text itself says about its significance for the writer and first readers (2:11), using this as a touchstone for what it may say to another audience in another time.

THE FIRST CONFRONTATION: JESUS AND THE TEMPLE AUTHORITIES (2:13–22)

In all three Synoptic Gospels, the story of Jesus driving the salespeople and money changers out of the temple in Jerusalem appears very near the end of his public ministry and serves as the trigger for events leading to his death.[1] Why does the fourth evangelist place a confrontation that Jesus initiates at the beginning of his Gospel? The scene has puzzled Christians, engaged the attention of New Testament scholars, and complicated relations between Christians and Jews. Before trying to defend or attack the text or any of its characters, one should seek to understand it.

Exploring the text

According to John, the setting (vv. 13–14) is the first of three Passover festivals in Jerusalem during Jesus' public ministry, one at the beginning, one in the middle (6:4), and one at the end (11:55; 12:1; and 13:1, which establishes the time for chapters 12–20). Church tradition has seen these as temporal markers that, taken with the "festival of the Jews" of 5:1 (debatably identified as Passover), have led to the understanding of a three-year ministry for Jesus, over against the Synoptics, which mention only the last Passover and associate this temple scene with it.

John specifies that it is "the Passover of the Jews." The prominence of the principal Jewish feasts in this Gospel is one of many indications that the author as well as Jesus is Jewish, but the phrasing of 2:13 (like that of 2:6) indicates that the intended readers included some who would need to have even basic Jewish matters explained to them.

The commerce described in 2:14 might need further explanation for readers today. Jewish pilgrims who came to Jerusalem for Passover needed to buy Passover lambs, and many took advantage of the occasion to offer sacrifices in the temple—animals for the wealthy and doves for the poor. The coins of this Roman-occupied country were not acceptable to the temple authorities, because they bore an image of the Roman emperor, who was given divine honors. The authorities therefore issued their own tokens, which alone could be used to buy sacrificial animals and birds in the temple precincts. This requirement entailed the changing of the money pilgrims had brought with them into temple currency, for a fee. Like other pilgrims who entered the temple at Passover time, Jesus noted this commerce.

Jesus' Action (2:13–17)

Many may have muttered about it, but Jesus took action (2:15–16). John alone mentions that Jesus made a whip of cords to use in driving them all out. The Greek text is so worded that the readers can envision Jesus using the whip on the animals only (TEV) or on the merchants as well (most translations). He poured out their coins and overturned their tables. Jesus said to the owners of pigeons, "Take these things out of here!" adding, to merchants and money changers, "Stop making my Father's house a marketplace." There is no suggestion in John that the merchants are dishonest ("robbers," Jer. 7:11), only that they have profaned God's house by turning it into a market. Only in John does Jesus in this context call the temple "My Father's house," drawing attention to his unique relationship to God.

John's detailed description of Jesus' indignation gives rise to the first reaction of his disciples, who remembered a different Old Testament text: "Zeal for your house will consume me" (Ps. 69:9). "Zeal" is a hot word, like "ardor," with the root meaning "to burn." The whip of cords may or may not have been used on human beings, but along with Psalm 69:9 it underscores the hot indignation that the commercialization of the temple aroused in Jesus.

The evangelist's note in 2:17 is the first of two appearances in this narrative of the comment, "his disciples remembered" (see 2:22). This account is a striking example of the retrospective point of view that surfaces often in the Fourth Gospel. In this way the author/evangelist shows that he believes the life and significance of Jesus Christ can only be understood backwards (see note on 2:4b), after his resurrection and with the help of the Holy Spirit (14:26; 16:13).

The Response of "the Jews" (2:18–22)

Given the disruptive nature of Jesus' indignant words and actions, the response is remarkably mild. They simply ask for a sign (2:18) that would warrant what he has said and done. This request expresses skepticism, but not yet rejection or hostility. It is, however, the first use of "the Jews"[2] in a pejorative sense in relation to Jesus' own religious community, which, in a series of increasingly hostile confrontations, comes finally to reject him and to conspire with the Romans to kill him. In the present scene, the term applies to all who were surprised and upset by Jesus' disruptive behavior: the authorities in charge of the temple, the money changers, and the merchants, all of whom had a personal financial interest in the smooth operation of the institution. As 2:23–25 indicates, the term does not apply to all of the Jewish crowd keeping Passover in Jerusalem, much less to the Jewish people as a whole.

Jesus' reply is enigmatic (2:19). He does not reject the request for a sign. He gives them a sign, but it is unintelligible to the hearers for two reasons. First, it is another example of the evangelist's retrospective viewpoint. It makes sense only to hearers and readers on this side of the resurrection of Jesus. Second, the hearers fail to understand because they apply Jesus' words to the actual stones of Herod's temple, an extensive enlargement of Zerubbabel's temple begun about 20 B.C.E. and still under way.

In an explanatory note (2:21), the evangelist points out that Jesus was speaking metaphorically of the temple of his body, thus offering the first example of a narrative device that is used repeatedly in the Gospel. By means of someone's misunderstanding in the narrative, the evangelist instructs the understanding of the reader.

In a second explanatory note (2:22), the evangelist informs the reader of the effect on Jesus' disciples when, after his resurrection, they remembered the word that Jesus had spoken (v. 22b). Jesus, speaking of the temple of his body, had said, "In three days I will raise it up" (v. 19), whereas according to the New Testament as a whole it is God who raised Jesus from the dead. John the evangelist places on Jesus' lips a claim to this act of God and wishes his readers to equate the word of Jesus with God's word in Scripture and to believe both.

By placing this incident near the beginning of Jesus' earthly ministry, the fourth evangelist introduces the theme of controversy that is so necessary to a plot whose climax is the death and resurrection of Jesus.

REACTIONS TO JESUS (2:23–25)

This brief paragraph serves as a transition between Jesus' confrontation with the temple authorities in Jerusalem during Passover and the encounter with Nicodemus that follows in chapter 3. It consists of two parts.

The *reaction of the crowd* is altogether positive: "many believed in his name because they saw the signs that he was doing" (2:23). To believe in his name is here equivalent to believing that he is who the Gospel thus far has said he is, without repeating in detail his messianic titles.

The *reaction of Jesus* to the crowd's belief based on signs (2:24–25) is as skeptical as was the reaction of the temple authorities to him. A literal translation of these two verses, using the same verb as the text, would read: "Many trusted in his name . . . but he was not entrusting himself to them." The remaining words are the first example of another quality in the narrator's point of view: he is omniscient and offers an inside view of Jesus' mind.[3] The evangelist tells readers why Jesus did not entrust himself to the crowd; namely, Jesus himself was omniscient (2:24b–25). In the Fourth Gospel, unlike the Synoptics, omniscience is a quality shared by the evangelist and Jesus.

This transition introduces chapter 3, in which Nicodemus is presented as an example of the many in Jerusalem who were attracted by Jesus' signs but whose response to him is not yet genuine faith. In 2:1–11 a sign of Jesus leads his disciples to see his glory and believe in him. In 2:13–22 the religious authorities respond to another sign proposed by Jesus with an incredulous question. In 2:24–25 Jesus does not entrust himself to a signs-based faith he knows to be shallow, but in 3:1–21 he seeks to lead one of the more open religious authorities beyond the signs to what they signify, and so to eternal life.

Preaching and teaching the Word

1. Jesus and the institutional church. When Jesus' disciples (including the evangelist) remembered this incident, it reminded them of Psalm 69:9, in which "zeal for your house" means fervent devotion to the temple.[4] Jesus, as a devout Jew, shows deep reverence for the temple and is outraged at its desecration. This was surely part of his motivation in confronting the commercial profanation of the temple. Jesus' warning raises questions about church bazaars and deeper questions for anyone whose livelihood is dependent upon institutional religion. What has the text to say about such concepts as "job description," "salary package," and "career security"? Religion in America at the beginning of the twenty-first century is big business, as was Herod's temple. How will Jesus demonstrate to us this zeal for his Father's house? How can his living presence in the Holy Spirit make of a local church more than a context for successful programs and an equal opportunity workplace? At what cost to us can he make of every church a place to meet God? These particular questions are but specific instances of the question the Fourth Gospel poses about institutional religion.

2. Reverence and zeal. In attacking the practices of those who were using the temple to advance their own interests, Jesus shows reverence for the temple as God's house. In a secular society this text calls not for the destruction of religious institutions but for a recovery of reverent awe before the God to whom they point and zeal for the mission they were instituted to accomplish. Preachers and teachers of this text can call Christians beyond superficial piety and attachment to familiar buildings and programs to genuine faith in God as revealed in Christ and to effective action in the world.

3. Responding to the Word. The Fourth Gospel juxtaposes the reaction of Jesus' disciples to his turning water into wine at a village wedding feast (2:11) and the reaction of the religious authorities in Jerusalem (2:18 and 20). In the confrontation in the temple (2:13–22) Jesus gives all who observe it an enigmatic sign, but they only scoff at it. Preachers and teachers can urge their hearers and learners to stop demanding signs, as those in Jerusalem did, and to see the remarkable signs given in everyday circumstances, so that they, like those first disciples at a village wedding, may come to believe in Jesus and have life in his name (20:31).

4. A word of caution. The feeling of hot anger that pervades this scene and the fact that in it Jesus takes the initiative in a vehement confrontation with "the Jews" has encouraged anti-Semitic attitudes through the centuries. To avoid a tragic perversion of the gospel of Jesus Christ, readers and interpreters of this text should recognize the influence of the historical situation of the evangelist and his community of faith some six or seven decades after Jesus' death.[5] The intention of the text is not to demonize Jews, but to show how Jesus reveals the glory of God when he confronts self-interested religious hypocrisy (2:13–22), as well as when he helps out at a wedding feast (2:1–12).

JESUS' ENCOUNTER WITH NICODEMUS (3:1–21)

Nicodemus is the first of several significant individuals who appear only in the Fourth Gospel as examples of different ways of responding to Jesus Christ. The immediate context suggests that he was one of those who saw the signs that Jesus was doing in Jerusalem during the Passover festival (compare 2:23 with 3:2). Many believed in Jesus' name, but Jesus did not entrust himself to them because he knew their faith was shallow (2:25). Immediately following this comment, the evangelist introduces a prominent Pharisee who is also attracted to Jesus by the signs that he does (3:1–2). Can this seeker be led beyond his initial attraction and curiosity to genuine faith? Two other appearances of Nicodemus in the Fourth Gospel (7:50–52; 19:39–42) throw further light on this question, but his encounter with Jesus in chapter 3 ends on a note that is less than promising.

Exploring the text

Several of the distinctive literary marks of this Gospel appear here for the first time, like this basic structure of the passage:

Narrative setting   3:1–2a
Dialogue   2b–10
Monologue   11–21

Narrative Setting: A Pharisee Visits Jesus at Night (3:1–2a)

Instead of a thoroughly Jewish name, like Nathanael (gift/God), Nicodemus (victory/people) is a common Greek name that was also found among Jews.[1] His name itself suggests a person who, while he was a committed Pharisee, reflected the more open attitude of Hellenized Judaism. His coming to Jesus by night further suggests a sincere but cautious inquirer, who does not wish to be pushed to commitment.

Nicodemus, an individual, is at the same time representative of a whole class.[2] Besides representing the many Jews who believed because of the signs Jesus did (2:23), this "leader of the Jews" represents the Jewish authorities whom Jesus engages in bitter debate as the Fourth Gospel unfolds. He represents those who do not dare to confess their private belief for fear of being put out of the synagogue (12:42).

Dialogue: Jesus and Nicodemus (3:2b–10)

The dialogue proceeds in three exchanges, each consisting of a remark from Nicodemus and Jesus' reply to it.

Nicodemus first addresses Jesus respectfully as a fellow teacher. "We know" represents a careful concession on the part of a religious leader and at the same time a claim to the knowledge that a good teacher should possess. "A teacher come from God" means a teacher whose miracles suggest a close relationship to God that Nicodemus could wish for himself and for all those he represents.

Jesus does not even acknowledge the religious leader's flattery. His response seems at first to be a non sequitur. Jesus responds not to what Nicodemus has said, but to what he knows to be in his visitor's heart (see 2:25). He recognizes Nicodemus's individual spiritual hunger expressed in terms of a yearning for the kingdom of God–an expression close to the heart of traditional Jewish theology but used only here in the Gospel of John. Jesus affirms that neither Nicodemus nor any religious authorities can even see that kingdom unless they are given new life from above.

Nicodemus then asks two questions, each of which indicates his failure to understand what Jesus has said. Misunderstanding is one of the basic techniques by which the evangelist communicates.[3] In this instance, the misunderstanding indicates that, for all his confidence about what "we know," this inquirer who comes to Jesus by night has, in fact, been in the dark.

Nicodemus's first question (3:4) turns upon a misunderstanding of the term *anothen,* which can mean either "from above" or "again," just as *da capo,* literally "from the top," in a musical score means "play it again." Jesus intends to say, "You must be born from above," as in the NRSV and NJB, but Nicodemus understands him to say, "You must be born again (or anew)," as in the AV, RSV, TEV, and REB. The latter is a misunderstanding of Jesus' intention, but a correct rendition of what Nicodemus heard. Both meanings are necessary to the proper understanding of the text. "Born from above" expresses Jesus' intention in this context; "born again" is a misunderstanding until it is filled with the meaning Jesus gives to it in verse 5, "born of water and Spirit." This kind of double entendre is another of the Fourth Gospel's characteristic literary traits.

Jesus' reply is also open to at least two different interpretations. Does "born of water" refer simply to the amniotic fluid of physical birth? This understanding has dominated evangelical interpretation, according to which physical birth into a Christian family is not sufficient for assurance of salvation, but only the experience of being "born again" through the power of the Holy Spirit. Or does "born of water" refer to the sacrament of baptism, whereby believers were initiated into the church? This interpretation, based on indirect allusions to baptism throughout the Fourth Gospel (beginning with the water Jesus turned to wine at Cana, chap. 2), has dominated Catholic exegesis. Here again a two-level understanding of John's Gospel is helpful. In Jesus' day there was no church into which Nicodemus might be baptized. At the time of the Gospel writer and first readers near the end of the first century, however, the reference to baptism as a public statement of commitment to Christ would be true to the intention of the text. Jesus seeks to lead Nicodemus beyond his institutional status as a leader of the Jews who comes by night as an inquirer, to a personal faith in Jesus and a public commitment in faith that only the Spirit can inspire. Catholic and evangelical elements are both present in the text.

Pneuma is another of the words with two meanings frequently found in John. It can mean either "(God's) Spirit" or "wind," and Jesus' explanation in verse 8 is typical of the wordplay the evangelist often uses. Water is not enough, whether it be the water of baptism or of natural birth. Entrance to the kingdom of God, or as John usually prefers, into eternal life, comes only through the action of the wind of God, which blows where it chooses.

As a religious authority, Nicodemus is perplexed by Jesus' explanation of birth from above. His second question, "How can this be?" (3:9), echoes that of verse 4. Jesus replies with a sharp question about this teacher's dullness and the dialogue is over. Nicodemus utters not another word and disappears until 7:45–52.

Monologue: Jesus and the Evangelist (3:11–21)

Much of the theological freight is carried by the monologue, whose vocabulary and style are unlike the words of Jesus in the Synoptic Gospels, but virtually identical to the vocabulary and style of the evangelist throughout the Fourth Gospel. This fact has led people to ask where the words of Jesus end (v. 12? 15? 16? 21?). The question is moot, because in John the narrator and Jesus are indistinguishable in vocabulary and in thought.[4] In terms characteristic of Johannine theology these verses echo and develop the sweeping claims of the prologue (1:1–18) that Jesus Christ, the only Son of God, made flesh as Son of Man, came from God to bring light and life to the world; that his own people did not receive him; and that whoever does believe in him is born of God into eternal life.

In verses 11–12 the accent shifts from Jesus as an individual ("I" in 11a and 12) to Jesus as vehicle for the testimony of the Johannine community ("we/our" in 11b and c). The polemical ring of these two verses ("you people do not receive our testimony . . . you people do not believe," author's translation) probably reflects the embattled situation of the evangelist and first readers of this Gospel. These verses also refer to Jesus' preceding words to Nicodemus about the wind/Spirit as "earthly things," and introduce the teaching that will follow in verses 13–21 about "heavenly things."

Verses 13 through 16 make three bold affirmations about Jesus as Son of Man and Son of God. First (v. 13), Jesus is the Son of Man who descended from heaven and who alone can reveal heavenly things, since no one else has ascended there. This affirmation ignores the Old Testament stories of Enoch and Elijah (Gen. 5:24; 2 Kgs. 2:1, 11) and other prophets and seers who claimed to have received revelations by means of "heavenly journeys."[5] Ruling out the claims of revealers purporting to have come down from heaven, this verse also excludes the notion that God, having made the world, has left it alone. The understanding of Jesus as the unique Son of Man who came down from heaven to reveal heavenly things underlies the overall pattern of descent and ascent in the Fourth Gospel. Chapters 1–12 focus on Jesus' coming from God to bear witness to the truth and to open the way to abundant life; from 13:1 onward the focus is on Jesus' departure from this world to go to the Father.

Second (vv. 14–15), the purpose of the Son of Man's coming down from heaven is that whoever believes in him may have eternal life through the death of Jesus Christ on the cross. Jesus' crucifixion is here spoken of in a figure of speech based on a story in Numbers 21:4–9. Just as Moses at God's command made a bronze serpent and put it on a pole so that Israelites dying of snakebite in the wilderness because of their sin could look at it and live, so Jesus, the Son of Man, must be lifted up on the cross, "that whoever believes in him may have eternal life." Sin, so prominent in the Numbers text, is not mentioned in John; "lifted up," which does not appear in Numbers, is the focus of the text in John, where Jesus' crucifixion is regularly thought of as his glorious exaltation (e.g., 12:23–24). The evangelist is interested not in a literal explanation of the Numbers text but in lifting up before the reader a powerful visual image that conveys one dimension of the meaning of Jesus' death on the cross. The image of the snake on a stick as a symbol of healing and salvation had important religious connotations in the world of John's first readers: the staff of Asclepios (Greek demigod of healing, whose Roman name was Aesculapius) and the wand of Hermes (Mercury, to the Romans), the messenger of the gods, whose wand assured recipients that his word was of divine origin and authority. The caduceus, symbol of the medical profession in Western culture today, is one form of this ubiquitous allusive image. Its use in this text is a good example of the Fourth Gospel's proclivity for adapting symbols drawn from Judaism and combining them with symbols of the surrounding culture to give them new meaning.[6] This text proclaims the power of the incarnate Word, lifted up on a cross for the healing of all who will look and believe and be saved.[7]

Third (v. 16), Jesus' descent from heaven, his servant life, and his death on the cross are the supreme expression of God's great love for the world. "World" here means the entire human race as the object of God's love. God's love for, in, and through the Son is a recurrent theme in the Fourth Gospel. In John 3:16 that great love is summed up in the gift of God's only Son.[8] God loved; God gave. The goal of the gift is eternal life, a theme that is developed elsewhere, as in 3:36–eternal life begins now–and 10:10–it is abundant life as well as eternal. The present text affirms that a loving God has not left the world to its own destructive devices. In the life, death, and resurrection of Jesus Christ, God has intervened to give life to everyone in the world who will receive the gift. This is the central witness of the Fourth Gospel: who Jesus is and what he does. This is what the evangelist sees when he looks at Jesus on the cross, and what he invites his community, his Jewish neighbors, and all the world to see as well. The man on this cross is the unique one from heaven, Son of Man and Son of God, giving his life for the world as the last, full measure of God's love for humankind.

The focus of verses 17–21 is on the human response and the element of divine judgment that is implicit in that response. The element of human response has already been introduced in the purpose clauses of verses 15 and 16 ("so that everyone who believes . . ."), and the theme of judgment is alluded to in the word "perish" (be destroyed, ruined, lost; die).

Verse 17 continues to reflect on God's initiative, "God sent . . ." The latter part of this verse affirms that God's purpose in sending the Son was not to condemn the world but to save it. "Condemn" makes explicit the idea of judgment and alerts the reader that in the following verses "judgment" means not "discernment" or "considered opinion" but "condemnation." "Saved" is used as the antonym of "be destroyed" ("perish"), and is synonymous with having eternal life.

Verse 18 reaffirms that God's purpose in sending Jesus is to save, but it adds that the human response to that initiative determines its actual effect. The alternative is stark; there is no middle ground. The conclusion of the verse is added to clarify. "Name" in Semitic usage refers to what is essential in a person; the name of the Son of God is Jesus, which means "savior."[9] Not to believe in Jesus is to reject the essential quality of God, in whom all of time is *now,* so that rejecting him is of ultimate significance. "Condemned already" in verse 18 is echoed by the contrasting parallel statement in the present tense in verse 36: "Whoever believes in the Son has eternal life." John's "realized eschatology" (the last judgment is now) lends urgency to Jesus' dialogue with Nicodemus and to every reader's encounter with this text.

Verses 19–21 develop the idea of judgment. Judgment was not God's intention in sending the only Son, but judgment is what happens when light comes into a dark place. "World" here is still neutral, designating the realm of human history, but the echo of 1:5 and the emphasis on darkness suggest the pejorative understanding of "world." In Jesus Christ, the Son of God, light has come into the world, and its very presence constitutes a judgment. Doers of evil hate the light and do not come to it, while doers of truth are drawn to the light. It is like turning on a light in a dark kitchen: moths will come to the light and circle around it in fascination, but roaches will flee from it and hide in dark crannies. The purpose of turning on the light was not to judge at all, but in the presence of the light different creatures judge themselves by their response. In the text, that response is rooted in the good or evil deeds of different people. Here doing is just as important as believing and is its inevitable corollary.

The doctrine of the Trinity was not fully elaborated until two centuries later, but its components are evident in this and other texts of the Fourth Gospel. Readers today can see the unity of the passage in the flow of its theological emphases. It is about *the Spirit*, the wind of God that brings birth from above and entrance into the kingdom of God (3:3–10). It is about *the Son* who came down from heaven to tell us about heavenly things and to give us life by being lifted up on a cross (3:11–15). It is about *God the Father* who loved the world and gave the Son so that we need not be condemned, although judgment inevitably occurs when light comes (3:16–21).[10] All is the action of the one God who was in the beginning, whose Word made flesh encountered Nicodemus, and whose Spirit may still encounter readers and hearers through the words of John 3:1–21.

Preaching and teaching the Word

In John 3:1–21 many of the basic elements of the gospel message, its insights into the human condition and its revelation of the heart of God, are concentrated in brief, limpid statements. They suggest these themes:

> The image of the Spirit as the wind of God (v. 8), which gives life and breath to teaching and preaching about the Holy Spirit.
>
> Jesus' wry comment to a leading teacher of Israel who yet did not understand the basic facts of life in relationship to God (v. 10) as a warning about the danger of specializing in religion.

The affirmation that Jesus has come down from heaven to reveal heavenly things (vv. 12–13) and to be the living expression of the love of God (vv. 16–17) as a reminder that we are not alone, that ours is a visited planet.[11]

The striking analogy between Jesus on his cross and the serpent on the pole that Moses lifted up in the wilderness (v. 14), which calls attention to the importance of where one fixes one's eyes in life. This image suggested to Charles Spurgeon that "There is life in a look *at* the crucified One, because there is life in a look *from* the crucified One."[12]

The proclamation of God's boundless love and saving purpose in John 3:16. With verse 17, it says who God is. With verses 18–21, it says who we are. The linking of unbelief and condemnation (v. 18) underscores the ultimate importance of one's daily response to Jesus Christ. The image of judgment by light (vv. 19–21) is a helpful alternative to that of judgment by law.

The combination of believing (vv. 15–16) and of doing (vv. 19–21), a salutary corrective to the easy assumption that only one or the other matters.

The story of Jesus' encounter with Nicodemus is of particular significance, however, for those who come to Jesus "by night." They may come from the darkness of sin, a context in which evangelists have preached this text from time immemorial and to which the text does have a powerful word to say. Nicodemus, however, represents not sinners but devout people who, despite their loyal service to the dominant religious institution of their place and time, know the darkness of an unsatisfied hunger for God. These people may, like the Pharisees in Jesus' time, exemplify reverence for God and the Scriptures, personal rectitude, disciplined devotion, and intellectual acumen. They are the pillars of many a Christian church. But they still experience darkness in their lives and often, like Nicodemus, they are afraid to confess Jesus in public.

In every congregation and class there are devout Christians who come to Jesus by night, wondering wordlessly, "Are you really who the Fourth Gospel says you are?" Perhaps they come with another question, their own mixture of faith and caution, their own hungers and fears. Just who the Nicodemuses may be in any gathering, only they themselves, guided by the Holy Spirit, may say.

Can they be led to genuine faith and to unreserved discipleship? Jesus' word for them cuts to the essence of our human yearning for God and to the heart of the hindrance to its fulfillment. He does not say, "I'm so glad you came; let's talk about it and then we'll pray." No readjustment of the old forms will do, nor more diligent observance of established patterns of piety. Instead, "You must be born from above," and in a manner of speaking that means being born again. More is needed than the amniotic waters of birth into a good, religious family; more than the water of baptism into a true church. These are good, but not enough.

And more is available. There is the love of God. One can believe God's love itself and come to its burning light.

There is the death of the Son on the cross. Those who keep their eyes fixed on him discover in him eternal life, for one tends to grow like that which one steadily contemplates.

There is also the fresh wind of the Spirit of God that braces the mind and clears the eyes to see the kingdom of God. Though none can predict or control the action of that Spirit/wind, anyone can long for it, pray for it, wait for it, and expect it. And who knows? Perhaps even now, in the presence of this encounter between Jesus and a seeker, some cautious, predictable church leader may be blown away by the wind of God, and some thirsty soul in the waiting congregation will experience–anew or for the first time–what it means to be born again, from above. It might even happen to the preacher or the teacher.

JESUS AND JOHN: FIRST SUMMARY (3:22–36)

John 3:22–36 signals that the cycle of first witness to Jesus, first disciples of Jesus, and first encounters with Jesus is complete. The unity of John 3:1–36 is best appreciated if one stands in the place of the Gospel's first readers and views Nicodemus and the disciples of John the Baptist as representative of two groups related to but distinct from the Johannine community of faith.[1] Nicodemus represents devout Jews who, initially drawn to Jesus by seeing the signs he performed, come to believe in him but remain secret believers for fear of expulsion from the synagogue. This group needs the breath of the Spirit to give them courage to declare their faith and, through baptism, to make public their adherence to Jesus Christ. The disciples of John the Baptist represent a rival group who look to John as their founder and the channel of God's word. This group needs to realize the subordinate role of John and to move on to faith in the one to whom John points.

Exploring the text

In 3:22–36 the evangelist brings back on stage the chief protagonists from the first scenes in the Gospel: John, Jesus, and the disciples of each.

This brief narrative features a dialogue between John the Baptist and his disciples, shading into a summary in which the evangelist recapitulates the testimony to Jesus thus far.

Narrative Setting (3:22–24)

Jesus and John are baptizing out in the country, both accompanied by their disciples. These verses contain three puzzles for anyone who reads John as a historical, factual account. With regard to place, the scene is set on the west side of the Jordan. Jesus and his disciples are in the country-side of Judea, while John and his disciples are at Aenon, not necessarily on the river bank but in a place of abundant springs. With regard to the time, the Synoptics state explicitly that Jesus' public ministry did not begin until after John was imprisoned (Mark 1:14), while a period of simultaneous ministry, clearly affirmed in verse 24, is basic to the meaning of the present text in the Fourth Gospel. On this as on most other points of divergence, the weight of evidence favors the historical accuracy of the Synoptics, while John may reflect the historical situation of the evangelist and of Jesus' disciples in the Johannine community as rivals of the followers of John the Baptist. The evangelist introduces the final testimony of John here as an appeal to John's disciples to recognize Jesus as the greater one whom they should follow, just as the encounter with Nicodemus constitutes an appeal to serious inquirers or secret believers among the leaders of the synagogue. John and his disciples dominate the scene in 3:23–30 but then disappear from the pages of the Fourth Gospel.

Only here in the New Testament is it affirmed that Jesus himself baptized (3:22, 26; 4:1), and this is corrected by the note in 4:2. The discrepancy is best accounted for by the hypothesis that the evangelist was using a source (oral or written) that he chose to correct. The reference is to water baptism, since the only baptism attributed to Jesus in the preaching of John the Baptist, and indeed throughout the New Testament, is baptism with the Holy Spirit, which occurs only after the resurrection of Jesus (20:22).

Dialogue between John and His Disciples (3:25–30)

A dialogue recalls and concludes the testimony of John the Baptist with which the body of the Fourth Gospel began (1:19–36). What gave rise to the dialogue was "a discussion (debate, REB; argument, NIV, TEV) about purification between John's disciples and a Jew" (3:25). This "Jew" could be any one of the many who believed in Jesus (2:23; 4:1). The only other use of the term "purification" (*katharismos*) in John is in 2:6 with reference to the six stone water jars. The text is silent about the substance of the discussion about purification, but the context of baptism in this scene suggests a debate about whose ritual washing is most effective for spiritual cleansing: that of official Judaism, that of John the Baptist, or that of Jesus. The report in verse 26 suggests that many were leaning toward that of Jesus, and the reaction of John's disciples suggests that they are jealous.

In verses 27–30, the heart of the paragraph, John the Baptist makes four statements about Jesus–and about John's relationship to Jesus–that the evangelist wishes to impress upon the reader:

> Jesus' power of attraction is God's will and God's gift, since whatever success anyone enjoys is the gift of God (v. 27).
>
> John's disciples should not be upset, because the baptizer had already stated plainly that he was not the Messiah, but the Messiah's herald (v. 28; cf. 1:19–23).
>
> Indeed, John's disciples should be glad, because John, the herald, is related to Jesus the Messiah as the best man at a wedding is to the bridegroom: John's joy is fulfilled when Jesus is the center of attention (v. 29).
>
> Jesus is to become more and more important, his herald less and less so. This pronouncement clinches John's speech (v. 30).

These words attest the genuine humility and accurate self-image of John. They portray John as an example for his disciples in the time of Jesus, and for a continuing community of John's disciples when the Fourth Gospel was written some decades later.[2] They also address disciples of Jesus then and now.

Monologue (3:31–36)

The monologue can be viewed as part of John's speech (NIV, NJB) or as commentary by the evangelist (NRSV, RSV, TEV, REB). The King James Version (AV), like the Greek text, uses no quotation marks at all. This avoids identifying the speaker and is probably closest to the intention of the text. In this monologue, as throughout the Fourth Gospel, the voice of the protagonist in the story (Jesus in 3:11–21, John in 3:27–36) is the voice of the evangelist.[3] Verses 31–36, building on the witness of John the Baptist, continue to urge upon readers the truth about Jesus Christ and the importance of how one responds to him. These verses affirm that:

Jesus comes from heaven and speaks the truth about God with the authority of personal knowledge that neither John nor any other human witness possesses.

Jesus is God's beloved Son, sent by the Father to speak the words of God.

In Jesus, God gives the Spirit without measure.

The Father has placed all things in Jesus' hands.

How people respond to God's initiative in Jesus Christ is of immediate and ultimate importance, because all who believe in the Son receive eternal life now, while those who disobey him never even see what true life is, but are the objects of God's wrath.

This paragraph (3:31–36) is a summary of Johannine theology thus far. In the style and vocabulary characteristic of the Fourth Gospel, it focuses on the person of Jesus Christ, his relation to God on the one hand and to believers on the other, and on the importance of believing the truth that is incarnate in Jesus, since eternity is now.[4]

The wrath of God, familiar in the letters of Paul (e.g., Rom. 1:18–3:20), is explicitly mentioned only once in John (3:36). The judgment of the Father and the Son is usually presented in John as the judgment of light, which judges only by the response people make to its presence. Light can burn, but it does not grow angry. The evangelist, however, was clearly angry with the religious authorities who rejected the message that Jesus is Messiah and who expelled from the synagogue those who affirmed that he is. The harsh words about "the Jews" that the Fourth Gospel attributes to Jesus probably reflect that anger, as does this word about "the wrath of God" that those who disobey the Son must endure.[5]

While obeying Christ's commandments usually refers in the Fourth Gospel to loving and serving God, Jesus, and one another, "disobey" in 3:36 is used as the opposite of "believe," reflecting the early Christian view that the supreme disobedience was a refusal to believe their gospel.[6] For John, the most important thing for anyone to do is to believe in Jesus Christ, and to live that belief out in loving service (13:15–17, 34; 14:15, 21; 15:10, 12, 14).

The statement in verse 32b, "no one accepts his testimony," followed immediately by "whoever has accepted his testimony" in verse 33a seems incongruous, but it is simply one among many examples of hyperbole in the New Testament.

Overfamiliarity with the ideas in this text due to their repetition throughout the entire Gospel and in evangelistic preaching tends to dull the reader's mind to their power and vital significance. Repetition, however, is characteristic of Scripture and of any literature written for an oral culture. Modern advertisers have also learned the power of repetition. The enduring effectiveness of the Fourth Gospel vindicates its repetitive style.

Preaching and teaching the Word

1. The witness in art. John the witness's final testimony to Jesus in the Fourth Gospel concludes with a short and pithy punch line, "He must increase, but I must decrease" (3:30). A lesson on this text might focus on the crucifixion panel of Matthias Grünewald's Isenheim Altar (ca. 1513–15).[7] Like the fourth evangelist, the artist is not primarily concerned with historical accuracy: John was long dead when Jesus went to the cross. Yet this painting is a true and powerful representation of John's role in salvation history. According to medieval artistic convention, the size of figures in a painting was dictated by their importance. In this painting John is second only to Jesus. Although John the evangelist might assign that position to the Beloved Disciple, other details in Grünewald's representation of John the Baptist come straight out of the Fourth Gospel: the disproportionately large hand, whose index finger points to Jesus, the gesture of a witness (1:7–8, 34); the open Scriptures in the other hand, on the basis of which John bears witness (1:23); the lamb whose blood spills into a chalice at the foot of Jesus' cross, itself bearing the cross as an emblem (1:29, 36); and, above all, the Latin text printed in large, clear letters between John's forefinger and his face: *ILLUM OPORTET CRESCERE ME AUTEM MINUI* ("He must increase, but I must decrease").

Karl Barth, whose christocentric theology of the Word of God is also thoroughly Johannine, thought this the most powerful painting in the Western world. John's greatness consists precisely in his subordination to the incarnate Word, to which he points till the end of time. The humility of John in this text is of towering proportions and has theological depth. John models the role of disciples in every time, a role to which Barth gave the caption "The Christian as witness."[8] Such witness involves courage, as in the case of the author and signers of the Barmen Declaration.[9] It also involves in all true disciples of Jesus a willingness to play second fiddle.

2. On self-importance. In every successive generation John the Baptist continues to address disciples of Jesus whose self-importance is wounded by the success of other heralds or servants. The text rebukes every sect, movement, or church that points to itself as the way to God; senior ministers who keep associates in their place; church members who seek prominent positions; and all persons in the public eye who tend to put down those who show promise of eclipsing them in importance. It is a call to a generosity of spirit that evaluates one's own role positively but gladly acknowledges the potentially greater role of another. It invites us to love others as we love ourselves. Above all, it bids believers to recognize and testify to the greatness of Jesus Christ, whose Spirit breathes into every disciple a proper self-esteem unsullied by self-importance.

3. The demand for decision. The prologue (1:1–18) introduces Jesus Christ as the eternal Word of God that came into the world, bringing life and light, glory, grace, truth, and the possibility of new birth as children of God. Now, after hearing the message of Jesus' first witness and watching Jesus gather his first disciples, perform his first sign, engage in his first confrontation with organized religion, and encounter a religious seeker, every reader is faced in 3:31–36 with a call to decide. It is not the last such call in this Gospel, and, God willing, it will not be the last such invitation in the earthly life of hearers today. But the punch line of this paragraph (3:36) proclaims that whoever hears this call and walks away from it unmoved or undecided in fact decides not to see the life Christ offers, but rather to walk in darkness. The evangelist says to every reader or hearer, "Get a life!" The hearer may be unmoved by the call, but God is not unmoved by the decision. Every decision not to decide weakens the next call to an encounter with Christ, and the evangelist says that to walk in darkness without Christ is to endure the self-imposed judgment of God.

4. The wrath of God. This subject is an embarrassment to mainline churches in our time. It is largely avoided by preachers, committees preparing curriculum materials, and resources for worship. Yet under the surface of many a heart lurks the suspicion that maybe the sterner though loving God of earlier generations is closer to the truth than our own sanitized representations. The present writer remembers the question of a neighbor whom he had bailed out of the county "drunk tank" early one Sunday morning. "God don't get mad, does he?" the neighbor asked.

Preachers wishing to probe the question would find more material in Paul than in John, whose only mention of the wrath of God is in this text. It is not a Johannine theme, but in 3:36 the Fourth Gospel confirms the uniform witness of Scripture that God is angered by our disobedience to the Word and that anger is not inconsistent with parental love.

Responses to the
Coming of the Light

(John 4:1–12:50)

The first half of the Gospel of John is about meeting the living Word (1:19–12:50). The summary section at the end of chapter three (vv. 22–26) marks the end of Jesus' contacts with John, which bracket his first encounters with other individuals and groups. His next meeting introduces the largest single block of material in the Fourth Gospel (4:1–12:50), in which varying responses to Jesus show the growing depth of belief in some and the growing intensity of unbelief in others. All are designed to lead different types of readers to believe in Jesus and find a new quality of life in him. After Nicodemus, who will it be?

THE SAMARITAN WOMAN (4:1–42)

The unnamed woman whom Jesus encounters in chapter 4 is quite a contrast to Nicodemus, the male teacher of Israel, who met Jesus in chapter 3. He has a respected heritage; she has a questionable past. He has seen signs and knows Jesus is "from God"; she meets Jesus as a complete stranger.[1] He takes the initiative to find Jesus, but under cover of darkness. She is approached by Jesus under the burning sun of high noon. He represents official orthodoxy; she represents a despised heresy. Nicodemus belongs to the religious in-group of his time; the Samaritan woman is an outcast.

The structure of this contrasting pair of encounters is parallel: the revelation of Jesus, 3:1–21 and 4:1–30, is followed by an account of the witness of others to the revelation, 3:22–30 and 4:31–42.[2]

Exploring the text

After a description of the setting, the story unfolds in three scenes of unequal length.

Setting (4:1–6)

Four verses (1–4) situate the story of Jesus and the Samaritan woman in the overall narrative of John's Gospel. The Pharisees (4:1) were first mentioned in chapter 1 as the particular group of Jews who sent priests and Levites from Jerusalem to investigate John (1:14, 24). The next explicit mention of them is in the person of Nicodemus, a Pharisee and leader of "the Jews" (3:1–10). Chapter 4 marks a distinct stage in the relationship between Jesus and the Pharisees, a relationship marked by a growing distance that will culminate in Jesus' crucifixion.

That Jesus was making and baptizing more disciples than John was introduced in 3:26 as the basis of jealousy between John's disciples and those of Jesus. Now that phenomenon becomes a subject of jealousy on the part of the Pharisees in Jerusalem. The parenthetical remark about Jesus himself not baptizing (4:2) is inserted to correct the statement in 3:22, 26 that Jesus and his disciples were baptizing in the Judean countryside (see comment at 3:22, 26). Even if the first disciples did baptize, but not Jesus, word of the rapid growth in the number of his followers might well be expressed as "Jesus . . . making and baptizing more disciples than John" (4:1).

These verses underscore the geographical location of the ensuing story: Samaria (4:4), a setting that has historical and theological significance. Originally one of the designations of the northern kingdom of Israel, whose capital city was Samaria, in the time of Jesus the term applied to the whole region. Direct travel from Jerusalem to Galilee was through Samaria.

The more precise location, Jacob's well near Sychar, is specified in verses 5–6a. Sychar is probably a corruption of the name "Shechem," forty miles north of Jerusalem.[3] The well in question is probably the one located a quarter of a mile from the edge of ancient Shechem, now found in the crypt under a Greek Orthodox church built to shelter it. The text situates it on the plot of land that Jacob gave to his son Joseph (Gen. 33:18–20, 48:22) and calls it "Jacob's well." The tie with Joseph, whose mummified body the Israelites brought up from Egypt and buried here when they entered Canaan (Gen. 50:25–26; Josh. 24:32) links this site to the northern tribes, and especially to Joseph's son, Ephraim, another synonym for Samaria and the northern kingdom. Mention of Jacob means that the tradition about this well belongs to all of Israel: Judeans, Samaritans, and Galileans.

The time is about noon (v. 6). The well is on a plain under the heat of the noonday sun. Jesus, tired out by his journey, sits by the well.

Jesus and the Woman (4:7–26)

Only two characters are on stage, a Samaritan woman and Jesus. Jesus' disciples have gone into Sychar to buy food (4:8). Jesus makes contact with the woman in the first three of six exchanges; in the last three he comes to the point and the woman must decide how to respond. The expression "Samaritan woman" marks this person as an outsider on two grounds, yet Jesus takes the initiative to make contact with her.

In the first exchange (4:7b–9a) Jesus asks the woman for a drink of water, and she expresses surprise that a Jewish man would ask a drink of her, a woman of Samaria. Of the two strikes against any contact with this person, the evangelist explains only the second (presupposing Gentile readers): "Jews do not share things in common with Samaritans" (4:9b). This editorial note alludes to a long and unhappy history. The inhabitants of Samaria were of mixed blood, occasioned by the deportation of its inhabitants by the king of Assyria after the fall of Samaria in 722–721 B.C.E. and the settlement of non-Israelite colonists in the region. The paganization of the region described in 2 Kings 17:24–41 is overstated, for some of the descendants of these mixed marriages continued to worship Yahweh and built a temple to him on Mount Gerizim in the fourth century B.C.E. A significant Jewish sect developed that viewed this as the only true temple of Yahweh and the five books of Moses as the only authoritative Scriptures of Israel. The Yahwists of Samaria were viewed as heretics and were not allowed to help rebuild the Jerusalem temple after the exile (Ezra 4:3). In addition to these ethnic and religious tensions, there was a political basis for the hostility between Jews and Samaritans (Neh. 2:9–10, 19–20; 4:1–23; 6:1–19; cf. 13:28). Samaria vigorously opposed the Persian reestablishment of the Judean province. Jewish troops in the Maccabean period (from ca. 165 B.C.E.) destroyed the temple on Mt. Gerizim, deepening yet again the hostility between Jews and Samaritans. They even viewed each other's eating vessels–including drinking cups–as unclean. This hostility is what gives force to Jesus' parable of the Good Samaritan (Luke 10:30–37) and the healing of the ten lepers, only one of whom–a Samaritan–returned to say thank-you (Luke 17:11–17), as well as to this scene by Jacob's well.

Jesus ignores the woman's initial rebuff and initiates a second exchange (4:10–12). If the woman had known who he was, she would have asked a drink from him and he would have given her living water. This draws attention to the question of Jesus' true identity, which lies beyond the fact of his Jewishness. The expression "living water" gives rise to the kind of double entendre the fourth evangelist loves so much–like *anothen* and *pneuma* in chapter 3. The woman's first response (4:11) shows that she hears "living water" in its ordinary sense of fresh, running water from a spring or stream, misunderstanding Jesus' figurative use of the expression. The second focuses attention again on Jesus' personal identity, as she says, in effect, "Who do you think you are?" (4:12).

In the third exchange (4:13–15) Jesus says who he thinks he is when, in Johannine language, he expands the image of the living water that he gives and that satisfies permanently one's thirst (for God). Unlike well water, this water is a gushing, life-giving spring inside oneself, and the life it gives is eternal (4:14). The reference is doubtless to the Holy Spirit, which is subtly linked with water throughout the Gospel of John (3:5, 2:1–12, and 7:37–39).

Absence of such direct claims for himself on the lips of Jesus in the Synoptic Gospels, together with the thoroughly Johannine thought and vocabulary, suggests that the voice of Jesus is here mediated through the words of the fourth evangelist and his experience of the risen Lord.[4] What Jesus promises is not something that will be used up after he gives it, but the gift of himself in the person of the Paraclete. The Nicene Creed expresses the cumulative force of this passage in the words, "We believe in the Holy Spirit, the Lord, the giver of life, who proceeds from the Father and the Son."

Only much later did early Christians come to this understanding of the living water that Jesus gives. The woman's response is finally the request Jesus was looking for, but she still misunderstands: "Sir, give me this water, so that I may never be thirsty or have to keep coming here to draw water" (4:15). She is now open to Jesus' offer. Even though she doesn't fully understand, she is on the way to believing.

These first three exchanges reveal three stages in the woman's response to Jesus. First, she reminds Jesus of the barrier between them (4:9); next she expresses a somewhat mocking doubt that he can deliver what he has offered (4:11b–12); and then, responding to his offer (though she misunderstands it), she echoes Jesus' initial approach to her by asking him for a drink of water (4:15).

In a fourth exchange (4:16–18) the dialogue comes to the point. Jesus will give his living water freely, but there is a condition attached. The woman must be open and honest with him. Jesus again takes the initiative by raising the subject of the woman's past: "Go, call your husband." The woman responds with a half-truth, "I have no husband." Jesus' answer shows that he knows this woman's history in full.

Many interpreters assume that the woman had a lurid history of promiscuous living, that the reason she came to the well at high noon was to avoid facing the other women of the town in the cool of the morning. If true, it would be a third strike against this woman who is a Samaritan: she would also be a woman of questionable reputation. She might as easily be a victim as a sinner in this uncommon series of relationships,[5] but the text is silent on this subject.

Jesus' comment prompts the woman to initiate a fifth exchange (4:19–24), on a new topic of her choosing. For the first time she takes the initiative and seeks to ingratiate herself by saying, "Sir, I see that you are a prophet." Readers will recognize this as a common and correct but inadequate understanding of who Jesus is, a point on which John and the Synoptic Gospels are in full agreement (Mark 8:28 and parallels; John 9:17). She then raises the issue that lay at the heart of the hostility between Jews and Samaritans. "Let's don't talk about my past," she suggests. "Let's talk about worship" (4:20, paraphrased).

Several explanations are possible. The woman may be trying to keep her distance from Jesus by changing the subject. Her comment may reflect the human desire to stay in control of a conversation and the reluctance to be totally honest with a stranger. Her question could also be an honest effort to answer a theological question that had plagued her.

Whatever the woman's motives may have been, the evangelist uses her question to introduce a revelatory discourse. Jesus replies, what matters is to know *who* we worship, and on this we Jews have it right. What matters for all of us is that we worship the one we both acknowledge as Father in spirit and in truth, for that is the kind of worship the Father wants.

Again the voices of Jesus and the evangelist are indistinguishable. "Hour," "spirit," and "truth" are significant terms in the Johannine vocabulary. For all the tensions between Jesus and the temple authorities in Jerusalem, the evangelist insists that Jesus was a Jew, that the God known through the Jewish Scriptures is the true source of salvation, and that the Samaritan Yahwists were on the wrong track. Through words attributed to the historical Jesus, the spirit of the risen Lord here affirms that the true worship of God is not to be identified with Pharisees or Samaritans, with Gerizim or Jerusalem.

In a sixth exchange (4:25–26) the key to such worship is provided. The woman is not prepared either to deny or to affirm Jesus' weighty affirmation in 4:21–24. She needs time to think about it. She says, "I know Messiah will come and will explain" (4:25, paraphrased).[6] Jesus' answer is what the story has been building toward all along: "I am he, the one who is speaking to you" (4:26).

The woman's comment has shifted the direction of the conversation to the subject of greatest interest to the evangelist: the identity of Jesus. Once again, John's love for double entendre shapes the way he reports Jesus' answer, which reads literally, "I AM, the one talking to you." At the obvious level, that means, "I am the Messiah." But when Jesus says, I AM, he uses the answer God gave at the burning bush in Exodus 3:14, a text as sacred to Samaritans as it was to Jews. The point is not lost on the woman, whose astonishment becomes evident in the following verses.

Transition (4:27–30)

The disciples return to Jesus as the woman rushes off to the city, with the Samaritans of Shechem (Sychar) just offstage in the wings.

The disciples are amazed that Jesus is speaking with a woman, but out of deference to his authority they do not question his action (4:27). Their surprise mirrors the woman's first words to Jesus, "How is it that you, a Jew, ask a drink of me, a woman of Samaria?" (4:9). At that earlier point, the evangelist's comment underscored the fact that she was Samaritan, now the fact that she is a woman.

The woman is so flustered that she leaves her water jar and rushes back to the city (4:28). Unlike the disciples, who had left Jesus to find something to eat, she leaves her jar and her quest for drinking water in order to bring people to Jesus. She says to the people of Sychar/Shechem: "Come and see a man who told me everything I have ever done!" The hyperbole is understandable in light of the claim she has just heard from Jesus' lips.

"Come and see!" These were the words of Jesus to Andrew and an unnamed disciple of John the Baptist who asked where he was staying (1:39), and of Philip to Nathanael, who asked if any good thing could come out of Nazareth (1:46). Through these words, the Samaritan woman takes her place beside Andrew and Philip as one of the earliest witnesses to Jesus Christ.

Her words about Jesus as Messiah are framed as a question, not an affirmation. She is not yet sure what to make of Jesus. Maybe–just maybe–he is who he says he is. She is prepared to entertain that possibility, and she invites her friends to do so, too. The people of Sychar hear her tentative but compelling witness and set out to see for themselves (4:30).

Jesus and the Disciples (4:31–38)

This scene reports the conversation between Jesus and his disciples by the well while the woman is gone. A brief dialogue about food introduces a slightly longer monologue about Jesus' vocation–and the vocation of all his witnesses. The disciples initiate the dialogue with an invitation to their teacher to have something to eat (4:31). Jesus replies, "I have food to eat that you do not know about" (4:32). Once again the evangelist uses a misunderstanding based on double entendre to communicate with readers. The disciples are speaking of physical food, Jesus of what nurtures the soul.

Jesus knows what they are saying to one another—one of many examples of his omniscience in the Fourth Gospel (e.g., 1:47–48; 2:24; 4:16–18; 6:15)—so he explains why he is not hungry. His conversation with the woman so satisfies the deepest hunger of his life that he feels no physical hunger at all. Jesus' desire to do the will of God is the essence of his sense of purpose in life.

In the monologue of verses 35 to 38 Jesus indicates that he will finish his work of bearing witness to the truth, drawing people into the kingdom of God, and giving them eternal life through his disciples. Jesus invites his disciples to partake of the spiritual food that he is enjoying. The disciples seem to be guided by a proverb about harvest being four months away— a saying that gives farmers time to rest after they have done the sowing and cultivating. Jesus, however, suggests that there are plenty of people ready for harvesting right now, if the disciples would just notice the outcasts (4:35). Continuing the analogy of sowing and reaping, Jesus says to disciples of all succeeding ages, that those who see the harvest all around them are already gathering fruit for eternal life, their own and that of the people who receive their witness (4:36).

This talk about completing the work of the one who sent Jesus sounds like a word that John the evangelist would address to the community for which he writes this Gospel. That impression is heightened in the words that follow. The Fourth Gospel has no account of Jesus sending out disciples during his earthly ministry. The words apply directly to the community that will have heard the command of the risen Lord in John 20:21. Jesus' vocation is to love the world as God does and thus to bear witness to the world about who God is and what God wants of disciples. That is Jesus' calling and work; it is also that of his disciples in every generation.

Jesus and the Samaritans (4:39–42)

In the brief denouement the Samaritans come to believe. As a result of Jesus' reaching out to one outcast, many cease to be outcasts and are included in the fellowship of believers. When the woman reached town with her astonishing news, many believed in him because of her testimony (4:39).

When the Samaritans of Sychar/Shechem believed, they did not just say, "That's interesting," and go about their business. They left town and came to Jesus. The text does not say anything more about the woman. Her essential role as witness has been accomplished. The people of the city returned, taking Jesus with them, "and he stayed there two days." During that time, many more believed because of his word, not just because of what the woman reported, but because of what they heard for themselves (4:41–42).

The last clause in the text states what they came to know, summing up the main point of the entire pericope: "We know that this is truly the Savior of the world" (4:42b), the Savior of the whole world, including outcasts. This scene in which a group of Samaritans becomes part of the community of believers in Jesus Christ is one of the pivotal moments in the New Testament.

The Samaritans heard and appropriated the truth of John 3:16: "God so loved the *world* that he gave his only Son, so that *everyone* who believes in him . . . may have eternal life." "Everyone" includes women, people of a questionable past, Samaritans, Greeks, Romans, and every reader of the Gospel of John. But according to John 4:1–42, God seems to have a special concern for outcasts, and Jesus counts on his disciples to finish his work.

Preaching and teaching the Word

1. Jesus meets a woman at the well. This story is admirably suited for teaching through a dramatic reading (for mature learners who read well) or role play (for energetic, imaginative youth). The six exchanges between Jesus and the Samaritan woman touch on many relevant themes that would be overload for a sermon but can spark lively interest and discussion in a study setting. The teacher can set the scene briefly, assign parts judiciously and determine how much of the text to read at a time, invite response by observers and readers, and draw together salient comments and themes at the end. A good way to close might be to play the popular 1960s song, "Jesus Met the Woman at the Well," sung by Mahalia Jackson or by Peter, Paul, and Mary.

2. Evangelism. The subject of Jesus' dialogue with his disciples (vv. 31–38) is evangelism. These verses suggest a proper respect and appreciation for our predecessors, through whom we have come to know Jesus; commitment to do the will of God as the answer to our yearning for a sense of purpose in life; and the promise of fruit and therefore of joy to any who will hear this word and act on it. Evangelism is also a key for interpreting the whole story. Jesus models the way to establish contact with those we normally seek to avoid. The woman—an unlikely evangelist in that time and place—became a witness to him even before she was sure about who he was. She challenges us to share with friends and neighbors any significant contact we have had with Jesus, even if we are uncertain about theology. Telling others about one's own experience of Jesus Christ is more important than giving money for programs of evangelism, or worrying about declining denominational membership.

Addressed to those who do not know Jesus and feel shunned by those who think they do, the text offers an example of how Jesus reaches out to them and by patient, tough love leads them gradually to faith. Here the accent is on the boundless love of God that takes the initiative to make contact with those who have been left out; the penetrating love of God that cuts through masks, sees into the heart, and probes sore spots; the patient love of God that stays with the loved ones until they recognize the lover, first on the basis of someone else's testimony and then on the basis of their own experience.

3. The inclusive love of God. This story invites teachers and preachers to search their own hearts and ask, "Who are my Samaritans–the ones I do not know and seek to avoid?" Answers to that question indicate the parts of God's field into which God sends us to build bridges of understanding, to labor and to reap. We can find a well and discover what help we need from those other folks. In the process we preachers and teachers will learn more about who Jesus Christ really is.

4. Sparring with Jesus. A sermon might recount the way this woman tried to keep Jesus at a distance and how he led her to faith, relating this to the way people today, even those in church pews, relate to Jesus. Sometimes his probing questions of us are painful, but there is no hiding place from Jesus. His seeking love will never give us up–as Francis Thompson discovered and testified in his famous poem "The Hound of Heaven" (1893)–until we, too, come to "know that this is truly the Savior of the world."

5. Worthy worship. As a distraction, the woman raises a question about worship, but Jesus treats it seriously. In congregations experiencing differences of opinion about styles of worship, a sermon or Bible study on John 4:19–24 might help move the discussion beyond external and secondary matters to the question of what it means to worship in spirit and truth, informed by the words of the text and guided by the living Spirit of Jesus, who is Christ and who is himself the way, the truth, and the life (14:6).

TRANSITION: FROM SAMARIA TO GALILEE (4:43–45)

Jesus continues his journey (4:3) from Judea to Galilee, after the significant two-day interlude in Samaria. Verse 45 completes the travel note by reporting a warm welcome in Galilee by those who had also gone to the festival in Jerusalem (2:13) and seen the signs that Jesus had done there (2:23).

An editorial note in verse 44 injects a puzzling element when it reports an aphorism of Jesus about a prophet having no honor in his own country. This saying appears in all three Synoptic Gospels in the account of Jesus' rejection in his hometown of Nazareth (Mark 6:4//Matt. 13:57; Luke 4:24), as well as in the Gospel of Thomas (saying 31). The contrast between the proverb and Jesus' favorable reception in Galilee in John 4:45 has led interpreters from Origen onward to debate what John considers to be Jesus' "own country." Theologically, the religious leaders in Jerusalem are his own people (1:11), the Jerusalem temple is his father's house (2:16), and a predominant portion of Jesus' public ministry in the Fourth Gospel takes place in Judea. Yet John, like the Synoptics, repeatedly refers to Jesus' Galilean origins (1:46; 2:1–2; 7:41–42, 52; 19:19) and does not even report that he was born in Judea. What is clear in this transitional note is that Jesus is welcomed in Galilee as well as Samaria. Clear references to his rejection still lie ahead. Some occur in Galilee (6:41, 59), but most are in Jerusalem and Judea (7:1, 32; 8:59; 10:31, 39; 11:7–8, 49–57; 19:6, 15, 17–18).

THE ROYAL OFFICIAL'S SON (4:46–54)

Sign, miracle, and believing in Jesus, major Johannine themes, converge in this story of a devoted parent who moves from a desperate quest for help, through astonished realization of Jesus' power, to personal commitment as head of a household.

Exploring the text

References to "Cana in Galilee where he had changed the water into wine" (4:46) and to "the second sign that Jesus did after coming from Judea to Galilee" (4:54) mark the limits of this narrative unit and situate the healing of the royal official's son in a series of miraculous signs in the first twelve chapters of John. The first two signs end with a note linking each with believing. In the present text, Jesus' first response to the father's request (4:48) is typical of the ambiguous role of signs in the Fourth Gospel. **Signs** are powerful symbols of who Jesus is, but faith based on miracle is disparaged as inadequate.

Verse 46b identifies the petitioner as a royal official who belongs to yet another social group. The term "royal official" implies a regional civil authority subservient to the Romans. This man is not a religious leader like Nicodemus, nor a social outcast like the Samaritan woman, but a respected citizen of local importance. Thus the evangelist provides a range of personalities with whom readers of all sorts and conditions can identify.

The account is a miracle story, remarkably similar to the healing of a centurion's servant (Matt. 8:5–13; Luke 7:1–10) despite some striking differences. The Synoptic story involves a Roman centurion whose slave is deathly ill and who believes in the authority of Jesus' word even before it is pronounced. Jesus says of him, "Not even in Israel have I found such faith" (Matt. 8:10//Luke 7:9). The present text involves a civil official whose son is deathly ill, who realizes the power of Jesus' word only after the son is healed, and then believes. Both depict men in authority who send or come to Jesus for help out of concern for someone else, and in both cases the word of Jesus has power to heal even at a distance. There are also points of contact with the story of the Syrophoenician woman (Mark 7:24–30). Important elements include the urgency and persistence of the father's request, Jesus' initial rebuff of the father, the stages by which faith grows, the identical timing of Jesus' word and the son's recovery, and the concluding note that the royal official and all his household believed.

Some striking interpersonal dynamics are revealed in the dialogue between Jesus and the desperate father. In his distress this royal official is not ashamed to beg an itinerant rabbi for help. Jesus interprets his approach as a typical desire to see a miracle and rebuffs faith based only on signs (4:48). Unwilling to give up, the father addresses Jesus with a term of respect and an appeal for compassion toward a dying child (4:49). Jesus then utters the authoritative word. The official believes the word of Jesus and starts back to Capernaum. Along the way he learns that his son began to mend at the very hour Jesus spoke the healing word. At this point his faith in the miracle worker's word is confirmed, and the narrative suggests—though it does not state—that his faith has grown into believing Jesus in the full, Johannine sense of "believe" (see glossary).

The stages of faith in the Fourth Gospel include (1) willful blindness to the signs, (2) seeing the signs as wonders and regarding Jesus as a wonder worker sent by God, (3) seeing beyond the signs to their true significance and coming to believe in and know Jesus for who he really is, and (4) coming to believe in Jesus even without signs.[1] The second and third of these stages come into play here. Jesus' initial response expresses his dim view of faith based only on signs (see 2:23–25) and his impatience with those who come to him simply looking for a sign (see 6:2, 26, 30). The denouement in 4:53, however, reflects the fourth evangelist's nuanced position on signs, which tends to be more positive than negative. Faith based on a sign is not enough, but it can be a stage on the way to a personal relationship with the one to whom the sign points.

The text is silent about the subsequent relationship of the royal official and his household to Jesus, but the place of this story in the structure of the Gospel leads readers to keep on reading and see what believing means.

Preaching and teaching the Word

1. Miracles and faith. Belief in miracles is one of the elements used in some quarters as a litmus test for Bible-believing Christians. All four Gospels present Jesus as a miracle worker and healer–an exorcist as well, in the Synoptics. According to the Fourth Gospel, "Did Jesus really perform miracles?" is the wrong question to ask. Miracles were an accepted, if not common, phenomenon in the world of the Old and New Testaments. The appropriate questions are, "What does this miracle mean?" and "Who is this one whose word has such power?"

For those who have eyes to see, Jesus' signs reveal his glory (2:11), which is the glory of God. Not everyone sees that way. Most people today think of events like this one as coincidences. Others regard them as miracles but are only fascinated, while some see in them the gracious hand of God. These are, or might become, Jesus' disciples.

Where belief in miracle is denied or belittled as shallow enthusiasm, careful teaching and preaching of this text–together with sensitive pastoral care–could deepen insight and lead to the kind of personal relationship with Jesus Christ expressed in John's use of "believe." As Jesus' compassion moved him to say the word in this text, so the beneficiaries of his gracious action today may see Jesus Christ in the work of his living, present Spirit and respond in faith, love, and gratitude. Such a response can be the foundation of a durable relationship, which the Fourth Gospel calls "abiding in Christ," a kind of believing that no longer depends on seeing signs.

2. Jesus and a VIP. Part of the significance of this text lies in the identity of the distraught parent. Royal officials were not prone to come as petitioners to itinerant Jewish rabbis, but this official, pushed by desperate concern for his child, does. There are no atheists in foxholes. Jesus does not respond as one who is flattered by the official's approach. He puts the official to a test, a test that the official passes. The royal official is not looking for a sign; he is begging for the life of his son. Seeing this official's genuine distress, Jesus manifests himself as emissary of a much greater king, yet one to whom recipients of his grace can relate personally in grateful love.

THE PARALYTIC BY THE POOL (5:1–18)

Must one actively oppose Jesus in order to be against him? Jesus is reported to have said, "Whoever is not with me is against me" (Matt.

12:30). John 5:1–18 offers a good example of what that disturbing saying might mean.

Exploring the text

The story of Jesus' healing of a sick man at the pool called Bethzatha in Jerusalem combines an individual response to Jesus (5:1–9a) with the first full-fledged rejection of Jesus by the authorized religious leaders (5:9b–18). This healing, paired with Jesus' second **sign** (4:46–54), is the third miracle by which Jesus reveals who he is and implicitly calls for a decision. The controversy between Jesus and "the Jews"[1] occasioned by the healing plays a prominent role in the plot through chapter 12, and again in the passion narrative (chaps. 18–19).

Setting (5:1–3)

Verse 1 situates the story at an unnamed Jewish festival that Jesus has come from Galilee to Jerusalem to attend. Verse 2 further specifies the location: by the Sheep Gate at the pool, probably the twin pool just north of the temple area, whose name appears variously in early manuscripts as Bethzatha, Bethesda, and Bethsaida.[2]

The nature of the man's illness is not specified in the most reliable manuscripts. The word "paralytic" at the end of verse 3, together with all of verse 4 about an angel stirring up the water and the healing of the first person who stepped in afterward, appears to be a scribal note added in some ancient manuscripts to explain the man's comment in verse 7. This diagnosis, however, states explicitly what is implicit in the story itself. The legend about the angel, relegated to a footnote in most modern translations, may accurately reflect an ancient popular tradition about the pool.[3]

Healing (5:5–9a)

Just as the encounters with Nicodemus and the Samaritan woman form a contrasting pair, so the healing of a passive paralytic contrasts with the healing of the son of the energetic and determined royal official at the end of chapter 4. Both stories follow the pattern for miracles of healing: the severity of the problem is set forth, a dialogue with Jesus ensues, Jesus pronounces a word of command, and proof of healing is reported. The stories, however, reveal encounters with two very different personalities. In the earlier story, the desperate father took the initiative to find Jesus. In the present story, the patient had lain for thirty-eight years beside a potential source of healing but had found no way to take advantage of it. Jesus knew he had been there a long time (a divine clairvoyance frequently attributed to Jesus in this Gospel), so he takes the initiative (5:6).

The sick man finds in the question an implicit criticism, a common human response. He makes an excuse, blaming his condition on the fact that he has no one to do for him (5:7). The power of Jesus' healing word then transforms the situation (5:8). The evangelist reports that "immediately the man was made well, and he took up his mat and began to walk around" (5:9a, author's translation). The man's response indicates an obedient faith that sets this passive person on his feet and makes him well.

Controversy (5:9b–18)

Verse 9b introduces the account of Jesus' first major controversy with the custodians of Mosaic law. The controversy over Sabbath observance escalates into a major theological discussion of Jesus' relation to God that fills the remainder of chapter 5, drives the plot forward through most of the remainder of the Gospel, and still marks a boundary between Judaism and Christianity.

The action shifts to an encounter between the healed man and the Jewish religious authorities. This is the clear referent of "the Jews" through the remainder of chapter 5. They chide the man that "it is not lawful for you to carry your mat" on the Sabbath.[4]

The man seeks to avoid blame, saying, in essence, "I am only doing as I was told." Earlier he laid on others the responsibility for his having not been healed. Now he lays on his healer the responsibility for his breaking the Sabbath. The healed man had failed to thank his benefactor or even to learn Jesus' name.

Once again Jesus takes the initiative. Finding the man in the temple, Jesus warns him not to sin any more (5:14). In the Fourth Gospel, failure to recognize Jesus and to believe in him is called sin (9:41; 15:22–24; 16:9). On this understanding of sin, Jesus' warning to the man makes good sense. He had not turned to Jesus in gratitude for his healing but had blamed his benefactor. Jesus warns him against doing this again. The man has not shown active antagonism, but Jesus views his passive attitude as irresponsible and sinful.

Far from heeding Jesus' warning, the man now acts on his own initiative for the first time. He goes away to tell the Jewish religious authorities that it was Jesus who made him well (5:15). At best, this is thoughtless acquiescence with the powers that be. At worst, it is cowardly collaboration with Jesus' enemies. It is certainly a negative reaction to Jesus' gracious initiatives. At this point the man disappears from the story. The contrast with the royal official (4:46–54) is complete.

Three transitional verses report the reaction of the religious authorities to Jesus (5:16–18). Their dedication to the purity of the community and the sanctity of the Sabbath blinds them to what has happened to the paralytic. They now start persecuting Jesus. Jesus justifies his action: "My Father is still working, and I also am working" (5:17). The foundation for observing the Sabbath states that God rested on the seventh day (Gen. 2:2–3), but Jesus appeals to common sense. God works even on the Sabbath to give and sustain life. After all, babies are born and rain falls on the Sabbath without objection from the guardians of Mosaic law. They interpret Jesus' response as a claim to be equal to God, and having just begun to persecute him, they seek now to kill him (5:18). In so few words the controversy escalates from a dispute about Sabbath observance to a far more serious issue, which is elaborated in the rest of the chapter: Jesus' relationship to God the Father.

Preaching and teaching the Word

1. Apathy, self-pity, and healing. John 5:1–9 is the alternative Gospel reading for the Sixth Sunday after Easter in the Revised Common Lectionary. This truncated portion of Jesus' encounter with the paralytic by the pool suggests a sermon on Jesus' power to heal those who want to be healed (v. 6). The paralytic provides a mirror for people to whom life has dealt a hand that is far from satisfactory and who have given up on ever being whole. They may fall into apathy. Some tend to ask for pity. Their blaming others (v. 7) may thinly veil an urge to blame God. When Jesus comes into the paralytic's life, refuses to play the self-pity game, ignores the question of who is to blame, and tells him to get up and walk, this weak person is suddenly flooded with strength and acts without hesitation upon Jesus' command. It's a miracle! His willingness to step out in faith gives practical proof of the healing power of Jesus' word. Examples abound today in which faith has brought healing or positive acceptance of a limitation, deliverance from apathy, and a fruitful life.

2. Healing and response. Inclusion of the entire unit (vv. 1–18) offers richer grist for the preacher's mill, for it depicts the paralytic's reaction to his healing as well as that of the zealous enforcers of the Sabbath law.

> How do people today respond to healing? Do we recognize the miraculous quality in all healing and turn to God in gratitude and praise, or do we, like the paralytic, simply walk away without acknowledging the hand of the Great Physician? Can this be the sin of which Jesus speaks when

he finds the healed man later, or was he speaking of the possibility of falling back into apathetic dependence?

Instead of thanking Jesus, the paralytic responds to his heal-ing by identifying him to the authorities. Could this thoughtless conformity to the pressures of the surround-ing cultural and religious context be the sin against which Jesus warns the healed man? In our affluent culture, con-formity to traditional norms of religion is often praised, while challenging them can lead to serious conflicts.

The religious authorities are so focused upon their role as upholders of the law that they see only the infraction of carrying a mat on the Sabbath and are blind to the won-der of the man's healing. When Jesus explains his action by analogy to the ceaseless, healing work of God, his Father, they ignore that point and press his words into a charge of heresy. There are analogies today.

The end of the story is not edifying, for it shows negative responses to Jesus by the healed man and by the author-ities. But Jesus' healing word to the paralytic (v. 8) can be a means of grace, provided we understand that we have the freedom and write our own ending. It is as if Jesus says again and again, "Stand up, take your mat, and walk." We make our response every day.

3. *"Do not sin any more."* Twice in the Fourth Gospel Jesus tells a person he has graced to look to the future and not sin any more (5:14 and 8:11). Comparing the healed paralytic with the woman caught in adultery and the nature of the sin referred to in these two stories could produce an illu-minating lesson or sermon.

THE SECOND CONFRONTATION: DOES JESUS CLAIM EQUALITY WITH GOD? (5:19–47)

Exactly what does Jesus claim here about his relationship to God?

That Jesus of Nazareth was the unique revelation of God in human flesh is the basic affirmation of the Fourth Gospel and a distinguishing mark of the Christian faith. This claim sets Christianity apart from Judaism, from Islam, and from all other faiths, secular and religious. It has occasioned faith and commitment on the one hand and controversy and rejection on the other, ever since the first Christians set out to preach sal-vation in the name of Jesus Christ. According to John this claim originated with Jesus himself and was articulated with increasing clarity throughout his earthly ministry. This is not Jesus' first confrontation with Jewish religious authorities (see 2:13–22), but it is the first major articulation of his claim to a unique relationship with God. It grows out of an incident in which Jesus healed a sick man on the Sabbath (5:1–18). At the conclusion of that narrative the evangelist comments that the Jewish religious authorities were seeking all the more to kill Jesus (5:18). Jesus' reply to their accusation of Sabbath breaking had resulted in the accusation that he was making himself equal to God. The remainder of chapter 5 is Jesus' sustained response to the latter accusation. The polemic between Jesus and the Jewish religious authorities begins in earnest with this passage and is a major factor throughout the rest of the Fourth Gospel, culminating in the crucifixion of Jesus. The argument is still a crux in the relationship of Christians and Jews and in the presentation of the gospel to the world.

Exploring the text

Jesus answers this question in an unbroken monologue addressed to "the Jews" (5:18)[1] who do not believe what he says (5:47). The monologue consists of two parts, didactic and polemic. In the first part (5:19–30) Jesus explains his relation to God. In the second (5:31–47) he points to three witnesses to the truth of what he says and attacks the Jewish authorities for rejecting him.

The Son and the Father (5:19–30)

Jesus clearly calls God his own **Father.** The language is masculine, but the reference is to relationship, not gender. Jesus claims a relationship to God that is like the intimate, personal, relationship of parent and child. But does he claim to be equal to God? Jesus' very first affirmation (v. 19), echoed by the last in this subunit (v. 30), claims not equality but subordination. Jesus insists that he can do nothing on his own, but only what the Father does and what the Father delegates to the Son to do (vv. 22, 26). It is true that the Son does things that only God the Father can do: gives life to whomever he wishes and executes ultimate judgment on all, now and after the general resurrection at the end of time. That is why the Son is due the same honor as God the Father (v. 23). The verb translated as "honor" in most English versions, repeated four times in this verse, is the verbal form of the noun for value or worth. It can mean setting a price on something, or holding someone in high esteem. Here, it affirms that the Son is to be held in the same high esteem as the Father, to be honored and reverenced equally with the Father. However, Jesus makes a clear distinction between himself and God. The authority, power, and honor that

Jesus claims here is in every case delegated and derivative. He appeals to his listeners to hear him, but to believe in the one who sent him (5:24).

On the other hand, the relationship between Jesus and God appears to be a distinction without any functional difference. The Son works because the Father works, does what he sees the Father doing, gives life as the Father gives life, and exercises judgment according to the will of the Father.

These verses are punctuated by three of the twenty-five "amen, amen" sayings of Jesus that appear in the Fourth Gospel (vv. 19, 24, 25). John's use of the expression probably echoes Jesus' own, though it was by no means original with or peculiar to Jesus.[2] John alone has the doubled form, perhaps an example of the Fourth Gospel's tendency to heighten the authority of the risen Christ. English versions and commentators translate the phrase variously, but the purpose of the formula is to claim the attention of its hearers. The reader is to understand that Jesus here speaks as the one sent by God, with God's full authority.

The expression "greater works" (v. 20) alludes in part to the healing of the paralytic as a basis for comparison with what is to follow, while raising the dead and giving them life (v. 21) foreshadows the astonishing story of the raising of Lazarus in chapter 11.

Two types of eschatology appear side by side in this passage. Verses 25 and 26 express the realized, present eschatology characteristic of the Fourth Gospel. This refers to those who, during the earthly ministry of the Son of God, hear the incarnate Word, believe, and are not condemned but pass from death to life in a birth from above (3:16–18a). Verses 27–29, however, presuppose a future, apocalyptic eschatology in which the Son of Man will call the dead from their graves and execute judgment.[3] Among the messianic functions of the Son of Man in Jewish and Christian apocalyptic writings is that of judging the world. Those who recognize in Jesus' words the eternal Word of God and respond in reverent faith have already passed from death to life. Nevertheless, at the end they, with all those who are in their graves, will be raised to life or condemnation based on what they have done. It is rare that John suggests anything other than belief in Christ and love for one another as a criterion for acceptance with God. This is perhaps the only text in John that points to the last judgment as a reason for doing good in this life. This inclusion of this characteristically Synoptic view of God's judgment suggests that exhortations in the Fourth Gospel to keep Christ's commandments (14:15, 21; 15:10) should also be read in canonical context to include more than the single commandment to love.

Judging and giving life are divine prerogatives that Jesus says God has delegated to him (vv. 21–22, 26–27). Jesus' judgment is just, because he does the will of the one who sent him (v. 30c). It is also just because it confirms the self-judgment of individuals as they respond to God's light ("as I hear, I judge," v. 30b). The will of God for all, according to the Fourth Gospel, is eternal life as children of God through believing in Jesus (1:12; 3:16–18; 20:31).

Witnesses to Jesus (5:31–47)

There is a change in subject and in tone at 5:31. In verses 31–38 Jesus calls attention to four witnesses who corroborate what he has just said about himself: the witness of John the baptizer (5:32–35), the works or miraculous signs that he is doing (5:36), the Father who sent him (5:37–38), and the Scriptures (5:39). Jewish law required two or three witnesses in various circumstances (see Num. 35:30; Deut. 17:6; 19:15). In adducing four witnesses Jesus meets the Torah specialists in their own court with superior evidence to support his case.

At 5:37 the tone of the monologue becomes distinctly polemic. The rather neutral use of "you" in verses 33 and 35 changes into direct accusations and a hammerlike repetition of "you" thirteen times in verses 37–44 and four more in 46–47. The accusation in 37b–38 recalls John 1:18. Because Jesus' adversaries do not believe the Son, they do not have God's word abiding in them.

A graver accusation is introduced at 5:39. "You search the scriptures" reflects the meticulous study of biblical texts that often gave rise to heated debates among various rabbinic schools. "It is they that testify on my behalf" is echoed in 5:46, where Moses by synecdoche stands for all the Scriptures. No specific text is cited here, but the earliest Christian preachers and writers all insisted that Jesus was the one to whom the Hebrew Bible pointed. Jesus accuses the Jewish religious authorities of basing their hope on their meticulous exegesis of Scripture.

Such pulpit-pounding language probably reflects the heated debates between the evangelist and his community on the one hand and the Jewish religious authorities and their followers on the other. The chief point of 5:39–40 is that eternal life is not to be found in erudite exegesis of Scripture, but in personal commitment to the one to whom the Scriptures point–the Word made flesh.

Preaching and teaching the Word

1. Jesus' relationship to God. This text lends itself to teaching as well as to preaching. It has been important for efforts to understand who Jesus is, from the theological debates of the third and fourth centuries to the present day, and it is significant whenever a child of any age asks, "What is God like?"

When the church formulated the doctrine of the Trinity, "subordinationism" (the doctrine that the second and third persons of the Trinity are inferior to the first) became a dirty word to orthodox Christians. These verses clearly teach that the Son is subordinate to the Father, yet they insist that the honor due to the Father is due also to the Son because the Son is the Father's surrogate in giving life and in judging. In a "Prayer of the Kasai" a Congolese theological student used African traditional wisdom to arrive at the conclusion reached by the theologians of Nicaea, "The ancestors said that a son equals his father, thus you are truly God."[4] The same inference is drawn by Jesus' adversaries in John 5:18. Jesus does not refute it in the following verses, but neither does he flatly affirm it. Instead, the text states the relationship between Jesus and the Father as a paradox that points to the mystery of God's nature without reducing it to a rational formula. The best answer to the question "What is God like?" is not to be found by logical discourse or theological definition but by pointing to Jesus and saying, "God is like that."

According to the Synoptic Gospels, Jesus proclaimed not himself but the coming kingdom of God and only after his death and resurrection commissioned witnesses to preach throughout the world the good news about what God had done through him. According to the Fourth Gospel, however, Jesus from the very beginning proclaimed himself to be the Son of God, the Messiah, and the light of the world, and engaged in vigorous debate with those who rejected that claim. The present passage reads like the abridgment of an extended debate that had started before the Fourth Gospel was written and had reached boiling point at the time of writing. The sharpness of the debate was forcing clearer definition of terms, a process that led to the definition enshrined in the creed of Chalcedon. Yet the definition does not fully satisfy the questing heart that asks who Jesus is and what God is like. All four Gospels respond to this hunger and thirst.

2. How can I know who Jesus is? "Jesus Christ, Superstar, do you think you're who they say you are?" This question from the 1960s Lloyd Webber and Rice rock opera of the same name captures the attraction of Jesus, mixed with doubts about him, that has permeated scholarly and secular circles for half a century or more. The pastor/preacher who senses that it lurks in the hearts of people in the pew may find it appropriate to call attention to John 5:31–46. According to these verses Jesus cites witnesses to authenticate the truth attested by the text, but is the text still credible? No reader of these lines has heard John the Baptist preach, and few grant Moses the authority here accorded to him and his writings, but Jesus still has witnesses. There are preachers who, like John the Baptist, point to Jesus and testify that he is the Lamb of God who takes away the sin of the world. Dedicated disciples of Jesus still do godly works in his name, some public and spectacular, though most are not miraculous and are known only to those blessed by them. Scripture is still a witness, including the Gospel of John itself and the writings of the Hebrew Bible ("Moses and the prophets") as interpreted throughout the New Testament. The conclusive testimony, however, is that of God, who in the person of the Holy Spirit says in our hearts concerning Jesus Christ, "This is who I really am."

3. On "getting a life." The biting words in the latter part of the text (37b–47) are particularly significant to preachers and teachers, including this commentator. We are challenged to consider that the "you" (plural) who are addressed by Jesus here includes each of us. Jesus underscores the importance and the limitation of the right interpretation of Scripture (5:45b–46). He affirms Scripture as a witness to him, but he brings to Scripture an interpretation that was new to his learned opponents and therefore unacceptable to them.

Verses 39 and 40 are significant for all believers. They point beyond study to commitment, beyond words to the Word. The kind of relationship with God that the Fourth Gospel calls eternal life is to be found not in exegesis or theology, but in coming to Jesus Christ. This polemic passage ends with an accusatory, rhetorical question, but preachers and teachers today might consider concluding a sermon or lesson on this passage by linking the accusation in 5:39–40 ("you refuse to come to me to have life") with the promise of 5:24, "Very truly, I tell you, anyone who hears my word and believes him who sent me has eternal life, and does not come under judgment, but has passed from death to life."

OVERVIEW OF CHAPTER 6 (6:1–71)

In this, the longest chapter in the Fourth Gospel, several characteristically Johannine patterns converge: action/dialogue/monologue, encounter with and reaction to Jesus, miraculous signs, and "I am" sayings. Two of the seven signs are here (feeding five thousand people, 6:1–15, and walking on the sea, 6:16–21), and one of the seven sayings ("I am the bread of life," 6:35, 51). In addition, the theme of conflict between Jesus and those who reject him reaches a new level of intensity, and the revelation of the eternal Word of God finds here a new depth in his monologue about the bread of life. This theme governs the limits of three of the five lectionary pericopes in John 6, slightly adapted as units in the pages below.

Exploring the text

The chapter consists of the two miraculous signs (6:1–21) followed by dialogues with a hungry crowd (6:22–40), angry adversaries (6:41–59), and ambivalent disciples (6:60–71). The dialogues melt into monologue at verses 35, 43, and 53. Jesus' interaction with these groups continues the series of encounters through which various reactions to his words and deeds are depicted. An appropriate goal for preaching and teaching this chapter today is to encounter Jesus in a way that leads hearers to echo Peter's profession of faith, "Lord, to whom can we go? You have the words of eternal life" (6:68–69).

Jesus Feeds Five Thousand People and Walks on the Sea (6:1–21)

In the first five chapters the Fourth Gospel has presented vignettes of vivid encounters between Jesus and a wide variety of people, most of whom appear only incidentally or not at all in the other three Gospels: namely, Philip (1:43–48; 6:5–7; 12:20–22; 14:8–9), Nathanael (1:45–51; 21:2), Nicodemus (3:1–9; 7:50–52; 19:39–42), the Samaritan woman at the well (4:1–42), and a paralytic by a pool (5:2–15). The stories of Jesus feeding a hungry crowd of five thousand people and walking on water to rejoin his disciples after dark, however, do appear in all four Gospels, and in all but Luke they are linked together (see Matt. 14:13–33; Mark 6:30–52; Luke 9:10–17). In John the main point is indicated by the word **"sign"** which is introduced as the theme of chapter 6 (vv. 2, 14, 30). The first of the signs in chapter 6 is for the crowd; the second is for the disciples. Both show Jesus' authority over nature. Like the water turned into wine, they are signs that even material bread and physical waves are subject to the Word that was in the beginning, a Word that is not a "which" but a "who," through whom all things came into being and who can feel the hunger of a crowd and the fear of his disciples.

Jesus Feeds the Crowd (6:1–15)

In all four Gospels the text follows the usual structure of a miracle story: setting (vv. 1–4), problem (vv. 5–9), Jesus' resolving of the problem (vv. 10–11), proof that the miracle has occurred (vv. 12–13), and response of those who saw it (vv. 14–15). The Fourth Gospel, however, emphasizes points that differ from the Synoptics. The setting in John (vv. 1–4) gives the Roman name for the Sea of Galilee (Tiberias, v. 1) for the benefit of readers acquainted with imperial terminology, mentions Jesus' healings ("signs") as the reason crowds were following him (v. 2), and specifies that it is Passover time (v. 4), when memories of the deliverance from Egypt and of God's provision of bread in the wilderness were fresh in the mind of the Jewish crowd. This reminder also prepares the reader for Jesus' discourse on the bread from heaven that follows (vv. 32–58).

The words "Jesus went up the mountain and sat down there with his disciples" (6:3) do not appear in the Synoptic parallels to this story, but they are like an echo of the introduction to the Sermon on the Mount in Matthew 5 in which Jesus, as the living Word, "taught them as one having authority, and not as their scribes" (Matt. 7:29). Jesus offers the crowds the words of God in Matthew and the Word of God in John. These are the true staff of life without which mortals cannot live (see Jesus' response to Satan in Matt. 4:4 and Luke 4:4).

The brief dialogue with the disciples about the problem of food for the crowd is presented quite differently in John (vv. 5–9). In the Synoptic accounts the disciples initiate the conversation, but here Jesus broaches the subject with a question to Philip that suggests that Jesus and his disciples, as hosts to the crowd, ought to buy bread for them but lack the means to do so (v. 5). In an editorial aside characteristic of the Fourth Gospel, the evangelist says that the question was only to test Philip, since Jesus himself, being omniscient and omnipotent, already knew what he would do (v. 6). This interchange, found only in John, provides an occasion for the evangelist to suggest to the reader who Jesus is—one who shares the attributes of God—and what the sign is intended to signify—that he is the bread of life (v. 35).

Philip replies that two hundred denarii would not buy enough bread for each one of the crowd to get even a little bite (6:7). The denarius to which the Greek text refers was a small, silver coin about the size of a dime stamped with the emperor's name and face (see Mark 12:15–16//Matt. 22:19–20; Luke 20:24, Gk. text and some versions) and worth a day's labor (see Matt. 20:2, 9, 10, 13, Gk. text and some versions). Contemporary translations are correct when they render the equivalent of two hundred denarii as six (NRSV) or eight (NIV) months' wages.

Other details found only in John enrich this particular version of the familiar story.

> Only John has Andrew say that a little boy standing there had the five loaves of bread and two fish mentioned in the other accounts, and only John specifies that the loaves were of barley (common, peasant bread) and that the fish were small (*opsaria* instead of *ichthyas,* 6:9). These details suggest the boy's willingness to share his lunch and heighten the miraculous contrast between the insignifi-

cance of the lad's gift and the abundance of what was eaten.

All four Gospels mention the twelve baskets of leftover fragments, but only John has Jesus order that they be gathered up "so that nothing may be lost" (6:12). This detail is echoed in 6:39, 17:12, and 18:9, which speak of Jesus' guarding safely all of those whom God entrusts to him. The number twelve was doubtless included in the earliest oral form of this traditional story about Jesus. Although many early interpreters interpreted it allegorically, the evangelist refers to it only as proof that the crowd had eaten their fill (6:12, 26).

Only John reports that the crowd said, "This is indeed the prophet" (6:14), and adds, "Jesus realized that they were about to take him by force to make him king" (6:15). Although all four Gospels reflect common misconceptions about Jesus' kingship in other contexts, John here contrasts the crowd's misunderstanding with the understanding of Jesus that is presented in the following dialogues.

Preaching and teaching the Word

The feeding of the five thousand is a favorite for preaching and teaching in the church, often used to point to the compassion of Jesus and to exhort hearers to emulate the generosity of the boy who shared his lunch (a significant feature in John but not mentioned in the Synoptics). The temptation of the interpreter is, on the one hand, to get so carried away with the boy and his shared lunch as to overlook the miraculous power of Jesus Christ or, on the other hand, to be so caught up in proclaiming the Son of God as to lose sight of the Son of Man who felt for the hungry crowd and, before commanding that they be seated, noticed that there was lots of grass in that place (6:10).

1. Christology. A sermon on Christology (under a more appealing title, of course) is a way to tackle this challenge head-on, using the response of the crowd as the text: they said he was a prophet and they wanted to make him king (6:14–15). Both are presented as inadequate understandings of Jesus, though each is in some sense true. The Westminster Shorter Catechism (questions 23–26) and Larger Catechism (questions 42–45) affirm that Christ is prophet, priest, and king. This text offers an occasion to reflect on that truth in light of John's proclamation of Jesus as Son of God, Word of God, and bread of heaven. When "he withdrew again to the mountain by himself," was he really alone? What is Jesus' relation to God? What is the relationship between his time with the crowd and his time with God? How can he be known today as he really is? Any sermon on this theme would be didactic, and any teaching session should be kerygmatic (proclamatory), respecting the close tie between teaching and preaching in all the Gospel presentations of the ministry of Jesus. The interpreter, like Jesus himself, would need to find in the particular teaching/preaching context points of contact with the lives of the hearers.

2. The fragments left over. Another approach to preaching, less theologically substantive perhaps but easier to relate to contemporary life, would focus on Jesus' command to "gather up the fragments left over." What a mess that hillside would have been had the fragments not been gathered up! To suggest that Jesus was thereby constituting his disciples as a cleanup crew in an antilitter campaign is an anachronism so blatant as to defer the onset of drowsiness in a congregation. The preacher could, however, call attention to the fact that in the Synoptic accounts the fragments were gathered up without any command–evidence of a subsistence economy in which the wastefulness of American culture would be unthinkable–while in John the gathering up shows Jesus' concern that nothing and no one be lost, reiterated in 6:39. It is a Johannine way of presenting God's special concern for the lost, presented in parable form in Luke 15 and in the figurative language of John 10 about Jesus the good shepherd who guards and keeps all his sheep (17:12) and lays down his life in order to gather other sheep into his fold (10:16). The present text shows the divine will to preserve the results of every feeding on the bread that Jesus gives, recognizing the danger that the nourishment may simply be dissipated and lost in the routine of life after some intense experience of the presence and power of Jesus Christ.

3. The role of the boy. Even closer to daily life would be a sermon on the boy's role in the miracle of loaves and fishes. Bishop Desmond Tutu, in an address to a Student Christian Movement gathering in North Carolina on December 31, 1998, pointed out that "the divine miracle requires the thoroughly inadequate human contribution," adding a pithy saying from Augustine: "We without God cannot; God without us will not." The boy did not have much, but what he had, he brought to Jesus. What God did with it was so amazing that it is remembered after two millennia.

4. A communion meditation. Communion is another context in which to interpret this text, focusing on Jesus' action in taking, giving thanks, and distributing the loaves (6:11). All four Gospels report this sequential action, but only John uses *eucharisteo,* the verb for "give thanks" that also designates the Eucharist, to describe Jesus' prayer, which the Synoptics refer to as a "blessing," before he distributed the bread. John does not report the institution of the Lord's Supper in connection with the Last Supper before Jesus' death (13:1–30), but in the discourses that follow this text in chapter 6, and especially in verses 52–59, Jesus himself is reported to have interpreted the feeding miracle in sacramental terms. If, however, the lectionary should offer John 6:1–21 as the Gospel text on a Sunday on which the sacrament of the Lord's Supper is observed, the preacher may wish to consider John 6 as a whole and preach those portions of it that are appropriate to the celebration of the Eucharist, beginning with John 6:11.

Exploring the text (continued)

The shorter of the pair of nature miracles in chapter 6 is the account of Jesus' walking across the Sea of Galilee (Lake Tiberias) on a stormy night and joining his terrified disciples in their boat (6:16–21).

Jesus Walks on the Water (6:16–21)

In the basic story as it appears in Mark 6:45–51, the destination is Bethsaida, two to four miles east of Capernaum. But in John they start across the sea to Capernaum (6:17), where he confronts his Jewish opponents in the synagogue on the next day (6:59). Matthew expands Mark's account considerably by adding to it the story of Peter's attempt to walk on water like Jesus (Matt. 14:28–33). John reduces the Markan story to its bare bones, leaving just enough for readers to recognize that it is a theophany, a manifestation of God. Three elements mark it as such: the strong wind (6:18; see, for instance, Elijah at Mount Horeb, 1 Kgs. 19:11, and the disciples in Jerusalem on the day of Pentecost, Acts 2:2); the **"I Am"** (*ego eimi*) **saying,** translated here as "It is I" (6:20; see Moses at the burning bush, Exod. 3:14); and the command "Do not be afraid" to those who tremble in the presence of God or God's messenger (6:20; see God's word to Abram at Gen. 15:1 and Gabriel's to Mary at Luke 1:30). The sayings in which Jesus uses "I Am" without a defining term are of great importance in the Gospel of John. These, together with "I am" followed by a predicate nominative (defining term), are a major way in which the Fourth Gospel presents Jesus' claim to speak for and as God.

The essential elements of the story of Jesus walking on water are the same in all three Gospel accounts, but the climactic line of this text is peculiar to the Fourth Gospel: "They wanted to take him into the boat, and immediately the boat reached the land to which they were going" (6:21). John heightens the element of wonder by having the boat and all its occupants miraculously transported to Capernaum the moment the disciples want to take Jesus into the boat. In Matthew and Mark Jesus gets into the boat with the disciples, who react with astonishment in Mark and with faith in Jesus as Son of God in Matthew; but no reaction is reported in John. The evangelist is more interested in the response of the reader.

Preaching and teaching the Word

The story of Jesus' walking on water is less often the text chosen for a sermon, as it seems to offer few clues for application to the life of hearers or readers. The miraculous arrival of the boat and its occupants at their destination, however, may suggest experiences in which a period of darkness, rough sailing, and fear was suddenly and miraculously terminated by a clear sense of God's powerful presence in the person of Jesus Christ. The association of the disciples' wanting Jesus in the boat and their immediate arrival at their destination (6:21) may be compared with the solution to problems in our lives becoming immediately apparent when we really want Jesus in our boat with us.

Preachers of the common lectionary may be tempted to read the entire pericope for the Seventeenth Sunday in Ordinary Time, year B (John 6:1–21), but to preach only on the first of this pair of miracle stories. Before deciding to go this route, however, it might be fruitful to reflect on why the fourth evangelist, who felt free to pick and choose among the stories of Jesus (20:30–31), decided to keep these two together, as they seem to have been in the earliest Gospel (Mark) and in the underlying oral tradition.

For one thing, in John 6:1–15 Jesus reveals his divine power to the crowd and in 6:16–21 to the inner circle of his disciples. John wishes to show Jesus' encounters with both groups and their reactions to him. For another, the focus of the two stories is different but complementary. John 6:1–15 highlights certain individuals in both of those groups: Philip and Andrew among the disciples and, in the crowd, the little boy with the loaves and fish. It offers abundant material for reflection on the interaction of various personalities in the story and leaves open the possibility of interpreting away entirely the material miracle of the multiplication of the loaves, transforming it into a psychological "miracle" whereby ordinary, self-centered people are led to share their provisions with their neighbors, inspired by the unselfish example of the little boy. Understood so, it becomes a down-to-earth example story that no longer embarrasses minds that have no room in them for miracle.

John 6:16–21, however, focuses almost entirely on Jesus himself. To be sure, the disciples' fear is a factor, as in the parallel story about the stilling of the storm (Mark 4:35–41//Matt. 8:23–27//Luke 8:22–25), but here the object of their fear is not the storm; it is Jesus. John's account is that of a divine manifestation—in this case a "Christophany" (an appearance or manifestation of Christ). Even the words about the storm, "the sea became rough because a strong wind was blowing," are reminiscent of the theophanic winds at Horeb and on the day of Pentecost. In the context of a Gospel about the coming of the eternal Word as light, one thinks of Samuel Terrien's remark about the experience of the presence of God. "For Israel and for the church," he writes, "there has always been 'a great wind of light blowing, and sore pain'" (*The Elusive Presence* [San Francisco, Harper & Row, 1978], 95). The story is entirely designed to elicit reverent awe and to inspire faith in Jesus as the revelation of God's powerful and protective presence.

Keeping these two stories together ensures that the interpreter will hold in tension, as the evangelist did, the human and the divine elements in Jesus Christ. He is as near to us as our physical hunger yet as far beyond us as the eternal Word that was in the beginning with God, through whom all things were created. Hymns like "O thou in all thy might so far, in all thy love so near" do this too.

The Crowd's Search for Bread (6:22–35)

How do different people respond to Jesus?

John 6:1–21 contains two miracle stories that set the stage for Jesus' interaction with three groups: the crowd (6:22–40), "the Jews"[1] (6:41–59), and his disciples (6:60–71). First, the scene shifts from the place where Jesus fed five thousand people to his meeting the crowd in Capernaum (6:22–24). A dialogue between Jesus and the wrongly motivated but persistent crowd (6:25–34) sets the stage for a long discourse in which Jesus speaks directly of himself as the bread of life (6:35–58), a discourse that continues beyond this pericope. It is punctuated by two responses from "the Jews" (6:41–42 and 52) and ends at 6:59. A section on the response of Jesus' disciples closes the chapter (6:60–71).

Exploring the text

The transitional paragraph (6:22–24) makes sense if one remembers that Tiberias is on the western shore of the Sea of Galilee, Capernaum on the northern shore just west of the point where the Jordan River empties into it, and the unidentified place of the feeding (6:1–15) somewhere on the eastern shore. Verse 24 suggests that the crowd has shrunk from the five thousand who ate the loaves to a number small enough to get into some boats from Tiberias that picked up people at the site of the miracle on the next day and followed Jesus to Capernaum. What they lack in number is made up for in persistence. The exact location of the initial dialogue between Jesus and the crowd in Capernaum (6:25–34) is not specified.

The uneven flow of this conversation can be clarified by a paraphrase: When they found him there, they said, "Teacher, when did you get here?" (6:25).

Instead of answering the question, Jesus accuses them of following him for the wrong reason. "You're not looking for me because you saw what that miracle signified, but just because you filled up on bread and now want some more." Then he starts to lecture them: "Don't exert yourself to get material food that only lasts as long as the digestive process, but direct your energy toward getting nourishment that produces and sustains eternal life–the kind of food the Son of Man will give you. This is the food that carries God's seal of approval."

Their response to this piece of advice shows that they have understood it only partially, or not at all. "What must we do to perform the works of God?" they ask (6:28). Perhaps this is a legitimate question, or perhaps, like Simon Magus, they want to be bread makers, too!

Jesus tries again: "The work of God is for you to believe in the one whom God has sent."

"You want us to believe in you?" they reply. "Well, what sign–what further 'work of God'–will you show us so we can see it and believe you? How about some more bread like the manna Moses gave our ancestors in the wilderness (Exod. 16)? Remember what it says in the Scriptures, 'He gave them bread from heaven to eat'" (6:30–31).

"Listen to me," says Jesus. "It wasn't Moses who gave you [*sic!*–not just your ancestors] heavenly bread, but my Father who gives you the true bread from heaven. God's bread is what comes down from heaven and gives life to the world" (6:32–33).

"Right, sir," they answer. "Give this bread to us continually!" (6:34).

So in the discourse that follows (6:35–58), Jesus does exactly that, by means of words that are the Word of life.

The key term in the opening dialogue is "bread," used in two senses–another example of the double entendre and consequent misunderstanding that are characteristic of this Gospel. The crowd is interested in more loaves (6:26; the Greek word for bread is translated "loaves" when it is plural) like those they had eaten the day before (6:23). They speak of the manna (6:31) that their ancestors had eaten in the wilderness. They quote as Scripture words based on (though not identical with) Psalm 78:24, referring to Exodus 16:4, 15. Jesus is interested in another kind of food (6:27) when he speaks of the true bread from heaven, the bread that God–not Moses–gives (6:32–33).

Another example of word play is the crowd's use of "work of God" to refer to the miraculous multiplication of the loaves, which they view as a "sign" (6:28, 30) and Jesus' teaching that the work of God is something quite different from a miracle, but which is worth working for (6:27, 29). Jesus had given a sign that discloses something about God, but all they saw was the miracle that satisfied their appetite. The interplay of work and sign in the context of two miracle stories (Jesus and the loaves, Moses and the manna) leads to the specifically Johannine understanding of the relationship of "seeing" and "believing." The crowd had seen and eaten the bread, but they did not see what it signified.

The pericope concludes with the crowd's request that Jesus will give them this bread and keep on giving it, a request reminiscent of the Samaritan woman by the well (4:15). Jesus does not brush the crowd's request aside, for it sets the stage for what Jesus and the evangelist most want the crowd and readers to hear: "I am the bread of life."

In literary terms, this text moves from a discussion about a sign (the feeding of the crowd) to the affirmation of a symbol (Jesus is the bread of life). In general literary usage today, signs more or less arbitrarily point to something other than themselves and, to be effective, a sign can point to only one thing. There is no intrinsic connection between a sign and the thing or person to which it points. Symbols, on the other hand, are connecting links between two different spheres. They bear some inherent analogical relationship to that which they symbolize. The reader or viewer understands that the symbol means or expresses something more or something other than its plain or superficial meaning. What that something is may be assumed from the shared background of writer and reader, and it may point to or suggest many meanings, even when the symbol stands for a particular referent. "Symbols often span the gap between knowledge and mystery. They are the meeting point between the finite and the infinite. They call for explanation and simultaneously resist it."[2] National flags and wedding rings, for example, are symbols.

In the Gospel of John bread, water, light, and vine are symbols that are sometimes closely related to signs. John 6:22–35 opens with a reference to seeing signs and closes with an appeal to believe in Jesus, whose words are words from God and who is himself the bread of life. Jesus seeks to lead the crowd from seeing a miracle, to seeing a sign, to the deeper seeing that is synonymous with believing.

Preaching and teaching the Word

"I am hungry, but I don't really know what I want." This common complaint offers a way into John 6:24–35, the Gospel reading for the Eighteenth Sunday in Ordinary Time, year B. To get through to this crowd, Jesus had first to get past their full stomachs, their satisfaction with so little.

Americans are the envy of many in the world because they have so much. This passage suggests that Jesus would chide most Americans, including those in church pews Sunday morning, because they are satisfied with so little. In John Bunyan's *Pilgrim's Progress* Interpreter takes Christiana and her children into a room

> where was "a man that could look no way but downwards, with a Muck-rake in his hand. There stood also one over his head with a Celestial Crown in his hand, and proffered him that Crown for his Muck-rake; but the man did neither look up, nor regard, but raked to himself the straws, the small sticks and dust of the floor. . . .
> Then said Christiana, O deliver me from this Muck-rake.
> That prayer, said the Interpreter has lain by till 'tis almost rusty. *Give me not Riches*, is scarcely the prayer of one of ten thousand. Straws and sticks and dust with most are the great things now looked after.[3]

The preacher or teacher could explore the deeper hungers that the American way of life does not satisfy, and the kinds of joy experienced by those who feed on Jesus as the bread of life.

Another approach to this text might be to focus on the crowd as one of the case studies in responses to Jesus in the Fourth Gospel. In addition to the present dialogue, the crowd interacts extensively with Jesus at the festival of Booths in Jerusalem (7:10–44) and at his triumphal entry into the city and his final teaching there (12:9–36), with only two further references in this Gospel (5:13 and 11:42). The crowds come in response to Jesus' signs, and their appearance is always in the context of controversy over the meaning of the signs. "The crowd represents the struggle of those who are open to believing, but neither the scriptures nor the signs lead them to authentic faith. They are the world God loves (3:16)."[4] In John 6, so long as those who come looking for Jesus are still open to his teaching, they are called "the crowd" (6:22–34). But when they begin to complain about him, they are called "the Jews" (6:41). Responses to Jesus in the Fourth Gospel include that of insiders (disciples), those on the margin (the crowd), and unbelievers ("the Jews"). There may be some from each group in any congregation, and Jesus has goals for all three. An appropriate goal is so to preach or teach as to move those who identify with the crowd in 6:24–35 to find their place with the disciples in 6:60–69.

A closely related approach is to preach or teach about seeing signs and believing. Jesus reproaches the crowd for not seeing in the miracle a sign of God's presence and providential power to satisfy the hunger of the heart. He invites belief in the one whom God sent as the work of God and offers himself not just as an object of belief but as the very bread of life. John 6:22–34 offers an opportunity for the preacher to urge hearers to reflect more deeply on the signs of God's presence and power in their own lives. The sermon could invite hearers to see the sacred in the common things of life—to reflect on daily bread, for instance, long enough to discern in it the gift of God and a means of communion with Jesus Christ.[5] A teaching session on the text might point to the pattern of faith development in the Gospel of John[6] from a simple openness to faith in the presence of a sign (like the crowd in the present passage), to a faith based on signs (like those at the first Passover in 2:23, whose faith was not yet trustworthy), to a mature faith that no longer depends on signs (which Jesus declares blessed in 20:29, and to which the evangelist invites all who read or hear this Gospel). Educators might relate the pattern of faith development in the Fourth Gospel to contemporary faith-development theory.[7]

Those who appreciate the Bible as literature could study John 6:22–35 with an eye to the relationship between signs and symbols. The teacher might explore various available resources that would clarify, expand, and perhaps correct ideas about these two distinct but related modes of communication that were sketched in the exegetical notes above. Such a study would consider the use of these terms in general literary criticism, then note the particular way that "sign" is used in the Gospel of John. The feeding of the five thousand is a prime example of John's "sign" language, and "bread of life/bread from heaven," like all the "I am's" of Jesus, is a prime example of symbolic language in the Fourth Gospel. Such language allows the Word himself to enter the heart and nourish it. Sometimes a light surprises Christians when they study.

"I Am the Bread of Life" (6:35–51)

To read "I am the bread of life" (6:35) as a believer is to have one's heart warmed by Jesus' promise of satisfying our human hunger and thirst for God.

The words lie at the heart of John's longest chapter (chap. 6). Verse 35 serves as the climax of Jesus' dialogue with the crowd (6:25–35) and also as the lead sentence for a discourse (6:35–58) whose conclusion is marked by a geographical note at verse 59. The discourse is divided into three sections (6:35–40, 43–51, 53–58) by two interventions from "the Jews" (6:41–42, 52). The present passage, which is abridged as the Gospel pericope for the Nineteenth Sunday in Ordinary Time, comprises the first two sections of the discourse.

The intent of the text is to call all who read it to believe in Jesus as the one who came down from God in order to feed the inner life of believers and so to give life to the world. Verses 36–40 are omitted from the pericope in most lectionaries, an unfortunate choice that ignores the concise summary of the gospel in verse 40 and diminishes the cumulative effect of the passage as a whole. The entire pericope is like a compendium of Johannine theology. It rewards those who are prepared to contemplate three mysteries, two promises, and one implicit question–subjects that are explored below.

Exploring the text

The initial words constitute the first of the seven **"I Am" sayings** of Jesus with a defining term that is characteristic of the Gospel of John. The warm light of this saying is clouded by several puzzling elements in the text: the aggressive tone of verse 36, the alternation of personal and impersonal pronouns in verses 37 and 39–40, and the difficulty of following the line of reasoning from one verse to the next. This difficulty stems partly from the fact that the text is less a verbatim report than a digest of Jesus' teaching, and partly from the nonlinear, dialogical, and contemplative nature of the evangelist's reasoning. His way of reporting the teaching of Jesus does not seek to convince by logical argument, but rather to invite readers to reflect upon truths which, by their very nature, lie beyond reason and pertain to mystery.

It is no wonder that this evangelist is called John the Theologian. This is a revelatory monologue in which the voice of the evangelist merges with the words of Jesus to speak the gospel message directly to readers.[1]

(a) Three mysteries. The mystery of the two natures in Jesus Christ is what gives rise to the complaint of those who know very well that Jesus, son of Joseph, is a flesh-and-blood human being "whose father and mother we know" (6:41). They have understood Jesus' claim to have come down from heaven. "Heaven" is a way to speak of God without using the divine name, and Jesus' speaking of God as "my Father," whom he alone has seen (6:46), suggests an intimate relationship with the Almighty that other mortals do not share. To the hearers, Jesus is claiming a relationship with God that is incompatible with his human status as the son of Joseph and Mary. The question they raise in verses 41–42 could be paraphrased, "How can this Jesus claim to be both human and divine?" That way of putting the question emerged only later, but the question itself, already explicit in this text, is implicit in every account of Jesus' earthly ministry. The rational answer is, "This cannot be." But suppose God transcends the limits of human reason? What if, in coming to Jesus, one discovers a person who cannot be explained by ordinary human categories, yet who is

obviously, even quintessentially, human? What if, in communion with him through prayer and meditation, the hunger of the soul is fed and its thirst assuaged? That was clearly the experience of the evangelist and members of the Johannine community, who, in their abiding in Jesus Christ, heard him say, "I am the bread of life."

The preponderant weight of this discourse is on the divine side of Jesus' nature as the Son of God who came down from heaven, yet in the last phrase of the pericope Jesus says that the bread he will give for the life of the world is his flesh–that human flesh that hung on a real and cruel cross.

The mystery of election and free will emerges in Jesus' response to those who have seen him and yet do not believe (6:36) with his rebuke of their incredulity (6:43) on the one hand and his affirmation that all whom the Father gives him will come to him (6:37, 45) and that none can come to him unless drawn by the Father (6:44) on the other. Here, as throughout the Fourth Gospel, these two themes stand side by side, irreconcilable and inseparable. "Whoever comes, whoever believes, [and] whoever eats" (6:35, 51) are open invitations to the free choice of hearers and readers, but the predominant teaching of this passage and of the Gospel as a whole is that these choices are predetermined by God, whose will is "that I should lose nothing of all that he has given me" (6:39). The doctrines of election and of the perseverance of the saints, so often associated with the apostle Paul, Augustine, and John Calvin, are not strangers to the Fourth Gospel. What is different in John is that there is no attempt to work out the paradox rationally. It is a mystery to be grasped by coming to Jesus and believing in him. All human beings experience in their own lives the paradoxical fact of being free and also being determined. Those who know Jesus experience the fact of free will and know the mystery of election as the ground of a sure and certain hope based on Jesus' revelation of the will of God.

A third mystery, *the interaction of present fulfillment and future hope* is evidenced here by the juxtaposition of the characteristic Johannine understanding of eternal life as a present possession (6:47) closely kin to immortality (6:50–51) and a future hope for resurrection at the last day repeated three times in the present pericope (6:39, 40, 44) and again in the final part of the discourse (6:54). Analytic minds have seen here a disparity so sharp that some have supposed that an editorial hand added language about the last day to a Gospel that otherwise offers a consistent view of eternity as now and heaven as here in Jesus Christ.[2] Others have found a third, "heavenly" eschatology in the Fourth Gospel and have proposed various ways to resolve the rational tension among the three,[3] but the fourth evangelist shows no interest in this endeavor. Popular piety has harmonized these conflicting versions of the Christian hope for so long that they no longer seem a mystery. While Paul speaks in terms of salvation as being "already" and "not yet" and wrestles with the theological problem intellectually, John's Jesus speaks of eternal life as here and now and, in the same breath, of resurrection at the end of time. John finds here no problem at all, but a mystery arising from the fullness of God's love and grace.

(b) Two promises. The promise of satisfaction for the heart's hunger and thirst appears at the very beginning of the passage (v. 35) and is reiterated in the promise of eternal life as a present possession (vv. 40, 47), a quality of life that never ends (vv. 50–51). Referring back to the crowd's request that he give bread from heaven like the manna in the wilderness that was given daily (vv. 30–31), Jesus promises to assuage a far deeper hunger and thirst than they had in mind initially.

The promise is expressed in terms that cause a problem for many. Even taken figuratively, the promise "Never be hungry . . . never be thirsty" is simply not true to the experience of those who have known dry times when God seems absent and Christ a distant figure. But truth can be expressed in hyperbole, the kind of overstatement or language of excess often found in Hebrew poetry (for example, 1 Sam. 18:7; Isa. 11:6–8; 35:1; 43:20; Amos 9:13) and sometimes in the teaching of Jesus (for example, the log in the eye, Matt. 7:3–5, and the camel and the needle's eye, Matt. 19:24). The promise may be hyperbolic, but those who experience an inner communion with Jesus Christ have found it to be true.

The promise of resurrection at the last day may be a theological puzzle for those looking for a coherent view of eternal life in the Gospel of John and a biological scandal for literalists who ask, "What body?" But for those who stand beside an open grave and share the faith of the Fourth Gospel, it is pure promise. The death and resurrection of Jesus are inseparable in all four Gospels and in the Christian message, but they are underlined differently by different New Testament writers. The pivotal place of the raising of Lazarus in this Gospel (11:1–53), its understanding of the cross as exaltation and glorification rather than tragedy (3:14; 12:23, 32–33), and its powerful accounts of Jesus' resurrection and subsequent appearances (20:1–21:23) mark it as a resurrection Gospel. Resurrection at the last day crowns the Johannine promise of eternal life.

In verse 39 the promise of life in Christ applies to every *thing* (echoing v. 37a), but in verse 40 it applies to every *one* (echoing v. 37b). The Fourth Gospel as a whole is intensely personal, but verses 37a and 39 mirror the way in which God's promise in Jesus embraces the whole world (as in 1:1–3 and 3:16) and point to the final redemption of all creation (as in Rom. 8:19–21 and Col. 1:20).

(c) One question. The basic question that confronts readers of the bread of life discourse is *"Will you believe?"* This question is implicit in the "whoever believes" of verse 35 and "yet [you] do not believe" in verse 36. It surfaces in Jesus' formulation of the will of the Father in verse 40 and again in verse 47, where "whoever believes" is reiterated and linked to eternal life as a present fact for those who do believe. Verses 48–51 recapitulate the entire discourse, placing the implicit question once more squarely before the reader. The question remains implicit, for its explicit form is not a question but an invitation and a promise. "Whoever eats of this bread will live forever" (6:51b) is restated as the purpose of the entire Gospel: "so that you may come to believe that Jesus is the Messiah, the Son of God, and that through believing you may have life in his name" (20:31).

Verses 41–42 introduce into the discourse a major objection to believing in Jesus, which divides this pericope into two sections. Jesus' hearers in the first section (vv. 35–40) are designated as "the crowd" (see verses 22, 24, and 25–34), the term for groups with differing reactions to Jesus. In 6:41–42, however, the hearers' words of complaint show their rejection of Jesus' teaching, so they are no longer called simply "the crowd" but "the Jews." It is possible that the scene shifts to the synagogue at this point (see 6:59), but no mention of priests or Pharisees suggests that "Jews" here refers to Jewish religious authorities. What is at issue is the hearers' rejection of Jesus and his teaching, and the term "Jews" here (like "the world" in other texts) refers to those who refuse to believe in Jesus.[4]

Preaching and teaching the Word

The puzzling or paradoxical elements in this passage ("mysteries") suggest a possible series of three sermons (or Bible studies): one on the humanity and deity ("two natures") of Jesus Christ; one on election and free will based on the open invitation to come to Jesus (6:35) and the assertion that "no one can come to me unless drawn by the Father" (6:44); and one on the present and future dimensions of eternal life (the interaction of present fulfillment and future hope in the Fourth Gospel and in Christian experience). The first two topics lend themselves to teaching, which would allow exploration of traditional statements of the Christian faith in the creeds of Christendom and a sharing of individual struggles with these issues. The third is perhaps best approached through a sermon on one or both of the great promises in this passage, dealing with the *present* dimension of God's great offer to us in Jesus Christ—satisfaction for the heart's hunger and thirst for God here and how—and the *future* dimension of that offer—resurrection at the last day.

Any sermon on this passage, whether on its mysteries or its promises, should confront hearers with the basic question that the text poses. The preacher or teacher needs to reflect on the degree to which the group she or he addresses is best described in Johannine terms as a crowd (people with various attitudes toward Jesus but open to hear him), or "Jews" (people who complain about what Jesus says), or disciples (people who accept what Jesus says and are trying to follow him). Whatever may be the audience addressed, the approach to preaching that is most faithful to the intention of the text must be an appeal to believe in Jesus, accept his invitation, and claim his promises.

The basic metaphor in this passage is bread, and hunger is the basic situation addressed. In the prayer Jesus taught his disciples, the only petition for a material blessing is the prayer for daily bread (Matt. 6:11; Luke 11:3). In John 6:35–51 Jesus offers himself as the bread of life and invites all to come to him and believe in him. The preacher might bring these texts together, using "not by bread alone" (Matt. 4:4; Deut. 8:3) as a connecting link. The sermon could take as a starting point the hunger of the hearers, at whatever level, using a concrete illustration of that hunger drawn from the recent experience of the hearers–just as the evangelist does by joining this discourse to the feeding of the crowd (6:1–15).

Preachers and teachers could explore the richness of bread as a symbol. In English-speaking countries, it is "the staff of life." It is the carbohydrate that–like rice, potatoes, and manioc in other cultures–is our basic source of energy. Bread is the stuff that makes human beings go, but it sustains us only when eaten regularly. By analogy, Christians need to feed upon Christ, the living bread, through a regular discipline of private prayer and readings in the Gospels, as well as regular communion with Christ through the Eucharist (or Lord's Supper), in company with fellow disciples. These are ways of coming to Christ in our time. They are the means of grace whereby the energy of the Holy Spirit is communicated to those who believe in Christ. Together with service in Christ's name, they are the soul food that sustains his indwelling presence in believers and allows us to abide in him.

In the present text, bread is primarily a symbol for the revelation of God's Word in Jesus and his teaching. William Farel, one of the pioneers of the Protestant Reformation, prayed, "Give us the bread of thy word."[5] A sermon on this topic might relate the bread of life discourse to Jesus, the Word of God, in John 1:1, 14, 18. It could tie the reference to Isaiah 54:13 in John 6:45 ("And they shall all be taught by God") to the divine invitation in Isaiah 55:1–2 to all who are hungry and thirsty to come and buy wine and milk without money and to eat bread that really satisfies. In Isaiah, the reference is to a messianic banquet. In John 6, it is an invitation for all who hunger and thirst (6:35) to feed on Jesus Christ by coming to him in faith and abiding in him as a way of life.

"Eat My Flesh and Drink My Blood" (6:52–59)

Were the earliest Christians cannibals?

Not really, but Christian apologists in the second century had to defend them against this charge.[1] The present text, coupled with the fact that non-Christians were excluded from the celebration of the Lord's Supper, could easily have given rise to the accusation. The language is still shocking, even to many Christians, in the twenty-first century. What does it mean?

Exploring the text

(a) Relation to the remainder of chapter 6. Verses 52–59 constitute the conclusion of the bread of life discourse, pointing back to the sign of the feeding (6:1–15) and forward to the Eucharist in the early church, which is both sign and symbol.

The strongly eucharistic flavor of 6:52–59 has led some to the opinion that this paragraph was inserted to correct the basically antisacramental theology of the Johannine community, in order to make the Fourth Gospel acceptable to the larger church. Others, noting the parallels between verses 35–50 and verses 51–58, suggest that these may be two forms of the bread of life discourse, both made up of sayings passed down in the Johannine preaching tradition. In both units Jesus is the bread of life, but in the first the reference is primarily to his teaching, whereas in the second the reference is to Jesus' flesh, given for the life of the world (6:51).

Verse 58 recapitulates the main point of the entire dialogue and discourse (6:25–51). This theological summary is sealed by the evangelist's closure of the unit in verse 59, and an account of responses to the discourse among Jesus' disciples brings the chapter to a close (vv. 60–71).

(b) Language. John 6:52–59, linked to the body of the bread of life discourse by verse 51c, contains language that refers unmistakably to the Christian Eucharist: eat, drink, flesh, blood, bread. The unit, about eating the body and drinking the blood of Jesus, the Son of Man (6:53), is in the form of a monologue, prompted by a question from those who found Jesus' claim in 6:51 to be incredible. The question takes Jesus' language literally; the monologue enlarges upon it figuratively. Its intent is to lead the reader beyond a literal understanding to reflection on the figurative meanings of eucharistic symbolism.

While eucharistic texts in the Synoptic Gospels and letters of Paul speak of Christ's body and blood, this text speaks of flesh and blood. At this point John is probably closer to the original language of Jesus, since the word for "flesh" (*basar*) in Hebrew and Aramaic serves for both flesh and body. "The bread that I shall give is my flesh for the life of the world" (6:51c) may well reflect the words of institution used in the Johannine community.[2] Indeed, this passage could be viewed as an abbreviated homily on the eucharistic words (intelligible only to the initiated), preserved in a Gospel that omits the account of the institution of the sacrament.

The Fourth Gospel elsewhere uses "flesh" fairly frequently as a synonym for "human," "human nature," or "humanity" (1:13, 14; 3:6; 6:63; 8:15; 17:2), and this is a pointer to the figurative meaning of "flesh" in 6:51c–56. To eat Jesus' flesh is to take his humanity into our own, identifying with him in lowly service at the cost of life itself. "Body" is used in only three contexts in the Gospel of John (2:21; 19:31–40; 20:12), and in every case it refers to the physical body of Jesus that was crucified and raised from the dead.

The text uses two words for eat. The common one, *phagein,* is used three times (vv. 52, 53, 58). A harsher synonym, *trogein,* was originally used of animals and meant to eat noisily or chomp. It is used four times in the present text (vv. 54, 56, 57, 58) and only once again in the Fourth Gospel (13:18, quoting Ps. 41:9, "The one who ate my bread has lifted his heel against me"). Its only other appearance in the New Testament is at Matthew 24:38, which refers to those who were mindlessly eating and drinking in the time before the flood until the day Noah entered the ark (see Gen. 6:11–7:1). It appears to be used here to counter the tendency to "spiritualize" the concept of eating Christ's body so that nothing physical remains in it,[3] a tendency that blossomed as Docetism in the second century.

Preaching and teaching the Word

The Gospel reading for the Twentieth Sunday in Ordinary Time, year B is John 6:51–58. Verse 51 is important as the context for the dispute among the Jews in verse 52 and Jesus' response to it. It is also good for the preacher to begin–and end–with the promise of verse 51c.

"How can this man give us his flesh to eat?" (6:52). Although the question is that of "the Jews" who were complaining about Jesus because he claimed to be the bread from heaven (6:41), it is a reasonable question which may lurk in the hearts of many hearing a sermon on this text. It should alert the preacher to the outrageous nature of the Christian claim that in Jesus the eternal word of God–the bread of heaven–became human flesh. To minds nurtured in reason and science it is literally incredible, and a preacher who expects anyone to believe it must lean hard on the work of the Holy Spirit. But abiding in Jesus through faith is the goal of the sermon, since that is what feeds the hunger of the heart. Prayer is therefore the most important element in the preacher's preparation.

The natural occasion on which to meditate on this text is the celebration of the Lord's Supper. One approach to a communion meditation on this text would be to relate the expression "sign and seal" from the Presbyterian *Directory for Worship* (W-2.4001a) to the use of the term "sign" in the Fourth Gospel and its association with bread as a symbol of Jesus Christ, the living Word, in John 6. This approach should be used with discernment, because the historic confessions of the Reformed tradition, unlike contemporary literary critics, use sign and symbol interchangeably.[4] Also, the term "seal," so common in Reformed sacramental language,[5] although used twice in the Fourth Gospel (3:33; 6:27), is not there associated with the flesh and blood of Jesus Christ. The evangelist does not use the language of literary criticism or of church ordinance, but chapter 6 does deal with sign and symbol throughout. Reflecting on 6:51–58, the preacher could suggest what the Lord's Supper points to as a sign, and how the language of flesh and blood, while pointing to Jesus' death, symbolizes also his real presence at the communion table and in the hearts and lives of those gathered there.[6] The liturgical word of invitation, spoken as the bread and the cup are held out to the people, "The gifts of God for the people of God," reflects the central affirmation of John 6: Jesus himself is the gift of God for the life of world (6:35, 51, 58; 3:16).

In contemporary American idiom, "bread" means money. This particular usage represents a devalued currency, for in Christian hymns and devotional literature through the ages, "bread" refers to Jesus Christ, echoing the discourse in John 6. Consider the depth of devotion that gave rise to Bernard of Clairvaux's "We taste thee, O thou living bread,"[7] and the refrain of a Jamaican communion calypso, "Jesus lives again, earth can breathe again, pass the Word around: loaves abound!"[8]

Any exposition of or meditation upon this passage should mention that it is the conclusion to the bread of life discourse, which, taken as a whole, is an extended parallel of Jesus' gracious invitation to come unto him and find rest (Matt. 11:28–30) and an echo of the institution of the Lord's Supper (1 Cor. 11:23–24). Thomas à Kempis saw this and expressed it in eloquent simplicity as a caption above his reflections concerning the sacrament in Book Four of *The Imitation of Christ*:[9] "Come unto me, saith our Lord, all ye that labour and are heavy laden, and I will give you rest. And the bread that I will give is my flesh, which I will give for the life of the world. Take, eat: This is my body which is broken for you: this do in remembrance of me. He that eateth my flesh, and drinketh my blood, dwelleth in me and I in him. The words that I speak unto you they are spirit, and they are life."

John 6 in its entirety is Jesus' word of invitation spoken through the fourth evangelist.

Responses of Disciples (6:60–71)

What are we to do with the hard sayings of Jesus?

If politics is the art of compromise, Jesus is no politician. He does not bend his teachings to accommodate us. We must decide how to respond to him, just as he is.

Exploring the text

A major theme of the entire Fourth Gospel is the reactions of various individuals and groups who encounter Jesus. The present text, the concluding section of chapter 6, shows reactions of belief and disbelief among Jesus' disciples. It consists of two paragraphs. The first shows the disbelief of many disciples (6:60–65). The second focuses on the response of the chosen Twelve (6:66–71).

Jesus and a Large Group of Disciples (6:60–66)

This paragraph follows the earlier pattern of an objection to Jesus' teaching phrased as a question (vv. 41, 52, 60), followed by Jesus' response and further teaching. The response of the larger group of Jesus' disciples appears in verse 66, which properly concludes this paragraph but also introduces the following one (6:66–71).

Many of Jesus' disciples find his teaching difficult (6:60), for two reasons. First, the reference to eating the flesh of the Son of Man and drinking his blood (6:53), universally abhorrent, would be especially offensive to Jesus' hearers (all of them Jews), since eating blood of any sort is explicitly forbidden in Leviticus 17:10–14. As a scarcely veiled reference to the Christian Eucharist, the teaching is difficult for interpreters today because it seems to point to something Jesus' hearers could not have understood and whose origin the Gospel of John does not report in its account of the Last Supper. This teaching might have been even more difficult for the first readers of the Fourth Gospel, who would have understood the eucharistic reference perfectly well. By the time this Gospel was written, baptism and the Eucharist had become defining rites for the earliest disciples of Jesus. The call to believe in Jesus, even at the cost of excommunication from the synagogue, may underlie this discourse and the disciples' response to it, just as it does the encounter with Nicodemus

(3:1–21) and with the man born blind (9:1–41).[1] For those facing such a decision, this teaching is difficult indeed, and many cannot accept it.

The second teaching that would have been difficult for Jesus' hearers is his claim to be the bread that came down from heaven, which, unlike the manna in the wilderness, assures eternal life to those who eat it (6:58, echoing 6:35, 48–51). His claim to a unique relationship with God infuriated the Jewish authorities in Jerusalem (5:18) and offended many of his disciples in the all-Jewish crowd in Capernaum (6:61).

Jesus answers their skeptical question by another question: "What if you were to see the Son of Man ascending to where he was before?" (6:62). This verse deals with one difficulty by posing another, for by using the verb "ascending," Jesus points to a future event that will validate his claim. To return to the Father is John's way of expressing what Luke depicts as ascension (compare Luke 24:50–51 and Acts 1:1–11 with John 13:1, 36; 14:1–4; 16:17; 20:17). Jesus' question suggests that when disciples have seen–and when readers have followed–the whole drama of Jesus' death, resurrection, and return to God, his words about being himself the bread that came down from heaven will make good sense. The present text is an expression of John's theology of the descending and ascending Son of Man, who, as Son of God and Word of God, came down from heaven and who, as the risen Lord, returns to God, where he was before.

Two significant features of Johannine theology are expressed in verse 63: the basic dichotomy between flesh and spirit (paralleling the dualism of light and darkness, life and death) and the gracious affirmation that Jesus's words are spirit and life, since he is himself the living Word (1:4, 9, 14). Jesus' affirmation that "the flesh is useless" (6:63) is difficult when juxtaposed to "unless you eat [my] flesh you have no life in you" (6:53–54, author's paraphrase) until one realizes that John uses certain terms–for example, **"world"**–in more than one sense. "Flesh" in verse 53 refers to bread on a table symbolizing the physical body of Jesus who died on the cross; it carries the metaphorical sense of Jesus' humanity. "Flesh" in verse 63 refers to the realm of reality that is visible and temporary, as contrasted to the realm of spirit, which is invisible and eternal. When the intended meaning is read from the context, the seeming contradiction disappears, and the mystery of the incarnation comes into view. In the person of Jesus, a flesh-and-blood human being, the invisible, eternal realm of God invaded the fleshly world of space and time, so that in him spirit and flesh were truly one. This paradoxical truth transcends the bounds of human reason (fleshly understanding). To perceive that it is true–that Jesus really is the living bread that came down from heaven–is the work of the life-giving Spirit. The NIV and TEV opt for this interpretation and capitalize

"Spirit" in verse 63, which can be paraphrased, "The Spirit gives life; the flesh is useless." The prologue expresses the same idea when it affirms that those who believe are born "not of blood or of the will of the flesh or of the will of man, but of God" (1:13).

Another difficulty arises when Jesus affirms that some of his disciples in the crowd do not believe; then the evangelist affirms that Jesus has known from the first who they are and which one would betray him (6:64). For those who saw Jesus as "the son of Joseph, whose father and mother we know" (6:42), this would be hard enough to accept. The difficulty is compounded when Jesus adds, "That's why I told you that no one can come to me unless it is granted by the Father" (6:65, author's paraphrase). Jesus seems to chide his followers for not believing, then repeats that only God can grant the gift of believing (see 6:44). This apparent assault on human freedom repelled Jesus' ambivalent disciples. "Because of this many of his disciples turned back and no longer went about with him" (6:66). This comment functions as the denouement of the preceding paragraph about the response of disbelief (6:60–65) and also as the occasion for Jesus' question to the Twelve and Peter's response of belief in the following verses (6:67–69).

Jesus and the Twelve (6:66–71)

The final paragraph of chapter 6, introduced by the evangelist's note about the many disciples who turned back, consists of a question by Jesus to the inner circle of the Twelve, Peter's affirmation of faith, and Jesus' prediction of his betrayal by Judas Iscariot.

The main verb of Jesus' question is significant: "Do you also *wish* (want or will) to go away?" (6:67). Jesus puts a question that assumes the freedom of the human will. He offers to the inner circle the option of turning back if they want to. His offer can be read as a wistful question springing from disappointment at the disbelief of the majority of disciples, or as a strong question testing the faith of those who remain. In either case, the question is real and confronts the Twelve with a genuine decision.

Here, as in many circumstances in the Synoptic Gospels, Peter is spokesperson for the intimate group. The Fourth Gospel, however, frequently calls him Simon Peter, retaining his birth name along with Jesus' designation of him as "the Rock." The first part of his reply is a question that may be paraphrased as, "What are our alternatives?" (v. 68a). The clear implication is that the alternatives have little appeal for Peter. His question may reflect a resigned world-weariness, or it may simply be a bold affirmation of the surpassing worth of Jesus. Either way, it serves as the backdrop for an affirmation of faith (6:68b–69) that is parallel to the one at Caesarea

Philippi (Mark 8:29//Matt. 16:16//Luke 9:20), enlarged to include basic terms of the theology of the Fourth Gospel–eternal life, believe, know.

At the end of the Fourth Gospel the evangelist states that its purpose is "that you may come to **believe** that Jesus is the Messiah, the Son of God, and that through believing you may have life in his name" (20:31). In the present text, Peter says on behalf of the Twelve, "We have come to believe and **know** that you are the Holy One of God" (6:69). Peter makes a heartfelt profession of the faith the evangelist seeks to elicit in the hearts of readers. Only the titles given to Jesus differ, and this is a distinction without any substantial difference. Peter was introduced to Jesus as Messiah at the very beginning of John's story (1:41). Now he and the Twelve have come to believe and therefore know[2] that Jesus is the Holy One of God, the one whom God has sanctified and sent into the world (10:36). He is the one, and the only one, who has the words of eternal life, for he is the Word that was in the beginning with God (1:1–2), the one in whom was life (1:4), and the one who gives life to the world (6:33).

Instead of a joyful acknowledgment of this exalted affirmation of belief, Jesus reminds the disciples that he chose (*exelexamen,* elected, 6:70) all twelve of them, yet one would betray him. Jesus calls him a devil, one of the New Testament terms for the Adversary (compare 6:70 with 13:2, 27). The traitor, Judas son of Simon from Kerioth, is named in an editorial note that underlines the perfidy of betrayal by a chosen disciple (6:71) In Mark's account of Peter's great confession of faith, Jesus immediately afterward calls Peter "Satan" (Mark 8:33). Here Jesus calls Judas a devil, thereby stating the paradox of divine election and human freedom in the baldest terms. Jesus chose them all. Peter will not go away, but Judas will and does. "Election is no substitute for the decision of faith."[3]

Preaching and teaching the Word

This is a good passage to preach or teach in *churches that are losing members.* Jesus, too, had the experience of watching the numbers of his disciples shrink. His reaction was astonishing. Instead of upbraiding them or seeking more effective ways to attract them, he asks the faithful remnant if they will also go away. Resigned to the shallowness of what passes for faith among his disciples, he understands that any remedy must spring from the heart of those who set out to follow him. Peter's reply acknowledges that there are alternatives which others may find more attractive. Instead of coming up with a ringing christological confession, Peter counters Jesus' question with one of his own, "To whom shall we go?" Any real commitment in life rests on a considered leap of faith, whether it be the choice of a spouse or a decision for Jesus Christ. The text calls for its readers and hearers to make that leap in response to our encounters with him in ourselves and in others. This approach is not guaranteed to stanch the flow of young blood from old churches, but it is a reminder that the basic issue is our relationship to Christ, in whom we hear the appealing voice of a Good Shepherd who knows and keeps his own (10:14–15; 17:12).

The brutally frank picture of Jesus' disciples in John 6:60–71 suggests a sermon on *the sifting effect of the gospel*. The passage emphasizes problems about Jesus' teaching, rejection of it, and finally betrayal of the teacher. Peter's faith develops in the face of the hostility to Jesus that characterized the vast majority even of those who initially followed him. Faithful pastors can take heart from the honest report in John 6 in which Jesus interacts first with a huge crowd (6:2), then with a crowd persistent enough to follow him to Capernaum (6:22, 25), then with those in the crowd who were becoming hostile to his teaching ("the Jews," 6:41, 52), then with "his disciples," those in the crowd who had stayed to hear his teaching (6:60, 66), and finally with the inner circle of the Twelve and their spokesperson, Peter (6:67–69, 70–71). The gospel has always had a sifting effect. Jesus' first disciples included many who did not believe in him, one who betrayed him, and a few who stayed with him through thick and thin, not out of enthusiasm but because they knew of no lively and life-giving alternative.

The text addresses pastors. Given the broad spectrum of discipleship present in a typical congregation today and the indifference to Jesus' teaching in the world, preachers and teachers may empathize with the discouragement and incipient sense of abandonment discernable behind the words, "Do you also wish to go away?" Those who are not themselves tempted to go away may at least want to water down Jesus' demands. Jesus' approach is not a formula for church growth. It is an uncompromising call to faithful discipleship.

The text invites consideration of the religious alternatives to which so many are drawn. In Jesus' day these included a plethora of divinities and philosophies in the Hellenistic world, and among Jews the dream of a military Messiah who would deliver them from Roman oppression. In our day hedonism, other world religions, reverence for nature, the God within, social activism, and philanthropy all attract adherents and offer spiritual satisfaction. Many of these alternatives are not bad and should be explored, not summarily dismissed. Preachers and teachers who dare, like Jesus, to leave open the question, "Will you also go away?" may engage honest seekers in serious dialogue. How is Jesus' offer of himself as the bread of life unique? Why stick with him? While a sermon or lesson may appropriately address these questions, one-on-one conversations are probably the contexts in which pastors and teachers can most effectively give their own honest answers.

JESUS AT THE FESTIVAL OF BOOTHS (7:1–8:59)

Chapters 7 and 8 tell about Jesus in Jerusalem during and after the Festival of Booths. They take him back from Capernaum (6:59) to Jerusalem, where he had already experienced hostility (5:18). The first section of chapter 7 (7:1–13) describes the circumstances surrounding Jesus' return from Galilee.

The occasion for this journey was the Festival of Booths or Tabernacles, still known among Jews by its Hebrew name, *Sukkoth*. It was one of Israel's three great annual festivals, celebrated as a harvest festival for an entire week in the fall (Exod. 23:16; 34:22–24; Deut. 16:13–15). It drew pilgrims to Jerusalem, where celebrants would eat and sleep in booths made of plaited branches like those once used to guard orchards and vineyards at harvest time, reinterpreted as a reminder of Israel's years of wandering in the wilderness.

Among the features of the Festival of Booths was the ritual pouring out of water each morning to commemorate how God provided springs in the desert during the wilderness years. At night four huge golden candlesticks, each having four golden bowls with wicks made from the worn-out garments of priests (Mishnah *Sukkah* 5:2–4; for the allusion, see Deut. 8:4; 29:5), lit up the temple area and, according to the Mishnah, the entire city. Jesus takes advantage of this setting to invite all who are thirsty to come to him for living water (7:37–39) and to offer himself as the light of the world (8:12). These claims give rise to the extended confrontation with the Jewish authorities that makes up the bulk of chapters 7 and 8. In the midst of this controversy, the scribes and Pharisees set a trap for Jesus as he is teaching in the temple (7:53–8:11).

These two chapters are made up of four major blocks of material:

7:1–13   Transition from Galilee to Jerusalem
7:14–52   Encounter and response at the Festival of Booths
7:53–8:11   A sinful woman and her sinful accusers
8:12–59   Further confrontation in the temple

In the following notes, the larger blocks (7:14–52; 8:12–59) will be divided into smaller units for the convenience of preachers and teachers.

Transition from Galilee to Jerusalem (7:1–13)

Chapter 7 takes stock of the responses to Jesus up to this point. Some are positive but most are negative. The transitional unit explores responses of Jesus' brothers, the world, the crowds at the Festival of Booths, and the Jewish authorities.

Exploring the text

The change of scene from Galilee to Jerusalem is reported at length. It includes an unusual glimpse of the dynamics of belief and unbelief within Jesus' own family.

Jesus and His Brothers (7:1–10a)

Their mother's implicit faith in Jesus was reported earlier (2:1–5). Now the evangelist states, "Not even his brothers believed in him" (7:5). John assumes a nuclear family of father, mother, and several siblings in a way that makes the argument for the perpetual virginity of Mary difficult. The evangelist's comment about his brothers' unbelief, inserted where it is, suggests that their urging Jesus to make the traditional pilgrimage to the Festival of Booths in Jerusalem "so that your disciples may see the works you are doing" (7:3) was not kindly motivated. Their invitation to "show yourself to the world" (7:4) is rebuffed by Jesus, who knows that the time has not yet come for his final confrontation with the Jerusalem authorities, equated with "the world" (7:7).

This text is a prime example of the Johannine use of **"world"** to denote all those who reject Jesus' gracious invitation and refuse to believe in him, in contrast to its use to refer to "everybody," as in John 3:16 and 7:4. By their unbelief his own brothers at this point choose the world's response to Jesus.

Jesus' rebuff of his brothers, followed immediately by doing what they suggest, echoes the interaction with his mother at the wedding in Cana. Readers today may see here an example of the human quality of changing one's mind, but the more likely intention of the evangelist is to show that Jesus is always in full command of the situation. His actions are not determined by the opinion of others, whether friend or foe, but by his understanding of the will of God.

The Authorities and the Crowd (7:10b–13)

Here the evangelist reports the division of opinion about Jesus that has been growing throughout the narrative to this point. The response of "the Jews" is negative; they are the custodians of the Law who are seeking to kill Jesus because he has broken the Sabbath and called God his own Father (5:18). They are out to get him ("Where is he?" 7:11).

The crowd's response is mixed. Some, while not determined to get rid of Jesus, complain about his teaching and think he is a deceiver, while others are favorably disposed ("He is a good man," 7:12). The more important but unspoken factor, however, is the fear inspired by the hostility of the Jewish authorities (7:13).

Preaching and teaching the Word

There is a difference between being widely known and being deeply appreciated. It is true that "no one who wants to be widely known acts in secret" (7:4), but Jesus went to the feast in secret (7:10), disregarding his brother's advice. The connection between this incident and the wedding at Cana (2:1–11) consists in advice given by family members that Jesus declines with the comment "My hour [time] has not yet [fully] come" (2:4; 7:6). Yet privately he provides wine (2:6–8) and privately he goes to the festival (7:10). These incidents show Jesus' sovereign control of the situation all the way to his death and resurrection, but they also point to one whose desire to do the will of God overrode the desire for popular acclaim. It is a good example to point out to youth, whose unwise decisions are often based on peer pressure. It is appropriate to reflect that in the Synoptic Gospels Jesus teaches his disciples to place faithfulness to God even above family ties (Mark 3:31–35//Matt. 10:37–38), and in these Johannine texts he practices what he preaches. Preachers and teachers of John 7:1–13 can help disciples today wrestle with the tensions that sometimes rise between loyalty to family and loyalty to God.

Encounter and Response at the Festival of Booths (7:14–52)

Jesus' encounter with the crowds and the religious authorities in Jerusalem at the Festival of Booths represents the third major confrontation with "the Jews" in the Fourth Gospel. The first was when he drove the money changers out of the temple at Passover time (2:13–21), and the second when he healed a paralytic near the Sheep Gate on a Sabbath day (5:18–47). With each of these three confrontations Jesus' discourses become longer, the subject matter wider, and the chasm between him and his adversaries deeper.

The long report of controversy in chapter 7 is enlivened by dialogue and punctuated by time references that divide the material conveniently into two parts, the first "about the middle of the festival" (7:14–36) and the second "on the last day of the festival" (7:37–52).

About the Middle of the Festival (7:14–36)

The first section of this confrontation includes four paragraphs, each on a different subject.

Exploring the text

(a) "The Jews"[1] *are astonished at Jesus' teaching and by his reply about its source (7:14–18).* This paragraph raises two questions: Where does Jesus' teaching come from, and whose glory is he seeking? The authorities

in Jerusalem pride themselves on their mastery of the traditional curriculum of religious studies and are astonished that this man "knows his letters" (*grammata oiden*, v. 15) without the benefit of formal education. Jesus replies that his teaching comes from God, and that anyone who wants to do the will of God will recognize that his teaching is true (7:17). He then contrasts his teaching with that of the official religious leaders, whom he accuses of speaking on their own and seeking their own glory (7:18a), implying that such teaching is false. Jesus, on the other hand, seeks only the glory of the one who sent him (God), and his (Jesus') teaching is true, unadulterated by anything false at all (7:18b).

(b) Jesus argues with the crowd and the authorities about the law of Moses (7:19–24). Here Jesus addresses those who are seeking to kill him because he was breaking the Sabbath law (5:18). The Jewish crowd apparently knows nothing of this determination on the part of the religious authorities, whom John designates as "the Jews." "You have a demon!" they say. "Who is trying to kill you?" (7:20). Jesus replies to the crowd and to the authorities among them when he engages in a bit of rabbinical exegesis about what is lawful on the Sabbath (7:22–23). He then urges the crowd and the authorities alike to judge not by appearances, but with right judgment. It is decision time (7:24).

(c) The crowd wonders if Jesus is the Messiah (7:25–31). In this paragraph "some of the people of Jerusalem" raise the question of Jesus' messiahship. When they say "we know where this man is from" (v. 27), they are thinking of Nazareth (1:46; 19:19) in Galilee (7:41, 52). Jesus acknowledges that they know where he is from in the usual sense of place of origin (7:28a); then, in a play on words characteristic of the Fourth Gospel, Jesus teaches them that where he comes from is not a place but a person. "The one who sent me" (7:28b–29) refers to God the Father.[2] The authorities understand this veiled reference and try to arrest him (v. 30). The crowd understands but is divided in its response. All wonder if he could be the Messiah (7:26), but most doubt it because of the widespread belief that "when Messiah comes, no one will know where he is from" (7:27). After hearing Jesus' teaching and seeing his signs, however, "many in the crowd believed in him" (v. 31).

(d) The Pharisees order Jesus' arrest and he teaches about his imminent departure (7:32–36). The Pharisees who are in the crowd grow alarmed by what they hear and presumably report it to the chief priests, who have authority to send temple police to arrest Jesus (7:32, also 30). These are the religious authorities to whom the fourth evangelist often refers by the expression "the Jews."[3] Their move to arrest Jesus leads him to recognize that he has not much time remaining to accomplish the purpose for which

he was sent (7:33), but this thought inspires in Jesus no fear at all. "You will search for me but you will not find me," he says (7:34). Double entendre and misunderstanding come into play again. The authorities assume he is speaking of the inability of the arresting party to find him. Through their speculation about going to teach the Greeks of the Dispersion (*diaspora*, 7:35), the evangelist speaks over their heads and directly to his readers in the Hellenistic Jewish milieu of the end of the first century. But when he has the authorities repeat Jesus' words, "You will search for me and you will not find me" and "Where I am, you cannot come" (7:36), the evangelist wishes readers of every age to understand that Jesus speaks of his return to the Father, to whom no one can come except through him (14:6) and at the Father's initiative (6:44).

Preaching and teaching the Word

Much of the argument between Jesus and the zealous followers of the law of Moses in John 7 seems irrelevant in our time, but the relationship between knowing the truth of Jesus' teaching and willingness to live by it is perennially pertinent. "Anyone who resolves to do the will of God will know whether the teaching is from God or whether I am speaking on my own" (7:17). "Doing what is true" (literally, "doing the truth") in 3:21 also pins spiritual discernment firmly to obedient action. Those who resolve to be doers of the word and not hearers only (James 1:22) will find that Jesus' words in this chapter and throughout the Gospel ring true in their hearts. Jesus' teaching really is from God, and in doing what he teaches that conviction will be validated in the kind of knowing that comes only from experience. A sermon or lesson on this text would be appropriate for individuals and groups in our own time who tend to make judgments and deliver opinions about Jesus without first hearing him and trying to find out what he is doing in the hearts and lives of people today.

On the Last Day of the Festival (7:37–52)

This section of chapter 7 consists of three brief but important paragraphs.

Exploring the text

(a) Jesus invites all thirsty souls to come to him (7:37–39). Jesus' gracious invitation to anyone who is thirsty is as richly allusive as it is inclusive. "Come to me" (7:37) is synonymous with "believe in me" (7:38). Materially, the invitation refers to the water that was poured out ritually each morning of this weeklong festival. Metaphorically, it is Jesus' offer of himself as the water of life–almost, but not quite. A Bible teacher or preacher might wish that Jesus had said, "I am the water of life," to form a trilogy with "I am the bread of life" (6:35) and "I am the light of the

world" (8:12). Verse 39 explains why the parallelism is broken here: water in the Fourth Gospel refers not to Jesus but to the Spirit. The invitation is to come to Jesus, believe in him, and receive the Holy Spirit, which believers were to receive after Jesus returned to the Father ("was glorified," 7:39).

The Scripture quotation in verse 38 raises interesting questions for translators. The Greek says, "Out of his belly," translated literally in the AV but softened in contemporary translations (NRSV, "heart"; NIV, "from within him"). The more significant translation issue, however, is the antecedent of "his," which can and probably does refer to Jesus rather than to the believer as the source of living water. Read in this way, the thirsty one comes to Jesus, the believer drinks from Jesus, and the Holy Spirit proceeds from Jesus (7:39). This makes sense of the evangelist's remark that at his death water came from Jesus' side (19:34). It is also consistent with John's belief that it is Jesus who gives the Spirit (20:22). The Eastern church fathers denied that the Spirit proceeds from the Father *and the Son* (the *filioque* controversy, dating from the fourth century and still unresolved). They interpreted "his" in John 7:38 to make the verse speak of the believer's heart instead of Jesus,[4] the interpretation adopted by the King James Version (AV) and followed by the RSV, NRSV, and NIV.

The source of the Scripture citation is difficult to identify because these exact words are not found in the Hebrew Bible or Greek Old Testament. They might allude to the rock in the desert that Moses struck so water flowed from it, a scene described in the Pentateuch (Exod. 17:1–7; Num. 20:2–13; Deut. 8:15), echoed in Second Isaiah (43:20; 44:3; 48:21) and in the Psalms, where it is twice related to the bread from heaven (78:15–16, 19–25; 105:40–41; 114:8), and used as a type of Christ in the early church (1 Cor. 10:4). On the other hand, the citation might allude to Zechariah 14, a text that was read at the Festival of Booths, and in particular to the prophecy that "on that day living waters shall flow out from Jerusalem. . . . And the Lord will become king over all the earth" (Zech. 14:8–9). Given the fact that no Old Testament text is quoted verbatim here, the interpreter may well point to more than one allusion suggested by the rich imagery of this paragraph.

(b) The divided response of the crowd (7:40–44). These verses echo the earlier divided opinions about whether or not Jesus is the Messiah (7:25–31). Those favorably disposed to Jesus thought he was "the prophet" (7:40), that is, the prophet like Moses (Deut. 18:15; John 6:14), or Elijah, whose return would herald the appearance of the Messiah (Mal. 4:5; Matt. 3:4; 11:14 and parallels). Others said Jesus was himself the Messiah (7:41) but were challenged by those who pointed out that according to the Scriptures Messiah was to come from Bethlehem and not Galilee. There is no indication here or elsewhere in the Fourth Gospel of any tradition that Jesus was born in Bethlehem. He was known to be from Nazareth in Galilee (see [c], p. 94). Again the crowd is divided in its response, and again there is the suggestion of his arrest, but no action on it.

(c) The division of opinion among the authorities (7:45–51). The final paragraph in this section and in the chapter as a whole reports a division of opinion among the authorities as well as among the crowd. It is the sequel to the final paragraph in section 1, in which the chief priests and Pharisees send the temple police to arrest Jesus (v. 32). The dialogue between the religious leaders and the police when they return empty-handed depicts two contrasting opinions about Jesus. The chief priests and Pharisees berate the police for not arresting Jesus, ask if they too have been deceived, and point out that nobody who is anybody believes in Jesus (vv. 45, 47). The police, in reply, offer a pointed witness to Jesus and his teaching: "Never has anyone spoken like this!"

Jesus has another friend among the authorities. Nicodemus, "who was one of them" (that is, a Pharisee, 3:1), raises a legal question about the propriety of judging someone without due process. The reply of his peers invites readers to hear a tone of contempt and to visualize a superior sneer. Their unbelief comes to expression in words of sarcasm and disdain, bringing to a provisional close this inventory of responses to the person and teaching of Jesus.

Preaching and teaching the Word

Is Jesus really who he says he is according to John? This question underlies the controversy reported in John 7 and still causes division in the crowd, in the church, and in the secret heart of many a believer.

John 7:37–39 is one of the two Gospel readings proposed for the Day of Pentecost–the only lectionary reading from chapter 7. It captures the vivid moment when Jesus, on the last day of the Festival of Booths, cries out, "Let anyone who is thirsty come to me, and let the one who believes in me drink!" (7:37–38). This is the basic invitation to faith that the entire Fourth Gospel presents to the world, and the interpreter has the privilege of giving voice to it.

Jesus' ringing invitation to come to him and drink lends itself to evangelistic preaching to any crowd, whether in the church or elsewhere. Only as the will to come to Jesus is awakened in people will they be able, on the basis of personal experience, to form a valid judgment of who he is. "The thirst that from the soul doth rise doth ask a drink divine,"[5] and many who have come to Jesus have found in him a satisfaction akin to that of thirst assuaged on a hot, hot day, expressed in an old cowboy song, "Cool Water."

The density and richness of the text make it an apt subject for teaching. In whatever context, a faithful interpretation of this text will blend preaching and teaching, for it invites all to come to Jesus, believe his teaching, and drink deep of its living water, which is the Holy Spirit. A teaching situation allows the interpreter to explore the fluidity of the water symbolism, in which there is no real conflict between water as the teaching of Jesus, water as the Spirit who gives life to that teaching and to the one who believes it, and water as a symbol for the Spirit communicated through believers to others who may receive eternal life through their witness. The *filioque* controversy (does the Spirit proceed from the Son as well as the Father?), which contributed to the division of the Eastern and Western churches in the eleventh century, loses its steam when one recognizes the fluidity of symbolic language. The terms of debate have changed over the years, but misunderstandings of John's symbolic language still abound, offering to teachers the challenge of clarifying through teaching who Jesus is and what God intends for the world. They can heed Alexander Pope's sage advice,

> A little learning is a dangerous thing;
> Drink deep, or taste not the Pierian spring:
> There shallow draughts intoxicate the brain,
> And drinking largely sobers us again.[6]

The police sent to arrest Jesus said, "Never has anyone spoken like this!" (7:46). Their wonderment has sparked many a meditation on the uniqueness of Jesus Christ, some that lift up particularly powerful words from his teaching and others that reflect on the global impact of his personality.[7] The preacher whose heart leaps up in recognition at the words of the temple police may still, by the inspiration of the Spirit, become a channel through which Jesus' matchless words are heard again.

A Sinful Woman and Her Sinful Accusers (7:53–8:11)

Sometimes what appears to belong is actually out of place, and sometimes what appears to be out of place really belongs. In a way characteristic of the Fourth Gospel, these seemingly contradictory statements are both true of the story of a woman caught in sin and her accusers caught off base.

It appears to be out of place because many early manuscripts omit it or include it here within the ancient equivalent of brackets, while other early copies of the New Testament place the story in different contexts: some after John 21:25, some after Luke 21:38, and at least one after John 7:36

before the last day of the festival. The style and vocabulary of the text are more typical of the Synoptic Gospels, especially Luke. The Gospel of John is characterized by long discourses, but this text is a short narrative in which Jesus says little. Indeed, at the heart of the drama Jesus is silent. With regard to vocabulary, "Mount of Olives" and "scribe" appear nowhere else in John but are used in all the other Gospels. Furthermore, if a reader skips from 7:52 to 8:12, John's account of Jesus at the Festival of Tabernacles reads smoothly. For these and other reasons, it is almost certain that the story was not originally a part of this Gospel but was an early, free-floating unit of tradition.

On the other hand, the story fits well here because it highlights the eagerness of the authorities to bring a charge against Jesus (8:6a), continuing the theme of their attempt to arrest and try him (7:32, 45–52) and introducing the theme of judgment that is developed in chapter 8 (see 8:13–18). The incident is thoroughly congruent with Jesus' compassionate relationship with other women in the Fourth Gospel (the Samaritan in chap. 4 and Mary Magdalene in chap. 20). This vivid narrative also continues the pattern of encounters with Jesus that sustain the plot of the Fourth Gospel through chapter 12. It maintains reader interest in the middle of two full chapters of heavy theological discussion.

Some scholars have suggested that the reason this text had no fixed home in the Gospels was fear that it might lead to leniency in dealing with adultery—contrary to the early church's stern penitential discipline[1]—and because it testifies against a male-dominated status quo by making male religious leaders look bad.[2] However that may be, the story has all the earmarks of early, authentic tradition about Jesus that the Christian community cherished and retained.

Exploring the text

The text takes the form of a pronouncement story, so frequent in the Synoptic Gospels, in which a situation is described with only enough narrative to serve as a setting for a brief, memorable saying of Jesus. This account of a woman accused of adultery and of her judgmental accusers enshrines two words of Jesus that are memorable (8:7, 11)—three, if we count his eloquent silence as a nonverbal word (8:6, 8).

The structure of the text is important for its understanding. Three brief verses (8:53–7:2) tie the narrative to its present literary context, provide the setting (time and place) for the story, and place its central character, Jesus, at center stage. Verse 3 introduces the other characters: religious authorities (scribes and Pharisees) on the one hand and a woman caught in flagrant violation of Mosaic law on the other. Focusing on Jesus' conversation partners, the scene then develops in two parts:

1. The authorities and Jesus (8:4–9a)
    The authorities question Jesus (8:4–5) and the evangelist explains why (8:6a)
    Jesus is silent, bends down, and writes on the ground (8:6b)
    The authorities continue to question, then Jesus stands and speaks a word not of judgment but of justice: "*Let anyone among you who is without sin be the first to throw a stone at her*" (8:7b).
    Again Jesus is silent, bends down, and writes on the ground (8:8).
    The authorities are silent and depart, one by one, beginning with the eldest (8:9a).

2. Jesus and the woman (8:9b–11)
    Jesus, still bending down, is alone with the woman, standing; both silent (8:9b).
    Jesus rises and questions the woman, "Has no one condemned you?" (8:10).
    The woman speaks her only line: "No one, sir" (8:11a).
    Jesus speaks a word of grace: *"Neither do I condemn you. Go your way, and from now on do not sin again"* (8:11b).

Two parallel sequences about Jesus' actions appear in the two parts of the story:

Jesus bends down and writes on the ground	8:6b	8:8
Jesus stands up to address his conversation partners	8:7b	8:10a
Jesus speaks	8:7c	8:11b

The latter analysis highlights the fact that Jesus has two sets of conversation partners–the scribes and Pharisees, and the woman. In both cases sin is an issue, but the nature of the sin, the level of the sinners' awareness, and Jesus' way of dealing with it differ widely.

The pattern of speakers is significant, as is the pattern of speech and silence. The scribes and Pharisees speak first and most. Their interruption of Jesus' teaching and their outraged accusation against the woman are motivated by their desire to bring a charge against Jesus. Jesus is silent for some time, writing with his finger on the ground. What he wrote will never be known, nor does it matter. The silence gives the accusers time to reflect on what Moses commanded in the law (Lev. 20:10; Deut. 22:23–24). In both contexts, the law targets primarily the guilty man, with the woman as an accessory to his sin. Reflection on the law could lead the accusers to realize that bringing only the woman to Jesus is a miscarriage of justice. When Jesus finally speaks, he says very little–just enough to invite them to test themselves rather than him (8:7). Jesus bends down and writes on the ground again (8:8), and in the ensuing silence the accusers realize that they also are sinners and quietly leave. Jesus now speaks again, asking a brief two-part question of the woman (8:10). Her answer is even briefer, just two words in Greek (*oudeis, kyrie*) and three in English, "No one, sir" (8:11). She expresses relief at freedom from her accusers, but perhaps also apprehension about what Jesus might say next. The final words belong to Jesus. He first relieves her anxiety, "Neither do I condemn you," then in a memorable sentence that combines mercy and justice, grace for the sinner and condemnation of the sin, he adds, "Go your way, and from now on do not sin again" (8:11b).

Silent reflection on the psychological dynamics of this succinct narrative will yield for the interpreter rich insights into human relationships, social as well as individual. Such reflection should always come back to the central figure, Jesus, whose treatment of this woman and of her accusers reveals the heart of God.

Preaching and teaching the Word

The title for this passage given above has avoided its usual designation because the story is not primarily about adultery; it is about passing judgment. To be sure, adultery is the presenting issue, but the real issue is how Jesus deals with the woman's judgmental accusers and how he deals with the woman herself.

An interpretation *focusing on Jesus and the accusers* should recognize that the text has direct implications for the preacher or teacher, who often stands in the position of a religious authority. Ask not, "What can I say about this text?" but first of all, "What is this text saying to me?" What issues are raised when the accusers quote and apply the Scriptures and use the law to conceal their real motives? Notice the finesse with which Jesus uses silence in dealing with hostility and how he ignores their question about what he would do. He exemplifies the wisdom and eloquence of silence in such a situation, then he points to what they want to do in a way that redirects their accusing fingers from the woman to themselves. The central point of this part of the story (8:3–9a) is Jesus' statement in verse 7, "Let anyone among you who is without sin be the first to throw a stone." Preachers who feel a judgmental attack coming on might find it good medicine to tuck this story under their tongue from time to time and let it melt. They might then refrain from judging their judgmental congregations, but preach with an empathy that leads hearers to judge themselves.

Alternatively, the interpretation could *focus on Jesus' interaction with the woman.* He deals first with the fact that she was being used by the religious authorities; then he deals with her shame, her fear, her anger at being used, and her sin. For Jesus, people are persons, not pawns. People are also sinners, and many are wrestling consciously or unconsciously with their own sense of guilt. The interpreter might look closely at Jesus' sensitive questions to the woman, and especially at his lapidary, two-part word, "Neither do I condemn you. Go your way, and from now on do not sin again" (8:11). The woman's response is not recorded, but that need not inhibit a sermon on grace and gratitude. Jesus' nonjudgmental word is the incarnation of the grace of God. A sermon on it should help flagrant sinners and pious hypocrites alike to move from guilt and shame to forgiveness and new beginnings. Jesus' injunction is a prescription for the proper expression of any forgiven sinner's gratitude.

A sermon *encompassing the entire story* could be called "sinners anonymous," for it is about two kinds of sinners, and in both cases anonymity is involved. In the case of the scribes and the Pharisees, the sinners are identified, but the sin—judgmentalism—is not named. In the case of the woman caught in adultery, the sin is named, but the woman is anonymous. The interpreter could explore the two kinds of sin. The first is closely related to hypocrisy and seldom publicly recognized; the second is publicly recognized but until recently it was talked about only in private. Jesus offers no word of condemnation for either of these sins, though it is evident that for him judgmentalism is a more serious sin than adultery. In both cases, the response of Jesus is gracious, and his goal is liberation from the sin. He expects his adversaries to recognize their sin and to desist from it, which they do. He offers the freed woman the chance to live out her gratitude by leaving off her sin, which she (and the reader or hearer) may do.

This approach offers an occasion to explore the *interplay of justice and mercy* in the text. Jesus' concern for justice dominates his dealing with the scribes and Pharisees; his concern for mercy determines his response to the nameless woman. The latter case shows how it is possible to love the sinner while hating the sin. Jesus does not condemn the woman, but he does not condone adultery.

The interesting thing is that the text does not present any of these ideas explicitly. Jesus does not preach a sermon! This suggests that the best way to interpret the text might be just to tell the story, perhaps by letting one of the characters tell it in a first-person sermon. Even better, in a teaching-learning setting the interpreter could let the learners tell the story themselves. The text could be explored in a group study session that would include reading it aloud, assigning parts to the participants. For a deeper experience, participants could be invited to write their own dramatization of the story and role-play it at the next gathering of the group. The teaching possibilities for an imaginative leader are as rich as they are varied.

The Light of the World: Confrontation in the Temple (8:12–59)

John 8 presents some of the most startling contrasts in the Fourth Gospel. In 8:3–11 Jesus is portrayed as laconic, nonjudgmental, and compassionate. In 8:12–59 he is portrayed as wordy, judgmental, and aggressive. Even within the present unit (8:12–59) the contrasts are startling. "I judge no one" (v. 15) is followed by "I have much to say about you and much to condemn" (v. 26). "I am the light of the world" (8:12) stands close beside "you are of your father the devil" (8:44). This harshest of Jesus' judgments upon his adversaries follows immediately upon his shaming their judgmental attitude in 8:2–11. It is hard to reconcile with "Do not judge, so that you may not be judged" (Matt. 7:1), and it stands in sharp contrast to his gracious promise "to the Jews who had believed in him, 'If you continue in my word, you are truly my disciples; and you will know the truth, and the truth will make you free'" (8:31–32). How is the preacher to understand this text? How should it be interpreted for others?

Exploring the text

The Fourth Gospel as a whole presents encounters Jesus had with all sorts of individuals and groups. John 8:12–59 is the fourth in a series of confrontations with the religious authorities who rejected Jesus.[1]

The encounter is reported in the style of heated rabbinic debate. Jesus' adversaries are variously identified, and each of four smaller units is introduced by an expression that suggests a new topic and perhaps a new occasion: "Again Jesus spoke to them. . . . Again he said to them. . . . Then Jesus said to the Jews who had believed in him" (8:12, 21, 31). The fourth unit begins with a harsh accusation by Jesus' adversaries (8:48). Each of the four deals with topics that recur in Jesus' ongoing debates with Jewish religious authorities, this time treated with increasing vehemence.

The Pharisees (8:12–20)

Jesus introduces his teaching in the treasury of the temple (8:20) with the second of the seven **"I Am" sayings** with a defining term in the Gospel of John, "I am the light of the world. Whoever follows me will never walk in darkness but will have the light of life" (8:12). This powerful affirmation is occasioned by the special illumination at the Festival of Booths. It is elaborated in the story of the man born blind (chap. 9), but not in the verses that follow in chapter 8. Instead, the Pharisees start an argument about what constitutes valid testimony in a lawsuit. When Jesus promises that whoever follows him will have the light of life, the specialists in Scripture take exception, because they understand themselves to be the exclusive custodians of God's word, which is a lamp to the feet and a light on the path (Ps. 119:105). Instead of receiving, believing, and following Jesus, they reject what he says and set off on a side trail of scriptural interpretation. The implication of the text is that they walk in darkness–a reverse image of Isaiah 50:11, in which the Lord's faithful servant walks in darkness yet trusts in God, while the majority walk in the light of flames they have kindled.

The theme of testimony, which figures prominently in chapter 5 (5:31–37) and elsewhere in the Gospel (1:6–8; 3:11, 32–33; 19:35; 21:24), dominates the argument in verses 13–18. Other major Johannine themes that surface here are Jesus' knowledge of where he has come from and where he is going (8:14b; see also 8:21b–23 and 42), and judgment (8:15–16, exemplifying John's paradoxical use of the verb *krino,* which can mean either "judge" or "condemn").[2]

When Jesus calls his Father to witness (8:18), his opponents reopen the major question of Jesus' relationship to God by a thinly veiled allusion to questions about his paternity (8:19). The affirmation that Jesus is Son of God, introduced as the basis for his adversaries' rejection of him in 5:18, is stoutly maintained throughout the polemic in chapter 8 (8:16–20, 38–40, 54–58) and later (10:30–36). The revelation of Jesus' unique relationship to God is a basic element in the witness of the Fourth Gospel to Jesus, the Christ.[3]

"The Jews" (8:21–30)

The theme of Jesus' coming from God and going to God, introduced at 5:43a; 7:28, 33–36; and 8:14b, opens this section of the debate with "the Jews"[4] (8:21–24), although the word "God" is not used. In the Fourth Gospel "the Father," "heaven," and "above" (8:23) are all ways of referring to God. The affirmation that Jesus has come down from the Father and will return to the Father runs like a thread through the Gospel of John,[5] to which is added his return to be with his disciples beginning at chapter 14 (14:3; 16:16–19; 21:22–23).

At verse 25 his adversaries introduce the basic question of the entire Fourth Gospel when they say to Jesus, "Who are you?" Jesus asks why he is wasting his breath on them (8:25b), adds that he has much more to condemn in them (8:26, judgment theme), then points out that only after his crucifixion and resurrection will they realize who he really is (that "I am,"

8:28, Greek text). As evidence of his unique relationship to God, he states that he does and says only as he was instructed by the Father, who is always with him (8:29).

To close this subunit and introduce the next one, the evangelist notes that "as [Jesus] was saying these things, many believed in him" (8:30), an echo of the response of many during his first visit to Jerusalem (2:23).

Preaching and teaching the Word

Against the dark background of the polemic reported in this unit of Scripture, several points of light attract the eye. The first is the verse that opens the unit, "I am the light of the world. Whoever follows me will never walk in darkness but will have the light of life" (8:12). The whole of chapter 9 is the evangelist's own sermon based on this text. Both passages are based on the metaphor of light. The preacher or teacher could profitably explore what light is—a significant question to physicists—and how it functions in laboratory or darkroom, in the natural world, and in the experiences of everyday life. To which of these characteristics might Jesus have referred in his time? How does the expanded understanding of light in our time enrich the potential meaning of this text? What common experiences today might elucidate the scope and thrust of Jesus' words about light and darkness in our own time?

In its biblical context, the point of John 8:12 is the importance of following Jesus, not arguing with or about him—just following, and so living in the light. The real and present danger today is not so much our propensity to argue with Jesus as it is to acquiesce but not to follow him. Only followers can claim the promise.

The Jews Who Had Believed in Him (8:31–47)

Exploring the text

This section of the confrontation begins on a promising note as Jesus addresses "the Jews who had believed in him" (8:31). Within the crowd and even among the authorities, some are favorably disposed toward Jesus (7:45–52; 8:30). To these first-level believers Jesus addresses a memorable promise: "If you continue in my word, you are truly my disciples; and you will know the truth, and the truth will make you free" (8:31–32). "Believe" in verse 30 seems to refer to intellectual assent, while "disciple" in verse 31 means "learner" or follower. True discipleship is conditioned on "continuing in Jesus' word," that is, learning his teachings and coming to know him through following him. To know him is to know the truth (18:37–38), and to know the truth in this sense is to experience freedom.

Instead of asking Jesus to elaborate on the promise, these potential disciples seize upon the term "free" and pick fault with Jesus. Their objection introduces the theme of slavery versus freedom, and their claim to be descendants of Abraham (8:33) raises the question of their own paternity.

In reply Jesus develops both themes. He states emphatically that sinning is a kind of slavery (8:34) and develops the metaphor of sin as slavery by contrasting the place of a slave with that of a permanent family member (8:35). He claims authority as the Son [of God] to grant the freedom that makes people full members of God's household (8:36). He then takes up their claim to be descendants of Abraham. He grants them the biological fact but points out that their behavior does not match their claim (8:37). Verse 38 contrasts what Jesus has seen in the Father's presence with what his adversaries have heard from their father. The NRSV adopts a form of the Greek text that omits "your" from the second "father" and translates the verb "do" as an imperative. This reading of the text is entirely possible,[6] but the more probable sense is "I talk about what my Father has shown me, but you do what your father has told you" (8:38 TEV; similarly RSV, NIV, REB, NJB).

In verse 39 the potential disciples insist that Abraham is their father, but Jesus replies (8:39b–41) that if they were Abraham's children, their behavior would reflect Abraham's. Jesus has granted (v. 37) that they are Abraham's descendants ("seed," *sperma*), but he does not grant that they are his children (*tekna*). The shift is significant, for in Hebrew and Aramaic usage, "child of X" is used to describe someone's dominant quality, as when Barnabas is called a "son of encouragement" (Acts 4:36). The fact that these descendants of Abraham do not recognize the revelation of God when confronted by it shows that they do not share Abraham's characteristics. Their behavior demonstrates another paternity (8:41a).

They protest that they are not illegitimate children and insist that their one ultimate father is God (8:41b). Jesus' extended reply (8:42–47) is based on an if-then argument (8:42), and three rhetorical questions. One question (8:46a, "Which of you convicts me of sin?") is left unanswered. Jesus answers the other two (8:43, "Why do you not understand what I say?" and 8:46b, "Why do you not believe me?") in a series of sentences containing four statements of cause (8:43, 44, 45, 47), the gist of which is summed up in a shocking affirmation: "You are from your father the devil," buttressed by "you choose to do your father's desires" and "he was a murderer from the beginning" (v. 44). This vehement denunciation, addressed in the text to "the Jews who had believed in him," reflects hostility that Jesus himself experienced plus that experienced by the evangelist and his community.[7]

This text also brings us to the heart of the paradoxical relationship between foreordination and free will. "Because" does not appear in 8:44, but "choose" does. The text itself can be read either as an affirmation that "the Jews" involved in this controversy with Jesus cannot believe in him because they are children of the devil, or that their free decision to reject him shows whose children they really are. At the beginning of this sub-unit Jesus offers them the choice of continuing in his word as a real possibility that carries a real promise (8:31). At its end Jesus states that the reason they do not hear his words is that they are not from God (8:47).

Preaching and teaching the Word

Another point of light is Jesus' word to the Jews who had believed in him, "If you continue in my word, you are truly my disciples; and you will know the truth, and the truth will make you free" (8:31). The text invites those who accept what Jesus says to discover the truth of his words—and to know Jesus as the truth—in faithful, persistent practice of them. For John, Jesus' basic teaching is communion with him (15:4) and love for the community of disciples (15:12). For the other evangelists, it is to love God and love one's neighbor (Mark 12:28–31//Matt. 22:34–40//Luke 10:25–28). Continuing in the whole word of Jesus, as mediated by the whole New Testament, is the way to knowledge of the truth (in John, Jesus himself) and the experience of free and open relationships with God and with others. Jesus' first tentative believers did not recognize their enslavement to sin, and neither do most of us. For that reason, *Speaking of Sin*[8] is still appropriate.

Jesus takes up the theme of slavery, introduced by self-confident new believers who objected to the implication that they were not born free (v. 33), and links it with sin: "Very truly, I tell you, everyone who commits sin is a slave to sin" (v. 34). A sermon based on this "Amen-word" of Jesus affords the opportunity to explore the meaning of sin in the Fourth Gospel. In this case it is not simply the refusal to believe in Jesus (9:41; 15:22–23; 16:9) but a matter of acts committed or omitted. The preacher could reflect on how we are still blinded to sin as one thing leads to another, comparing and contrasting verses 34–36 with Paul's great passage on enslavement to sin (Rom. 6:15–23). Above all she or he could proclaim the freedom of God's children for open relationships with God and each other in and through the Son (vv. 35–36): "So if the Son makes you free, you will be free indeed."

Jesus and "the Jews" (8:48–59)

Exploring the text

The final subunit of the confrontation refers to Jesus' adversaries only as "the Jews" rather than "the Jews who had believed in him" (8:48). They have made their disbelief quite clear, and in response to Jesus' harsh words about their paternity they reply in kind: "You are a Samaritan and have a demon" (8:48). Several earlier themes are repeated (glory/honor, judging, keeping Jesus' word, Jesus' intimate knowledge of his Father, and acknowledgment that Abraham is the ancestor of the Jews). One more significant Johannine theme is introduced into the debate: eternal life. It is underscored by two of the "Amen-sayings" of Jesus.

Jesus' solemn promise that whoever keeps his word will never see death (8:51) is incredible if one understands him to be speaking of physical death. His adversaries understand it that way and cite Abraham and the prophets as proof of the fact that even the most godly people die (8:52–53), adding "Who do you think you are?" (author's paraphrase). When Jesus in reply states that Abraham "saw [my day] and was glad" (8:56), he refers to a kind of life that does not eliminate but transcends physical death.

In another example of Johannine misunderstanding based on double entendre, the opponents ridicule Jesus for claiming to have seen Abraham although he was not yet fifty years old (8:57, the only reference in the Fourth Gospel to Jesus' age). Jesus' reply, underscored by *amen, amen,* is another of the texts in which the claim for his unique relation to God is made by the absolute use of the verb "to be": "Very truly, I tell you, before Abraham was, **I am**" (8:58). His opponents move one step closer to fulfilling their hostile intention by picking up stones to kill him, but Jesus slips away unobserved (8:59).

Preaching and teaching the Word

Two "Amen-words" in 8:48–59 suggest a sermon on one of the great Johannine themes, eternal life, and its opposite, death. Jesus' promise, "Very truly, I tell you, whoever keeps my word will never taste death" (8:52), refers not to physical death but to that second death that is separation from God. Many fear the first more than the second. To believe (that is, entrust oneself to) this word of Jesus is to find freedom from the fear of death, both physical and spiritual. And Jesus is trustworthy, because he is the Word that was with God in the beginning, in whom was life (1:1–5), who is the resurrection and the life (11:25), as well as the way, the truth, and the life (14:6). That is why those who keep (= continue in) his word already have abundant life (10:10) and will never taste death (8:52). The promise of life beyond death is an article of faith that lies beyond verification in this world, but experiences of Jesus' trustworthiness in this life nurture faith in his promises for its continuation beyond physical death.

This chapter is a rich compendium of Johannine theology. Most of the themes interwoven here center on the question of who Jesus is, as does the entire Gospel. Many of the polar opposites that characterize the dualistic thought of the Fourth Gospel come into play in these dialogues between Jesus and those who reject him (light/darkness, life/death, slave/free, above/below, truth/lie). These merit exploration and discussion, using selected portions of John 8 and related texts.

The bitter polemic of this chapter does not make either Jesus or his adversaries look good, which may be one reason John 8 does not appear in any of the major lectionaries in use today. Yet it stands in Scripture as a resource and challenge for interpreters. Here are a few guidelines for those who struggle with the questions it raises.

1. *Recognize that the voice of Jesus and the voice of the evangelist are merged* in the Fourth Gospel. The evangelist was not a court reporter. He was a witness, testifying to what he heard from his risen Lord.[9]

2. *Appreciate the influence of the evangelist's own circumstances and audience* upon the way events are reported, as well as the influence of the interpreter's own circumstances and audience upon the way they are interpreted. In a time of deep hostility and tension between Jews who were excluded from the synagogue because of their persistent belief in Jesus and those who excluded them, the vehemence of the evangelist's report of what Jesus said would be understandable. In a time when believers in Jesus are not being persecuted by Jews, but when prejudice against Jews is a real and present danger in many places, interpreters need to use special care in the treatment of texts which, read in this totally different context, can fuel anti-Semitism.[10]

3. *Read Jesus' words in this chapter in the light of his other words* according to John and the Synoptic Gospels. Set Jesus' harsh words in John 8:12–59 alongside his gracious words in John 8:2–11 and in his teachings about love of enemy and not judging in the Sermon on the Mount (Matt. 5:43–45; 7:1–2). Do not let words spoken by Jesus and the evangelist in the heat of controversy obscure the overall message of love, light, and life in John's portrait of Jesus, of warm compassion in Luke's, of healing power in Mark's, and of gracious invitation in Matthew 11:28–30.

4. At the same time, *do not underestimate the significance of ignoring or rejecting the revelation of God in Jesus Christ.* Do not allow the Fourth Gospel's strand of determinism to diminish the fact that encounter with the Word confronts all who hear with a real choice that has real and permanent effects in this life and the next. Voltaire's clever word, "God will forgive me; that's his business," is not the message of the Fourth Gospel. According to John, Jesus' message is:

> I have come from God
> I am going to God
> You come too

The interpreter must not let the desire to make Jesus look nice cut the nerve of John's testimony that one's response to this invitation is a life-and-death decision (3:35–36), not only for the world to come but because of its effect on how life is lived here and now.

THE BEGGAR BLIND FROM BIRTH (JOHN 9:1–41)

"Come and see," said Jesus to Andrew and his companion (1:39); Philip to Nathanael (1:46); the Samaritan woman to her neighbors (4:29). This sequence belongs to the pattern of seeing and believing that is vividly portrayed in the story of Jesus' giving sight to a beggar blind from birth.

Several Johannine patterns and themes converge in this rich text: one of Jesus' encounters with a wide variety of people,[1] one of the seven miracle stories which John calls **"signs,"** one of the seven dramatic claims of Jesus based on the expression **"I Am"** followed by a defining term, and the theme of **light/darkness** in the form of a case study in seeing and blindness.

Exploring the text

John 9, like good drama in general and the Fourth Gospel as a whole, operates at two levels: that of the interaction among characters in the story, and that of the dramatist and the first readers.[2] Both levels are taken into account in the following exegetical notes, and a third level is introduced in suggestions about how the story might be communicated to readers and hearers today.

The drama unfolds in seven dramatic scenes.

Scene 1. Jesus Heals a Man Born Blind (9:1–7)

Actors in the opening scene are Jesus, his disciples, and a man who had been blind from his birth. His disciples ask whose sin was responsible for this man's condition (9:2). Jesus' answer (v. 3) changes the man's blindness from a result to a possibility—an occasion for the revelation of God's glorious work. Neither Jesus nor the evangelist is interested in speculations about where sin and darkness come from. The world is blind, and God's work is to heal it.[3]

The seeming anomaly in verse 4, " *We* must work the works of him who sent *me* while it is day," bothered early scribes, who thought to correct it by alternate readings. The text as we have it, however, is probably the original reading. Through it the evangelist has Jesus speak directly to his first disciples and also to all subsequent ones, since "night is coming when no one can work" (9:4b). This saying about daylight and dark has meaning at three levels. At the moment of his encounter with the blind beggar, Jesus knew his death was imminent; John's first readers and we know only that ours might be.

Jesus' affirmation "I am the light of the world" (9:5) is one of the seven "I Am" statements with a defining term in the Gospel of John. Jesus here uses the image of light to say who he is, echoing what was already said in 8:12. The evangelist means for us to read the healing of this blind beggar as a dramatic example of the fact that Jesus is who he claims to be: the light of the world.

In verses 6 and 7, Jesus uses saliva and anointing with mud to heal the blind man, an element that appears in many healing stories from the Greco-Roman world. This scene is depicted in the art of the Roman catacombs to illustrate the meaning of baptism. The anointing practiced at the time of baptism from ancient times till today in some traditions is based on the connection of baptism with this text and the idea of illumination.[4] The evangelist, however, finds significance at two other points. First, among Jews kneading was among the thirty-nine categories of work explicitly forbidden on the Sabbath, and Jesus violated the law by mixing spittle with dirt to make a medicinal mud. The other point has to do with Jesus' command to go wash in the pool of Siloam. The evangelist inserts an editorial note, reminding his readers that "Siloam" in Hebrew or Aramaic means "sent" (9:7). In doing this work of the one who sent him, Jesus, as the Son whom God sent into the world not to condemn the world, but that the world might be saved (John 3:17), sends this beggar to wash in a pool called "sent." Furthermore, the pool of Siloam was the source of the water that was poured out ritually on the last day of the Festival of Tabernacles or Booths (7:37–38), when Jesus cried out "Let anyone who is thirsty come to me!" This is a good example of the way John uses language more to suggest connections than to define ideas.

Scene 2. First Reaction: The Neighbors (9:8–12)

In the first of a series of scenes depicting various reactions to this miracle of healing, Jesus is no longer on stage–an unusual situation in the Fourth Gospel. He does not reappear until near the end of the chapter (9:35). The main actors in this scene are the blind man and his neighbors and acquaintances. The latter discuss whether or not this is the blind man who used to sit and beg. Their difference of opinion is quickly settled by the man's own affirmation: "I'm the one!" (9:9, author's paraphrase).

The more significant reaction is revealed when the blind man answers their question, "How were your eyes opened?" He replies, "The man called Jesus . . ." (9:11). It is the first in four progressive steps toward his seeing who Jesus is.

As for his "I don't know" (9:12) in reply to the question about Jesus' whereabouts, how could he know? After all, being blind, he had not ever seen Jesus, and by the time he could see, Jesus had disappeared into the crowd.

Scene 3. Second Reaction: The Pharisees (9:15–17)

In the next three scenes, instead of Jesus it is the Pharisees who are present throughout, in dialogue with various actors. Early in their dialogue with the cured man, the evangelist adds a note: "By the way, it was a Sabbath day when Jesus made the mud and opened the man's eyes" (v. 14, author's paraphrase). This detail is important at the moment when the Pharisees are introduced, for they are the custodians of the Sabbath laws and other traditional observances.

The Pharisees, like the friends and acquaintances, also ask the man how he received his sight (9:15). When he tells them how it happened, they argue among themselves about whether the healer is a Sabbath-breaking sinner or someone with powers from God (9:16). They are not moved by interest in the man, either as a human being or as a medical case. Their concern is about Jesus, who seems not to be careful about observing the law as it was traditionally interpreted. They pursue the investigation by asking the blind man (whom they'd never known as anything but "the blind man"), "What do you say about this man? It was your eyes he opened."

"He is a prophet," the cured beggar replies (9:17).

This scene focuses on the Pharisees but actually shows three reactions to Jesus. Some of the Pharisees consider only the remarkable signs that Jesus is doing and conclude that he must get this power from God. Others consider only that he doesn't observe the Sabbath and conclude that he is a sinner. The affirmation of the blind man (9:17) marks his second step toward seeing who Jesus really is.

Scene 4. Third Reaction: The Parents (9:18–23)

The religious authorities do not want to believe that Jesus has done this thing, so they call the parents of the man who has received his sight. "Is this your son," they ask, "who *you say* was born blind? If that is true, how do you explain the fact that he now can see?" (v. 19, author's paraphrase). The parents affirm that the man is their son and that he was born blind, but as to how he now sees, they say, in effect, "Don't ask us; ask our son. He is of legal age; let him speak for himself" (vv. 20–21).

The editorial note in verses 22–23 is important to the dynamics of the story. First, it explains this evasive reply of the parents, who perceive that the religious leaders have no real interest in their son but are looking for a way to discredit Jesus. They fear that the Pharisees wish not only to trap Jesus but to trap them as well. Second, the evangelist explains the basis of the parents' fear: "the Jews" [the religious authorities] "had already agreed that anyone who confessed Jesus to be the Messiah would be put out of the synagogue"–that is, would be excluded from the Jewish family of faith.[5] "Put out of the synagogue" appears only in the Gospel of John, and the only other references in the Gospels to disciples of Jesus being attacked by authorities of the synagogue are in predictive contexts about what will happen in the future.[6] According to this note, however, the parents understand that a confession of Jesus as Messiah would entail social and economic ostracism, and they choose to save their own necks, even at the possible cost of their son's expulsion.

Scene 5. Second Interview of the Healed Man by the Pharisees (9:24–34)

Frustrated in their first effort to discount the significance of this healing, the Jewish leaders call the man who had been born blind for a second interview. The anonymous beggar stands before the leading biblical scholars of his time. "Give glory to God" (v. 24), they say, using a traditional oath formula by which people were enjoined to tell the truth.[7]

In the first exchange of the present dialogue (9:24–25) the Pharisees, relying on their knowledge of Scripture and their expertise in its interpretation, know that violation of the Sabbath is a sin and that Jesus, therefore, is a sinner. The beggar is not prepared to debate theology with them ("Whether he is a sinner or not, I do not know"), but he knows his own experience: "Though I was blind, now I see."

In a second exchange (9:26–27) the authorities, having finally decided to grant that this man really was born blind and that Jesus has in fact healed him, ask again what Jesus did to open his eyes.

"I have told you already," replies the man with irritation, adding sarcastically: "Why do you want to hear it again? Do you also want to become his disciples?"

The next exchange (9:28–33) grows more heated. The authorities call the beggar the most insulting thing they can think of at the moment: "You are his disciple!" Then they add, "But we are disciples of Moses. We all know (there it is again!) that God has spoken to Moses, but we don't know who this man is or where he is from" (vv. 28–29, author's paraphrase). They imply that there is some question about Jesus' hometown, and even about his parents.

The healed man now warms to his subject. "Here is a wonder for sure: you don't know where he's coming from, and yet he opened my eyes! We know, as you say, that God does not listen to sinners, but he does listen to one who worships him and obeys his will. That's what you teach us, isn't it? Well, did you ever hear of anyone opening the eyes of a person *born* blind? If this man were not from God, he couldn't do this, or anything else worth mentioning, could he?" (vv. 30–33, author's paraphrase).

The man has decided he can argue theology with the experts after all. Since they have granted him the truth of his basic claim, he grants them their own major premise: God listens to those who worship him and obey his will; God does not listen to sinners. This is the synagogue's teaching, not that of Jesus, whom the man has not yet seen, and whose teaching he has not heard. But when this man joins the synagogue teaching to his own experience of Jesus, he arrives at a conclusion diametrically opposed to that of the Pharisees: Jesus comes from God. It is the man's third step toward full understanding.

The authorities have no answer to the man's reasoning, but they do have the last word: "You're a low-born sinner, and you're trying to teach us?" (v. 34a, author's paraphrase). In saying to the man, "You were born entirely in sins," they revert to the same presupposition that led to the disciples' question at the beginning. They assume that the misfortune of being born blind must be the result of sin, a presupposition that Jesus had rejected out of hand (9:3).

The closing sentence of the narrator, "Then they drove [literally: threw] him out," means at the first level that his interrogators drove the healed man out of their presence. At a second level it could refer to the experience of those who, at the time the Gospel was written, confessed that Jesus is Messiah and were driven out of the synagogue.

Scene 6. Jesus Finds the Outcast, Who Makes His Final Response to Jesus (9:35–39)

Jesus hears that the religious authorities have driven out the man who had dared to stand up for him, so he takes the initiative to look him up, as he had done when he healed the man. Jesus is at center stage again, this time with the man only. Jesus puts the question that the evangelist poses to the reader: "Do you believe in the Son of Man?" (9:35).

The man recognizes that this title refers to someone of importance, but he does not know who it might be. He replies, "And who is he, sir? Tell me, so that I may believe in him" (9:36). His reply shows a respect for and trust in the one who befriended him, even though the man does not yet fully understand who his friend is, and he certainly cannot identify him in traditional theological terms.

"Why, you have seen him," said Jesus. "Not only so, but the one speaking to you is he!" (9:37, author's paraphrase).

The man's reply constitutes one of the earliest, simplest, and most fundamental professions of Christian faith, "Lord, I believe." Now he sees—really sees—who Jesus is: the Son of Man, before whom he kneels in reverent awe (9:38).

Scene 7. Jesus' Concluding Word to the Man, to the Pharisees, and to Us (9:40–41)

"Son of Man" in the Old Testament was associated with a future judgment by one who will come on the clouds of heaven. Jesus' closing word as Son of Man has to do with judgment but corrects the idea that it lies only in the future: "I came into this world for judgment so that those who do not see may see, and those who do see may become blind" (v. 39).

The coming of the light as judgment is discussed at length in the discourses of chapters 3, 8, 10, and 12. The present text does not specify to whom this aphorism is addressed, but it is pertinent for three audiences.

To the once-blind man Jesus says, in effect, "I came into this world for your sake, so you may see. And as for those who have cast you out of the synagogue, their response to me and their treatment of you have made it clear that they are blind."

To the self-assured religious leaders of Jesus' time, the Pharisees, and to those who had probably excluded Christian Jews from the synagogue in the time of the evangelist and his first readers,[8] Jesus says, in effect, "I came so that the bright light of my presence will make crystal clear just how blind you are."

Some of the Pharisees standing nearby hear Jesus' words and respond, "Surely we are not blind, are we?" (9:40). Jesus' frank reply seems almost pitiless: "If you were blind, you would not have sin. But you have extensive knowledge of the Scriptures and a long tradition of sound theology, which should have prepared you to recognize me, but they have only filled you with proud self-confidence. You say, 'We see,' when in fact the things you think you see so clearly have blinded you to the light. That is why your sin remains—the sin of rejecting the very light you think you see" (v. 41, author's paraphrase).

Preaching and teaching the Word

Preachers who always follow the lectionary will never preach on this text, but recognition of Jesus as the light of the world is surely one of the pillars of the Christian faith, just as the coming of the light is a major theme of the Fourth Gospel. The task of the preacher is not simply to repeat these verities, however. It is to help hearers come to the light, to see themselves and the world by that light, and to walk in it. This might be done by reflecting on how Jesus helps me to see myself as I really am, exposing all my darkness and lifting all that is good in me to the light. Again, the sermon might ask how the world today looks to Jesus, inviting hearers to consider world affairs in the light not of national self-interest but of God's saving love. The evangelist's sermon on the text "I am the light of the world" (8:12 and 9:15) is to tell the story of how Jesus healed a blind beggar. Preachers could do worse than simply tell this story with empathy and conviction, but that was then. They might do better by telling stories from their own experience of how Jesus has brought light to dark lives and desperate situations. The goal would be to help people know Jesus better and thereby to see everything in a new light.

We can identify with various actors in the drama. Are we, like the blind man, stunned recipients of some great gift of God that we do not fully understand, but that we will not deny, and are we moving steadily toward ever fuller understanding of and commitment to the giver? Are we like the neighbors who can't believe a miracle has happened? Are we, like the parents, aware of what Jesus is doing in the world but too concerned about our own social and economic status to stand up as witnesses for him, or to offer costly support to those who do? Are we, like students and teachers of the Torah in Jesus' day, so sure of our Bible and theology as to be ready to write off those who have some other experience and understanding of Christ, since we are the custodians of the peace and purity of the true faith? Are we, perhaps, on some days like one and on some days like another?

Jesus' final word warns us against saying too quickly, "We see," even when the question is where we see ourselves in the text. Before seeing ourselves in the blind man, we might ask ourselves what we are blind to and who has ostracized us because of our stand for Jesus. Friendly observers have sometimes called Presbyterians the Pharisees of the Christian family, keen on the interpretation and implementation of Scripture. Before seeing ourselves in the Pharisees, however, we might ask to what degree we really know the Bible and theology, and really care about the peace and purity of the church.

This story lends itself to dramatic reading, role play, or mime. The length of the story, the variety in its cast of characters, and the abundance of dialogue offer clues that are a challenge for a teacher to pursue and a joy for learners to act out.

One might entitle a sermon on John 9 "Daylight Saving Time." It is rare that a grammatical irregularity suggests a sermon, but the shift from plural to singular in verse 4 does. "*We* must do the works of him who sent *me* while it is day" makes good sense as a first-level statement about Jesus and his disciples then, but the plural form of the subject calls attention to its applicability at a second level to the evangelist and first readers and, at a third and more immediately relevant level, to hearers today. None of us has unlimited time before death. Like Jesus and his disciples in this story, we have time right now to do God's work, and that time is limited.

One might also think that the name of the pool where the blind man washed the mud off his eyes made no difference, but for John it is important. The definition given in 9:7 (Siloam, "which means sent") may be etymologically dubious,[9] but it points to a major theme of Johannine theology. Jesus is sent from God (more than twenty texts), and as the Father has sent him so he sends us (20:21). This theme is not developed in chapter 9, however. Before preaching on "sent," it would be appropriate to explore 3:16; 4:34; 6:29, 38, 57; 7:28–29; 13:20; 17:8; and especially 20:21, where the idea of God's sending Jesus and his sending us is central.

Most congregations include people at various stations on the way to believing in its full, Johannine sense. The Fourth Gospel holds up the man born blind (chap. 9) and the woman of Samaria (chap. 4) as positive models for coming to believe in Jesus. Tracing the development of the blind beggar's faith from "the man called Jesus" (9:11) to "he is a prophet" (9:17) to "not a sinner . . . but from God" (9:30–33, author's summary) to "Lord, I believe" (9:38) is a fit point of entry into teaching or preaching this major theme of the Fourth Gospel. Once in, hearers and learners could consider what "believing in Jesus" means in practice today.

The exchange between Jesus and the Pharisees (9:40–41) is an important moment in the development of the Johannine understanding of judgment. Jesus did not come to condemn the world (3:17) or to judge the world (12:47), yet he came into this world for judgment (9:39), and those who do not believe in him are condemned already (3:18). The paradox is apparent only. God's judgment in and by Jesus Christ is the judgment of light (see notes on 3:17–21). In Jesus' presence a man who had lived in darkness all his life is given sight and drawn to him, while those who trusted in the lesser lights they lived by are blinded by his light. It is not so much that Jesus judges them; by their response to him they judge themselves—and so do we.

"Blinded by the light" suggests to some today a song by Bruce Springsteen made popular in the 1970s by Manfred Mann. The lyrics of the song are not very helpful for preachers, but the story of Saul, the Pharisee, being blinded by a light from heaven on the road to Damascus (Acts 9:1–9) suggests a sermon that brings these two texts together. Preachers can explore why the Pharisees, during Jesus' lifetime, remained in their blindness, while Saul, confronted by the risen Christ, regained his sight and became Paul, the apostle.

THE METAPHOR OF THE SHEEPFOLD (JOHN 10:1–21)

Mixed metaphors tickle the funny bone: "You have buttered your bread, now lie in it." But sometimes mixed metaphors speak to the heart, as in Psalm 23 and John 10. Psalm 23:1–4 is about God as shepherd, while verses 5–6 are about God as host. John 10:1–4 is about Jesus as gate of the sheepfold and also as shepherd. The theme of the good shepherd binds these texts together and speaks to the human need for someone to care.

Exploring the text

According to John 10:1–21, Jesus does just what the Father does. He is God at work as our shepherd.

The Basic Metaphor: A Sheepfold (10:1–6)

Introduced by the emphatic expression, "Very truly I tell you" (v. 1), this important teaching of Jesus is given in the form of a "figure of speech" (*paroimia*, v. 6). Although John 10:1–21 includes several actions (entering, calling, leading out, going ahead), the text is not a true narrative and cannot be properly called a parable (*parabole*). And although thief, bandit (v. 1), and stranger (v. 5) refer to the Pharisees (9:40; 10:6–7), while gate and shepherd (vv. 2–3) refer to Jesus, with the gatekeeper left to puzzle over, the text is not an allegory, for this text is not a story, and it offers no one equivalent for Jesus. The evangelist's term, "figure of speech," is careful and accurate. This series of word pictures is a riddle (another meaning of *paroimia*)[1] or an extended metaphor with elaboration and response.

The metaphor itself (vv. 1–6) is mixed, for in it Jesus describes himself as the gate or door to the sheepfold and also as the shepherd who enters through the gate. Understanding the metaphor depends on a visual image of a Palestinian sheepfold or sheep pen, an enclosure made of stones or briars where several shepherds could bring their sheep at night to keep them safe from predators. A section of the enclosure was left open to serve as an entryway in which the shepherd could lie to keep sheep from straying out and predators from getting in. The fact that a person might serve as both shepherd and gate or door should not obscure the fact that in the text these are two distinct metaphors. The umbrella image covering both metaphors is that of the sheepfold.

The dominant image is that of the shepherd who enters the enclosure, calls his own sheep by name, and leads them out from among the mingled flocks (v. 3). His own sheep follow him out because they know his voice (v. 4). Two elements in this picture are important. Unlike the cowboy who drives a herd, the shepherd leads a flock. Second, unlike cattle that respond only to physical prodding or visual signals, sheep follow the sound of the shepherd's well-known voice.

The language of thieves and bandits (v. 1) continues the argument of the preceding chapters, but the tone in chapter 10 is much less strident. Jesus' teaching in this passage is pastoral rather than polemic. The fold or pen is a place of safety for a flock. The same claims are made for Jesus here, and the same sharp distinction is drawn between him and his opponents as before, but these points of conflict are mere shadows in the picture of the Father's love and care expressed through Jesus, the good shepherd. So muted is the polemic that the Pharisees whom Jesus had just accused of being blind (9:41) and to whom he now refers as thieves and bandits (10:1) "did not understand what he was saying to them" (10:6).

The Entryway (10:7–10)

To introduce and emphasize the first explanation of the figure of speech, Jesus says again, "Very truly, I tell you" (v. 7a), and adds a claim in the Johannine form of an "I Am" saying: "I am the entryway for the sheep" (v. 7, author's translation). *Thyra* is usually translated "door" (AV, RSV, REB), but in this text many current English translations use "gate" (NRSV, NIV, TEV), since "door" connotes a wall, door frame, and roof, which are not in view here. The problem is that "gate" also connotes posts and a barrier that swings open and shut, as in a barnyard cattle pen–again an image that is not in view here. What is intended is the entryway through which sheep and shepherds go in and out of the enclosure. This understanding is reinforced when Jesus says, "Whoever enters by me [*dia mou*; literally, through me] will be saved, and will come in and out and find pasture" (v. 9). Jesus as the way in and out finds echo when he later describes himself to his intimate flock as the way to the Father (14:6).

In this paragraph the earlier polemic comes to the surface. "All who came before me" (v. 8a) cannot refer to Abraham, Moses, and the great prophets of Israel, for whom Jesus shows the greatest respect throughout the Fourth Gospel. These "thieves and bandits" to whom the sheep did not listen (v. 8b) are, rather, the official interpreters of Moses with whom Jesus has been tangling from chapter 5 onward. They are the self-styled gatekeepers who threatened to put out of the synagogue anyone who confessed Jesus to be the Messiah (9:22) and who had just thrown out the blind beggar whom Jesus healed (9:34). The statement that the sheep did not listen to them makes sense in the case of the man born blind. It would make even more sense to John's first readers who, heedless of the threats of synagogue authorities of their time, decided to follow Jesus. Of all religious authorities who are more interested in their own prestige than in the welfare of God's flock, the text says: "The thief comes only to steal and kill and destroy" (10:10a).

In contrast, Jesus offers himself as the entryway through which the sheep have free access to security on the one hand and sustenance on the other. "I came" from the Father–a prominent Johannine theme–so that God's people "may have life, and have it abundantly" (10:10b). This verse adds a significant dimension to the meaning of eternal life in John. What Jesus promises and gives is a quality of life in intimate communion with God, life that does not end, and life that is rich and overflowing. Good pasture, indeed.

The Good Shepherd (10:11–18)

At the heart of the text the shepherd image is set, like that of the entryway, in an "I Am" saying, but without the emphatic formula. The image draws depth and power from its use in the Old Testament. There the shepherd represents ideal kingship, whether divine or Davidic, in which the sovereign is depicted as the shepherd of Israel (Pss. 23:1–4; 80:1–3; 100:3–5; 2 Sam. 7:8; 24:17; Isa. 40:10–11; Ezek. 34:11–16, 23–24). When this ideal was betrayed, the prophets denounced bad shepherds, expanding the image to include bad priests and false prophets as well as self-indulgent and power-hungry kings (Ezek. 34:1–10, 17–22; Jer. 23:1–6; Zech. 11:4–17). In John 10, Jesus draws upon this rich tradition to portray the contrast between himself and the religious authorities of the time, whom he characterizes as worse than bad shepherds. They are hired hands (vv. 12–13), earlier called thieves, and bandits (vv. 1, 8).

Jesus contrasts what the hired hand does with what the shepherd does when a wolf appears. The hired hand sees danger coming, leaves the sheep, and runs away (v. 12–13), whereupon the wolf snatches the sheep and scatters them. The fluidity of the metaphor allows one to think of the parents of the blind man in the preceding story, who, to save their own good standing in the community, forsook their son during the inquisition of the wolflike authorities (9:18–23), and of the authorities themselves, who have little or no real concern for the man whose welfare they were appointed to protect.

Unlike the hired hand, the good shepherd owns and cares for the sheep (vv. 12–13), knows and is known by his own sheep (v. 14), and above all lays down his life for the sheep (vv. 11, 15, 17, 18). He stays with the sheep and cares for them at whatever cost. That Jesus lays down his life for the sheep is clearly the main idea in this paragraph, emphasized by fourfold repetition and by further explanation in verses 17–18. This is John's way of expressing one of the core affirmations of the Christian message, "Christ died for our sins" (1 Cor. 15:3; Rom. 5:8; 1 Pet. 3:18). While Peter accuses the Sanhedrin of putting Jesus to death (Acts 4:10) and, with Paul and the other apostles, affirms that God raised him from the dead (Acts 2:32; 4:10b), John's Jesus insists that he lays down his life of his own accord, and in his own power takes it up again, adding "I have received this command from my Father" (v. 18).

Two significant elements in Johannine theology emerge here: Jesus' complete mastery of the situation as the drama of his impending death unfolds, and his unique relationship to God. That relationship is described in this text as one of intimate knowledge ("I know my own and my own know me, just as the Father knows me and I know the Father," v. 15), a mutual knowledge in which Jesus' sheep are privileged to share. It is also a relationship of love. In genuine care for the sheep, the good shepherd lays down his life, and for that reason the Father loves the shepherd (vv. 11, 15, 17). It is a relationship of subordination, for it is at the command of the Father that Jesus lays down his life and takes it up again (v. 18). At the same time, it is a relationship of identity, for it is through this gift of the Son's life that God loves the world (3:16).

After more than two centuries of argument Jesus' followers tried to resolve the mystery of his relationship to God in the rational, philosophic language adopted by the ecumenical councils of Nicaea and Constantinople (325, 381 C.E.). The fourth evangelist found Jesus' enigmatic metaphor of the sheepfold to be a provocative, nurturing statement of who Jesus is and what God is like, as well as how they are related to each other and to all of God's sheep.

Another enigmatic element in the metaphor of the sheepfold is the reference to "other sheep that do not belong to this fold," whom the good shepherd must also bring (literally "lead"). These sheep, too, will listen to Jesus' voice and, together with all who follow him, will constitute one flock under the leadership of the one good shepherd (v. 16). In the context of the Gospel narrative about Jesus' earthly ministry, the Samaritans of chapter 4 might exemplify the "other sheep" Jesus had in mind. However, the future tense of two verbs in this verse points toward developments after the death and resurrection of Jesus, and particularly to the inclusion of Gentiles, which was already a significant fact about Jesus' flock by the time the Fourth Gospel was written. The term is open to new understandings with each successive generation of readers.

Divided Response (10:19–21)

The evangelist notes that "the Jews" (v. 19) were divided in their response to Jesus' words about the sheepfold, the entryway, the shepherd, and the hired hands. The term could refer to the Judean crowd that heard this teaching of Jesus. More likely, however, it refers to the same religious authorities represented by the Pharisees in 9:40.[2] The harsh way in which some of them accuse Jesus of having a demon (v. 20) echoes the exchanges of 8:44 and 48 ("You are from your father the devil"; "you are a Samaritan and have a demon"). This reprise of the bitter polemic is softened by the note that others of "the Jews" found nothing demonic in Jesus' words, adding, "Can a demon open the eyes of the blind?" (v. 21). Their reference to the healing of the blind man ties this unit to the preceding chapter and thereby wraps up the Fourth Gospel's exposition of three of Jesus' **"I Am" sayings**: "I am the light of the world" (8:12; 9:5), "I am the door/gate of the sheep" (10:7), and "I am the good shepherd" (10:11, 14).

Preaching and teaching the Word

The dominant images in this text answer some of the deepest longings of the human heart.

The basic metaphor of a sheepfold resonates with our desire to belong. Human individuals may be more or less "gregarious," a term derived from the Latin word for "flock," but all of us need not to be utterly alone. We crave the companionship of others like us, and the care of someone to whom all of us are dear. God's people are likened throughout the Bible to a flock of sheep with God as their shepherd and their appointed leaders as undershepherds.[3] The task of a pastor (the Latin word for "shepherd") is to foster in church members the sense of belonging to each other as well as to God. The image of flock, fold, and shepherd is basic to a proper understanding of our relationship to God and each other. A sermon on John 10:1–6 (part of the Gospel lection for the Fourth Sunday of Easter, year A) is a fine way to nurture this relationship.

Two important elements in our relationship to Christ as shepherd are that when he calls we recognize his voice, and that where he leads we follow. How do we recognize the voice of others? When Jesus calls someone by name, his voice evokes recognition at a deep level (10:3–4). The recognition scene in which the risen Jesus calls Mary Magdalene by her name (20:16) shows how much this meant to the evangelist and suggests that perhaps he too had such an experience. Undershepherds might ask themselves, "Do I spend so much time with the Good Shepherd that my flock can hear in my voice the unconscious echo of his?"[4]

A major function of a sheepfold is to protect the flock from danger (10:1, 5). Pairing the text with Ezekiel 34:1–10 lifts up the real and present danger to leaders in the church at any level–from Sunday school teachers to bishops–of themselves becoming bad shepherds. It is no accident, however, that the OT reading paired with John 10 in the lectionary is Psalm 23, which underscores the principal and positive teaching of the Gospel rather than its dark background.

The latter portion of this lectionary pericope (10:7–10) lifts up the image of Christ as the gate or entryway who enables the sheep to "come in and go out and find pasture" (10:7, 9). "Whoever enters by me will be saved," says Jesus. A sermon on salvation could point to elements in the metaphor of the sheepfold that clarify its meaning: safety in the fold, freedom of movement in company of the shepherd, sustenance in the pasture, and abundant life.

Explanation of the visual image of door or gate as reference to an entryway affords the opportunity to reflect on Jesus as the way in to the fold, the way out to the world, and the way up to God . Such a sermon could be linked profitably with John 14:6, "I am the way," and related to concrete examples of how Jesus does in fact lead his own today to live in God's way.

What is the meaning of abundant living in our consumer culture? What do we Americans tend to thank God for on the fourth Thursday of each November? Is eternal life simply lagniappe–something extra–on top of material blessings? Preoccupation with these things may effectively foreclose our entrance into the kind of life to which Jesus offers access, but there are people who exemplify a different kind of abundant living.

"I am the good shepherd" states succinctly the major image in the Gospel reading for the Fourth Sunday in Easter, year B (John 10:11–18). The hired hand serves as a dark background for the text's glowing affirmations about the good shepherd who lays down his life for the sheep

(10:11, 15, 17–18), who knows his own and whose own know him (10:14), who knows the Father just as the Father knows him (10:15), and who promises to bring together other sheep not of this fold so there will be one flock, one shepherd (10:16). The text is all about relationships: shepherd to sheep, sheep to shepherd, shepherd to God, and sheep to others not now in the fold. What binds all these in one is the love that is displayed in the cross of Jesus Christ, where Jesus of his own accord laid down his life to show us what God is like.

Jesus' fourfold reference to laying down his life for his sheep suggests to all undershepherds–those to whose care others are in any way entrusted–something less ultimate and more daily: expending one's time and energy on behalf of the sheep. Those who do this will never be lonely or bored.

"Other sheep not of this fold" (v. 16) raises the question of who today are the sheep whom Jesus wishes to bring into a fold that now excludes them. Running the risk of posing publicly this provocative, controversial, and important question might be one of the ways a good pastor is called to lay down his life for the sheep, including those not yet "of this fold."

REVIEW OF THE ARGUMENT (10:22–42)

This passage may seem unnecessarily repetitive until one understands its place and function in the Fourth Gospel. Jesus' dialogue with representatives of the religious establishment in Jerusalem at the end of chapter 10 recapitulates and summarizes the hostile confrontation that underlies and sometimes dominates the evangelist's account from chapter 5 to this point. John 10:22–42 is the theological summary of Jesus' argument with those who reject him.

Exploring the text

The pericope includes an introduction or setting (10:22–23) and a conclusion (10:40–42) that takes Jesus again to the place where John had been baptizing and underlines for the last time John's true witness to Jesus (10:40–41). Each of the two paragraphs within these brackets ends in the authorities' attempt to get rid of Jesus (10:31, 39). Verse 31 serves as the conclusion to the first paragraph (10:24–31), which turns upon Jesus' identity as Messiah, and also as the introduction to the second paragraph (10:31–39), which focuses on Jesus' identity as Son of God (10:36). Through the argument in these two paragraphs, the evangelist works to achieve his objective of leading readers to believe that Jesus is the Messiah and Son of God (20:31), even though the religious leaders of the time do not.

Introduction (10:22–23)

Jesus is still in Jerusalem, as he has been since the autumn harvest Festival of Booths (7:2, 10, 14). It is now the time of the winter Festival of the Dedication (*Hanukkah,* in Hebrew) and Jesus is walking in the portico of Solomon, the long, covered walkway (*stoa*) on the east side of the temple, which afforded shelter from the wintry wind. This three-month period in Jerusalem in confrontation with the religious establishment is unparalleled in the Synoptic Gospels, whose only report of a visit to Jerusalem after age twelve is at the springtime Passover festival during which Jesus was crucified. The setting described in 10:22–23 is appropriate for the increasingly icy rejection of Jesus by those who do not/will not/cannot believe in him.

Jesus the Messiah (10:24–30)

In this setting "the Jews" could refer simply to the crowd of Jewish worshipers who were in the temple on this occasion and who are undecided about who Jesus is, or it could refer to the responsible leaders of the Jewish establishment who have consistently rejected Jesus' message and are hostile to him.[1] Their opening question is, literally, "How long will you take away our life?" (10:24). This idiomatic expression can indicate either suspense—as indicated by the translation in the NRSV and most other versions—or it can signify irritation ("How long will you continue to annoy us?"), as in modern Greek and some ancient examples as well.[2] The former translation (suspense) reflects the translators' judgment that "the Jews" in 10:24 are still divided in their opinion about Jesus (as in 10:19). If they have already rejected him (as in 10:31), the question indicates irritation that they do not yet have a plain claim to messiahship from Jesus' lips (10:24b) to justify their intention to do him in.

In this text Jesus does not make the messianic claim that his questioners want, but he does claim a special relationship to God (Father-Son, 10:30) and a special relationship to those who believe in him (shepherd-sheep, 10:27–29). The text underscores several ideas presented in the metaphor of the shepherd and the sheep in the first half of this chapter. Jesus' sheep hear his voice and know him; he knows them and calls them by name; they follow him (10:27//10:3–4). "You do not believe, because you do not belong to my sheep" (10:26) reiterates and emphasizes the idea of election, which the reader has encountered earlier (6:44, 6:65, and 8:43–44).[3] The present paragraph (10:24–31) does not speak of human freedom at all, but it speaks eloquently of the positive as well as the negative side of election. That Jesus gives eternal life to his sheep (believers) has been a theme throughout the Fourth Gospel. An important new dimension is added here: the assurance that "no one will snatch them out of my hand" (10:28) or "out of the Father's hand" (10:29). God's election of the sheep is good news.

The NRSV translation of verse 29 calls attention to a textual problem by placing "*What* my Father has given me is greater than all else" in the text and relegating "My Father, who has given them to me, is greater than all" to a footnote. The difference in these translations reflects "a nest of variant readings in the earliest Greek manuscripts."[4] Although the more difficult form of the text adopted by the NRSV and TEV is more likely to be original, other translations (AV, RSV, NIV) agree with D. Moody Smith's judgment that "One can scarcely imagine that the sheep are 'greater than all'! . . . the evangelist must have meant–if he did not clearly write–that the Father is greater than all."[5]

The affirmation, "The Father and I are one" (10:30), gathers up the cumulative evidence about Jesus' relationship to God that has been building throughout his confrontations with his adversaries in chapters 5–10. He does only what the Father does and accomplishes the work (including judgment) that the Father has sent him to do (5:19–30); he is the true bread from heaven, the bread of life that the Father gives (6:27–58); he knows God, because he comes from God who sent him (7:29). He is from above, the "I am" in whom we must believe or die in our sins, who speaks as he was instructed by the Father, and who always does what is pleasing to God (8:23–30); he is the Son who makes slaves free, who declares what he has heard in the Father's presence, the "I am" who was before Abraham (8:34–58); he is from God (9:33); he knows the Father just as the Father knows him, and he lays down his life for the sheep and takes it up again just as the Father has commanded him (10:11–18).

In the context of this sequence of affirmations, Jesus' statement that "The Father and I are one" (10:30) means that the Father and the Son are one in what they do. Those to whom Jesus addressed the claim, however, understood that more was at stake than obedient subordination and a family resemblance. Jesus here claims a union with God that is unique. There is no functional distinction between him and God. Those who heard the claim clearly did not believe it, for they picked up stones to kill him (10:31; see also 8:59). According to Jesus' teaching in this text, they *could* not believe it (10:26).

Jesus the Son of God (10:31–39)

The move to stone Jesus (10:31) concludes the first paragraph of the dialogue and introduces the second. Jesus again calls attention to the good things he has done ("works"), which should have alerted observers to his special relationship to God, and asks for which of these they intend to stone him. They ignore the evidence to which Jesus points and focus solely on his claim to be one with the Father. Earlier, when Jesus defended his healing a paralytic on the Sabbath on the ground that "my Father is still working," they interpreted it as "making himself equal with God" because he called God his own Father (5:17–18). Now when he says, "The Father and I are one," their accusation is heightened: "You, though only a human being, are making yourself God," and they call this "blasphemy" (10:33, 36).

The accusation of blasphemy appears on two occasions in the Synoptic Gospels (Mark 2:7//Matt. 9:3//Luke 5:21 and Mark 14:64//Matt. 26:65), but only here in the Gospel of John. The Greek word *blasphemia* basically means "evil speech" and is translated "slander" when it is directed against humans (as in the vice lists of Matt. 15:19, Mark 7:22, Eph. 4:31, and Col. 3:8). With reference to God, it is translated "blasphemy" and means to speak ill of God or in any way to violate God's majesty. For a mere human to claim to be God would be to demean God's sovereign power and to affirm faith in more than one god; hence the charge of blasphemy by Jesus' adversaries in the present text.

The charge is as serious as it is understandable. Jesus answers it by quoting Psalm 82:6, "I said, you are gods," and using it in a way that makes sense only if the speaker is God and the "you" refers to "those to whom the word of God came" (10:35). In the psalm those addressed are the lesser gods, gods of the nations, assembled in the divine council. This vestige of primitive Israelite henotheism was unacceptable to later Judaism, which interpreted "you" in the way presupposed by Jesus in this rabbinic argument.[6] On the basis of their own interpretation of the Scriptures, which Jesus and his interlocutors all accept as authoritative, Jesus insists that he has said nothing offensive to God–the more so since he had not said he was God, but God's Son (10:36). He then reverts to the claim of functional equivalence (he does what God does, 10:37), and despite his earlier assertion that they do not belong to his sheep (10:26), he once more appeals to these guardians of the Torah to believe on the basis of his works (10:38). The key phrase here, parallel to "the Father and I are one" at the end of the first paragraph (10:30), is "the Father is in me and I am in the Father." The union of which Jesus speaks here is later opened to all believers (15:4, 10; 17:21).

Ignoring Jesus' appeal to believe and confirming their response of rejection, "they tried to arrest him again, but he escaped from their hands" (10:39; see also 7:30, 32, 44, 45).

Conclusion (10:40–42)

The closing geographical note (10:41) harks back to the role of John the baptizer as the first witness at the beginning of Jesus' public ministry, which is now drawing to a close. The crowds who had come to John then now come to Jesus and remember what John had said about this man. Their remark about signs (10:41) points back to those that Jesus has performed thus far (chaps. 2–9) and ahead to the climactic sign about to be reported in chapter 11. The positive response of many (10:42) balances the negative responses of other Jewish hearers and their leaders (10:31, 39). The paragraph as a whole serves as an important bracket in the unfolding story of Jesus and as a theological summary for what is often called "the book of signs" (the first half of the Fourth Gospel).

Preaching and teaching the Word

John 10:27–30, an important part of the lectionary reading for the Fourth Sunday in Easter, year C, is God's word of assurance to believers: Sheep may safely graze.[7] Salvation is here defined as eternal life (10:28), and its promise is secure, not just because we believe it, but because we belong to the Good Shepherd. This term refers to Jesus and also to God because, with regard to the shepherd's holding the sheep in his hands, Jesus says, "The Father and I are one."

The intensity and vitality of an individual's faith may fluctuate, so that Christians may sometimes doubt their good standing with God. The Westminster Confession of Faith deals with this issue in a chapter entitled "Of the Assurance of Grace and Salvation,"[8] as does the Larger Catechism in questions 80 and 81.[9] The language of the confessions addresses the mind. The promise that nothing can snatch us out of the shepherd's hand appeals to the heart. Both are appropriate for teaching as well as preaching.

Like many other passages in John, this text (10:22–42) depicts people who do not believe in Jesus (10:24–39) as well as those who do (10:40–42). In every age most people in the world do not believe in Jesus. Is it because they will not, or is it because they cannot? "You do not believe, because you do not belong to my sheep," says Jesus to those who rejected him (10:26). This seems to suggest that they cannot believe because they are not among the chosen, which raises questions about election and free choice that are also found in other passages in the Gospel of John.[10] This theological problem, often debated in college bull sessions and by learned theologians, could be treated through lecture and discussion in a teaching session.

On the other hand, the text lends itself to an evangelistic sermon based on Jesus' appeal to those who do not believe in him to "believe the works, so that you may know and understand that the Father is in me and I am in the Father" (10:38). Even those who have initially rejected Jesus can believe and follow him if they will. Jesus' sheep are those who hear his voice and follow him (10:27). Like those who followed Jesus across the Jordan (10:40–42), anyone can pay attention to the works he is doing and come to believe in him. It is better to follow Jesus and then believe than to believe but not follow him. It is the following that shows who the sheep are, not just a profession of faith.

Another approach to the text is to focus on the identity of Jesus. Leading readers to believe that Jesus is Messiah and Son of God is the stated purpose of the Fourth Gospel (20:31), and the identity of Jesus is its central concern. Conventional wisdom often contrasts the Fourth Gospel, in which Jesus speaks early and often about his identity and demands that people believe in him, with the Synoptic Gospels, in which Jesus is virtually silent about himself and speaks only of the kingdom of God. This perception is accurate but overstated. In John 10:22–42, as in John 5:18, Jesus' opponents accuse him of claiming deity for himself ("making himself equal to God," 5:18; "making yourself God," 10:33). In both texts, Jesus replies by saying, in effect, "Not really." To be sure, he affirms that he does what the Father does (5:19–20, 30), gives life as the Father gives life (5:21, 24–26), and judges as the Father judges (5:22, 27–30), so that our response to him is in fact our response to God (5:23). And in the present text he affirms that "the Father and I are one" (10:30) and that "the Father is in me and I am in the Father" (10:38). Yet neither here nor anywhere else in John does Jesus say plainly and directly "I am the Messiah" or "I am God." At significant moments his affirmations about himself are in response to someone else's statement (the Samaritan woman, "I know that Messiah is coming," 4:25–26) or question (Pilate: "So you are a king?" Jesus: "You say that I am a king," 18:37). The highest affirmation about him is from the lips of a disciple (Thomas: "My Lord and my God!" 20:28). In John as in Mark, Jesus' reticence about using traditional titles to describe himself is intended to lead those he met then and those he meets now to come to realize who he is by observing what he does and to respond in faith.

In a teaching session, the narrative approach of the Gospels to the question of Jesus' identity could be compared with the philosophical approach of the fourth-century theologians who hammered out the creeds of Nicaea and Constantinople. A study group could discuss the difference between the way Christology is treated in the Fourth Gospel and in the later creeds, as well as the basic continuity between the two. Now as always, some

Christians stress creedal statements as the best way to tell others about Jesus, and some prefer to invite others to believe Jesus' works, love and obey him, and thereby come to know who he is. Exploration of these different modes of expressing faith in Jesus might lead to a clearer understanding of the gospel and the creeds as well. Such a study, guided by the Holy Spirit, could also result in a deeper commitment to the one to whom they all bear witness.

THE RAISING OF LAZARUS (11:1–44)

At the midpoint of the Fourth Gospel the evangelist takes up a major theme of the prologue, life (1:3–4), and offers a preview of the climax of the Gospel, the resurrection of Jesus Christ (chap. 20). The story of the raising of Lazarus is the final sign performed by Jesus in his public ministry (chaps. 1–12), foreshadowing the supreme revelation of God's glory in raising the Son of God from the dead. While chapter 10 summarizes the growing rejection of Jesus by the religious authorities but closes with a brief notice about the positive response of many (10:42), chapter 11 tells of Jesus' life-giving power and the response of faith (11:27, 45) but closes with the authorities' determination to kill him (11:45–57). This chapter also presents the last of Jesus' significant encounters, this time with a family group: two sisters–Mary and Martha–and their brother, Lazarus.

Exploring the text

After a brief setting, the story unfolds in four closely interwoven scenes.

Setting: Bethany Near Jerusalem (11:1–3)

The setting introduces Lazarus, the name given also to the poor beggar lying at a rich man's door in one of Jesus' parables, to whom father Abraham says, "If they do not listen to Moses and the prophets, neither will they be convinced even if someone rises from the dead" (Luke 16:31). Although there is no evidence of any literary or historical link between the parable in Luke and the narrative in John, Abraham's prophecy in Luke is applicable to the reaction of the chief priests and Pharisees when Lazarus is raised from the dead in John (11:47, 53).

In the sisters' message to Jesus, Lazarus is further introduced as "he whom you love *(philein)*" (11:3). This description of Lazarus has led to the suggestion that he was "the disciple whom Jesus loved *(agapan)*" (13:23; 19:26; 21:7, 20). This identification is not likely, however, either on internal literary grounds or on the external basis of early church tradition that identified the beloved disciple as John the apostle and son of Zebedee.[1]

Bethany (11:1) is a village situated about three kilometers (less than two miles) from Jerusalem–fifteen stadia as the Romans measured distance (11:18). The two sisters are introduced, and Mary is identified as "the one who anointed the Lord with perfume and wiped his feet with her hair" (11:2), a story which will not be told until the following chapter (12:1–8). This is an example of the Fourth Gospel's frequent allusion to previous or coming events in order to help the reader keep in mind the flow of the plot and to read each part of the Gospel in light of the whole.[2]

Scene 1. Jesus and His Disciples (11:4–16)

The scene opens on the east side of the Jordan River, where John had earlier been baptizing (10:40), another Bethany as reported in John 1:28. Its exact location is unknown, but it must have been far enough away for the journeys reported in the text to add up to the four days Lazarus was in the tomb (11:17, 39).

Jesus' affirmation that "this illness does not lead to death" (11:4) merits careful reflection, since Lazarus did die before Jesus came to him, and his raising Lazarus did lead to Jesus' death (11:53). But at a deeper level, Lazarus's illness led beyond death to life when Jesus called him out of the tomb, and Jesus' death and resurrection still lead not to death but to eternal life for all who see in them the glory of God and believe what God has done.

"The **glory** of God" (11:4, 40) is the clue to the interpretation of the entire story. The raising of Lazarus is not only a glorious sign pointing to the resurrection of Jesus; it is a manifestation of the splendor and majesty of God, in whom is life and light.[3]

In the evangelist's note, "Jesus loved Martha and her sister and Lazarus" (11:6), Martha is given the prominent place that she occupies throughout this narrative.

Jesus' word about twelve hours of daylight with the commonsense observation that people stumble if they walk in the dark (11:9–10) is suggestive. In context, it means that Jesus must use to the full the short time that still remains to him on earth and he must go now to "awaken" Lazarus, even at the risk of his own life. On reflection, disciples then and now realize that we too have only a short time on earth, which we must use to the full.

After a brief exchange between Jesus and his disciples about Lazarus's falling asleep (11:11–12), the evangelist adds the comment that Jesus was talking about Lazarus's death, but the disciples took the word "sleep" literally and therefore misunderstood him (v. 13). They cannot yet understand that this trip to Judea to give life to Lazarus at the risk of death is necessary if Jesus is to bring life to everyone. Once more the evangelist uses the misunderstanding of characters in the story to clarify the understanding of the reader.

The scene ends with a word from "Thomas, who was called the Twin *(Didymos)*" (11:16). Thomas *(Te'oma)* is the Aramaic word for "twin," and Didymus (retained here in AV and NIV) is the Greek word for twin, so in both languages Thomas was called Twin. According to later tradition among gnostic Christians, he was the twin brother of Jesus.

In scene one, Jesus is presented as having divine omniscience and power: he knows what is going to happen, and he decides when it will occur. The response of the disciples is fearful prudence, and that of Thomas is resigned loyalty.

Scene 2. Jesus and Martha (11:17–27)

The detail about many Jews coming to console Martha and Mary after their brother's death, in conjunction with the note about how near Bethany was to Jerusalem (11:18–19), indicates that Judean mourning customs of that time included coming to sit with the family after a funeral (as in many cultures today). These are not hostile religious authorities but members of one or more synagogues in Jerusalem who were showing solidarity with their friends and fellow believers at a time of grief.[4]

After Lazarus's death Martha becomes the head of household who takes the initiative to go meet Jesus as he is approaching Bethany (11:20). The dialogue on the road is poignant. There is a note of reproach in Martha's "if only" comment to Jesus (11:21) and an indication of a wistful faith in Jesus' power to bring Lazarus back to life even now (11:22). One can imagine what might have been the tone of voice when each speaks. Jesus assures Martha that her brother will rise again (11:23), but Martha takes this to be a routine word of comfort based on the common hope of many Jews at that time. "I know that he will rise again in the resurrection on the last day," she says, but this does not really deal with her emotional pain and grief at the present moment. Jesus then speaks to her heart by adding, perhaps in the authoritative tone that once made even the police sent to arrest Jesus turn back in awe (7:45–46):

> "I am the resurrection and the life.
> Those who believe in me, even though they die, will live,
>   and everyone who lives and believes in me will never die.
>   Do you believe this?"
>
> (11:25–26)

These words embody a central proclamation of the Fourth Gospel: resurrection is not something that happens only after death, nor is eternal life. Both are present in Jesus Christ, and available now to whoever believes in Jesus. So the hope Jesus offers is not just life after death; it is spiritual resurrection now, bodily resurrection after death, and eternal life, beginning the moment one believes.

Martha's reply, "Yes, Lord, I believe that you are the Messiah, the Son of God; the one coming into the world" (11:27), echoes a basic affirmation of the prologue (1:9) and expresses the seeing/knowing/believing in Jesus that is the goal of this Gospel, expressed in almost identical words at its end (20:31). Martha of Bethany is the first disciple to make that full confession of faith.

Scene two is about Jesus and Martha, who takes precedence over Mary here. Jesus is presented as the resurrection and the life, and Martha as his down-to-earth, commonsense disciple who responds to Jesus by believing that Jesus is the Christ, the Son of God, and the one in whom God breaks into the world and into our lives.

The key word in this scene is "believe": "Those who believe in me . . . everyone who lives and believes in me . . . Do you believe this? . . . Yes, Lord, I believe." The scene is about seeing God's glory in Jesus, the resurrection and the life, and about Martha, who comes to Jesus and believes.

Scene 3. Jesus, Mary, and the Jewish Friends (11:28–37)

Although these verses narrate what happened at two different places–the place where Martha had met Jesus just outside the village (11:30, 32–37) and the house in Bethany where Mary was sitting with friends of the family (11:28–29, 31)–they present essentially one scene: Mary's encounter with Jesus on the occasion of her brother's death. Verses 28–31 prepare the way for this encounter.

Mary's initial comment is identical to that of Martha: "Lord, if you had been here . . ." (11:32). Jesus' response, however, is different this time. When Jesus saw Mary and her friends weeping, he was gripped by powerful emotion (11:33), variously translated as "greatly disturbed in spirit," "deeply moved," "troubled," "he groaned in the spirit," and "his heart was touched." These English versions reflect the understanding of the family's Jewish friends (11:36): Jesus' feelings sprang from his love of Lazarus, grief at his death, and sympathy for his loved ones' grief.

Another reading is possible, however. The Greek verbs used in verse 33 are *embrimaomai*, whose root meaning is "to snort," connoting anger and indignation, and *tarasso,* which means "agitated" or "troubled." The NEB is very close to the sense of the Greek when it translates this expression, "He was moved with indignation and deeply distressed." Many patristic writers, Martin Luther in his German Bible, and many current scholars agree with this interpretation. The tears in verse 35 can be interpreted in more than one way—just as *anothen* and water can be in the Nicodemus passage, for instance (3:3, 5). Here, as in other cases in the Fourth Gospel, onlookers may see only one of the possible meanings and miss the deeper one.

But why is Jesus indignant? Some interpreters think Jesus is angry because of the lack of faith of all those present: friends, family, and comforters alike. Perhaps a better explanation in the context of Jesus' own time and culture is that he is indignant at the suffering caused by Satan, sin, sickness, and death. He has come to display the glory of God by overcoming death, but at this moment death seems to have the upper hand, and Jesus is flooded with the emotion a strong person feels in the presence of a mortal enemy.

The friends of the family are not wrong when they say, "See how he loved him," but Jesus' love here moves not only at the level of individual sympathy. It is Jesus' love for the entire human family that moves him to raise Lazarus, even at the cost of his own death, knowing that his death will open the door to life for everyone.

Scene three, though initially about Jesus and Mary, is mostly about Jesus' powerful feelings of human sympathy and divine indignation. Its closing note is about the Jewish friends, some of whom were sympathetic (11:36), others of whom were hostile (11:37).

Scene 4. Jesus and Lazarus at the Tomb (11:38–44)

The fourth scene is introduced by another reference to Jesus' deep emotion ("greatly disturbed," *embrimomenos,* 11:38) as he comes to the cave in which Lazarus is buried. It is impossible to know whether this was one of the shallow caves that pockmark the Judean countryside, with Lazarus's body laid in the bottom and the stone laid horizontally across the top, or if it was a larger cave, natural or hewn into the hillside, with a stone on its edge leaning against the opening. In either case, the stone is there to keep animals out and the stench in.

The exchange between Martha and Jesus about the stench reveals that Lazarus has been dead four days (11:39) and underscores that only an act of God can bring him back to life (11:40). In words to Martha, then to God, and, through this prayer, to the witnesses standing by, Jesus interprets what is about to happen. Those who, like Martha, believe (11:40) see the glory of God, who gives life to the dead (5:21). In speaking to God as Father and doing what the Father does, Jesus reveals that he is the Son of God (11:41) and so is glorified (11:4). Through seeing the sign, those who are present are invited to believe that God sent Jesus (11:42).

Having prepared the way for understanding, Jesus cries out with a loud voice, "Lazarus, come out!" (11:43). Isaiah 42:2 says of the Lord's Servant, "He will not cry or lift up his voice." Only twice do the Gospels report that Jesus cries out, using this particular Greek word: once when, from the cross, Jesus cries out in anguish, "My God, my God, why have you forsaken me?" (Mark 15:34), and here, when Jesus, confronted by death, cries out in majestic power and the dead man comes out (John 11:44). Unlike Jesus, who at his resurrection leaves his graveclothes in the tomb, since he rises never to die again, Lazarus emerges with the traditional graveclothes still on his body. His hands and feet are bound with strips of cloth, and his face wrapped in a cloth. He will again experience physical death, though spiritually he will never die.

Jesus says to the bystanders, "Unbind him, and let him go" (11:44). With these words Jesus commands bystanders to become participants with him in loosing the bonds of death. Lazarus says not a word. He simply walks free, a living sign of Christian hope in the face of death.

Scene four is about Jesus and Lazarus, with the accent upon Jesus, whose word of command is a word of life.

Preaching and teaching the Word

John 11:1–45 is the Gospel lesson appointed for the Fifth Sunday in Lent, year A, in the Revised Common Lectionary. Although on literary grounds the narrative ends with verse 44, verse 45 provides a positive ending for the account of the raising of Lazarus.

1. Tell the story. The story is so tightly narrated that lifting out just one piece would be difficult, and so well told that it scarcely needs elucidation. Its impact lies in the cumulative effect of the whole. Instead of reading the entire text and then preaching on part of it, the preacher could absorb the story by reading it repeatedly and imaginatively over a period of time and then tell what happened, perhaps using verses 25–26 verbatim as a conclusion. Jesus' word to those who stood by at the tomb (11:44) can be his command to the preacher: just turn the story loose and let it go.

2. Resurrection now. "I am the resurrection and the life," said Jesus to Martha. "Those who believe in me, even though they die, will live, and everyone who lives and believes in me will never die" (11:25–26). These words evoke powerful memories in the hearts of believers who have heard them as they said good-bye to persons dearly loved. Like all the words of Jesus, they evoke faith and hope in some, doubt and disbelief in others. Jesus' question is highly pertinent: "Do you believe this?" The question has to do not with a general belief in life after death, but with trust that Jesus means what he says. When he says, "Those who believe in me, even though they die, will live," he speaks of physical death and what lies beyond it. But when he says, "Everyone who lives and believes in me will never die," he speaks of the eternal life that begins now and that physical death cannot bring to an end. A Johannine scholar wrote, "The future resurrection of Martha's initial belief becomes irrelevant in the face of the present resurrection that faith grasps."[5] One could do worse than to quote these words of Bultmann in bearing witness to the resurrection at a funeral, or in preaching this text at any time.

3. *Seeing the glory of God.* Another approach to the text would be to focus on the glory of God. To approach the story from this point of view is particularly appropriate when the Gospel pericope is John 11:32–44 (All Saints Day, year B). In this passage "Did I not tell you that if you believed, you would see the glory of God?" (11:40) echoes "[This illness] is for God's glory, so that the Son of God may be glorified through it" (11:4). What most people see most clearly in the face of death is evidence of our mortality and an occasion to mourn our loss. Jesus knew these human emotions (11:33–36), but in the face of the impending death of his beloved friend Lazarus he saw even more clearly an occasion to reveal the glory of one who is stronger than death (11:4). This glory is shared by the Father and the Son, for "just as the Father raises the dead and gives them life, so also the Son gives life to whomever he wishes" (5:21). In the authoritative word of command to Lazarus in the tomb, bystanders hear the echo of God's voice that called light out of darkness (Gen. 1:3; John 1:5), and when the dead man comes out despite the fetters of his mortality, they see the glory of the life which is the light of humankind (John 1:4). But only eyes of faith can see the glory. For such eyes, "Earth's crammed with heaven, and every common bush aflame with God."[6]

4. *The gift of time.* A sermon on the importance of living each day to the full might focus on "Are there not twelve hours of daylight?" and the proverbial wisdom sayings that follow (11:9–10). Light can be thrown on these puzzling verses by juxtaposing them with Jesus' words in 9:4, "We must work the works of him who sent me while it is day; night is coming when no one can work." In 9:4–5, the shift of the first person pronoun from plural ("we") to singular ("I") suggests that Jesus and the evangelist have in mind a principle that applies equally to Jesus in his earthly ministry and to his disciples in their earthly pilgrimage. The same principle governs 11:9–10 and 12:35–36: the time available to do the works of God

is limited. All three texts imply that time is given us in order to see clearly, walk surely, and accomplish God's work in the world by the light of Jesus' presence. Daylight saving time!

5. *The cries of Jesus.* Only at the grave of Lazarus (John 11:43) and from the cross (Mark 15:34) is Jesus reported to have cried out with a loud voice. In each case, the cry echoes a central note of the Gospel according to that evangelist. For Mark, the goal of Jesus' earthly ministry was his death on the cross in obedience to the will of God with vindication by his resurrection, and the mark of discipleship is taking up one's own cross to follow Jesus (Mark 8:31, 34; 9:31; 10:33–34). For John, the goal of Jesus' earthly ministry was to reveal the life that was with God in the beginning and to make eternal life available to all who believe that Jesus is the resurrection and the life. For John as well as Mark, the price of that gift was the life of God's only Son (John 3:16), but John subsumes Christ's death under the theme of resurrection and life. The cross is but a moment in God's act of lifting Jesus up in glory. Cross and resurrection are both essential to the message in both Gospels, and both perceptions of the central thrust of Jesus' earthly ministry are necessary for a full understanding of who Jesus is and of who we are to become.

6. *Browning's "Epistle . . . of Karshish."* A rich resource for teaching John's story of the raising of Lazarus is a reflection on it by Robert Browning, who in 1855 wrote a dramatic poem called "An Epistle Containing the Strange Medical Experience of Karshish, the Arab Physician."[7] Karshish, an apprentice gaining field experience, reports to Abib, a practiced physician, about a case he has encountered while traveling through the Roman province of Judea in 69 C.E. The case is a man named Lazarus, whose firm conviction is that he was dead and buried, but restored to life "by a Nazarene physician of his tribe." Out of the poet's imagination, Karshish describes how Lazarus takes up the "after-life," indulging every thoughtful reader's curiosity about what happened to Lazarus after he was raised. Browning attends not to events, but rather to changed attitudes that characterized Lazarus's new life.

Karshish is about to close his letter when he remembers one detail about the case that he has hesitated to mention, out of respect for a good man's name. Deciding he should hold nothing back from his mentor, he adds, "This man so cured regards the curer, then, as–God forgive me! Who but God himself, creator and sustainer of the world, that came and dwelt in flesh on it awhile!" But "after all, our patient Lazarus is stark mad," he says, and passes on from this "trivial matter" to remark on an herb he has found growing on the edge of a pool. He bids Abib farewell, but then, in a postscript, he writes:

The very God! Think, Abib; dost thou think?
So, the All-Great were the All-Loving too—
So, through the thunder comes a human voice
Saying, "O heart I made, a heart beats here!
Face, my hands fashioned, see it in myself!
Thou hast no power nor mayst conceive of mine,
But love I gave thee, with myself to love,
And thou must love me who have died for thee!"
The madman saith He said so: it is strange.

At the end of Browning's poem, the risen Lazarus points Karshish to the one who raised him—just as John wished his Lazarus to do for readers of the Fourth Gospel.

THE DECISION TO KILL JESUS (11:45–57)

The last thirteen verses in chapter 11 report several responses to the raising of Lazarus. They also move the narrative forward by means of changes in place and time.

Exploring the text

Two transitional verses (11:45–46) report the divided response to Jesus on the part of those who had witnessed the miracle concerning Lazarus. The scene then shifts to Jerusalem and the response of the religious authorities (11:47–53); next to a town called Ephraim, to which Jesus withdraws in response to their decision to put him to death (11:54); then back to Jerusalem at the time of Passover to note the attitude of the crowd and of the authorities (11:55–57).

Mixed Response (11:45–46)

"The Jews" in verse 45 are the Judean friends who had come to console the family after Lazarus's death (11:31, 33). They were all of the Jewish faith and probably belonged to one or more small communities of believers (synagogues) in Jerusalem. As a result of Jesus' ultimate demonstration of God's power at work in him, some believed in him (11:45), a comment that brings to a close the scenes in Bethany. "Believe" is not defined here, but the context suggests that they shared Martha's faith in Jesus as the Messiah, the Son of God (11:27).

Others of these same friends and eyewitnesses, however, went to tell the Pharisees what Jesus had done (11:46). Perhaps they only wanted to know what the authorities thought of Jesus, but more likely they viewed him as an imposter and a threat to the faith and order of the community. Their response shifts the action to Jerusalem and introduces the following scene.

The Response of the Religious Authorities (11:47–53)

An important new element is introduced here into the conflict between Jesus and the religious authorities in Jerusalem. "The Pharisees called a meeting of the council (*synedrion,* or Sanhedrin)" (11:47). This judicial body, composed of representatives of the local aristocracy (predominantly priestly and Sadducean), leading interpreters of Mosaic law (predominantly Pharisaic), and the high priest as presiding official, was the final authority in Jewish civil and religious matters, autonomous within the limits imposed by the Roman occupation. The claims made by Jesus and the large following he is attracting now become a matter for formal deliberation by this council, bringing to a head the conflict that has been building since chapter 5.

The convener of this meeting is Caiaphas, whom the text identifies as "high priest that year" (11:49, 51). This qualifying phrase reflects the stormy relationship between the high priest and the Roman procurator at this period of Jewish history. In principle, the high priest was appointed for life, but Annas, who was appointed in 6 C.E. by the Roman governor, Quirinius, was deposed in 15 C.E. by Valerius Gratus. A series of appointees followed him, whose terms of office depended on Roman favor. Annas's son-in-law, Joseph Caiaphas, was high priest from 18 to 36 C.E., a period that included the fateful year in which Jesus died.[1] Annas, however, was apparently still viewed by some as the legitimate claimant to that high office (18:13).

The council perceives in the popularity of Jesus a threat to the temple ("our holy place") and to the degree of national autonomy they then enjoyed ("our nation"), not to mention the threat to their own position in that system (11:48). The text does not state why a budding messianic movement would incite the Romans to destroy Jewish institutions, but the charge brought against Jesus at his trial appealed to Roman fear of sedition (19:12), and the Roman destruction of Jerusalem in 70 C.E. indicates that the Sanhedrin's fear of Roman intervention was not just a pipe dream.

The climax of this scene belongs to Caiaphas, who is presented as an arrogant man with little respect for the court over which he presided (11:49). His own prudent judgment is that "it is better for you [plural: you of the ruling class] to have one man die for the people (*laos,* the Jewish people apart from their leaders) than to have the whole nation (*ethnos,* Jewish religio-political entity including leaders and people) destroyed" (11:50). On the chief priest's lips, "people" and "nation" both refer to the Jews as the people of God.

In the editorial note that follows (11:51a) the evangelist reveals his respect for the office of high priest despite his low estimate of Caiaphas, for God spoke through him to prophesy (in this case, predict) why Jesus was about to die and with what effect. This aside is intended to guide the reader's interpretation of the events narrated in chapters 18–21. The evangelist takes up the chief priest's use of "nation" and shows how the death of Jesus expands his restrictive understanding of the people of God: "Jesus was about to die for the [Jewish] nation, and not for the [Jewish] nation only, but to gather into one the dispersed children of God" (11:51b–52). God's word through the evangelist here has the same theological force as the revelatory word of Simeon, whose aged eyes saw in the infant Jesus "a light for revelation to the Gentiles (*ethne,* "nations," plural) and for glory to your people (*laos,* singular) Israel" (Luke 2:32). Both point to a gathered community of faith that includes Gentiles as well as Jews.

The concluding verse in this paragraph marks an important turning point in the plot of the Fourth Gospel: "So from that day on they planned to put him to death" (John 11:53). It is not yet time for the plan to be put into action, but from this point on, the death of Jesus is a done deal.

Withdrawal to Ephraim (11:54)

The text refers to Ephraim as "a town . . . in the region near the wilderness." Scholars do not agree on its exact location, but most place it a dozen or so miles northeast of Jerusalem on the edge of the Judean hill country overlooking the Jordan valley. Earlier, Jesus and his disciples waited east of the Jordan until he judged it to be time to return to Bethany near Jerusalem despite the danger (11:7–10). Now he withdraws from the heightened danger in Jerusalem to an obscure town on the West Bank a short distance northeast of Jerusalem (11:54), not out of fear, but to await with his disciples the time he will choose for his betrayal and death.[2]

Transition (11:55–57)

The final paragraph in chapter 11 signals the passage of time as well as a return to the place where Jesus' death has been decided and where that decision will be carried out. Passover time approaches, for the third and last time in Jesus' public ministry (2:13; 6:4; 11:55). Crowds go up from the country to Jerusalem "to purify themselves "(11:55), that is, to perform all rites that might be necessary to assure that they are ritually clean and qualified to keep the feast.[3] The crowds speculate about whether or not Jesus will come to the festival. Many think he will not (11:56), for they know that the religious authorities have ordered that anyone who knows where Jesus is should inform them so they can arrest him (11:57). The suspense is almost tangible as the plot moves to its climax.

Preaching and teaching the Word

Although not included in the lectionary, John 11:49–52 (Caiaphas's opinion on what to do about Jesus and the editorial note inserted by the evangelist) commends itself for proclamation because it reveals John's understanding of the meaning of Jesus' death. Key points include the idea of one dying for many (11:50), of God speaking through Caiaphas ("he prophesied," 11:51), of Jesus' dying for God's chosen people, Israel (11:52a), and of that death being the means by which the dispersed children of God will be gathered into one (11:52b). The note about prophecy indicates that God's providential hand is in this death. The sermon could explore the meaning of "for," being careful not to push it to include a particular theory of the atonement. To die for the people and for the nation surely means "on behalf of " or "for the benefit of " those who otherwise would be destroyed. The high priest is not thinking of the idea of substitution. He simply wants to avoid the destruction of the people and nation and the loss of his job. Nor does the evangelist's editorial comment articulate any theory of atonement. John clearly believed that Jesus' death is the gift of God and evidence of God's love for the world (3:16), but he does not raise the question of how the death of one deals with the sins of many. What interests the evangelist is the intended result of Jesus' death: "to gather into one the dispersed children of God" (11:52b). This text addresses the question "Why did Jesus die?" not in the sense of "Why was it necessary?" but in the sense of "To what end?" God's purpose as stated here is to create a beloved community whose members love God, Jesus, one another, and the world that God loves. "The dispersed children of God" refers to all those whom the Father will draw close through the Son (6:44; 10:16), including Gentiles (12:20–23). The sermon could suggest how we today can live out in our communities of faith the intention of God expressed in the death of Jesus, drawing into our circle of love all whom God loves.

Important elements in this passage can be explored better through teaching than through preaching. Verses 45 and 46 show clearly the mixed reaction to Jesus that characterizes the entire first half of this Gospel, through chapter 12. Jewish friends of the family are divided in their response. Some believe in him (11:45); others report him to the authorities (11:46). Teachers can lead students to reflect on their own response to Jesus.

One can also reflect upon the interpersonal dynamics among characters in the story: the friends who did believe in Jesus, the friends who did not, the rigorous Pharisees and the acculturated Sadducees who were members of the council, the disdainful high priest who chaired it, the Roman occupying force whose off-stage presence permeates the deliberations, and Jesus who waits offstage. Beneath the black-and-white dualism of John's theology, his story reveals the interplay of many shades of light and darkness.

The evangelist uses changes in time and place and their implications for the plot to build suspense into a narrative whose ending is known in advance. In this way the reader's interest is held through the many events, discourses, and theological reflections that intervene between the crucial decision made at 11:53 and the narrative's denouement ten chapters later. Like the "Synoptic Apocalypse" of the first three Gospels,[4] John's plot is shot through with the delay of the expected ending. The suspense-laden section at the end of chapter 11 (vv. 54–57) is, in fact, followed by another scene in Bethany (12:1–11) that completes the Bethany cycle and introduces the next event.

John's message is communicated best through preaching and his literary art through teaching. The evangelist, however, seems to ignore this distinction. The text is teaching/preaching all the way.

THE ANOINTING AT BETHANY (12:1–11)

Some variation of this story, or one like it, appears in all four Gospels. Its significance in the Gospel of John is best discerned in light of its connection with what precedes and follows it. It is the final scene in a sequence of events in Bethany that began with a notice about the illness of Lazarus, brother of Mary and Martha (11:1), focuses on the raising of Lazarus from the dead, and closes with the report of the chief priests' plan to put Lazarus to death (12:9–11). In this context, Mary's act of costly love concludes a trilogy about Jesus' encounter with three distinctive disciples in the home of his friends in Bethany. Mary's anointing of Jesus' feet (12:1–8) also looks forward, as it anticipates Jesus' washing of his disciples' feet at the Last Supper (13:1–17). Both stories are about love, the heart of the relationship between and among Jesus and his disciples.

The plan to kill Lazarus (12:9–11) confirms the watershed position of chapters 11 and 12 in the Fourth Gospel's narrative. According to John, it was the raising of Lazarus that triggered the events leading to Jesus' death.

Exploring the text

The time of withdrawal and waiting is over (11:54). The Passover festival is near (12:1) and Jesus returns to Bethany, on the outskirts of Jerusalem.

The Setting and the Scene (12:1–3)

In the first of several scenes preparatory to the dramatic last act of crucifixion and resurrection, Jesus returns to the warm hospitality of a home, where a household of his close friends has prepared a dinner in his honor (12:1b–2). The text does not say how many of his disciples accompany him. Only at 6:67–71 and 20:24 does John mention a special group of twelve. Judas, at least, is present (12:4) along with the three hosts and the guest of honor.

The action itself is described in a single verse (12:3). Mary rubs on Jesus' feet about 12 ounces or 340 grams (a Roman pound) of ointment imported from the Himalayas and then wipes his feet with her hair. Nard, a costly oil extracted from the spikenard plant native to India, was used to perfume the head and hair (Song 1:12; 4:13–14; Mark 14:3) and to anoint the dead (Mark 14:8; John 12:7). All present are struck by the fragrance of the perfume (12:3b).

In this scene John seems to combine elements of two traditions: one in which an unnamed woman in the house of Simon the leper at Bethany anoints Jesus' *head* in preparation for his burial (Matt. 26:6–13; Mark 14:3–9), and another in which a woman of ill repute in the Galilean home of a Pharisee named Simon bathes Jesus' *feet* with tears and wipes them with her hair, then anoints his feet with ointment as an act of love and gratitude unrelated to his death (Luke 7:36–50).[1] In John, Mary of Bethany anoints Jesus' feet (not his head, as in Mark and Matthew) and wipes them with her hair (as in Luke), but does so in preparation for his burial (as in Mark and Matthew), not as an act of gratitude for forgiveness (as in Luke). The report of the action is very brief. More space is given to the reactions of a disgruntled disciple and a hostile religious leader.

Jesus' Verbal Exchange with Judas (12:4–8)

Judas, the disciple who is about to betray Jesus, is not pleased. "This perfume is worth a whole year's wages! Why wasn't it sold and the money given to the poor?" (12:5, author's paraphrase).

Here the evangelist inserts an aside to the reader: "Judas didn't really care about the poor; he just wanted the money to go into the common purse that he kept and from which he used to steal money" (12:6, author's paraphrase). John's is the only Gospel that names Judas as the one who objected to this waste of money, and only John suggests that, besides failing to realize the meaning of Mary's action, Judas was a thief—another step in the demonization of Judas (see 6:70–71), which, in our time as well as earlier, has moved many people to defend the betrayer.

Jesus says to Judas, "Leave her alone, so she can keep it for the day of my burial" (12:7, author's translation). The sentence does not make clear sense as it stands in Greek, so most translators add words to make it read smoothly. The NRSV says, "*She bought it* so that she might keep it for the day of my burial." The NIV says, "*It was intended* that she should save this perfume for the day of my burial." Some commentators have suggested, "Let her keep *the rest of it* (TEV: *what she has*) for the day of my burial." In any case, the evangelist wants readers to understand that Mary's gift is an act of generous love. Her intentional extravagance expresses her devotion in anticipation of Jesus' death.

Jesus continues his reply to Judas, but now includes all those present: "You (plural) always have the poor with you, but you do not always have me." This verse is one of the memorable aphorisms of Jesus that are so characteristic of the pronouncement stories in the Synoptic Gospels. It has sometimes been lifted out of context and distorted on the one hand to belittle any effort to alleviate poverty through social programs, and on the other hand to boost campaigns to raise money for a cathedral, an organ, a stained glass window, or even the preacher's salary. Such applications of the text are incongruous and self-serving, in the same way in which Judas' objection is depicted here as self-serving. What the evangelist wishes readers to hear in Jesus' words is the beauty of uncalculating love and its importance as a mark of true discipleship.

The Reaction of the Crowd and Their Religious Leaders (12:9–11)

"The Jews" (12:9) refers to the crowd from the Judean neighborhood who came to see Jesus, the miracle worker, and also to see Lazarus. It's not every day you can see someone who has come back from the dead! They are not hostile—just curious.

"Chief priests" (12:10) refers to Caiaphas and Annas (11:49; 18:13) and, by extension, to the religious establishment that was planning to put Jesus to death (11:53). As titular heads of that establishment, the chief priests, alarmed by the fact that many of their people are deserting and believing in Jesus because of this remarkable sign, now plan to put Lazarus to death also. The evangelist is interested not in Lazarus's afterlife or subsequent death, however, but in showing that Jesus' gift of life to him was the occasion for Jesus' own death to give life to all who will receive it. The chief priests, in the presence of life and light (1:4–5), turn their back on it and become agents of darkness and death ("his own people did not accept him," 1:11), unable to comprehend the light, but also unable to overcome it (1:5), as the Fourth Gospel makes clear in the ensuing narrative.

Preaching and teaching the Word

This text appears in the lectionary on two occasions. The anointing and the interchange with Judas (12:1–8) is the Gospel reading for the Fifth Sunday in Lent, year C, and the entire pericope treated above (12:1–11) is appointed for Monday of Holy Week every year.

1. Models of discipleship. In the Bethany scenes Mary, Martha, and Lazarus offer three models of discipleship. Martha believes, Mary loves, and Lazarus lives.[2] Anyone teaching a series on individuals who encounter Jesus and their various responses to him could group the entire series of scenes in Bethany (11:1–12:11) as examples of responses to Jesus.

Scene one (11:1–16) shows the disciples' fearful prudence and Thomas's resigned loyalty. Martha's statement in 11:27 (scene two) models faith for all disciples. In scene three (11:28–37) Jesus exemplifies human love and divine indignation at unbelief and death. Jesus' raising Lazarus from the dead in scene 4 still awakens hope in Jesus as the resurrection and the life (11:25). Scene five (11:45–54) depicts reactions of belief and unbelief, with accent on the unbelief of the chief priests and Pharisees in the highest religious governing body, the Sanhedrin. Scene 6 (12:1–8) shows Mary's response of love as she anoints Jesus' feet and wipes them with her hair. In a final note about unbelief, the chief priests plan to kill Lazarus as well as Jesus (12:9–11).

The Bethany cluster, like the Fourth Gospel as a whole, is about belief and unbelief, about life and love, and above all, about Jesus, whose death and resurrection are the way God's sovereign love has chosen to defeat death and bring life to the world.

2. Wiping feet. Another illuminating approach to the text lies in juxtaposing Mary's anointing Jesus' feet (12:1–8) and Jesus' washing his disciples' feet (13:1–17). Interpreters have noted that John uses the same Greek word for "to wipe" in the two stories (12:3; 13:5), so that Mary's action points toward that of Jesus.[3] Both stories are about expressions of love. Mary expresses a disciple's love for Jesus. Jesus expresses God's love for us. His example of the towel and basin shows us how we are to love God by loving one another.[4]

3. Extravagant love. In 12:1–4, Mary demonstrates the beauty of uncalculating love and its importance as a mark of true discipleship. Examples of extravagant giving today include flowers for the sick, who have time to "smell the roses." Judas's objection (12:5–6) represents "organized charity, scrimped and iced, in the name of a cautious, statistical Christ."[5] Any treatment of Jesus' memorable aphorism about the poor (12:8) should take care not to fall into any of the traps mentioned in the exegetical notes above.

JESUS ENTERS JERUSALEM (12:12–19)

The raising of Lazarus (11:1–44) marks the climax of Jesus' miraculous signs and the occasion for a firm decision on the part of the Jerusalem authorities to issue a warrant for Jesus' arrest in order to put him to death (11:53, 57). The first two scenes in chapter 12 announce the drama that is set in motion by these actions. When Mary anoints Jesus' feet in Bethany six days before the Passover (12:1–8), Jesus says her private act anticipates his death (12:7). When the crowd welcomes Jesus to Jerusalem the next day (12:12–19), hailing him as a victorious king (12:13, 15), they publicly though unwittingly anticipate his resurrection (12:16).

Exploring the text

The triumphal entry is reported in all four Gospels. Slight differences in the way the scene is reported reveal the particular interpretation given to it by each evangelist. The mention of palm branches and the title "King of Israel" appear only in John. The securing of the colt by two of Jesus' disciples introduces the scene in all three Synoptic Gospels but is omitted in John.

Setting, Scene, and Scripture (12:12–15)

The brief setting (12:12) establishes the time and place: five days before Passover in Jerusalem (compare verses 1 and 12). The scene depicts a great crowd carrying palm branches and shouting (12:13) as they come out of the city to meet Jesus, who is sitting on a young donkey (12:14). Jesus, fully in charge as always in the Fourth Gospel, needs no help with the donkey. He finds it himself and sits on it. The two Scripture citations (12:13, 15) make it clear that this is a regal act.

The crowd's acclamation comes from one of the psalms that were sung by pilgrims approaching Jerusalem for the major festivals (Pss. 113–18). Psalm 118 was used especially in observance of Passover. "Hosanna" (John 12:13), a Hebrew expression meaning "Save, I [we] pray" (Ps.

118:25), is transliterated as one word in Greek and English. Like the accla-mation "Alleluia," Hebrew for "Praise the LORD," its literal meaning in liturgical settings is less significant than its function as a praise word to cel-ebrate God's greatness.

The use of Psalm 118, however, on the occasion of Jesus' entry into Jerusalem is highly significant. It is an acclamation of praise to "the one who comes in the name of the Lord" (John 12:13; Ps. 118:26). In the psalm the reference is to an unnamed speaker who has been rescued from a situation of great distress (Ps. 118:5–9) and who celebrates his victory over enemies "in the name of the Lord" (Ps. 118:10–12). He also celebrates victory over death: "I shall not die, but I shall live. . . . [The LORD] did not give me over to death" (Ps. 118:17–18). Although the Psalm does not specify who it is that comes in the name of the Lord, the Gospel interprets the text messianically and names him: "the King of Israel!" (John 12:13; compare "Son of David," Matt. 21:9; "the kingdom of our father David," Mark 11:10; "the King," Luke 19:38).

The other Scripture, cited in John and Matthew, is Zechariah 9:9. This text comes from the chapter that introduces the second, apocalyptic half of the book of Zechariah. In the context of an oracle announcing the approach and victory of God as the divine warrior (Zech. 9:1–8, 14–17), the prophet calls the people of Jerusalem to welcome their king who comes "humble and riding on a donkey, on a colt, the foal of a donkey" (Zech. 9:9) to command peace to the nations and to restore scattered Israel (Zech. 9:10–13). Through the use of this text, the first and fourth Gospels confirm the identification of Jesus as king of Israel and shift the focus of his kingship from majesty to humility, from war to peace.

The Disciples, the Crowd, and the Pharisees (12:16–19)

The note about the disciples' failure to understand the significance of the scene at the time (12:16) expresses three traits characteristic of the Fourth Gospel. It calls attention to a misunderstanding that is then explained in a way that enlightens the reader's understanding. It uses "glorify" to refer to the crucifixion and resurrection as a single event through which the splendor of God is revealed in Christ, so that the cross is a symbol of exaltation—just as the lowly donkey symbolizes royalty and peace. It points out that the significance of the moment must be under-stood through memory illumined by the experience of Jesus' death and resurrection.

The crowd includes people who had been with Jesus the previous day when he called Lazarus from the tomb (12:17). They exemplify the role of witnessing, which is so prominent in the Fourth Gospel: they testify to what they have seen and therefore know.[1] The effect of their witnessing was to draw the crowd that came out to meet Jesus in response to the last and greatest of his signs.

The Pharisees' remark (12:19) points back to the negative result of that sign, namely, the decision of the Sanhedrin to put Jesus to death (11:53). Their disgusted "you can do nothing" (12:19) echoes the words of Caiaphas on that earlier occasion, "You know nothing at all" (11:49); like him, they then utter words that prove to be prophetic: "Look, the world has gone after him!"

Preaching and teaching the Word

Strangely enough, the only Gospel that mentions palm branches is not the primary Gospel reading for Palm Sunday in any year. John 12:12–16 is, however, the alternate reading in year B. In all three years Psalm 118:1–2, 19–29 appropriately accompanies the entry scene from any one of the four Gospels, and Zechariah 9:9–10 could be chosen as the Old Testament reading to accompany the Gospel text in which it is quoted (Matt. 21:1–9; John 12:12–16). Whether preaching from the lectionary or not, these three texts constitute a solid and significant basis for proclaiming the Christ as king and the surprising nature of the kingdom of God.

Intertextual relationships between Psalm 118 and the Gospel of John offer rich material for preaching on the festivals of Christ the King or Easter, as well as on Palm Sunday. The psalm, like the Gospel of John, celebrates one who is glorious in his humility, victorious though rejected, and triumphant even over death.[2] Such a sermon would give the preacher an opportunity to bear witness to Jesus Christ in a way that might at the same time bring fresh courage to Christians in the face of apparent failure, rejection, or death.

The so-called "triumphal entry" was hardly a triumph. It was a shabby show in the carnival atmosphere of a religious festival: a simply dressed provincial rabbi and miracle worker on a borrowed donkey being welcomed noisily by an enthusiastic but frothy crowd. It had no relevance for the fate of the honoree just days later, nor did his own disciples see any significance in it until after Jesus was crucified and had risen from the dead. Then those who believed in him and loved him saw it as the fulfillment of a prophecy about Israel's messianic king (Zech. 9:9) and understood that the royalty of Jesus as Messiah differs radically from what the world calls glory. Jesus' true glory had been revealed on a cross and by an empty grave.

This informed understanding of the nature of true glory is highly relevant in a society in which money, power, public piety, and their traditional trappings are so important for many people. Official occasions of church and state have become increasingly elaborate, and at the same time more empty. One thinks of the installation of pastors and church dignitaries, as well as the inauguration of presidents, and recalls the contrasting simplicity with which a U.S. president walked from the Capitol steps to the White House on inauguration day in 1977–not to mention the refreshing example of his work with Habitat for Humanity in his retirement. Are the outward rites and festivals of the church, such as Palm Sunday, sometimes noisy but hollow signs of the glory Jesus embodied and to which he calls us?

Another approach to the triumphal entry is suggested by the fact that it is reported in all four Gospels. Comparison of the four would allow differences to become apparent, some of which reflect what each evangelist thought was important about Jesus. The lesson or sermon could also note what is common to all four and relevant to the particular congregation or occasion. Important points might include the fact that Jesus is king; that he is humble and his reign is one of peace; and that we greet him with palm branches, the symbol of life, because he has conquered death.

"THE HOUR HAS COME" (12:20–36)

The coming of the Greeks and Jesus' ensuing teaching about his death mark the climax of his public ministry in John. From this point on, the narrative looks toward Jesus' death and resurrection. This passage is the fulcrum of the Fourth Gospel, as is the incident at Caesarea Philippi and Jesus' first passion prediction (Mark 8:27–9:1) in the Gospel of Mark.

Exploring the text

Under the choppy surface of the individual sayings which constitute this text there flows a coherent stream of teaching about the coming of the Greeks and of Jesus' hour, the glory of Jesus' death, finding life through losing it, and following Jesus as a servant. The passage interprets in advance the significance of Jesus' death and resurrection for Jesus himself, for the evil ruler of this world, and for all the world's people, with a closing exhortation to Jesus' disciples to walk in the light.

The Coming of the Greeks (12:20–22)

These Greek-speaking proselytes to Judaism[1] represent the Gentile world. Their coming begins the fulfillment of the Pharisees' prophecy in the preceding verse, "Look, the world has gone after him!" (12:19).

Andrew and Philip both have Greek names, one derived from *aner, andros,* "man," and the other bearing the name of Philip of Macedon, founder of the city of Philippi. They appear consecutively in the account of the calling of the first disciples, in which they respond to or issue the invitation, "Come and see" (1:39, 46). Both were from the town of Bethsaida in Galilee (1:44), a highly Hellenized region. Each plays a prominent part in John's account of the feeding sign (6:7–9). That Greeks should come to these disciples with Greek names to seek an audience with Jesus is not surprising. They too wanted to "come and see." The Greeks then disappear from the pages of the Fourth Gospel, but readers can recognize in them the forerunners of the Gentiles who, by the time the Gospel is written, are coming into the Johannine community of faith in Jesus.

The Coming of "the Hour" (12:23–24)

Jesus' answers Andrew and Philip–and through them the Greeks–by saying, "The hour has come for the Son of Man to be glorified" (12:23). In this text communication occurs at many levels, for Jesus' words in verses 23–26 are addressed to all disciples, then and now, and through Jesus' reference to "the hour" the evangelist signals to readers of the Gospel that a turning point has arrived.

Three times Jesus has said, "My hour has not yet come," once to his mother (2:4) and twice to his brothers (7:6, 8). Twice the evangelist has noted that "no one laid hands on [arrested] him, because his hour had not yet come" (7:30; 8:20). Now, with the coming of the Greeks, Jesus realizes that the time has come for the crucial event that will demonstrate God's love for the entire world (3:16). The Word has come to his own, and his own people did not accept him (1:11), but here are Gentiles ready to see what kind of God this Jewish teacher has come to reveal. So the hour has come for the Son of Man–a Jewish term with universal significance– to be glorified; that is, shown and seen as the splendor of God's character in human flesh. The heart of the Christian gospel is that the death and resurrection of Jesus Christ is the fullest revelation of what God is like, and that it has opened the way to God for all of humankind.

The meaning of the cross for Jesus himself is shown in verses 23 and 24 in terms of the paradoxical Johannine understanding of the cross as **glory.** Jesus will be glorified, but only at the cost of his death. Through the image of a grain of wheat, Jesus offers an oblique prediction of his passion analogous to those of the Synoptic Gospels. If his life on earth is to bear the fruit God intended in sending the only Son into the world (3:14–16), he must die. For Jesus, dying on a cross means reflecting the glory of God and bearing fruit (12:24).

The Meaning of Jesus' Death for His Disciples (12:25–26)

If the coming of the hour means death to Jesus, its meaning for his disciples is made plain in verses 25 and 26, which reiterate the instructions to disciples in Mark 8:34–36 and 9:35.[2] The teaching here is stated in distinctly Johannine terms. The image of the grain of wheat is found only here in the Gospels, with a parallel in 1 Corinthians 15:36. The teaching about saving life and losing it is common to all the Gospels, but only John speaks of "keeping it for eternal life" (12:25). The rule about following Jesus even at the cost of dying is common tradition, but John speaks of being Jesus' servant rather than his disciple (12:26) and adds the specifically Johannine promise, "where I am, there will my servant be also" (12:26b, 14:3). The promise that the Father will honor whoever serves Jesus (12:26c) is reminiscent of "glorified" in verse 23, since "to glorify" is also "to show honor." Dying glorifies the Son of Man because through it he brings forth the fruit the Father sent him to bear (12:24). This theme is carried forward as Jesus speaks with his Father in the following verses.

Jesus' Inner Struggle (12:27–28)

Realizing that the hour of his death is upon him, Jesus is troubled. The word is the same as one of the two used to describe Jesus' emotion at the tomb of Lazarus (11:33). Its literal meaning is "stirred up," as was the water in the pool of Bethesda (5:4, variant reading). These verses are John's substitute for Jesus' anguish in the garden (Mark 14:32–42//Matt. 26:36–46//Luke 22:39–46). The Fourth Gospel omits the Gethsemane scene entirely and interprets Jesus' prediction of his passion in thoroughly Johannine terms. The psychological moment is the same. Jesus is fully human and genuinely troubled by the sacrifice of himself that lies ahead. He considers asking God to be delivered from death (12:27).

In John, however, instead of praying to be saved from "this hour," Jesus prays that the name of God will be glorified through it. The hour that has come is the hour of glory. A voice from heaven says that God has already glorified the divine name—that is, revealed the essence of the divine character—through the signs and teachings of Jesus. Now his death will carry that revelation to a new level.

What Jesus' Death Means for the Undecided Crowd (12:29–36)

The remainder of this unit consists of two exchanges between Jesus and the crowd. These theologically packed paragraphs operate at three levels. The Jewish crowd (they know the Hebrew Scriptures, 12:34) represents those who are undecided about Jesus in his own time (he will be with them only a little longer, 12:35), in the time of the evangelist (they understand the Johannine expression "lifted up" [12:34]), and in every subsequent time, for through his words to them the risen Lord addresses us (12:30–32, 35–36).

In the first exchange (12:29–33), the people standing by first speculate among themselves whether the sound they heard (12:28) was thunder or the voice of an angel (12:29), two options suggested by the culture of the time. The evangelist, through Jesus' answer (12:30–33), makes it clear to readers that the voice is neither thunder nor an angel, but the voice of God, who also speaks through Jesus for the benefit of the crowd in the text and of readers ever since. The voice, with Jesus' interpretation of it, is intended "to indicate the kind of death he was to die" (12:33); namely, by being "lifted up from the earth" on a Roman cross (12:32). The essential revelation of these verses, however, points beyond the historical means of Jesus' death to its theological significance. God is glorified by Jesus' death because through it the world is judged already (present tense, v. 31a), and the expulsion of "the ruler of this world" (the devil, 6:70; 8:44; 13:2, or Satan, 13:27) is assured (future tense, v. 31b).

"The world" is used here in its Johannine sense of unredeemed humanity caught in the struggle between light and darkness.[3] "Judgment" is used in the Johannine sense of judgment by light. The willingness of the Son of God to give his life for the world holds up to the light the evil of rejecting Jesus' words, deeds, and person (see 3:19 and notes on that text). His resurrection gives the assurance, stated explicitly in this word of Jesus, that ultimately "the ruler of this world will be driven out" (12:31b).

Jesus also glorifies God by his death because through it he will draw all people to himself (12:32). Twice before the Fourth Gospel has mentioned the Son of Man's being "lifted up" (3:14; 8:28). In John, being lifted up includes three steps: lifted up on the cross, raised up from death, and lifted up to heaven. Only on this wider understanding of "being lifted up" does Jesus' statement that he will draw all people to himself make sense. Understood in this way, the promise is not yet fulfilled, but it is still valid.

In the second exchange (12:34–36) the crowd picks up on Jesus' reference to himself as "Son of Man" (12:23), equates the title with "Messiah" (12:34), and seems to understand that Jesus is speaking of his death when he speaks of being lifted up (12:32), for that would contradict their understanding of the Torah, according to which the Messiah remains forever. The scriptural allusion may refer to Psalm 89:36, which speaks of David's line continuing forever, or simply to the Hebrew Scriptures in general. Their question, "Who is this Son of Man?" (12:34c), recapitulates the question of Jesus' identity, which lies at the heart of his confrontation with those who doubt or reject him from chapter 5 onward. The question might be that of any reader of the Fourth Gospel still undecided about Jesus' claims.

Jesus does not answer this question directly but replies with an exhortation to walk in the light (12:35–36). This is not simply an evasion. There is no way to see who Jesus is except to walk with him. Parroting a title will not do. Jesus refers to himself when he speaks of the light here, as he has done earlier (8:12; 9:5). A fundamental way in which the Fourth Gospel communicates the revelation of God in Jesus Christ is by speaking of the coming of the light (1:4–5). Thus at the end of his public ministry Jesus' invitation to the crowd to walk in the light echoes his invitation to Andrew and his companion at the beginning, "Come and see" (1:39; see also 1:46 and 4:29).

The invitation is urgent because they will have the option to walk with Jesus for only a little while longer (12:35a, 36a), and the alternative to walking with Jesus is to walk in darkness and "not know where you are going" (12:35b). This proverbial saying, like the promise of eternal life, refers both to the present life and to what lies beyond it. Jesus then links walking and seeing with an invitation to believe, adding not a threat but a promise: "so that you may become children of light" (12:36a). Those who believe in the light and walk in it are the ones who serve and follow Jesus. They will be honored by the Father (12:26).

Jesus then departs and hides himself (12:36b), giving hearers and readers time to think the invitation over. It also makes space for the evangelist's summary of Jesus' public ministry (12:37–50).

Preaching and teaching the Word

John 12:20–33 is the Gospel reading for the Fifth Sunday in Lent in year B, and John 12:20–36 is the reading for Tuesday of Holy Week every year.

A sermon based on John 12:20–26 might focus on the rigors and rewards of serving Jesus Christ. The principle of dying in order to live is not just for Jesus; it is for all humankind, for "[all] who love their life lose it, and those who hate their life in this world will keep it for eternal life" (12:25). To follow Jesus means to lose one's own life in loving service and so to enjoy abundant life (10:10) now and hereafter. The rewards of following Jesus are that "where I am, there will my servant be also" (12:26b) and "Whoever serves me, the Father will honor" (12:26c). A pastor who has served the servants of Christ for a while can speak from experience and put flesh on these homiletical bones in such a way that the congregation ("the crowd") will hear again the inviting voice of Jesus.

A sermon on the John 12:20–33 pericope might focus on verses 27 and following, underlining the promise, "And I, when I am lifted up from the earth, will draw all people to myself " (12:32). A sermon or lesson on the three meanings of Jesus' being "lifted up" in John could be called, "What do you mean, 'Lifted up?'" (12:34 REB, adapted). The meaning for the fourth evangelist is laid out in the notes above. One meaning for followers of Jesus today is that if we will lift up Jesus in our lives (words and actions), Jesus will draw others to himself.

A sermon called "Indecision" could be based on the last two verses in the Gospel reading for Tuesday of Holy Week every year (12:20–36). Here Jesus, alluding to himself as the light of the world, urges us to believe in the light and walk in the light while we have it. We decide daily whether to walk in light or in darkness. Not to decide for Jesus is to walk in darkness and after a while to discover that we no longer have the light. To walk in the light of Jesus, on the other hand, to whatever extent we see it, sets us on the road to becoming children of light (see Luke 16:8; Eph. 5:8; 1 Thess. 5:8), who know where they are going and who goes with them. Such a sermon could, by the breath of the Holy Spirit, become a turning point for some hearer who heeds the word of Jesus and begins anew, or for the first time, to walk in his light.

Reflection on the role of Philip and Andrew in the coming of the Greeks (12:20–22) might spark a sermon or lesson on qualities that make disciples accessible to others who might want to see Jesus. Among these are personal knowledge of Jesus and excitement about what one has found in him; an openness to inquirers whose language and culture one understands; a willingness to be of service to Jesus and to others whose lives would be enriched by knowing him; the expectation that others will love Jesus too once they have met him. Such a sermon or lesson would be appropriate as preparation for a special period of evangelistic outreach.

Persons facing painful decisions, particularly decisions that involve personal sacrifice, might find guidance and nurture in John 12:27–28. In the parallel Gethsemane passages in the Synoptic Gospels Jesus prays first that God remove the cup from him—"if you are willing" (Luke 22:42)—but the bottom line of his prayer is that God's will be done (Matt. 26:39//Mark 14:36). In John, Jesus knows well what God's will is, but it is hard. His soul is troubled, yet he knows he has come to this hour for this very reason. The text will serve in sermon or lesson, but it might serve best in pastoral ministry to people today who know what God expects of them in a given situation but need to find the strength to do it.

ENTR'ACTE (12:37–50)

Two short paragraphs bring part one of the Fourth Gospel to a close: the evangelist's analysis of the response to Jesus' signs (12:37–43) and a summary of Jesus' teaching in his own words (12:44–50).

Exploring the text

These two paragraphs, situated between part one and part two of the Gospel, are like an entr'acte at a play.[1] With Jesus' invitation to the crowd to walk in the light (12:35–36), the curtain has come down on the first act of the Gospel of John. The playwright (= evangelist) now steps into the spotlight at the front of the stage to remind the audience that through the many signs that Jesus has performed in his encounters with all sorts of people, the living Word of God has come like light into the world. The response to the coming of the light has been mostly negative, however, and the evangelist offers an analysis of this shocking fact. The spotlight is then extinguished and the evangelist leaves the stage. Out of the darkness a voice comes from the wings, speaking now directly to the audience (= the reader and all who will listen), recapitulating the main themes of his teaching in this Gospel. The voice falls silent and all who read or hear are left to ponder this encounter with the living Word.

The Response to Jesus' Signs (12:37–43)

Two kinds of responses to Jesus are identified here: unbelief (12:37–41) and secret belief (12:42–43).

Verse 37 expresses the dismay of Jews who believed in Jesus at the unbelief of those who did not. How could anyone fail to see the significance of the signs that Jesus performed, especially when they bore out what Scripture had said (5:39; 6:30–33)? The evangelist, a devout Jew, turns to Scripture for an explanation of this enigma and chooses two quotations from the prophet Isaiah. The first (Isa. 53:1) introduces the body of the last and best known Servant Song (Isa. 52:13–53:12) in Isaiah 50–55. The poet/prophet describes an anonymous figure ("he" in Isa. 53:2–12) identified only as "my servant" (Isa. 52:13) and "the righteous one, my servant" (Isa. 53:11). In its original context the servant refers to exiled Israel, but from the first witnesses onward Christians have seen in this description the major traits of Jesus Christ. The fourth evangelist turns to this text, already widely recognized among believers as a testimony to Jesus,[2] to explain Israel's disbelief. "Who has believed our message?" (12:38) adapts Isaiah 53:1 for the new context.

The second text used to explain to readers the tragic blindness of Jesus' own people ("them" and "their," John 12:36–37; see 1:11) comes from the account of Isaiah's call (Isa. 6:1–13). In the temple Isaiah sees God's glory and hears the Lord asking for a volunteer for a mission. When Isaiah says he will go, God issues some disturbing orders (6:9–10). John 12:40 cites the second part of this command (Isa. 6:10), quoted freely. At God's command, Isaiah is to make the mind of the people dull (Isa. 6:10a//"[he has] hardened their heart," John 12:40b), to stop their ears and shut their eyes (Isa. 6:10b//"he has blinded their eyes," John 12:40a), lest they see (Isa. 6:10c//John 12:40c), and hear, and understand, and repent and be healed (Isa. 6:40 end//John 12:40 end).

John's introductory words, "And so they could not believe, because Isaiah also said" (John 12:39), heighten the idea of the divine purpose to harden the people's heart. John affirms that the prophetic word at the time of the exile was the effective cause of the people's unbelief in the time of Jesus. He also heightens the connection between seeing and believing by omitting Isaiah's references to hearing and the ears. The evangelist's further explanation of why Isaiah spoke includes a characteristic double entendre: "because he [Isaiah] saw his glory and spoke about him" (12:41). The text in Isaiah clearly refers to God's glory; the text in John refers to Jesus but presupposes that to see Jesus' glory is to see the glory of God.

The fourth evangelist is not alone in citing this text. According to all three Synoptic Gospels, Jesus used it to explain why he taught in parables (Matt. 13:14–15; Mark 4:12; Luke 8:10). In the book of Acts, the apostle Paul quotes Isaiah 6:9–10 in an eloquent closing statement evaluating his missionary labors and explaining why he has turned his major attention to the Gentiles.[3]

The response to Jesus was not completely negative, however: "Many, even of the authorities, believed in him" (12:42a) but would not declare themselves as Jesus' disciples. This presents another disappointment that the evangelist explains differently. It was not God's will that they remain secret believers. It was their own conscious decision, driven by fear and by the desire to be highly esteemed in the eyes of their peers (12:42b–43). Here, as earlier, the evangelist holds in tension the divine will and human freedom to choose (see notes on 8:31–47). Both come into play in the way his own people responded to Jesus. John does not condemn those who rejected Jesus outright; after all, they could not help it. However, those who believed but were afraid to confess it he holds fully responsible, attributing to them the motives of fear and vainglory.

Preaching and teaching the Word

In a teaching situation this passage in John offers an occasion to explore the problem of divine choosing (election) and human choice (free will) in the Bible. The teacher might recall God's choice of Abel rather than Cain

(Gen. 4:3–5), of Isaac rather than Ishmael (Gen. 21:12), of Jacob (Israel) rather than Esau (Gen. 25:23); God's hardening of Pharaoh's heart (Exod. 4:21; 7:3; 9:12; 14:8) versus Pharaoh's hardening his own heart (Exod. 7:13–14; 9:7, 34–35); and Paul's wrestling with this problem in Romans 9–11, concluding that God's judgments are unsearchable and his ways inscrutable (Rom. 11:33). These texts reflect a worldview that readily attributed natural events and human actions to the direct intervention of God. We tend, in our time, to seek natural causes and psychological or sociological reasons. Against this background, the teacher could point to texts in the Fourth Gospel that affirm both God's election and human freedom,[4] then encourage participants in the study to think of examples in human experience of the paradox of being or feeling at the same time programmed and free to choose.

A sermon on this unit might focus on the verses predicated on our freedom to choose (12:42–43) and call hearers to leave the ranks of secret believers and become bold witnesses to Jesus by love and service in church and community. Such a sermon could include the well-known image of the entry into heaven over which appears "Whoever will may come" and on the interior, visible only to those who have entered, "You did not choose me but I chose you."[5]

Exploring the text

The next verses present a summary of Jesus' teaching. The ideas that bracket this text are an appeal to believe in Jesus (12:44) and the promise of eternal life in his name (12:50a). They foreshadow the evangelist's statement of his purpose in writing this Gospel (20:31).

The Summary of Jesus' Teaching (12:44–50)

Nowhere is the contrast between the Fourth Gospel and the Synoptics more striking than in this paragraph, in which, at midpoint in the story, the evangelist allows Jesus himself to summarize what is most important in what he and the evangelist have been saying. Such a summary in any one of the first three Gospels might include the nearness of the kingdom of God, the need to repent, the basic commandments to love God and love one's neighbor, and the ethical demands entailed by following Jesus. Jesus' summary in the present text includes instead the importance of believing in Jesus as the one who reveals God, his being sent by God not to judge but to save, the reliability of his words as the word of God, and eternal life as the fruit of obedience to God's command.

The emphases and the words themselves embody and summarize the theology of the Fourth Gospel. Here as elsewhere the voice of Jesus and the voice of the evangelist coalesce.[6] The following notes do not enter the debate about whether or not Jesus, during his earthly life, spoke these words. They do, however, take the words to be the truth into which the Spirit of the risen Lord led the particular disciple who bears witness to him in this Gospel (15:26; 16:13).

Believe (12:44–45)

The theme of believing or not believing in Jesus runs like a scarlet thread throughout the Gospel. It is particularly prominent in the first twelve chapters, in which more than three-fourths of the uses of the verb **"believe"** in John appear. The theme is introduced with the sending of John the witness (1:6–7) and governs the first summary of the responses to Jesus in the prologue (1:11–12), as well as the summaries at the end of chapter 12 (12:37, 39, 42, 44). These summaries bracket the narrative of Jesus' public ministry and take stock of those who reject (do not accept) him on the one hand versus those who receive and believe him on the other.

Him Who Sent Me/the Father Who Sent Me (12:44–45/49–50)

In the Fourth Gospel, the most common terms used by Jesus to refer to God are **"Father"** and "him who sent me." Both terms are used in this summary of Jesus' teaching, once combined as "the Father who sent me" (12:49). Together they express Jesus' subordination to God, like that of an emissary to the sender, and at the same time his intimate relationship to God, like that of a son to his father. The relationship is uniquely close. To believe in Jesus is to believe in God who sent him (12:44) and to see Jesus is to see God who sent him (12:45). Jesus says only what God tells him to say and proclaims exactly what God has commanded (12:49–50), so that Jesus' words are God's word (12:47–48). These formulations of the relationship between Jesus and God pick up one of the major themes of the Fourth Gospel, broached often and developed extensively in 5:19–47 and 10:22–30. These passages lead the reader to view Jesus as the functional equivalent of God. The mystery of Jesus' relationship to God is preserved in this summary, with its paradoxical affirmations of subordination and functional equivalence. What Jesus' hearers, and the readers of the Fourth Gospel, are called to believe is that Jesus has come from God, is God's Word made flesh, God's only Son, the Messiah, through whom God shows his love for the world and in whom believers see God and are saved.

Light vs. Darkness (12:46)

Of the four **"I Am" sayings** with a defining term that have appeared thus far in the Fourth Gospel (bread of life, 6:35, 51; light of the world,

8:12; 9:5; gate, 10:7, 9; shepherd, 10:11, 14), the second is the one under-scored here ("I have come as light into the world," 12:46). The theme of the Fourth Gospel lifted up in this summary of Jesus' teaching is that of the opposites **light and darkness** (12:46). At the climactic moment of Jesus' final appeal to the crowd at the close of his public ministry Jesus urges all who will hear, "While you have the light, believe in the light, so that you may become children of light" (12:35–36). Because of the promi-nence of this theme, Lesslie Newbigin used it in the title of his fine expo-sition of the Fourth Gospel, *The Light Has Come* (Eerdmans, 1982). Here in 12:46 Jesus appeals to all who hear or read his words to believe in him and live in the light of God.

Judge/Condemn (12:47–48)

Two entire verses of this summary of Jesus' teaching are devoted to the theme of judgment. The verb "to judge," *krino,* is variously used in the Fourth Gospel. In one text it appears in the sense of forming an opinion about another person (7:24), but generally it is courtroom language, twice referring to a human court (7:51; 18:31) but usually referring to the divine tribunal. As a legal term it can mean simply to weigh cases and administer justice (5:27, 30), but it often refers to passing an adverse judgment, in which case it is sometimes translated "condemn" (3:17–18; 5:29; 8:10–11, 26; 16:11).

Jesus' attitude toward judging is paradoxical, a trait characteristic of the Fourth Gospel. He did not come to judge (3:17) and he judges no one (8:15b), yet he does judge and his judgment is valid (8:16a), for the Father has delivered all judgment to the Son (5:22) and exercises divine judg-ment through him (5:30; 8:16b), for the Father is the judge (8:50). Earlier, this enigma is addressed by the idea that Jesus' judgment is judgment by the coming of the light.[7] In this retrospective summary, it is the teaching of Jesus ("my words," 12:47a) that will judge those who have heard his words but not responded positively to them. By their response to Jesus' teaching, as by their response to his light, people judge themselves.

Words and the Word (12:47–50)

The shift from "words" (12:47) to "word" (12:48) is slight but significant. "The word that I have spoken will serve as judge" (12:48) still refers pri-marily to the teaching of Jesus, who has spoken not on his own but only in obedience to the Father's commandment (12:49–50). This teacher, however, is the one who in the prologue is referred to as "the Word" (1:1) that became flesh and thereby became a person (1:14). Jesus says only what the Father commands him to say, but paradoxically it is in such obe-dient speaking that Jesus reveals himself to be the eternal Word made flesh. That is why the words that Jesus has spoken as recorded in this Gospel placed hearers then and readers now in the presence of the Word of God.

"His Commandment Is Eternal Life" (12:50a)

When Jesus affirmed that he was laying down his life of his own accord, like a good shepherd, he added that he had power to lay it down and to take it up again because he had "received this command *(entole)* from my Father" (10:18). In the present text Jesus says, "I know that his commandment *(entole)* is eternal life." Jesus lays down his life of his own accord, but that voluntary act is the key to the eternal life that comes to all believers in obedience to God's command.

Eternal **life** is one of the major themes of the Fourth Gospel, occupying the place of the kingdom of God in the Synoptics.[8]

Preaching and teaching the Word

This unit lends itself to teaching, for it reads like a glossary of theological terms in the Gospel of John. It could serve as a starting point for a class session on the theology of the Fourth Gospel, using the subheads in the notes above as an outline for the session. Texts cited there and in earlier notes to which the comments have referred could be assigned by the teacher for participants to look up and read aloud as the class traces these themes through the Gospel. Time should be allowed for class discussion of each theme and the questions it raises in the minds of the learners, with practical examples of what this teaching of Jesus might mean in daily life. The session should be closed on a positive note, perhaps by reading verses 44–50 aloud together.

The opening words, "Then Jesus cried aloud," introduce a proclamation of great significance from the lips of Jesus. The preacher today has the privilege of putting herself or himself at the disposal of the risen Lord, just as the evangelist did, to say why faith in Jesus matters. If in teaching it is important to look closely at the text, in preaching it is essential to stand aside and let both text and preacher become transparent to the living Word. Jesus speaks here of his relation to the one who sent him, of God's purpose (expressed in Jesus) not to judge but to save the world, and of eternal life as the goal of the words God gave Jesus to proclaim in word and deed. Preachers who are able to speak of what they have seen of God in Jesus, of what believing in Jesus means to them, and of the quality of life Jesus has brought to them are likely to be good interpreters of this text, however they may organize their ideas about it. Such a sermon would focus on what it means to believe and be saved, pulling together exegesis and experience in order to become a channel for the Word of God.

PART TWO

Words to Live By

13:1–17:26

Preliminary Remarks

For twelve chapters John the evangelist has shown who Jesus is, and through him what God is like. Preceded by an eloquent prologue, the narrative has allowed us to come to know Jesus Christ through John the witness who first recognized him, through the disciples who first followed him, and through what he said and did as he encountered a wide variety of individuals and groups in Judea and Jerusalem, in Galilee and Samaria. By portraying responses ranging from immediate enthusiasm to puzzlement to seeing a dawning light and faith on the one hand, and from mild interest to hostility to rejection and execution on the other, the evangelist has confronted readers with the necessity of making a decision about Jesus on which their own eternal life or death depends.

In the next five chapters (13–17), the narrative focuses on Jesus and his disciples. The entire second part of the Gospel is set in a single place and time: an unspecified room in Jerusalem just before the Passover festival was to begin (13:1–2; 18:1). The structure of these chapters can be understood in more than one way. Here is the one used in the present commentary:

A. The Last Supper, footwashing, and prediction of betrayal (13:1–30)
B. The farewell discourse (13:31–16:33)
    1. Introduction (13:31–38)
    2. Table talk (14:1–31)
    3. Expanded discourse (15:1–16:4a)
    4. Recapitulation (16:4b–33)
C. The great prayer (17:1–26)

In these chapters Jesus gives to disciples of every time and place words to live by.

The Last Supper, Footwashing, and Prediction of Betrayal

13:1–30

In John the Last Supper is not a Passover meal (13:1a, 29) as it is in the Synoptics. Nor is it the Lord's Supper of Paul's epistles and of church tradition (1 Cor. 11:23–26; Matt. 26:17–30; Mark 14:12–26; Luke 22:7–23). There is no mention of "apostles" or of "the twelve," no command to "do this in remembrance of me," and nothing that suggests the life of an institution. Instead, John depicts an intimate supper at which Jesus, by wordless enactment of a symbol of lowly service, prepares his disciples to stay together as a community of faith even when he is no longer physically present among them.

Exploring the text

A weighty introduction (13:1–3) sets the stage for a symbolic action (the footwashing, 13:4–5), a dialogue with Peter in which Jesus suggests a first interpretation of the symbol (13:6–11), and a monologue in which Jesus gives a fuller explanation of the symbol (13:12–17), followed by an enigmatic allusion to his betrayal and death (13:18–20) and an explicit identification of Judas as the traitor (13:21–30). Judas's departure into the night marks the end of the unit.

Introduction (13:1–3)

These verses fix the time ("before the festival of the Passover") and the situation ("during supper"), though not the exact place. Jesus' omniscience is underscored: he knew that "his hour had come" (13:1), that "the Father had given all things into his hands, and that he had come from God and was going to God" (13:3). He also knew that betrayal was in the heart of Judas son of Simon Iscariot (13:2, 11).

This hour is the one that has been repeatedly mentioned but held in abeyance (2:4; 7:30; 8:20), announced as imminent (12:23, 27), and later referred to as present (16:32; 17:1). It is the hour of Jesus' death and res-

164

urrection (see notes on 12:23), spoken of here as the hour "to depart from this world and go to the Father" (13:1). In Luke, Jesus' departure through death is an *exodos* (Luke 9:31), suggesting Passover and deliverance, but the word John uses for depart (*metabaino,* "cross over," John 13:1) suggests transition from this world to the one above. Here, the hour of Jesus' death means a return to the state of glory which he enjoyed with God prior to his incarnation (1:1–5, 14; 17:5).

As narrative, this text marks the turning point from Jesus' public ministry to his death and resurrection and, for the disciples, from life with Jesus in the flesh to life in the community of faith, love, and service that his death and resurrection will call into being. As theology, it marks a turning point in the Johannine theme of descent and ascent. The eternal Word came from the realm of light and life into the darkness of this world (1:1, 9; 3:13) in order that the world might be saved through him (3:16–17). The Gospel as a whole portrays how, in a downward-upward parabola, Jesus has come from heaven (3:31), is about to finish the work God gave him to do on earth (17:4), and anticipates the moment when he will ascend to the Father (20:17). John 13:1–3 points to three significant elements of Johannine theology revealed by the coming of "the hour": Jesus' love for his own ("to the end," 13:1c, means "to the very end of his life on earth" as well as "to the uttermost"), the devil's power (Judas already has betrayal in his heart, 13:2), and Jesus' supreme authority, soon to be revealed when he departs from this world to return to the Father (13:1, 3)

Footwashing (13:4–5)

The simplicity with which John describes Jesus' symbolic action stands in striking contrast to its intricate introduction. Having vested the scene with profound literary and theological significance, the evangelist can let the scene unfold in total silence, its whole sense embodied in a few unforgettable gestures. "During supper Jesus got up . . . , took off . . . , tied around himself . . . , poured . . . , began to wash . . . and to wipe" (13:2b–5). The mind's eye readily supplies the table, the robe, the towel, the basin, and the disciples' dusty feet. No word is spoken yet. First the deed.

First Interpretation (13:6–11)

Peter's brash invasion of the silence initiates a dialogue in which Peter expresses surprise that his Lord and teacher would take the role of a slave to wash his disciples' feet and Jesus replies that only later–meaning after his death and resurrection–will Peter understand his action (13:6–7). Peter first refuses to let Jesus wash his feet, but upon hearing that his continuing relationship to Jesus depends on letting Jesus wash him, he impulsively blurts out a request that Jesus wash his hands and head as well (13:8–9). Jesus' reply in verse 10 refers to the customary hospitality of the time, which presupposed that guests at a dinner would have bathed before coming, but their feet, dusty from walking to the host's house, would be washed by a servant before the meal. The guests would then be entirely clean. Jesus adds, "And you are clean, though not all of you" (13:10b). The author's note in verse 11 explains the comment as a reference to Judas, whom Jesus knew would betray him. Readers who are familiar with the whole witness of the Fourth Gospel to the completed work of Jesus Christ can easily understand Peter's objection as a refusal to recognize and submit to a master who suffers and serves, like his rebuke of Jesus after the first prediction of the passion in Mark 8:32. Jesus' reply in both cases states in strongest terms that only by faith in and obedience to the servant Lord can one hope really to be Jesus' disciple.

This first, partial interpretation of the symbol of footwashing (13:6–11) suggests far more than it explains. It alludes to Jesus' sacrificial death as the Lamb of God (1:29, 36), to the cleansing that comes from accepting by faith what Jesus does for his disciples, and thereby "having a share in" (13:8) or enjoying communion with him as he enjoys union with the Father (17:21–23). Readers then and now may also see in the reference to "one who has bathed" (13:10) an allusion to baptism as a sign of cleansing through believing the Word that Jesus incarnates and the word that he has spoken (John 15:3; Rom. 6:3–4), but the text does not specify how it is that the disciples are already clean, or what further cleansing the footwashing represents.

Fuller Explanation (13:12–17)

After a note that concludes the symbolic action of footwashing (13:12a), the text presents Jesus' fuller explanation of his symbolic action in the form of a brief monologue. This time his words are straightforward and explicit: as master teacher, he has given his disciples an example of how they should relate to one another. If he, their Lord and Teacher (*didaskalos*, translated "master" in the AV) has washed their feet, they ought to wash one another's feet, as the master has done to them. In proverbial language, underscored by the doubled formula of emphatic assertion, "Very truly [*amen, amen*] I tell you" (13:16), that marks Jesus' solemn utterances twenty-five times in the Gospel of John, he reminds his disciples that they are in the position of servants and messengers. Servants are not greater than their master, and the disciples are surely not greater than their teacher, the one who sends them. He then drives the application home with an exhortation couched as a conditional word of blessing: "If you know these things, you are blessed if you do them" (13:17).

Taking Jesus' silent action as an acted parable, the initial explanation in 13:6–11 retains the open-ended, enigmatic quality of a parable, while the fuller explanation in 13:12–17 treats the parable as an example story. Both interpretations are important. The first focuses on the individual disciple's communion with Jesus, the second on the disciples' relationship to one another in a community of mutual service. The first calls for submissive faith in Jesus, the second for active emulation of him as servant Lord. Each interpretation is incomplete without the other. Taken together, they may be understood as the Johannine understanding of the marks of the true church: communion with Jesus Christ, and community with one another in emulating Jesus' loving service. They are words to live by.

Prediction of Betrayal (13:18–20)

Verses 18 and 19 carry forward the theme of betrayal introduced earlier (13:2, 10–11). They pose a problem. If Jesus knows those he has chosen (13:18), why did he choose one whom he knew to be "a devil" (6:70–71)? The text gives a traditional Jewish answer: in order to fulfill the Scripture, namely Psalm 41:9, which speaks of being attacked not by an enemy but by a bosom friend and table companion whom the betrayed one had trusted. Although this line of reasoning is alien to Western minds at the beginning of the twenty-first century, people in any culture who know the Bible find that it articulates their experience. "The one who ate my bread has lifted his heel against me" expresses aptly a pain that lies too deep for words. Jesus knows that pain in advance. He tells his disciples now so that when it happens to him, they will believe that "I am" (*ego eimi*)—that he knows as God knows (13:19).

Verse 20, another "Amen-saying" of Jesus, seems to be unrelated to the present context.[1] Receiving Jesus, however, is a positive counterpoint to betraying him. Like the footwashing and its first explanation, these words can be understood only after Jesus' resurrection. The promise of 13:20 makes sense in the context of 20:21–22, when Jesus commissions his disciples and breathes into them the Holy Spirit. It is fulfilled when disciples through the centuries, impelled by Jesus' Spirit and command, meet with hearts receptive to their witness.

The Betrayer Identified (13:21–30)

If Jesus' foreknowledge of Judas's betrayal (13:11, 18–19) is evidence of his oneness with God, his being "troubled in spirit" (13:21a) shows that he is one with us. His soul was troubled when he confronted the imminence of his own death (12:27), and his spirit is troubled by the thought of betrayal by one of his chosen disciples (6:70–71; 13:11, 18). His announcement of the impending betrayal is introduced by the solemn formula, "Very truly, I tell you" (13:21b).

The scene in which Jesus reveals the identity of the betrayer is important in all four Gospels,[2] but John's account is the most circumstantial. "The disciple whom Jesus loved" is introduced here for the first time, seated by Jesus at the Last Supper (13:23) and acting as intermediary between Peter and Jesus. He appears again at the foot of the cross (19:26), entering the empty tomb (20:2), and at the Sea of Tiberias (21:7). Rumor had it that he would live until Jesus comes again (21:20, 23). Although he is never named in the text of the Fourth Gospel, he is referred to as its chief witness and author (21:24). Church tradition since the late second century has identified him as John, the son of Zebedee, one of the Twelve. In recent years some have thought he symbolizes the community for which this Gospel was written. The debate about his identity is interminable and inconclusive. What the text states plainly is that he was an eyewitness who was particularly close to Jesus–literally, "reclining in Jesus' bosom" (13:23). In the prologue Jesus is described as "close to the Father's heart"–literally, "on the bosom of the Father" (1:18). For the evangelist, the beloved disciple is as close to Jesus as Jesus is to God, a closeness that Jesus prays might characterize all believers (17:23). The suggestion that the beloved disciple symbolizes the Johannine community is understandable.

When Jesus predicts that one of the disciples reclining with him at table will betray him (13:21), the beloved disciple, at Peter's request, asks Jesus, "Lord, who is it?" (13:25). Jesus answers by means of another symbolic act that he explains in advance to the beloved disciple (13:26). In a basic gesture of Oriental hospitality Jesus perhaps picks out for Judas a choice morsel of food as a special act of esteem (cf. Ruth 2:14). By accepting the piece of bread without changing his plan to betray Jesus, Judas shows that he has chosen for Satan.[3]

Jesus' command to Judas after he has received the bread and Satan has entered him–"Do quickly what you are going to do" (13:27)–is heard but not understood by the others at table. John uses their misunderstanding to inform readers that Judas is treasurer and purchasing agent for Jesus and his disciples, that the Passover festival still lies in the immediate future, and that as a group they give alms to the poor (13:28–29). Jesus is in full control of the situation. Judas should act quickly because Jesus' hour has come. Judas obeys and goes out into the darkness. The symbolic import of darkness throughout the Fourth Gospel (1:5; 3:2, 19; 12:35, 46) is underscored by the last four words of the text (three in Greek): "And it was night" (13:30). Judas's departure echoes the note at the beginning about Satan putting betrayal in his heart (13:2). It marks the conclusion of the supper and footwashing narrative.

Preaching and teaching the Word

Some portion of John 13:1–30 is the Gospel text for Maundy Thursday every year in all commonly used lectionaries. "Maundy" is derived from *mandatum*, "command," the first word in the Latin service for Holy Thursday, in which Christ's command "You ought to wash one another's feet" (John 13:14) is remembered. "Maundy" is an old ceremony of washing the feet of a number of poor people formerly performed by a sovereign or a church authority and still observed by the pope in Rome to commemorate Christ's washing his disciples' feet at the Last Supper. In any Christian community, Maundy Thursday is an appropriate time to preach on John's depiction of the Last Supper and to wash each other's feet.

1. Example story. The most obvious significance of the footwashing scene lies in its explanation as an example story in verses 14–15 and the punch line about knowing and doing in verse 17. Jesus washed his disciples' feet as an example of how his disciples of every age should relate to one another in mutual love and humble service. Furthermore, just knowing this is not enough; it is those who do it who are blessed. So important is this dimension of the text that the symbol of towel and basin has taken its place alongside bread and cup and the cross itself as a central expression of the Christian faith.

2. Communion meditation. The less obvious explanation of Jesus' symbolic action given in verses 7–10 makes this an appropriate text for preaching on communion Sunday (even though footwashing is not a sacrament), for it alludes to Christ's cleansing death to wash away our sin (1:29). This opens the possibility of combining Christ's commands to "Do this in remembrance of me" (1 Cor. 11:24) and "Do [for one another] as I have done to you" (John 13:14–15) in a single communion meditation around the symbols of bread and wine, towel and basin. The Lord's Supper represents our vertical relationship with God; the Last Supper and footwashing represent our communion with one another as disciples. Both are expressions of our communion with and in Christ.

3. "Unless I wash you." A sermon on John 13:6–11 might focus on how

Jesus cleanses us. "Unless I wash you, you have no share with me" (13:8) has been understood by Catholics as a reference to baptism and by Protestants as a reference to being washed in the blood of the Lamb (Rev. 7:14). In either case, intimate fellowship with or participation in Jesus Christ (having a share with him) hinges upon being cleansed by him. This purification comes through believing what Jesus says ("you have already been cleansed by the word that I have spoken to you," 15:3) and accepting what he does for his disciples by giving his life in sacrificial love (15:12–13). Probably everyone in any congregation will at one time or another have felt all dirty inside. To that common experience this text has spoken through the ages.

4. Servant discipleship. A sermon on John 13:1–5, 12–17 could reflect upon what the equivalent of washing feet might be in the life of a Christian individual or congregation today. The servant role, commonly assumed by women and African Americans in the past, has never been a popular one, particularly for those who once were confined to it. Yet it is an abiding element in the image of Jesus Christ and in the Christian understanding of discipleship. Nurses, Sunday school teachers, caregivers of small children and the elderly, janitors and garbage collectors all play a servant role.

Before women could be ordained, the Presbyterian Church in the U.S. created a institution to prepare women and men for service in the church called the "Assembly's Training School." Students and faculty made a motto of its initials: "Appointed to Serve." For decades its graduates did just that, often underpaid and underappreciated. Many problems in the institutional church might be avoided if more of its ordained servants still viewed themselves in this way.

5. Betrayal, foreordination, and judgment. The other major theme in John 13:1–30 is betrayal, which is prominent in the Gospel reading for Wednesday of Holy Week, years A, B, and C (John 13:21–32). Among Jesus' most intimate disciples was a traitor. This observation tends to lead the reader today to ask, with those first disciples, "Lord, who is it?" (13:25). Put in this way, the question led to bitter conflict in the Johannine community, one side of which is echoed in certain verses in 1 John (1 John 2:18–19; 4:1–6; 5:16b). Perhaps a more constructive way to phrase the question about betrayal is "Lord, is it I?" (Matt. 26:22; Mark 14:19 AV, RSV). Focusing upon the betrayal of Judas can be significant if it leads readers to reflect upon the ways in which they themselves betray Jesus, with a view to changing those patterns.

The text again confronts readers with the problem of foreordination and free will.[4] In the present text (13:18–27) Jesus foretells his betrayal by

Judas as if it were predetermined, yet he offers him food from the common dish as a gesture of special favor, as if Judas were free to change his mind. Furthermore, when Jesus dismisses him, he tells Judas to do quickly what he is going to do, not what he must do. Judas, by Jesus' choosing, is an instrument of God. Judas, by his own choice, is a tool of Satan. The betrayal by Judas serves as an illustration of the Johannine theme of judgment. Jesus did not come in order to judge anyone, but to bring life to all. Yet by Judas's response to the light he chooses death for Jesus and judgment for himself. It is no light matter when a chosen disciple of Jesus leaves the table of his or her Lord.

The Farewell Discourse

The last words of significant persons are often remembered and treasured. Farewell speeches, well known in classical literature, are a prominent feature of the Bible: Jacob (Gen. 47:29–49:33), Moses (book of Deuteronomy), Joshua (Josh. 22–24), David (1 Chr. 28–29), Paul (Acts 20:17–38 and 2 Tim. 3:1–4:8), and Peter (2 Peter). Christian tradition remembers Jesus' seven last words on the cross, three of which appear only in John's passion narrative (19:26–27, 28, 30). Of far greater importance in John, however, is Jesus' farewell address to his disciples, beside which the farewell speeches of famous persons in the Bible and in secular history fade into relative insignificance. Here are words spoken as if Jesus' death and resurrection were already accomplished, words of a living Lord, reported as the Paraclete brought them to the memory of his disciples (14:26b), words spoken from the far side of glory.

Judas's departure (13:30) has left Jesus alone with his faithful disciples, who cannot yet be aware of what Jesus, the evangelist, and the reader already know: Jesus is about to die. According to John, Jesus anticipated the dismay of his first disciples when he was gone. His farewell discourse addresses their search for meaning in his death and their sense of loneliness after his departure–and ours as well.

INTRODUCTION (13:31–38)

Exploring the text

Verses 31–35 introduce major themes of the ensuing discourse (13:31–17:26): the cross as the supreme revelation of God's glory in Jesus Christ; Jesus' death as a departure that separates him from his disciples; love as Jesus' new commandment to disciples and as their distinguishing characteristic. "Now" in 13:31 echoes "his hour had come" in 13:1 and adds that it will be the hour of his glorification; verse 33 picks up and elaborates the introductory notice in 13:1 of Jesus' impending departure from this world to go to the Father; and the love commandment in 13:34–35 makes clear that Jesus' disciples are to love each other just as he loved his own in the world to the very end (13:1).

Verses 36–38 report a brief dialogue with Simon Peter in which Jesus predicts Peter's denial. This dialogue parallels the notice of Judas's intention to betray Jesus in 13:2 and the elaboration of that theme in 13:18–19, 21–30. Jesus knew the character of both men. These themes, betrayal and denial, point beyond the farewell discourse. They are two major elements in John's passion narrative in chapters 18 and 19.

A striking characteristic of Johannine literary style comes into play here: the tendency to move forward in spiral fashion, coming back repeatedly to a restricted number of themes and adding something new each time a theme is revisited. The following notes underscore what John 13:31–38 contributes to the development of these themes in the Gospel as a whole.

Glory (13:31–32)

The theme of **glory** was introduced in the prologue.[1] The first hint of the cross seen as exaltation is given when John 3:14 speaks of the Son of Man being lifted up so that whoever believes in him may have eternal life. A further hint appears when the evangelist explains that Jesus was speaking about the Spirit that had not yet been given, "because Jesus was not yet glorified" (7:39).

From the resurrection of Lazarus forward the Johannine understanding of glory becomes increasingly clear. Chapter 11 as a whole points ahead to the resurrection of Jesus as a revelation of God's glory. In chapter 12 Jesus announces, "The hour has come for the Son of Man to be glorified" (12:23), and prays, "Father, glorify your name" (12:28), clearly referring to the hour of his death (12:24, 27, 32–33).

John 13:31, "Now the Son of Man has been glorified, and God has been glorified in him," echoes Jesus' prayer in 12:28, "Father, glorify your name." Both texts point to Jesus' imminent death and resurrection as the event through which his true nature is revealed, and with it the inner nature of God, weighty with honor and majesty, resplendent as light. With the departure of Judas to do what he is going to do, the hour of glory has come. In 12:28b the heavenly voice spoke of glorification in the past and future tenses; in 13:31–32 past, present, and future are conflated into Jesus' "now," a moment in eternity.

Departure (13:33)

Verse 33 serves as a fulcrum for another major theme in the Fourth Gospel: Jesus' coming and going. From the announcement in the prologue that "the true light, which enlightens everyone, was coming into the world" (1:9) to Jesus' recapitulation of his ministry and the response it met in the world (12:44–50), Jesus' coming has been a recurrent motif. Jesus has come "from above" or "from heaven" (3:13, 31; 6:33, 51; 8:23); he has been sent by God (3:16, 34; 4:34; 5:23–24, 30, 36–38, 43; 6:38; 7:28–29; 8:42); he has come not to judge but to save (3:17; 12:47), so that God's sheep may have life and have it abundantly (10:10); yet his coming has effectuated a judgment (3:18–19; 9:39).

During the Festival of Booths Jesus said to hostile religious authorities, "I will be with you a little while longer, and then I am going to him who sent me. You will search for me, but you will not find me; and where I am, you cannot come" (7:33–34). At the beginning of chapter 13 the evangelist announces the fulfillment of that prediction and specifies where Jesus is going: "Jesus knew that his hour had come to depart from this world and go to the Father" (13:1), adding that Jesus knew that "he had come from God and was going to God" (13:3). In the Fourth Gospel the Last Supper marks the transition between Jesus' coming and his going. Verse 33 takes up the theme of Jesus' departure and serves as an introduction to the ensuing discourse, in which Jesus prepares the disciples for his departure.

"Little children" (13:33) is a term of endearment found only here in the canonical Gospels and seven times in the First Epistle of John. Perhaps the term originated with Jesus himself, but if so, it was remembered only in the Johannine community. It seems more likely to be another instance in which the mind and heart of Jesus are presented in the words of the evangelist. The words that follow echo verbatim what Jesus had said to his opponents in 7:33–34, but in the intimate context of 13:33 their significance is quite different. Here they express Jesus' care for those who will desperately miss his physical presence. They will look for him but cannot go with him as he returns to the Father. What can sustain them individually and as a community in his absence? This concern leads to the introduction of a third major theme of the farewell discourse.

Love (13:34–35)

Jesus commands his disciples to love one another (13:34a). He then repeats the command with a qualification that gives it focus and depth:

they are to love one another just as he has loved them (13:34b). The love of God, incarnate in the Word made flesh (3:16), is now to be embodied in Jesus' followers. They will continue to feel his nearness in the love they give to and receive from one another, even when they cannot come with him where he is going (13:33). Introduced as a "new commandment" (13:34a), this theme is repeated and developed twice in the ensuing discourse (14:15–24, 15:12) and echoed in the First Epistle (1 John 2:7; 4:7–21). By loving one another, his followers continue their communion with Christ, preserve their community, and make their witness to the world, for this is how everyone will know they are Jesus' disciples (13:35).

Overconfidence and Denial (13:36–38)

This little dialogue with Peter is linked directly to the introduction to the farewell discourse by the repetition of Jesus' prediction, "Where I am going, you cannot come/follow" (13:33c/36b). It looks beyond the discourse to the passion narrative in chapters 18 and 19 (18:15–18, 25–27 in particular), as well as to the resurrection appearance to Peter in 21:15–22 ("but you will follow afterward," 13:36c).

Peter has understood that Jesus' words about leaving them referred to his death, but he has not understood that Jesus is in full control of the situation. He seems to think Jesus will need help. He intends to prove his love for Jesus by defending him to the death. It is, in fact, a noble thing to lay down one's life for a friend, as Jesus himself will soon say to Peter and the others (15:13). But Peter overestimates his courage, and he has not understood that the way to show love to Jesus is not to play the hero but to show love to fellow disciples who are far less attractive than Jesus is. When Jesus predicted his betrayal, Peter wanted to know, "Lord, who is it?" (13:25) with no suggestion of "Is it I?" Jesus is not favorably impressed by Peter's brash promise to lay down his life (13:37). He predicts that Peter will deny him three times; but he does not dismiss Peter, nor does Peter go out into the night. He stays there to hear and ultimately to heed Jesus' words to live by.

Preaching and teaching the Word

1. What glorifies God? The shock of the Johannine interpretation of Jesus' death can be realized today if one thinks not of the cross but of a contemporary means of execution: gallows, electric chair, gas chamber, lethal injection. To picture Jesus–the one dearest to God, sent to die for the whole world–lynched and hanging from a tree is incongruous. It baffles our understanding, but John finds it glorious.

A homely illustration catches this peculiarly Johannine understanding of "glorify" as the revelation of hidden, essential nature. To the casual eye, an onion may look like any other bulb, or even like a turnip. It looks quite ordinary. But if one peels the onion, its hidden essence is revealed and, though initially strong and offensive to the eyes (it brings tears!), lends savor to a meal. Peter and the other disciples did not understand how the death of their leader as an ordinary criminal could reveal the essential nature of God (Mark 8:32), but the fourth evangelist says, "God loves like that."[2] Substituting "reveal" for "glorify" when one reads verses 31 and 32 is one way to communicate this message.

Preachers on this theme might combine the present text with portions of the great prayer in which Jesus speaks of glorifying God through finishing the work God gave him to do (17:1–5). He even prays that God will give the same glory to those who will believe in him through the word of his witnesses (17:20–24). The latter text allows an expositor to apply the theme of glory to messengers and hearers today.[3]

2. The absence of Jesus. Jesus' departure was a problem for his first disciples. Most congregations today include people for whom Jesus seems only a memory, or who have moments when he seems to have left them. Jesus' assurance to Peter, "you will follow afterward" (13:36), offers hope that absence is not the last word in their relationship, but it is cold comfort for disciples who wrestle with the sense of Jesus' absence now. It can be linked, however, with the love commandment of 13:34–35 and with Jesus' promise, not to leave his disciples orphaned (14:18, "comfortless," AV), but to come to them in the person of the Holy Spirit whom the Father will give to them (14:15–19, 25–28; 15:26; 16:4–7). Christians often experience the fulfillment of Jesus' promise of the Holy Spirit through the love of other members of the community who support them through the bleak times when they look for Jesus and cannot find him. Even when we cannot go to Jesus, Jesus can come to us through the love of other members of the beloved community.

3. The love commandment. The Gospel reading for the Fifth Sunday in Easter of year C is John 13:31–35, a paragraph that is also appended to the reading for Maundy Thursday every year. The climax and conclusion of this reading is the love commandment in verses 34–35: "Just as I have loved you, you also should love one another" (12:34b). Jesus and the evangelist thought that love was important enough to mention it fifty-eight times, four of which are in the command "love one another" (13:34a and c; 15:12a, 17) and two in the qualifying phrase, "as I have loved you" (13:34b; 15:12b). Church tradition has imagined the apostle John on his death bed saying to his gathered followers, "Little children, love one another."[4] Even if legendary, the scene captures the importance of love as the tie that binds believers together in any community that lives by Jesus' farewell words to his disciples in the Gospel (13:34–35; 15:12–17). Love is the Johannine mark of the true church, for whoever claims to abide in Jesus ought to live as Jesus lived (1 John 2:6, author's paraphrase). Nor is this only a Johannine idea. "For to this you have been called, because Christ also suffered for you, leaving you an example, so that you should follow in his steps" (1 Pet. 2:21). A sermon on this theme could point to concrete examples of love in the community addressed by the preacher.

4. On making and keeping promises. Another sermon or lesson might focus on Jesus' words to a disciple whose self-esteem outran his real potential: "Will you really lay down your life for me?" (13:38). Peter had made a promise that Jesus knew he could not keep (13:37), though Peter thought he could. His subsequent denial of Jesus (18:15–27) is bad news for those of us who say, "Oh, I would never . . . ," before we are seriously tempted to do something we know is wrong. The good news is that Peter was given a second chance to keep his promise (21:15–19), and this time he kept it (21:18–19).

The familiar hymn "O Jesus, I Have Promised"[5] is an appropriate prayer for any who realize how hard it is to keep our promises to Jesus and how faithful Jesus is to keep his promises to us.

TABLE TALK (14:1–31)

Departure and Reassurance (14:1–14)

What did they talk about after supper?

Jesus is about to depart (13:1), and he has told his disciples they cannot come with him (13:33). He has even brushed off Peter's promise to follow him to the death (13:38). What words can Jesus leave with his disciples to reassure them after he is gone?

Exploring the text

As the table talk continues, Jesus is speaking directly to Peter, Thomas, Philip, Judas (not Iscariot), and the other disciples at the Last Supper. He also speaks through the evangelist to those in his time to whose remembrance the Holy Spirit has brought all that Jesus has said (14:26), and he still speaks through the Holy Spirit to those whose minds and hearts are open to what he has to say.[1] For all who will cooperate with the evangelist and the Holy Spirit to let the text become transparent and thus hear Jesus, risen and alive, speaking directly to them, Jesus' words in John 14 become words to live by.

The Father's House (14:1–4)

The discourse begins with *two exhortations*: Don't be troubled, and do believe (14:1).

Jesus knows about troubled hearts. Three times John reports that Jesus was greatly troubled: at the death of Lazarus (11:33), at the approach of the hour of his own death (12:27), and when he contemplated betrayal by one of his own disciples (13:21). Now, when he exhorts them to believe in God as an antidote for their troubled hearts, he does so as a wounded healer who knows the effect of the medicine he prescribes.

As an antidote to the fear engendered by the prospect of his death and perhaps their own, Jesus offers to his disciples trust in God, who is trustworthy, coupled with trust in Jesus himself, whose unique relationship to God allows him to make reliable promises (14:1). **"Believe"** is one of the major themes of the Fourth Gospel. Translations that render "believe" as "trust" in 14:1 rightly identify the major note in the semantic chord here. The text is not "believe *that*" but "believe *in*." Real believing–the believing that brings peace to troubled hearts–means a relationship of trust.

Since the Greek indicative and imperative forms of "believe" are identical in the second person plural, the verb (*pisteuete*) can be translated either as a statement ("You believe") or as a command ("Believe!"). Most recent translations read both forms as imperatives, so that Jesus urges the disciples to believe in–that is, trust–God and to "believe also in me." The AV and some recent translations, however, read the first clause as an indicative, so that faith in God is assumed as a premise. The ambiguity in the Greek original allows the text to speak to readers whose faith in God is secure but who aren't so sure about Jesus, as well as to those of little faith on either score.

Jesus then offers an encouraging disclosure, "In my Father's house there are many dwelling places" (14:2a), followed by two promises as ground for the trust that he has called for. Elsewhere in John, Jesus uses "my Father's house" literally to refer to the Jerusalem temple (2:16), but here the language is figurative. The words are spatial but their significance lies in the intimate relationship of those who live together. To dwell in the Father's house is to live intimately with God in this life and the next (an extension of its meaning in Psalm 23:6).

The Greek word for "dwelling place" is the noun form of the verb "to abide." When the Authorized (King James) Version was translated in 1611, "mansion" simply meant a dwelling or an abode. Today "room," "dwelling place," and "place to live in" are all appropriate translations. "Abiding place" might be even better, in light of the development given to "abide" in chapter 15. "Many dwelling places" signifies that the Father's house includes plenty of room for all who find in Jesus the way to God.

The discourse continues with *two promises*: "I go to prepare a place for you" (14:2b) and "I will come again and will take you to myself" (14:3b). These promises state in capsule form one of the Fourth Gospel's characteristic themes: Jesus' going and coming.[2] The overall pattern in the Gospel is that Jesus has come from God and, at his death, is going to God. This text extends the action to his coming again.

The translator's choice of rendering the first promise (2b) as a question or as a statement hinges on the presence or absence of the conjunction *"that."* This word is missing from many ancient manuscripts, including the one used by translators of the AV. In light of the manuscript evidence now available, most current versions include "that" and read the sentence as a question ("If it were not so, would I have told you that I go to prepare a place for you?"). This makes sense but creates a problem, since John has not hitherto mentioned Jesus' saying anything about going to prepare a place for his disciples. The omission of the conjunction makes for a smoother reading ("If it were not so, I would have told you," AV) and does not change the thought. On either reading, there is no doubt about what Jesus is promising here: "I go to prepare a place for you." He is referring to his imminent death on the cross and his return to the Father (13:1, 33). In Johannine theology Jesus' death, resurrection, and return are a single saving act through which the Lamb of God takes away the sin of the world (1:29, 36), makes his disciples clean (13:10; 15:3), and prepares for them an abiding place with the Father.

The second promise is that Jesus will come back and take his disciples to himself, so they can always be where he is (14:3). See "Preaching and teaching the Word" for four ways of interpreting this coming again, all suggested in the Fourth Gospel.

Continuing the theme of his departure, Jesus adds, "Where I am going you know the way" (14:4, author's literal translation). Some early manuscripts smooth out this rough sentence to read, "You know where I am going and you know the way," as in the AV. The word "place" does not appear at this point in the Greek text but is supplied in many current translations to make for easier reading, echoing the place mentioned in verses 2–3. It also states explicitly what Thomas understood Jesus to mean, judging by the question that follows (14:5). Jesus speaks of the Father's house as a place to which he goes and from whence he will come, but this "house" is figurative language for "where God lives."

The verb "to know" controls the thought of verses 4–7. In the Hebrew

Bible and in the Gospel of John "know" often expresses an intimate relationship rather than cognition.

Thomas's Question (14:5–7)

Four times in the farewell discourse a disciple interrupts with a question that advances and deepens Jesus' teaching through a brief exchange: Simon Peter (13:36–38), Thomas (14:5–7), Philip (14:8–10), and Judas (not Iscariot, 14:22–24). These exchanges make of chapter 14 not just a monologue but table talk, and each introduces a significant word to live by.

The exchange between Thomas and Jesus is another example of the Fourth Gospel's use of misunderstanding to allow Jesus to reveal a deeper truth. Thomas's objection in verse 5a uses "know" in its usual, cognitive sense, and his question in verse 5b gives to "way" its ordinary literal meaning. In verse 6 Jesus opens up new dimensions in the term "way," and in verse 7 he uses "know" in the sense of intimate personal relationship, analogous to the sense that he had given to "believe" in 14:1.

The significant affirmation in Jesus' response to Thomas is: "I am the way, and the truth, and the life" (14:6a). This is one of the seven **"I Am" sayings** with a defining term in the Gospel of John. Even more explicitly than the other six, this one presupposes the texts in which Jesus says simply and absolutely, "I am." The claim of a unique relation to and identity with God, implicit in those other texts (e.g., 8:58; 13:19), is stated with growing clarity in this passage (14:6–11).

Used in only two passages in John (here and in 1:23), **"way"** is prominent in the Synoptic Gospels as they tell of Jesus' teaching his disciples "along the way," and in Acts and the Epistles, where the term designates Christianity as a way of life–Jesus' way. The only times John uses "way" is in connection with one of the major themes of this Gospel: Jesus' coming from God and going to God. In canonical context and in light of Jesus' final command to Peter, "Follow me" (21:19), readers may rightly understand Jesus' claim as an invitation to follow in his way. Here, however, Jesus is identified as the way to the Father because he and the Father are one (10:30). This affirmation is clarified by two other terms that are characteristic of Jesus in the Fourth Gospel: truth and life.

Jesus and the evangelist sometimes use **"truth"** in its ordinary sense of reliable correspondence with objective reality, but its far more frequent and significant sense in the Fourth Gospel is in reference to the absolute truth that is the reality of God. Truth in this sense is introduced in the prologue ("truth came through Jesus Christ," 1:17) and illuminated by sayings like Jesus' word to the Jews who had believed in him, "If you continue in my word, you are truly my disciples; and you will know the truth, and the truth will make you free" (8:32). The present text (14:6) identifies Jesus as divine truth incarnate, and the exchange between Jesus and Pilate juxtaposes the ordinary meaning of truth with its pregnant, Johannine meaning of what is really real (18:37–38). This meaning is personal: Jesus Christ is not only a unique channel of truth; he himself is truth. To know the truth that sets us free, then, does not mean to know the formal truth of the facts in question; it means a concrete encounter with the person of Jesus Christ and following in his way. Knowing the truth means life in the Father's house all along the way.

Archbishop William Temple stated well the Johannine understanding of truth. "The ultimate truth is not a system of propositions grasped by perfect intelligence, but is a Personal Being apprehended in the only way in which persons are ever fully apprehended, that is, by love. The Incarnation is not a condescension to our infirmities. . . . It is the only way in which divine truth can be expressed, not because of our infirmity but because of its own nature. What is personal can be expressed only in a person."[3]

There are two Greek words which are translated by the English word **"life"** in the Gospel of John: *psyche* and *zoe.* John uses *psyche* about as often and in much the same way as the Synoptic Gospels do, except that the expression "lay down one's life" is used only in John. In John 12:25, a parallel to Mark 8:35, *psyche* is juxtaposed with *zoe,* the other word for life, in a way that shows the distinction between the two. John makes two significant changes to this well-known saying of Jesus: instead of losing and saving one's life or self as in the Synoptics (Mark 8:35; Matt. 16:25; Luke 9:24), Jesus speaks in John of loving and hating one's life (*psyche*) in this world and adds a significant promise: eternal life (*zoe*).

The characteristically Johannine word for life, *zoe,* is used thirty-six times in the Fourth Gospel, seventeen of which are in the expression "eternal life." In John, the functional equivalent of entering the kingdom of God is possessing eternal life through believing in and union with Jesus Christ. The importance of "life" in the Fourth Gospel is seen in the statement of the purpose for writing the Gospel (20:31); in the prologue, which enunciates the major themes of the Gospel (1:4); in the best-known verse in John (3:16); and in some of the most memorable of Jesus' words to live by: "I am the bread of life" (6:35, 48); "I came that they may have life, and have it abundantly" (10:10); "I am the resurrection and the life" (11:25); plus the present text, "I am the way, the truth, and the life" (14:6a).

Jesus has a *psyche* and he gives it up to death (10:11, 15, 17), but his *zoe* is not interrupted by death. Its continuation is what Jesus means when he speaks of "going to the **Father**." Truth and life are incarnate in him during his earthly life, and they are only enhanced by his death and resurrection, which open the way for his disciples to share in this abundant, eternal life. Thus Jesus' claim in 14:6 is also a promise, and it implies an invitation to disciples then and now to walk in his way, to know his truth, and to live his life. Paraphrased as a word to live by, Jesus says to disciples today, "I am the way to God, the truth about God, and the very life of God lived in and through you, my disciples."

Jesus then adds, "No one comes to the Father except through me" (14:6b). The intimacy of walking with God in Jesus Christ has an exclusive quality, like Israel's walk with the God who would not tolerate the worship of other gods, and like life together in a faithful marriage whose partners forswear intimacy with all others. Exclusiveness is basic to the law of Moses and to the wedding vows of Christian couples. It is set forth as a word to live by in Jesus' word to Thomas.

This claim that the only true knowledge of God is in and through Jesus Christ has become a stumbling block to generous spirits in a pluralistic world. Can it be understood in a way that is faithful to Jesus Christ and also true to the inclusive picture of Jesus elsewhere in John and the other Gospels?

At least four avenues of approach to this question are available to the interpreter:

1. The text is directed to Jesus' disciples: for Christians, there is no other way to come to God. Other religions are neither affirmed nor rejected here.

2. "No one comes to the *Father,*" that is, to the intimate relation with God that Jesus enjoyed, except through Jesus. The text does not exclude the possibility of other ways of knowing God, but no other is as full, as deep, and as warm as the knowledge of God in Jesus Christ.

3. "No one comes to the Father except through *me,*" that is, except through the Father/Son/Holy Spirit reality that Jesus embodied while he was in the flesh and that the Holy Spirit leads believers to recognize in Christlike individuals of other religions or of no religion as "the true light, which enlightens everyone" (1:9).

4. Accept what this verse affirms about Jesus as the way, truth, and life, but reject what it denies about other approaches to God. Committed to Jesus' way, remain agnostic about other ways, realizing that God is greater than the measure of our minds. Leave to God the acceptance or not of others' credentials.

Not all of these suggestions are mutually exclusive, nor are they exhaustive. They are meant to be suggestive as each interpreter listens carefully to what the risen Lord says in both parts of John 14:6, guided by the Spirit whom Jesus promised would come to guide his disciples into all the truth (16:13).

Verse 7 is transitional. In verses 4–6 Jesus has spoken to his disciples about knowing him as the way to the Father. In verse 7 he adds that to know and see Jesus is to know and see the Father. The theme of Jesus' unique relationship to God, which lay at the heart of his controversy with "the Jews" (5:18; 6:41–42; 8:19, 57–59; 10:30–31, 33), is further explored in verses 8–11.

The "you" in verse 7 is plural, as it is in verse 4. Thomas speaks for all Jesus' disciples, and Jesus' response is for all his disciples: "If you know me" (and you do), "you will know my Father also." This first part of the verse is a promise: If you know me as the way to God, you will discover that in following this way you are already in the company of God, the "I Am." The second part seems to point ahead ("From now on"), but it includes verbs in the present and past tense. Disciples know God the moment they understand that to know Jesus is to know the Father and realize that they have already seen God. In the narrative, "From now on" refers to the event of Jesus' exaltation through death and resurrection. In the reader's experience, "From now on" refers to the "Aha!" moment of insight in which Jesus' words about the truth become Truth incarnate through a personal encounter with him.

Philip's Request (14:8–11)

Philip's intervention, like that of Thomas (14:5–7), exemplifies the frequent use of a misunderstanding in order to let Jesus point to a deeper meaning. When Philip says, "Lord, show us the Father," he has in mind "see" with the physical eye. He also gives voice to a common human yearning: Just let me see God; show me, and I can believe and be satisfied.

The significant word, "see," appears in Jesus' response to Philip: "Whoever has seen me has seen the Father" (14:9). Jesus' reply (14:9–11) clarifies Philip's misunderstanding of what it means to see God. He shows that the seeing of which he speaks (14:9b) is a deep kind of knowing (14:9a; see v. 7), a knowing so closely related to believing (14:10–11) as to be almost synonymous with it. The interplay of seeing, believing, and knowing is a pervasive theme in the Fourth Gospel. The link between seeing and believing has been noted frequently (1:47–51; 6:22–34, 40; 9:1–41; 12:44–45). It becomes prominent again at the end of the Gospel (20:8, 25,

29). **Believe** and know are sometimes used as virtual synonyms (6:69; 17:7–8), and all three terms are conjoined in 3:11–12 and 19:35, as well as in the present text. The evangelist is not simply playing with words. Seeing, believing, and knowing God are all based on the concrete, physical works that Jesus has done in Philip's presence. To this companion of the road and table, Jesus says, "If you cannot believe that I am one with God as a metaphysical proposition, you can at least believe me for who I am, because the remarkable things I do show that I am in the Father and the Father is in me" (author's paraphrase). He invites an intimate disciple to recognize in him the functional identity with God that "the Jews" could not see.[4]

The kind of knowing of which Jesus speaks springs from seeing with eyes of faith. Such seeing and knowing is a kind of believing that issues in doing, as becomes evident in the following verses.

The Promise of Greater Works (14:12–14)

Jesus' reply to Philip ends with two remarkable promises to believers, the second of which is repeated for emphasis. Believers will do even greater works than Jesus does, because he is going to the Father (14:12) and he will do whatever they ask in his name (14:13–14). Both promises are predicated on believing in Jesus (see 6:28–29). They bring to a close a unit that begins with the exhortation, "Believe in God, believe also in me" (14:1), and ends with, "If you do not [believe that I am in the Father and the Father in me], then believe me because of the works themselves" (14:11). Jesus' union with the Father empowers him to do the works and now he promises that believers will do even greater works because he is going to the Father (14:12). The promise is clarified in Jesus' subsequent words about the Holy Spirit (14:16–20; 16:7) and the fruitful lives of those who abide in him (15:4–8). The promise is made to believers who show their love for him by keeping his commandments (14:15). The promised works will be greater not in quality but in their extent, when Jesus sends disciples into the world, just as the Father had sent him (20:21).

The reiterated promise to do whatever believers ask (14:13–14) belongs to a cluster of like promises in John (15:7, 16; 16:23–24) and in the Synoptic Gospels (Matt. 7:7–8//Luke 11:9–10; Matt. 18:19; Matt. 21:22//Mark 11:24). Most of these formulations of the promise are accompanied by one or another condition, and faith is the implicit or explicit condition in all of them. In the present text (John 14:13–14) two significant expressions qualify the promise: "in my name," which appears in both verses, and "so that the Father may be glorified in the Son" in verse 13. The promise applies to requests that are consistent with the character of Jesus and grow out of the believer's unity with him in heart, mind, and will–requests whose fulfillment will result in God's glory being seen in Jesus Christ.

Preaching and teaching the Word

The Gospel text for the Fifth Sunday of Easter of year A (14:1–14) contains several memorable texts that will preach (14:1–3, 6, 9, 12–14) because they are words to live by. When Jesus informed his disciples that he was going to leave them and they could not come along (13:33), their response was like that of children playing on the floor who look up, see their parents putting on coats and hats, and ask three questions: Where are you going? Can we go too? Then who is going to stay with us?[5] These are the questions that Jesus addresses throughout the farewell discourse, especially at its beginning when he says, "Do not let your hearts be troubled," . . . "and do not let them be afraid" (14:1, 27).

1. A word for troubled hearts. These words are most often heard at funerals and appropriately so, for at the departure of loved ones their absence is felt most poignantly, and those left behind may also fear the thought of their own death. But the text is appropriate any time a Christian feels keenly the absence of Jesus Christ or is for any reason lonely or afraid. Jesus' word for troubled hearts is "believe." The theme is announced in 14:1 and backed up by words of reassurance in the remainder of the chapter. In John 14:2–3 Jesus says what his disciples are to believe, but more importantly he says whom we are to believe in (14:1b; 7–11) and what power is promised to believers (14:12–14). Fred Craddock's image of the children on the floor would serve well for a sermon or lesson embracing everything from 13:31 through chapter 14. A sermon on "believe" in 14:1–7 (or 1–11) would not be satisfied with rational exposition of what disciples are to believe, but would aim at inspiring trust in the One who invites us to believe in him.

2. "My Father's house." The expression "my Father's house" (14:2) elicits in popular culture a picture of heaven as a place where good people go after they die. The concept is as superficial as it is pervasive. The spatial words "house" and "place" in this text (14:2) are metaphors for life together as family, and the "rooms" or "dwelling places" of which Jesus speaks are closely related to his invitation to abide in him (15:4–9). A well-known African American spiritual says, "When I get to heaven gonna put on my shoes." The deeper meaning of the text is that Jesus' death opens a way for believers to live as free people in intimate fellowship with God on both sides of the great divide. The relation of the future and present understandings of heaven for John is not either/or; it is both/and. The

Holy Spirit can use a sermon on this text to help disciples—even those who may feel like street people—to claim their heritage now.

3. "I will come again." The common understanding of Christ's second coming can also be greatly enriched by John's uncommon eschatology, using "I will come again" (14:3) as a point of departure.

The first coming again of Jesus to his disciples as reported in the Fourth Gospel is in three resurrection appearances: on Easter night (20:19–23), a week later in the same house (20:26–29), and later by the Sea of Tiberias (21:1–23). In these scenes Jesus deals with doubt and sends his disciples out rather than gathering them to himself.

A second way Jesus comes again is in the person of the Holy Spirit (Paraclete, Advocate, Spirit of truth), a coming promised variously in 14:18–19, 26; 15:26; and 16:7–20. In several of these texts the Spirit is an emissary, sent from the Father in Jesus' name (14:26), or from Jesus and the Father (15:26), or from Jesus alone (16:7), but his coming fulfills at least in part Jesus' promise to disciples, then and ever since, not to leave them orphaned but to come to them (14:18).

A third understanding of this promise applies it to each individual disciple at the hour of death. This interpretation combines 14:3b with Jesus' word to Martha at the death of Lazarus (11:25–26). It appropriately makes of this promise a word to die by as well as a word to live by.

The ultimate fulfillment of this promise, however, awaits the coming of Jesus "at the last day," when, as Son of Man, he will raise up believers and the world will be judged by the word he has spoken (6:39, 40, 44, 54; 11:24; 12:48). This future eschatology, characteristic of Paul's letters and the Synoptic Gospels, appears explicitly in John only in these texts, but it is implicit here (14:3) and at 17:24 and 21:22.

4. "I am the way, the truth and the life." "The way" is an important word in many of the world's religions and philosophies, of which the Tao of Lao Tzu is the most prominent example. In a memorable "I am" saying (14:6a), Jesus addresses the universal human search for the right way among a maze of alternatives, for truth among conflicting claims, and for a life that is worth living. Here Jesus says that the answer to our quest is not to be found in principles but in a person, a person who has come to show us the way by being the way.

Teachers who wish to explore the meaning of the three terms in this unforgettable word to live by will find help in the exegetical notes above. Preachers might choose just one of them and develop the personal and affective dimensions of the metaphor, drawing upon poems, hymns, and personal experience to proclaim who Jesus is for us.

5. "No one comes to the Father except through me." Roberta Bondi remembers the essential message of the fundamentalist church in which she was raised as, "Only believe that God loves you or he'll send you to hell forever."[6] Perhaps the best way to approach John 14:6b without giving this distorted understanding of its gospel message is in a teaching situation. There the four possible approaches to this exclusive text suggested in the exegetical notes (p. 182) can be presented, weighed, and discussed. Anyone preaching on this text should remember that Jesus said, "Except through me," not "except through the Christian church." Christ has other sheep not of this fold (John 10:16). An irenic Jewish scholar has said, "You don't have to hate the Jews to love Jesus." Indeed! On the contrary, if you love Jesus you will love Jews (and Muslims, Hindus, Buddhists, and animists) as God does and be eager to share with them the best thing you know.

6. Seeing and knowing God. The link between seeing and knowing in John 14:7–9 is exemplified when Christ is active today in situations and persons that allow us to see God. Alternatively, the focus might be on stories about what is hidden in plain view: Poe's *Purloined Letter*, the tourist standing at the base of a well-known skyscraper and asking the policeman on the corner where it is ("Look up!"); Tolstoi's cobbler who expected a visit from Christ and failed to recognize him in those whom he helped that day.

7. Greater works. A sermon on Jesus' promise that his disciples will do the works that he does, and even greater ones than these (14:11–14), might address the skepticism of those who mutter beneath their breath, "Surely you jest!" The promise appears elsewhere in John and in the Synoptic Gospels with other conditions attached, but the two qualifiers in the present text are that the request be made in Jesus' name and that its granting would manifest and exemplify the glory of the Father in the Son. To pray in Jesus' name goes far beyond the customary formula used at the end of Christian prayers; it means prayer growing out of the kind of union with Jesus to which "believe" refers in the Fourth Gospel. Jesus promises to answer such requests. Preachers should think of cases in which the promise has been fulfilled, drawing examples from life. Consider the Red Cross, Habitat for Humanity, communities of service like The Open Door in Atlanta, Georgia, and miraculous healings in which Christ works through committed disciples using the tools of modern science.

8. Teaching the passage as a whole. Participants in a teaching session could identify *words to live by* in John 14:1–14, post them on the wall, and share experiences that led them to view a given text as a word to live by. Through such sharing the Spirit of the living Christ may speak these words again to receptive ears and hearts.

The Promise of the Holy Spirit (14:15–31)

Jesus has spoken of going to the Father and of being the way to the Father (14:6, 12). Now he lays the foundation for a continuing community of his disciples by urging them to keep his commandments and by promising his continuing presence through the Holy Spirit (14:15–27). For the evangelist's community then and for readers today, the text reveals how Jesus' disciples can know him as risen and present even after he has died and left this world. The Holy Spirit assures us that Jesus is not really dead, nor is he really gone.

Exploring the text

Viewed verse by verse this text (14:15–31) appears somewhat disorganized, but like a painting viewed best from across the room, its individual strokes form a discernable pattern when seen as a whole. Its main feature is the promise of the Holy Spirit or Paraclete (14:26), inextricably tied to loving Jesus and keeping his commandments. These themes are announced in the opening verses, in which Jesus invites his disciples to show their love for him by keeping his commandments (14:15) and promises to ask his Father to send them the Holy Spirit (14:16).

The Paraclete (14:16–20)

Paraclete *(parakletos),* a key term in the text, is hard to represent in English. It appears four times during Jesus' final conversation with his disciples (John 14:16–17, 26–28; 15:26–27; 16:7–15) and nowhere else in the New Testament. Two of these occurrences are in the present unit (14:16, 26), where it is variously translated as Comforter (AV), Counselor (RSV, NIV), Advocate (NRSV, REB), and Helper (TEV), or left in Greek as Paraclete (NAB, NJB). Called the "Holy Spirit" in verse 26, the Paraclete is referred to as the Spirit of truth in three other instances (14:17; 15:26; 16:13). On the basis of a detailed examination of what the Fourth Gospel says about him, Raymond Brown concludes: "John presents the Paraclete as the Holy Spirit in a special role, namely, as the personal presence of Jesus in the Christian while Jesus is with the Father. . . . The one whom John calls 'another Paraclete' is another Jesus. . . . the Paraclete is the presence of Jesus when Jesus is absent. . . . Jesus will be in heaven with the Father while the Paraclete is on earth in the disciples. . . . the Paraclete [is] the continued post-resurrectional presence of Jesus with his disciples."[1]

The use of "Paraclete" in the Fourth Gospel shows how believers in Jesus who looked to the Beloved Disciple as the eyewitness par excellence (19:35; 21:20–24) faced two urgent problems. First, with the death of the last human link to Jesus, they felt orphaned. The Paraclete (the Holy

Spirit) becomes the one who teaches them everything, reminding them of all that Jesus has said (14:26), who dwells within them as he had in the eyewitnesses, and who declares the things to come (16:13). They need not depend on a succession of human witnesses for their connection to Jesus; the Paraclete is a living link to him. This perspective informed the evangelist in articulating Jesus' teachings throughout the Fourth Gospel. It can inform their interpretation today, removing anxiety about which words are to be attributed to Jesus and which to the evangelist, as well as easing discomfort with apparent anachronisms when they appear.[2]

The other problem that gave rise to the concept of the Paraclete was the delay of Jesus' second coming, which the Johannine community had expected before the death of the Beloved Disciple (21:23). The Fourth Gospel answers this problem by treating judgment, divine sonship, and eternal life as experiences that are already realities of the Christian life.[3] Furthermore, "I will not leave you orphaned," says Jesus; "I am coming to you. In a little while the world will no longer see me, but you will see me; because I live, you also will live" (14:18–19). Jesus promises that after his departure to be with the Father he will return to his disciples in a way that will enable them also to live the abundant life that Jesus intended for his own (10:10). In the person of the Paraclete, Jesus is present within and among all believers.

This understanding of the coming again of Jesus Christ transforms the meaning of the expression "on that day" in the Fourth Gospel. In many texts of the prophets, apocalyptic writings, and the New Testament, "on that day" refers to God's intervention at the end of history to judge and to save. In Mark 2:20, it refers to the time when Jesus is no longer present in the flesh and the believing community is learning to live with the sense of his absence. In John, however, Jesus says, "On that day you will know that I am in my Father, and you in me, and I in you" (14:20), referring to the time when believers will live on the strength of Jesus' presence as the Paraclete. John alone is predicated on an eschatology of immanence, for believers know "that I am in my Father, and you in me, and I in you" (14:20). Jesus also says of the Paraclete's coming, "Those who love me will keep my word, and my Father will love them, and we will come to them and make our home with them" (14:23). Mutual indwelling is a major theme of Jesus' table talk with his disciples, often expressed by "abide in" or "remain in" (*menein en*).[4]

Love Me, Keep My Commandments (14:15, 21–24)

The promise of the Holy Spirit is introduced by a conditional sentence about loving Jesus (14:15), an idea that is repeated twice in the following verses (14:21, 23). Jesus asks his disciples to show their love for him by keeping his commandments (14:15); he says keeping his commandments shows who it is that really loves him (14:21); and he affirms that those who love him will keep his word, while whoever does not love him does not keep his words (14:23–24). There is no significant distinction in meaning between "word" (singular) in verses 23 and 24b and "words" (plural) in verse 24a or "commandments" (plural) in verses 15 and 21. The only explicit commandment Jesus gives to his disciples in the Fourth Gospel is the "new commandment" given in the introduction to this lengthy conversation: "Love one another" (13:34). Now he adds to that the implicit command to love him and so share in the mutual love of Jesus and God the Father (14:21b, 23).

Although love for Jesus and each other is presented as the condition within which the promise of Jesus' presence in the person of the Holy Spirit will be fulfilled, it would be a mistake to conclude that a desire to receive the Holy Spirit is the reason disciples should love Jesus. They should love Jesus in order to enjoy his living presence and a quality of life that will not be evident to the world, but will be evident to Jesus' disciples.

The evangelist reports [the other] Judas's question[5] in order to pursue it with his readers: "In what way can disciples see Jesus when the world cannot?" (14:22, author's paraphrase). In answer Jesus pulls together the disciple's love for Jesus shown by keeping his word (or commandments), the Father's love for the disciple, and the coming of Jesus and the Father to make their home (*mone,* abode) with him or her (14:23). The world can know nothing of this mutual indwelling of Father, Son, and believer, but believers can and do. That is how they know Jesus, as they keep the commandment of love for Jesus and for each other.

Stepping back from the text, one can see that in 14:15–17 it is the Paraclete/Advocate/Spirit who will come to be with the disciples forever. In 14:18–21 it is Jesus who will come to live in the disciples and reveal himself to them. In 14:23–24 it is the Father who will come with Jesus to make a dwelling place within the disciples. All of these indwellings are thought of as accomplished through and in the Paraclete, who is the presence of Jesus while Jesus is absent, and all depend upon loving Jesus and keeping his commandments. These commandments are not simply words of Jesus; they come from the Father, who sent his Word to live with, among, and within us (14:24; 1:1–2, 10, 12, 14). His words are words to live by.

Recapitulation and Promise of Peace (14:25–31)

"I have said these things to you" (14:25) is a formula that recurs frequently in Jesus' last discourse with his disciples as a way of summarizing his preceding teaching (15:11; 16:1, 4, 33), usually followed by an explanation of why he has said it. In the present instance Jesus says a few sentences later, "I have told you this before it occurs, so that when it does occur, you may believe" (14:29, echoing 13:19). The evangelist wants readers to remember the essential points in Jesus' farewell words to his disciples in order to confirm their belief in him.

Repetition is a great aid to memory, and most of this concluding paragraph repeats ideas already expressed in the conversation that began at 13:12. Sometimes, however, an earlier idea is clarified by expansion, and sometimes something quite new appears.

Verse 26 expands the promise of the Paraclete by naming him the Holy Spirit and specifying his chief function: teaching and reminding disciples of all that Jesus said.

The promise of peace (14:27a) is an important new element. Jesus takes up the customary word of greeting upon arrival and of farewell upon departure and, by speaking of it as "my peace," makes of it his legacy to his disciples. If it is not what the world counts as legacy, neither is it given as the world gives (14:27b)–leaving to others what one has finished using or what one can do without. Jesus' peace comes at the cost of laying down his life when life still lay before him. It is himself he gives, and that is not the world's way of giving.

A significant expansion appears when Jesus adds to the opening words of this chapter, "Do not let your hearts be troubled," the further exhortation, "and do not let them be afraid" (14:27c). This marks the first good stopping place for Jesus' last discourse, since 14:1–27 would make a coherent unit. Any exposition of the first part of the chapter could well include 14:27, even if many intervening verses are omitted.

A new element is found in Jesus' observation that if his disciples really loved him, they would be glad about his departure rather than sad, since, from his perspective, going to the Father is returning to the greater one (14:28b). This is at the same time an expansion of earlier themes: Jesus' impending departure (7:33–36; 8:21–22; 13:33; 14:3, 28a) and the glory Jesus had shared with God in the beginning (1:1, 14).

Jesus' statement that "the ruler of this world" is coming (14:30) mirrors his prediction that this ruler is about to be driven out (12:31). He is identified in 13:2 as the devil, who had already put it into the heart of Judas to betray Jesus, and in 13:27 as Satan, who entered into Judas after he received the piece of bread from Jesus. Here, Jesus affirms that the ruler of this world has no power over him, since his impending death is to occur not because of the superior power of Satan but because of Jesus' obedience to the Father's command. This idea is not new, for it picks up the earlier affirmation that Jesus lays down his life of his own free will, in accord with God's will (10:17–18; see also 19:11).

A new element is added in the next verse: "I do as the Father has commanded me, so that the world may know that I love the Father" (14:31). According to Raymond Brown, this is the only verse in the New Testament that affirms that Jesus loves God.[6] Jesus demonstrates love for God by all that is reported of him in the gospel tradition, but he does not talk about it. Even here, it is by what he does that the world is to know that Jesus loves the Father.

Jesus' closing words in this chapter, "Rise, let us be on our way," suggest that this must at one time have marked the end of his table talk with the disciples, since the logical sequel, "After Jesus had spoken these words, he went out with his disciples," do not appear until 18:1. The hint is supported by verse 30, in which Jesus says he will no longer talk much with them (one Syriac version even leaves out "much") and then, according to the present form of the Gospel, continues to talk for three chapters before arising to go out. On the basis of these indications, chapter 15 is treated below as an expanded discourse and chapter 16 as a recapitulation.

Preaching and teaching the Word

1. Seeing Jesus. How can anyone who has left this world and is no longer seen or known by the people in it nevertheless be seen and known by his disciples (14:19–22)? Jesus' answer (14:23–24) to this question does not speak of heavenly visions or divine raptures, though through the ages many of Christ's disciples have experienced these. The Gospel of John, and this chapter in particular, has always and still does offer to many a thirsty heart the assurance of God's reality, nearness, and love, which leads to moments of insight and communion with the source of all life and light. The text honors experiences in which Jesus and the Father come to those who love them, but the text points to a love that keeps Jesus' word(s), the first of which is to love one another with a practical love (13:12–17, 34–35). In a community of disciples who show their love for Jesus and one another by acts of lowly service, Christians see Jesus in others, and others see Jesus in them. For John it is the basic way to see Jesus.

2. The promised Spirit. The text promises a divine indwelling of the Advocate, the Spirit of Truth, that results in a way of life lived in love. Some might doubt the reliability of the promise, since the Spirit, like the wind, is not visible (3:8). Unlike the wind, however, we cannot check on the Spirit by holding up a moist finger. Instead, we can know the Spirit by watching for signs of Christ's action in the lives of others and in our own heart. We can also, on the basis of Christ's promise, pray expectantly for the Spirit to breathe on us and spring up within us. Then, every time we feel the Spirit moving in our heart, we can get up and do what Jesus, through the Spirit, commands.

3. The meaning of love. Various portions of this unit are proposed as the Gospel reading for the Sixth Sunday in Easter of years A and B, and for the Day of Pentecost in year C. The opening sentence of this passage, "If you love me, you will keep my commandments" (14:15), offers one among many opportunities to preach a sermon or teach a lesson on the meaning of love in the Fourth Gospel. For John as well as Paul, love is what "binds everything together in perfect harmony" (Col. 3:14; compare 1 Cor. 13 and Eph. 4:2, 15–16). Only twice in the Fourth Gospel does Jesus directly ask his disciples to love him: here (14:15, 23–24) and in his dialogue with Peter after the resurrection (21:15–17). When love is commanded elsewhere in John, the obligation is to love one another in the community of disciples (13:34–35; 15:12, 17). Repeatedly, however, in the present text (14:15–16, 21, 23) and throughout the Fourth Gospel, love is described as the intimate relationship that binds together Jesus, God the Father, and all who love Jesus and keep his commandments.

4. Keeping Jesus' commandments. The alternation between keeping Jesus' commandments (plural) and keeping his word (singular) or words (plural) noted in the exegesis above raises the question, What commandments are we to keep? A correct but ambiguous answer is, "The love commandment." The answer is correct because the commandment to love lies at the heart of Jesus' teaching in all four Gospels. It is ambiguous because in the Synoptics, when Jesus is asked to name the greatest commandment, he names two: love God, and love your neighbor (Matt. 22:34–40//Mark 12:28–34//Luke 10:25–28). In the Fourth Gospel, however, the two love commandments are these: love one another (13:34–35; 15:12, 17), and love me (implied in 14:15, 23–24; 21:15–17).

The plural form "commandments" in the reciprocal statements about loving Jesus and keeping his commandments (14:15, 21) resists all efforts to reduce Jesus' will for his disciples to a single word. A sermon on "Keep my commandments" in John 14:15a would surely concentrate on loving Jesus and our fellow Christians, a command that in some cases is just as difficult as loving our enemies, but the text invites expanding the command to include all the commandments in the teachings of Jesus in all four Gospels, plus words of the Lord reported elsewhere in the New Testament. Such a reading includes all our neighbors and even our enemies in a world that has become a global village. Jesus' love commandment involves a whole way of life that is spelled out by specific teachings in all four Gospels.

5. The promise of peace. One of the memorable words to live by is "Peace

I leave with you; my peace I give to you" (14:27a). This word puts Jesus' gift of peace in the form of a bequest. This legacy of Jesus, delivered to us in the person of his promised Holy Spirit, makes his opening exhortation possible to attain: "Do not let your hearts be troubled, and do not let them be afraid" (14:27b). If the intricacies of the relationship of Father, Son, and Paraclete are best handled in a teaching situation, the gracious promise of peace can be most effectively conveyed by pastors who know their flock's need of it and preachers who have experienced it in their own lives. Such pastors and preachers will put down this commentary and read their own hearts and those of their congregation.

EXPANDED DISCOURSE (15:1–16:4a)

Chapter 15 is an uninterrupted monologue, most of which reiterates and expands themes already introduced in 13:31–14:31. Readers may be put off by the repetitive nature of the material, but these texts were meant to be read aloud, and repetition is an important aid to memory. The expansion includes Jesus' final **"I Am" saying**, "I am the true vine" (15:1), and weaves into that powerful image major themes of the last discourse expressed in memorable words to live by. One new theme is introduced: the world's hatred (15:18–25; 16:1–4a).

The chapter can be divided in several ways, recognizing that 15:1–17 is a true unit which can be subdivided at verse 6, 8, or 11. The following notes follow the divisions of the Revised Common Lectionary for the benefit of lectionary preachers.

The Allegory of the Vine and Branches (15:1–8)

Exploring the text

This passage and the metaphor of the sheepfold (10:1–18) are the closest John comes to the parables of Jesus in the Synoptic Gospels. The evangelist calls the sheepfold metaphor a "figure of speech" (*paroimia*, 10:6; see notes on that verse). The present text is an allegory in which the vine is Jesus, the vinegrower is God the Father, and the branches are Jesus' disciples. When the disciples later observe, "now you are speaking plainly, not in any figure of speech" (16:29), they are probably alluding to the figures of speech in chapters 10 and 15.

Behind the image of Jesus as the true vine lies the rich tradition of the vine as a symbol for Israel, enshrined in the Scripture, art, and liturgy of the Jewish people. Israel is God's vineyard (Isa. 5:1–7; 27:2–6), a vine God brought out of Egypt and planted in the land God cleared (Ps.

80:8–13). It was a choice vine that became wild (Jer. 2:21), a luxuriant vine that yielded abundant fruit to false gods (Hos. 10:1–2). Israel's faithless branches had to be stripped away (Jer. 5:10), its remnant gleaned (Jer. 6:9), and its withered stem consumed by fire (Ezek. 19:10–14). The prophets' thunder against the fruitless vine did not, however, obliterate the image of Israel as God's vine, an image that appeared on coins from the Maccabean period and adorned the entrance to the sanctuary in Herod's temple, sculpted in gold. The vine could also symbolize Wisdom (Sir. 24:17–19) and the Messiah (2 Bar. 39:7).[1]

The text does not specify what kind of vine is intended, but the referent was self-evident to Jesus' disciples and to John's readers. From the first mention of a phenomenal yield of grapes in the land of promise (Num. 13:20–24) to Jesus' allusion to "the fruit of the vine" in the account of the institution of the Lord's Supper (Mark 14:25 and parallels), the basic role of vineyards, grapes, and wine in everyday life in Palestine is clear. Three of Jesus' parables are set in vineyards: the wicked tenants (Mark 12:1–12 and parallels, in which the vineyard represents Israel), the laborers in the vineyard (Matt. 20:1–16), and the two sons (Matt. 21:28–32). As in all these other texts, the vine used as a symbol is a grape vine. For John, the **truth** is that what is symbolized is no longer Israel but Jesus himself. He is the true vine.

Against this background, Jesus' final "I Am" saying (15:1, 5) carried climactic force to John's first readers. Whereas they had previously counted on their being Israelites to assure their living relationship to God, Jesus' claim to be the true vine means that he is the vital link with God, fulfilling what Sirach affirms about Wisdom and what 2 Baruch later affirms of the Messiah.

In this Johannine figure of speech, God the Father is the vinegrower, a word also translated as "husbandman" (AV), "vinedresser" (RSV), and "gardener" (NIV, TEV, REB). The Greek word itself simply means farmer or cultivator (*georgos*, "earth-worker," from which we get the proper name George). In this text the farmer both owns and cares for the vineyard, functions that are sometimes separated in other biblical references to vines and vineyards.

The Father's work as caretaker is twofold, expressed through a play on words in Greek. The vinegrower removes (*airei*) or cuts off branches that bear no fruit and prunes (*kathairei*) or cuts clean those that bear fruit so they will bear more (15:2). The pun is played out further when, in the next verse, Jesus tells his disciples that they are clean (*katharos*) or pruned by the word he has spoken to them (15:3).

The idea of being "cleansed by the word" makes sense if "word" here means Jesus' whole teaching, as in 5:38. It is synonymous with "words" in 15:7. In both cases, "Jesus and his revelation are virtually interchangeable, for he is incarnate revelation, the Word."[2] As in 13:10–11 (see notes, p. 166), disciples are made clean through believing the Word that Jesus incarnates in his completed work of death, resurrection, and return to the Father, as well as through believing and putting into practice the words he speaks. As Jesus' word lives in them, they are pruned for fruitful, lowly service.

The third term in the allegory is made plain when Jesus says, "You are the branches" (15:5). Here and throughout the passage "you" is plural. An individualistic reading of the text violates the picture that it draws (a vine with one branch?!) and its intention as well. The vine and branches are a multiple, organic unity, like the unity for which Jesus prays in the great prayer that concludes his last discourse (17:21).

Jesus' direct command to his disciples, "Abide in me as I abide in you" (15:4a), is the heart of the matter. The expression translated "abide in" here (*meno en*) is one of the key terms in the Fourth Gospel. It is sometimes translated as "dwell in," "remain in," or "remain united with/to." In some contexts it connotes a deep, mutual indwelling; in others it simply means "stay connected to." Jesus has already introduced the theme of mutual indwelling in his teaching about the Paraclete in chapter 14 (14:16–18, 20). There the promise of indwelling spoke of an inward, spiritual union contingent on loving Jesus and keeping his word or commandments (14:21, 23). Here he points out the essential connection between abiding in him and bearing fruit (15:4–5), which is explained in the following verses in terms of sacrificial love for others (15:9–17). This is the connection that challenges a purely mystic or contemplative reading of the union of Father, Son, and believers. Abiding in Christ is not an end in itself; its purpose is to bear fruit (15:4b–5). The principle is stated first negatively: no connection between branch and vine, no fruit (v. 4b). Then it is stated in a balanced pair of propositions, one positive and one negative: abide in me, bear much fruit (v. 5b) *because* apart from me you can do nothing (v. 5c).

Picking up on the negative note at the end of verse 5, verse 6 brings a solemn warning. The passive forms–"is thrown away," "are gathered, thrown . . . , and burned" (15:6)–signal the action of God, the gardener. They echo the judgment pronounced in Ezekiel's lament for the princes of Israel (Ezek. 19:10–14). They do not depict eternal punishment, but they do indicate that fruitless branches are of no use to the keeper of the vineyard.

This warning is balanced by a repetition of the promise first made to those who believe in Jesus (14:12–14) and now reiterated to those who abide in him and in whom his words abide (15:7): "Whatever you ask in my name . . . I will do it" (14:13–14) is echoed by "ask for whatever you wish, and it will be done for you" (15:7). The promise is extravagant, but it is not incredible when appropriate attention is paid to the qualifying clauses, "If you love me [and] keep my commandments" (14:15, 23–24) and "If you abide in me, and my words abide in you" (15:7). To read this promise as a formula for manipulating God is to misread it. Its purpose is not to show believers how to get what they wish but to show the world the glory of God, "so that the Father may be glorified in the Son" (14:13), as those who abide in Jesus "bear much fruit and become my disciples" (15:8).

Preaching and teaching the Word

"What energizes you and makes life worth living?" The Gospel lesson appointed for the Fifth Sunday in Easter, year B (John 15:1–8) gives Jesus' answer to this question. It presents a command, a promise, and a warning (15:4–5) as it shows the direct relationship between staying connected to God and a fruitful life.

1. The command: "Abide in me." For both Paul and John, intimate union with Jesus Christ is a distinguishing characteristic of the believer's life. Paul expressed this conviction with the simple but theologically weighty term "in Christ."[3] In John, Jesus speaks of the same idea through the vivid word picture of a vine and its branches. A sermon or lesson on this text could use the various nuances of "abide in" to show the mutual flow of life from branch to vine and vine to branch, the necessity of a solid and continuous connection if life is to be maintained, and the impossibility of producing fruit if the connection is broken.

In the predominantly rural setting of Palestine in the time of Jesus and the evangelist, the image spoke directly to the experience of hearers and readers. Relatively few people today have worked in a vineyard, so the interpreter must provide ways for hearers to relate to the image. In our technological age one might think of how Christmas tree lights and home appliances are connected with the electrical power or how a computer terminal is connected with a network. Vines and their branches, however, are living things in which vital juices flow from root to leaf and from leaf to root. Electrical or electronic substitutes fall short of this vital feature of Jesus' analogy so more appropriate visual aids might be found in a nearby vineyard or (in a church sanctuary) in architectural or graphic representations of a vine and its branches. Allusions to the vine and branches can also be found in anthems, praise songs, and the second stanza of several hymns.[4]

The important interpretive move is from image to reality, suggesting how disciples today can stay vitally connected to Christ. The discipline of daily prayer and meditation (inward journey) and the obedience of sacrificial service (outward journey) would be good places to start. A composite text for the sermon or lesson would be appropriate: "Abide in me as I abide in you, . . . because apart from me you can do nothing" (15:4a, 5c). When Peter and John stood before the religious authorities in Jerusalem, their judges, "[realizing] that they were uneducated and ordinary men, . . . were amazed and recognized them as companions of Jesus" (Acts 4:13). That's what staying connected to Christ does.

2. The promise. Jesus' promise, "If you abide in me, and my words abide in you, ask for whatever you wish, and it will be done for you" (15:7), is a word to live by, but it is given only to those meeting rigorous criteria: "If you abide in me . . . if you keep my commandments" (vv. 7, 10). No interpretation should attend only to the subordinate clauses, for the main clauses, "ask . . . and it will be done . . . you will abide in my love," are a gospel promise. When this particular word of Jesus takes up its abode in us, it transforms the level of expectancy with which we pray.

3. The warning. The text also contains a word of warning. God is like a farmer who owns and tends a vineyard, and that involves cutting out dead wood as well as pruning lively branches. Both operations are essential to the health and productivity of a vineyard, a community of faith, or an individual disciple.

The relationship between the words "disciple" and "discipline" is organic, not incidental. God wills growth and fruitful life, and that requires discipline. The allegory of the vine and branches is a helpful way to understand this dimension of God's essential character, as is the analogy of a parent. The pruning function reflects God's concern for the well-being and fruitfulness of individual believers. The purging or cleaning function shows God's concern for the body of believers as a whole. Cutting out dead wood is the prerogative of the vinegrower, however, not of the branches. The primary concern of God conveyed by this allegory is not purity but fruitfulness, whether of the church or its individual members. We become disciples not just in a moment of decision but throughout a lifetime of disciplined fruit-bearing (15:8).

Perhaps the most fruitful idea for the reader of these notes is to find a quiet time and place in which, without distraction, to read John 15:1–8 just between yourself and your Lord. Read it slowly; read it aloud; read it several times; listen carefully for a direct personal word. Let the text speak to you about the vitality of your present connection to Jesus Christ. Let the Lord speak to you about the degree of fruitfulness he sees in your life just now. You might write your response to him in your journal and save it to reread from time to time. This could strengthen your connection to the true vine.

The Love Commandment (15:9–17)

In this subunit Jesus continues to develop and apply the allegory of the vine and branches. The form of the text is authoritative instruction; its function is to guide the life of the community of disciples after Jesus has departed from them to return to the Father.

Guidance is expressed in a series of lapidary sayings on loosely connected topics: abiding in the divine love (v. 9), keeping Jesus' commandments (v. 10), joy (v. 11), loving one another (v. 12), self-sacrifice (v. 13), slaves and friends (vv. 14–15), free will and election (v. 16a), bearing fruit (v. 16b), asking and receiving (v. 16c), and (again) loving one another (v. 17). Each is a little pearl among Jesus' teachings, and two are basic themes in the farewell scene (chaps. 13–17): the love commandment and the mutual indwelling of the Father and the Son. All the topics in this text are strung together by the theme of love, focusing in the first part on the vertical love that binds believers to God through Jesus (vv. 9–10) and in the second on the horizontal love that binds believers to each other (vv. 12, 17). Between these two series of pearls is a little gem on Jesus' joy in the love that binds him to God and to his disciples (v. 11).

Exploring the text

These ideas, tied together here on the analogy of a string of pearls, are linked in the text by the image of the vine and branches. No longer is the Father external to the vine, as in 15:1. What is depicted here is not a string or chain, but a vine in which love flows from the Father to the Son to each believer and to all other believers, uniting them organically.

Abide in My Love (15:9–10)

The first two clauses of verse 9, usually translated "As the Father has loved me, so have I loved you," can be translated as well or better by the present tense "I love you just as the Father loves me; remain in my love" (15:9 TEV).[1] The Father's love for Jesus and Jesus' love for the Father are not a past event but a permanent, steady state into which Jesus invites his disciples to enter and abide, staying connected to that love as a branch stays connected to the vine.

Jesus says he loves the disciples just as the Father loves him (15:9). The Father loves Jesus by showing him all that the Father is doing (5:20), and Jesus loves his disciples in the same way (15:15). Jesus lets his disciples know that God's love for the Son encompasses the Father's command to the Son to lay down his life for the world. This is, for the evangelist, the most important thing that God is doing. It is the highest and deepest expression of the love of the Son for the Father and of the love of God the Father and the Son for the world (3:16).

Jesus' love for God is expressed in concrete acts of obedience in time and space. Just as Jesus keeps the Father's commandments and abides in the Father's love, so Jesus' disciples are to keep his commandments and abide in Jesus' love (15:10).

Readers may wonder which of Jesus' commandments are intended in this verse. The immediate answer—the great commandment according to the Fourth Gospel—is, "Love one another" (15:12, 17). But before moving from the vertical love that enables believers to live in union with the Father and the Son (15:9–10) to the horizontal love that enables believers to live in community with one another (15:12–17), Jesus inserts a word about joy, which characterizes both dimensions of love.

Transition: Joy (15:11)

For Jesus, the love commandment is no burden; it is a formula for deep and abiding joy. To live in love for God and for one another is to share in the joy of doing the Father's will (4:32–34; 18:37b). John the Baptist testified to the joy of recognizing Jesus and standing in his presence (3:29). Jesus tells God that he wants his own joy to be made complete in his disciples (17:13). For fuller development of this theme, see John 16:16–24.

Love One Another (15:12–17)

Just as the source of Jesus' love for the disciples is God's love for him (15:9), so the source of his disciples' love for one another is Jesus' love for them. In both cases, the source is also the warrant and example of the love that is enjoined. "My commandment is this: love one another, just as I love you" (15:12 TEV).[2] The example Jesus gives to illustrate his love is an action, not simply a state of mind or attitude. Couching his teaching in the form of a proverb ("No one has greater love than this . . ."), Jesus points to the historic act by which he will lay down his life for his friends (15:13). For Jesus, love is a verb.

Paul states the same truth in more theological terms: "The proof of God's amazing love is this: While we were yet sinners, Christ died for us."[3] In John, Jesus focuses not on the sin of those for whom he died but on the quality of his love for them. It is not the love of a superior for an inferior, but of an individual for his friends. Furthermore, God did not force Jesus to die. Of his own free will (10:15b, 17–18) and at the time of his choosing (7:6; 11:9–11; 12:23–26) Jesus laid down his life for his friends. For Paul, Christ's death means that God calls us no longer slaves but sons and daughters (Gal. 4:7). For John, Jesus' death shows that he no longer calls us servants but friends (15:15).[4]

Next to his laying down his life for them, the primary evidence of Jesus' friendship or love for his disciples is the fact that he has made known to them everything that he has heard from his Father (15:15). The Fourth Gospel does not distinguish between *philia* (friendship) and *agape,* which are sometimes treated as two types of love. As revealer and redeemer, Jesus is our friend. For both Paul and John, the heart of the matter is love: God's love expressed in Jesus Christ.

There is a condition to be met, however, for Jesus inserts a proviso: "You are my friends if you do what I command you" (15:14), echoing the "if " in verse 10. To abide in Jesus' love means to love one another, for that is what he commands his disciples to do (13:34; 15:12, 17), and those who keep his commandments abide in his love (15:10a). Failure of disciples to love one another cuts them off from the organic unity of mutual love that binds them as friends to Jesus and to the Father, for they are no longer abiding in Jesus' love.

In verse 16 Jesus reiterates three themes introduced earlier in the Gospel. "You did not choose me but I chose you" (15:16a) drives home the mystery of election that has surfaced repeatedly throughout the Gospel (3:18; 6:44; 6:70; 8:44). Now he speaks to the disciples who have stayed with him after Judas went out into the night (13:30) and reassures them that they are both chosen and appointed.

A second theme is that of the vine and branches. The disciples are appointed in order to bear fruit, "fruit that will last" (15:16b). It is helpful to read this phrase in conjunction with the greater works promised in 14:12. The fruit of which Jesus speaks here is "love manifested in obedience and obedience manifested in love."[5] The disciples' works of love will bear witness to God's abiding presence in them. They are fruit that will last (*meno,* "abide") because they spring from the abiding presence of God within them, which is the very life of the vine.

The third theme repeated here is the promise of answered prayer, introduced at 15:7. There the promise was conditioned upon the mutual indwelling of the believer with Jesus and Jesus' words. Here (15:16b) the fulfillment of the promise hinges upon the disciple's bearing much fruit by demonstrating love in daily life. To those who lead such a life God grants whatever they ask in the name of Jesus, whose indwelling spirit produces the works of love.

Love is a prominent theme in Jesus' farewell discourse (13:1b; 13:34;

15:9), and his command to love one another brackets the paragraph with which the present unit closes (15:12, 17). In his great prayer for his disciples Jesus speaks again of loving and abiding (17:21–24), but verse 17 brings to a conclusion this theme in Jesus' table talk. The following verse (15:18) marks a radical shift of topic, from love to hate.

Preaching and teaching the Word

If one considers only the Fourth Gospel, the commandments that Jesus expects his disciples to keep are just two: love me and love one another, with the understanding that loving Jesus also means loving God (5:42–43; 8:42a; 10:30) and that loving one another includes acts of lowly service ("washing one another's feet," 13:14–15). The first sermon on the love commandment in the Gospel of John is found in 1 John 4:7–21. In John's Gospel and Epistle the love commandment is addressed only to the in-group of Jesus' disciples. This is one of the points at which it is important to read the Johannine witness in dialogue with the testimony of the other Gospels (for instance, Matt. 5:43–48) and of the Epistles (for instance, Rom. 13:9–10; Gal. 5:14–15; Jas. 2:8). Throughout the New Testament the basic Mosaic commandment to love one's neighbor is emphasized, and in the parable of the Good Samaritan Jesus interpreted "neighbor" to include any human being who is in need (Luke 10:29–37). In the Sermon on the Mount he extended the love commandment still further to include love for one's enemies (Matt. 5:44). The fourth evangelist may or may not have assumed that readers would have knowledge of these broader commandments of Jesus, but the disciples at the Last Supper did, and interpreters today should, take them into account as they preach and teach the Johannine love commandment.

1. Living in love. The Revised Common Lectionary lists John 15:9–17 as the Gospel for the Sixth Sunday of Easter, year B. Preaching and teaching the love commandment in the Fourth Gospel can be salutary in a culture where the currency of love has been debased. The term is used to cover everything from steamy bedroom scenes on TV through countless novels based on love triangles and lyrical poems about romantic love to exalted examples of selfless love in art, literature, and Scripture. In such a confusion of tongues about love, the clear voice of Jesus on the subject can satisfy a deep hunger of the heart.

By choosing the theme rather than a single text, the preacher or teacher can hold together the vertical and horizontal dimensions of love ("Abide in my love" and "Love one another"), just as they are held together in Jesus' farewell discourse. One way to do this is to note the prominence of the expression "unconditional love" in our time and in that light to examine the conditional sentences in John 15:9–17. They do not mean that if we don't love other people Jesus quits loving us. Jesus' love is as constant as that of the Father whose love abides in him. They do mean that if we don't love other people we are not abiding in Jesus' love and his words are not abiding in us. In such a situation, we cut ourselves off from the vital juice of love that flows from the Father through the Son and outward to others in the acts of love that are the fruit for which the vine exists. Life in Christ means living in love–in love with God, with Jesus, and with all those whom Jesus loves. The last part is tough love, for it embraces all the people in our particular church, in other churches, and in other religions. It includes all our neighbors and all our enemies in a time when the whole world has become our neighborhood and not all the neighbors are friendly. No way? There is life in the vine that makes it possible.

2. The church according to St. John. The image of the vine and branches with its associated love commandment can be preached appropriately on World Communion Sunday or at any celebration of the Lord's Supper. The image of the vine and branches, even though it does not speak explicitly of the church, is the Johannine equivalent of Paul's metaphor of the body of Christ. John's language stresses the members' dependence upon Christ and evokes a fellowship held together only by love for God in Christ and love for one another. Whenever and wherever the church has become for people at the table a burdensome institutional structure, characterized by endless programs and wearisome committee meetings, time spent in communion with the true vine and with one another can be a refreshing breath of life.

The Johannine model for the church is an organic unity of interrelationship, mutuality, and indwelling shaped by the love of Jesus. Preachers and teachers might reflect upon how the Johannine model can, without doing away with the church as an institution, renew it as a community whose life issues from communion with Christ.

3. The meaning of Christian joy. One of the words to live by in this section of the Fourth Gospel is Jesus' statement of the purpose of all these teachings: that his joy may be in us and that our joy may be complete (15:11). Joy is a significant theme for preaching and teaching in a culture in which people confuse joy with having fun and spend billions of dollars each year on entertainment.

Preachers who decide to lift up this text will find the paragraph division in the NRSV (after verse 11) most appropriate. It takes seriously the concluding function of the formula "I have said these things to you . . ." and suggests that the preacher extend the lectionary pericope for the Fifth Sunday of Easter, year B and read 15:1–11 as the Gospel lesson. This move has the advantage of leaving 15:12–17, a unit bracketed by the commandment to love one another, for the following Sunday.

The apostle Paul gave joy a prominent place in his list of the fruits of the Spirit, second only to love (Gal. 5:22). For him, joy in the Holy Spirit was one of the characteristics of the kingdom of God (Rom. 14:17), and a glance at the more than twenty references to joy in the Pauline Epistles will give a taste of the joy he experienced in his arduous service of Christ and the gospel.

For John the Baptist and for Jesus himself, joy was the name given to the deep satisfaction of fulfilling God's purpose for their lives (John 3:29; 4:34; 18:37b, "for this I was born"). That is the joy Jesus desires for his disciples when he teaches them about abiding in his love and loving one another (15:11).

A sermon on Christian joy might note the fact that in the text, joy is neither sought nor achieved. Christian joy is, rather, a by-product of one's union and communion with Jesus Christ, whose joy is of a different quality than that of the world. If such a sermon is to be a living word, it should be rooted in life experiences as well as in the text. It might also make use of an old adage: "Pleasure comes from the touch; happiness comes from the circumstance; joy comes from the Lord."

4. On choosing and being chosen. The theme of free will and election appears only once in this text (15:16), but it suggests a lesson or a sermon. Parents often observe that their children raise a terrible fuss to get something they want; then as soon as it is in their possession, they lose interest, put it aside, and cry for something else. Marketers depend on adults who do not act very differently. No matter how much people may have or what brands they may use, they can be persuaded that what they have is out of date or out of style and led to choose something else. Our society is built on obsolescence and impermanence.

Jesus approaches us differently when he affirms that, contrary to what we may think about our relationship to him, "You did not choose me but I chose you" (15:16). Though we may feel free to choose another master, we cannot escape the prior choosing of Jesus. Far from being a kind of enslavement, these words give us the assurance of knowing a love that is permanent. They tell us who we are and whose we are. They also give us a basic orientation as we seek to find out why we are here. We have been appointed to go and bear fruit for Jesus. Such a conviction, lodged in the heart, can become the cantus firmus or fixed melody that underlies a harmonious life. Such words are words to live by.

The World's Hatred (15:18–16:4a)

In sharp contrast to Jesus' repeated love commandment (15:9–17), his warning that in the world they must expect to be hated (15:18–19) comes like a blast of cold air. To disciples who still had hosannas ringing in their ears (12:13), such talk might have seemed about as appropriate as a sex education lesson in a class of first-graders. But these are the words of one who was misunderstood, rejected, and finally killed by the Roman occupying authority at the instigation of local religious leaders. They are written by an evangelist who addresses a community of Jesus' disciples who, fifty or sixty years after Jesus' death, would almost surely recognize their own experience in these words about being put out of synagogues and even threatened with death (16:2).[1] Historical certainty in this matter is impossible to come by, but it is unlikely that these words about the world's hatred were simply the product of the evangelist's paranoia. It is the Advocate, sent by the risen Christ to be with and comfort his disciples (14:16, 18; 15:26), through whom Jesus speaks these words to them and disciples of every age.[2]

Exploring the text

The pericope consists of three parts. The first (15:18–25) and third (16:1–4a) are warnings about and reasons for the world's hatred. The middle part (15:26–27) promises an Advocate to testify on behalf of Jesus, reinforcing the testimony of his disciples. "From the beginning" (15:27) is a stitch in the fabric that ties it to the following unit (16:4b–15).

The Warning (15:18–25)

"World" is used here in the characteristically Johannine sense of the realm of unbelief: those who fail to recognize in Jesus Christ the word, life, and light of God.[3] "Hate" covers a broad semantic spectrum in the New Testament, as it does in American usage today, but its meaning in this text is clearly focused and decidedly Johannine. "Hate" here refers to active hostility taking the form of persecution (15:20; 16:2; see 16:33) simply because these disciples are servants of Jesus Christ. It is the diametrical opposite of love (15:12–17), an example of the sharply dualistic thought characteristic of the Fourth Gospel.

Jesus predicts that his disciples will face rejection bitter enough to be called hatred, just as he did. He points out that servants should not expect any better treatment than their master, a warning that includes good news: "If they kept my word, they will keep yours also" (15:20).

Three reasons are given for the world's hatred, one of them reiterated in 16:1–4. First, "Because . . . I have chosen you out of the world–therefore the world hates you" (15:19b). As anyone who has a clear sense of being called or chosen may have noticed, those who are not chosen often dislike those who think they are. Jesus, who is so clear in enunciating the principle of election, is equally clear in foreseeing the hostility that such an idea will engender.

Second, disciples can expect to be hated because the world does not know either Jesus or the one who sent him (15:21b //16:3b). In the Fourth Gospel, knowing is synonymous with seeing, in its deepest sense ("Don't you see?"). Furthermore, seeing is believing, so that those who say, "We see," and yet do not believe are in fact blind (9:41; see also 14:9–11, 17–20). Those who have known God as Father see and recognize him in Jesus. For those who cannot see God in Jesus, his claims and those of his followers are heretical and dangerous, and therefore worthy only of rejection, here termed hate.

Third, the world's hatred fulfills "the word that is written in their law, 'They hated me without a cause'" (15:25). This reason is reminiscent of other points in John at which a human action is explained as occurring in order to fulfill Scripture: the crowd's response of unbelief (12:38) and Judas's betrayal (13:18). To the fourth evangelist, the Scriptures must be fulfilled. For him, the fact that two verses in Scripture affirm that "They hated me without a cause" is a valid reason for the world's hatred of Jesus and his disciples. Psalm 35 is the prayer of a weak and needy petitioner (35:10) for deliverance from enemies whose hatred is gratuitous, without cause (35:7, 19). Psalm 69 is a prayer for help by one who is derided, insulted, and shamed without cause (69:4, 6–12, 19–21) in terms so reminiscent of Jesus that this psalm is often read in Holy Week services.[4] The fourth evangelist had doubtless reflected on one or both of these psalms and concluded that these words of Scripture ("They hated me without a cause") were one of the reasons for the world's hatred of Jesus, strange as this notion of causality may seem today.

The text also gives two reasons why the world's rejection of Jesus is a sin: the words that Jesus has spoken (15:22) and the deeds he has done (15:24). Had they not seen and heard these things, they would be without sin. Because they have been exposed to the light and rejected it, they are without excuse (3:19–20).

The Promise (15:26–27)

The Advocate (Paraclete) has already been promised twice in the farewell discourse (14:16–18, 26). Now the Paraclete is introduced again as the Spirit of truth, in a role quite appropriately translated as Advocate. Foreseeing the persecution to which his disciples will be subjected in his name, Jesus promises to send the Advocate–insisting twice that he comes from the Father (15:26a, b)–who will be Jesus' attorney or witness by testifying to the truth on his behalf. What seems to be presupposed is a situation in which the disciples are on trial, formally or informally, because of their claims about Jesus. In such a situation the Advocate will persuade the disciples' opponents that what they say about Jesus is the truth. At the same time Jesus counts on his disciples to be his advocates too: "You also are to testify because you have been with me from the beginning" (15:27) and are therefore qualified to say who I am. The promise is at the same time a commission.

Reasons for the Warning and the Promise (16:1–4a)

"These things" (16:1) refers to the preceding teachings about the world's hatred (15:18–27). Two circumstances are mentioned in which these teachings will be highly pertinent. The first is excommunication from synagogues, already alluded to as an agreed-upon plan of Jewish religious authorities (9:22) and here prophesied as a future event (16:2a). The other is martyrdom at the hands of those who think that by killing Christians they are offering worship to God (16:2b). The two circumstances do not necessarily point to persecution at the hands of the same people.

The letters to the seven churches that introduce the book of Revelation refer to persecution at the hands of Jews (Rev. 2:9–10; 3:9–10) and of Roman authorities who viewed Christians as atheists because they would not worship the Roman gods (Rev. 2:13). Although the ancient tradition that the fourth evangelist also wrote the book of Revelation is hypothetical and dubious, it is evident that by the time the Fourth Gospel was written, disciples of Jesus Christ were being called upon to endure severe and sometimes mortal hostility. The world's hatred of which John 15:18–16:4a speaks was broader than the hostility felt by zealous Jewish traditionalists against the innovative messianic Jews in their synagogues.

The reason Jesus included in his farewell discourse the warning about the world's hatred and the promise of the Holy Spirit (and the reason the evangelist includes them in this Gospel) is twofold: to keep the disciples from stumbling under the blows they will undergo (16:1) and to remember Jesus' words and find strength to endure (16:4). This strength will come from the Holy Spirit, who, as their Advocate, will bring Jesus' words to their remembrance in that hour (14:26).

Preaching and teaching the Word

This commentary is written by and for persons who, with rare exception, have not been hated because they stand up for Jesus. There are many places in the world today, however, where Christians are looked down upon, ostracized, and persecuted for their faith. Preachers and teachers could be alert to news about incidents of persecution and try to keep their congregations informed about places where other branches of the true vine are suffering the world's hatred. Often the only time Western news media carry such stories is when Christian missionaries are involved. A word of caution is in order here. When Christian missionaries are subjected to abuse, it is often less because of their faith in Christ than because of the foreign policy of the nation whose passport they carry. Has religious conflict ever been simply a matter of standing for God's truth? It is often a deadly combination of religion, politics, and ethnicity in which motives are mixed and no single party can claim all the truth, for truth is the first casualty in any war.

The text is also pertinent to the hatred experienced by gays, lesbians, and certain ethnic groups in our society, often at the hands of professing Christians whose practice may fall short of their avowal. Many people who experience this kind of persecution are also Christians. These words of Christ are relevant for them, even though the hostility they experience is not because they are Christian but in spite of that fact.

The present passage lends itself better to teaching than to preaching because through this medium the historical context of the passage can be more fully explored and its inherent dangers—of self-righteousness on the one hand and demonization of the enemy on the other—can be more adequately recognized. In this passage the dark side of John's dualism comes to vivid expression. But truth is truth, and evil is evil. Through careful preparation and with the help of the promised Holy Spirit, a teacher of this passage can become a powerful witness for the truth.

RECAPITULATION (16:4b–33)

Chapter 16 introduces little that is new in the farewell discourse of Jesus. Topics that are reviewed include "I have said/did not say these things," Jesus' coming/going/coming, the promise of the Paraclete, the relation of the Father and the Son, the disciples' sorrow at Jesus' departure, joy when he comes again, asking and receiving, speaking in figures, false confidence, persecution, and peace. Because so much of the material repeats what has been said in the basic discourse (13:31–14:31), the following notes point readers to earlier passages where the same subject is treated and look more closely at ideas that appear for the first time in the present chapter.

The Departure of Jesus
and the Coming of the Advocate (16:4b–15)

Exploring the text

"I did not say these things" (16:4b) is the mirror image of "I have said these things" at 14:25, 15:11, 16:1, 4a (echoed at 16:6, 25). Alluding to things he has told the disciples about the hatred and persecution they must expect from the world (16:1–4a; 15:18–25), Jesus explains why he did not say them from the beginning of his ministry (16:4b). He was still with them then, but the time has come when he will no longer be with them.

Jesus announces that he is "going to him who sent me" and adds, somewhat reproachfully, that "none of you asks me, 'Where are you going?'" (16:5). The comment is strange, because Peter had earlier asked exactly that question (13:36) and because Jesus has just said where he is going. The following verse explains the hint of reproach, however, as well as the remark itself. It does not occur to the disciples to ask Jesus what returning to the Father might mean to him. Their hearts are filled only with sorrow at being left alone (v. 6).

Jesus recognizes that their concern is justified and deals with it by repeating the promise of the Paraclete (16:7–15; see 14:16–18, 26; 15:26). One new idea appears this time: If Jesus does not go away, the Holy Spirit will not come (v. 7). This reflects the characteristic Johannine concept that during his earthly ministry Jesus embodies the presence of God among humans, while after Jesus' exaltation through death and resurrection the Holy Spirit is the way the presence of the Father and the Son is experienced on earth. It is therefore to the advantage of the disciples that Jesus' physical presence be withdrawn so that his presence in the Spirit can work even more freely, anywhere and anytime.

In contrast to earlier statements of the promise, this time the Father is not even mentioned in connection with the coming of the Paraclete (Advocate, Spirit). Jesus simply says, "If I go, I will send him to you" (16:7). Distinctions about the sender apparently made no difference to the evangelist. The main point is what the Paraclete will do when the Spirit comes, and here the present passage introduces new material. "When he comes, he will prove the world wrong about sin and righteousness and judgment" (16:8). The key term can be translated "reprove" (AV), "convince" (RSV), "convict" (NIV), "show" (NJB), or "prove" (NRSV, NAB, TEV). At John 3:20 it is translated as "expose" ("For all who do evil hate the light and do not come to the light, so that their deeds may not be exposed"). The term is rooted in a judicial context, and its two meanings–expose and convict or prove wrong–both have to do with the work of the Holy Spirit in a courtroom situation. In the preceding unit the Advocate functions as a defense attorney, testifying on behalf of Jesus in favor of believers undergoing persecution (15:26). In this unit the work of the Paraclete is that of the prosecuting attorney who puts the world on trial, exposes its sin, and proves it wrong "about sin and righteousness and judgment" (16:8).

This enigmatic statement is explained in the following three verses. The world is wrong about sin, "because they do not believe in me" (16:9). They think that sin is failing to observe the law of Moses as understood by its official interpreters (for instance, Sabbath law, 9:16), but they are wrong because they do not see that Jesus is from God–the Lamb of God who takes away the sin of the world (1:29)–and their blindness to God's presence in their midst is sin (9:40–41; see also 8:24; 15:22, 24).

The world is wrong about righteousness, "because I am going to the Father and you will see me no longer" (16:10). The key term here can mean justice, or righteousness, or both, as is often true of ambiguous terms in the Fourth Gospel. Although most current versions use "righteousness," "justice" is the primary issue here; namely, the vindication of Jesus in the high court of God. A Jewish court found Jesus guilty of heresy, and a Roman court found him guilty of treason, but Jesus' departure to share the glory he had with the Father before the world was made exposes the world's error and vindicates Jesus as right, justified, and innocent of those charges.

It is possible, however, to understand "righteousness" in the sense of moral goodness and to read the verb as "expose" (see John 3:20). On this reading, Jesus' return to the Father exposes the world's error about what constitutes moral goodness. It is not strict adherence to the law, as the accusers of the woman caught in adultery (8:1–11) assumed. True righteousness includes mercy as well as justice, and "Jesus Christ the righteous," who receives the sinner without condoning the sin, is the model of the right way to understand the term (1 John 2:1–2, 29; 3:7). In the course of his ministry Jesus challenged his opponents with the question, "Which of you convicts me of sin?" (8:46). No one did. Now the tables are turned. The world is on trial, and the Paraclete will expose the world's error about Jesus and vindicate Jesus' claims about God.

The Paraclete will also prove that the world is wrong about judgment "because the ruler of this world has been condemned" (16:11). There is no doubt about the courtroom frame of reference in this echo of the conclusion to chapter 15. The ruler of this world, already referred to twice in this way (12:31; 14:30), is called elsewhere in the Gospel "the devil" (8:44; 13:2; see 6:70) and "Satan" (13:27). These more personal names are used when the evil one is at work in persons. He is referred to as "the ruler of this world" when God's ultimate judgment is in view. John 14:30–31 is a veiled reference to the cross and resurrection of Jesus as the time and place when this judgment occurred. When Jesus speaks with his disciples, the Paraclete's disclosing or proving activity lies in the future, but when the Paraclete discloses the meaning of the cross and resurrection to the evangelist and to readers of the Gospel, the judgment is viewed as past ("has been condemned," 16:11). Those who rejected Jesus thought that they had convicted and disposed of him. Jesus' return to the Father and his coming in the person of the Paraclete show that the world was wrong about judgment, for it is the world and its ruler that have been placed on trial and condemned.

Verse 12 serves as a transition to Jesus' final words about the future activity of the Spirit. The remaining verses in this unit are a mosaic of words and ideas introduced in the earlier passages about the Paraclete (14:16–17, 26; 15:26; 16:7–11) and reflecting affirmations about Jesus during his earthly ministry. The promised Advocate is the Spirit of truth (v. 13; see 14:17, 26). He will guide Jesus' disciples into all the truth (v. 13; see 14:6, 26). Just as Jesus does not speak on his own but says and does only what the Father does and says (5:19–20; 7:16–17; 14:10), so the Spirit will not speak on his own but will say only what he hears [from the Father and the Son] (16:13b). At the opportune time the Spirit will "declare to you the things that are to come"–that is, will prepare disciples to face the situations in which they will find themselves at that future time (16:13c), just as Jesus is, at the moment of this discourse, preparing the disciples to face his imminent crucifixion and departure (14:1; 16:1, 4a). After Jesus' departure the Spirit will glorify him (v. 14a), just as, in his earthly ministry and especially by his death and resurrection, Jesus glorified God.[1] In short, the work of the Paraclete will be to continue the work of Jesus after Jesus has returned to the Father.

"All that the Father has is mine" (16:15a) refers to all the qualities and attributes that made Jesus, during his earthly ministry, the functional equivalent of God the Father.[2] When Jesus promises and reiterates that the Spirit of truth "will take what is mine and declare it to you" (16:14b, 15b), he affirms that the Paraclete will continue the revelation of God, once present on earth in Jesus, after Jesus has returned to the Father (compare 14:26). In addition to reminding disciples of Jesus' words while he was on earth, the Spirit will tell them what he hears after Jesus has returned to the Father. In so doing, the Paraclete will glorify on earth the one who speaks from the glorious presence of God (16:14; 17:1, 5; 1:14, 18).

Preaching and teaching the Word

Lectionary preachers are offered on Pentecost Sunday every year the choice of Acts 2:1–21 and a text from the Gospel of John (in addition to readings from the Psalter and the Epistles). These choices reflect differing ways in which the Holy Spirit operates and is perceived in different persons, times, and places. Acts depicts the outward manifestations that accompanied the coming of the Spirit and narrates the exciting events of the first three decades of the church, as the Spirit led it into the Greco-Roman world. In John the Spirit is the presence of the risen Jesus, received as the breath of God and heard "like the murmur of the dove's song."[3] The Gospel reading for the Day of Pentecost in year B reminds readers of Jesus' promise to send the Holy Spirit (John 15:26) and describes the Spirit's work in human hearts (16:4b–15). Preachers and teachers can think of this text as Pentecost in the present tense, since the future of which Jesus speaks is available now to all who seek to know him as a living presence. The Paraclete bears witness to Jesus in our hearts and calls us to bear witness to Jesus in the world (15:26–27), working powerfully and pervasively in the lives of his disciples.

The enigmatic statement (16:8) about proving the world wrong (or exposing its error) about three things can be probed through a lecture/discussion session in a Bible study class whose members want to unravel some of the knots this text leaves in their brains. This can be intellectually satisfying, but the text calls for exposition that goes behind linguistic and logical puzzles to a more immediate contact with the Spirit of truth and glory to whom the text points. A sermon that pays attention to the verbs "testify" (15:26–27), "guide," "declare," and "glorify" (16:13–15), with examples drawn from personal experiences of the Spirit's action and carefully chosen hymns or poems,[4] could provide a context for the Spirit to work in corporate worship and private reflection.

The Gospel reading for Trinity Sunday in year C is John 16:12–15. Jesus, the Son of God, speaks in these verses, claiming that all that God the Father has is his, and promising that after the Son's departure from the earth the Holy Spirit will guide his disciples into all the truth. This text was written about two and a half centuries before the doctrine of the Trinity was hammered out at Nicaea and Constantinople, and the fourth evangelist would probably not have recognized the philosophical language of the fourth-century church fathers. Nevertheless, this text is part of the raw material from which the doctrine of the Trinity was fashioned, for it speaks of all three persons of the Trinity and of their interrelationship. Interpreters of this text today would do well to underscore John's way of stating what the Spirit does and how the Father and Jesus are related, trying to do so in language that makes sense to readers and hearers today. The text affirms that just as Jesus embodied the presence of God among humans while he lived on earth, so the Holy Spirit communicates that presence to us today by reminding us of what Jesus said then and by teaching us what God has to say to us now.

Scholars can, by rational criteria, make judgments and engage in debates about which biblical texts are more or less likely to contain the very words (*ipsissima verba*) of Jesus. According to the text, what the Holy Spirit provides is the living voice (*viva vox*) of Jesus. In the Fourth Gospel his voice is mediated through the words of the evangelist.[5] Through whom and in what ways is Jesus' voice mediated to us today? Any specific answer to this question may seem presumptuous to some, but Jesus here promises that the Spirit of truth will guide his disciples into all the truth. The text virtually dares us to trust that promise.

The dangers of such Spirit-guided interpretation surfaced early. Later disciples in the Johannine community were urged not to believe every spirit, "but [to] test the spirits to see whether they are from God" (1 John 4:1). Part of the Paraclete's guidance of Christ's disciples into all truth comes through teachers and preachers who are wise enough to submit their interpretation of his teaching for consideration by other believers who, in the bond of love, are also listening for the voice of Jesus.

On any occasion when John 16:12–15 is to be read, taught, or preached, its position as the last of six texts about the Holy Spirit in Jesus' last discourse with his disciples should be taken into account. In some teaching situations it might be appropriate to divide the learners into five groups, assigning one of the texts to each group (14:16–17, 26; 15:26; 16:7–11; 16:13–15), along with three questions: What is the Spirit called? How is the Spirit related to Jesus and to the Father? What is the Spirit going to do? After working in these small groups, the teacher can collate findings and then lead a general discussion—with examples—on the question, "How is the presence of the Father and the Son experienced on earth today?"

Conclusion: Joy and Peace (16:16–33)

Why does the evangelist insert a bit of dialogue here in which the words "A little while, and you will no longer see me, and again a little while, and you will see me" are repeated several times (16:16, 17, 18, 19)? For those who remember that the idea has appeared earlier (7:33; 14:19; 16:5, 10), its repetition may seem to be an insult to the reader's intelligence. But the sentence is a riddle, and riddles must often be repeated before the hearers "get it." The evangelist appears to be using the disciples' failure to understand to throw into sharp relief Jesus' explanation of the riddle to them and to successive readers as well.

Exploring the text

The explanation (16:20–22) leaves Jesus' disciples and John's readers to figure out for themselves that the riddle refers to the theme of departure to be with the Father and the promise of return introduced at the beginning of the farewell discourse (14:1–7, 28). While the reference to his impending death as a departure is clear enough ("a little while and you will no longer see me"), the repeated allusions to their seeing him again are ambiguous.[1] The most obvious reference of "again a little while and you will see me" is to the resurrection appearances on the third day after his crucifixion (20:11–29; 21:1–23), when the disciples' pain turned into joy at seeing Jesus alive again (16:20). Jesus prepares his disciples for their emotional roller-coaster during the ensuing week by warning them ahead of time of the pain they must endure and, at the same time, assuring them it will not last long and will end in joy. Joy is the theme of this paragraph, appearing in its first verse (6:20), its last verse (16:24), and three times in between–twice as a noun and once as the verb "rejoice." These verses are a fuller exposition of the joy referred to at 15:11.

In these verses Jesus uses the illustration of a pregnant woman whose pain in labor is swallowed up in the joy of a new life (16:21), an analogy that serves well to illumine the immediate experience that awaits the disciples but also points beyond it. "I will see you again" (16:22a) does not simply repeat the earlier expression, "you will see me" (16:16b, 17b, 19c). The disciples see him in the resurrection appearances, but the change in wording suggests the possibility of a later time when Jesus will see them but they will not see him. Again, when Jesus promises that their hearts will rejoice, he adds "and no one will take your joy from you" (v. 22b). But Jesus has just finished warning his disciples of the world's hatred, of coming ostracism, and of persecution (15:18–16:4a; see also 16:33b). The larger context suggests that the pattern of anguish followed by joy may be played out again in the experience of the evangelist and first readers and repeatedly thereafter, well beyond the fulfillment of the first Easter.

Clues to the deeper meaning of Jesus' analogy may be found in its Old Testament background and in other uses of birth imagery in the Fourth Gospel. The real-life image of a woman in labor was used by the prophets (Isa. 13:8; 21:3; 26:17; Mic. 4:10), and Israel's joy at deliverance from exile was likened to a woman's joy at the delivery of her child (Isa. 66:7–11). The Fourth Gospel uses the image of childbirth to describe what happens to those who receive the incarnate Word and believe in his name (1:12–13), who are born from above, by the Spirit (3:3–8), and Jesus begins his farewell discourse by addressing his disciples as "little children" (13:33). In the present analogy, the woman is in pain "because her hour has come" (16:21). Use of the "hour" language throughout the Fourth Gospel to refer to Jesus' death and resurrection (2:4; 7:30; 8:20; 12:27; 13:1) suggests that the culmination of Jesus' ministry on earth is the hour in which God's saving purpose to give life to the world comes to term. Jesus' analogy draws upon deep, subconscious associations to suggest more than it says.

This paragraph on joy also reverts to the theme of asking and receiving (16:23–24; see also 14:13–14; 15:7, 16; 16:26). "On that day" (16:23), like "hour" in the preceding analogy, refers to Jesus' resurrection, when the disciples will no longer need to ask him what he is talking about (16:18–19). The meaning of "ask" (*erotao,* "to ask a question") in verse 23a is correctly translated in the NRSV footnote, "[you] will ask me no question." It is not the same verb as "ask" (*aiteo,* "to make a request") in verse 23b. There is no real contradiction between "on that day you will ask nothing of me" (16:23a) and "if you ask anything of the Father in my name, he will give it to you" (16:23b). Jesus is saying that when they see him again after a little while, they will not need to ask him any question about his riddle in 16:16, and they will be free to bring their requests to the Father in his name. During his earthly ministry ("until now," v. 24a) they have not asked God for anything in Jesus' name. After his resurrection, however, they are to pray to the Father as they have come to know him in the Son, assured that their prayers will be heard and answered. The promise has been made earlier (14:12–14). From the perspective of the resurrection as an accomplished fact, it is repeated by the one who at the tomb of Lazarus had prayed, "Father, I thank you for having heard me . . ." (11:41; see 11:22). Now Jesus says, "Ask and you will receive, so that your joy may be complete" (16:24b). Answered prayer tops off the joy that Jesus' resurrection brings to his disciples.

The promise is reiterated in verses 25–27, this time from another temporal perspective. In this concluding paragraph of his reply to the puzzled disciples, Jesus speaks again of "the hour" (16:25b), but as a future time lying beyond the resurrection appearances reported in the Fourth Gospel. Of that time he says that he will tell them plainly of the Father, and "On that day you will ask in my name" (16:26a). He is alluding here to his earlier invitations to ask in his name (14:14; 16:23–24) and at the same time pointing to a time when he will not need to intercede with the Father on the disciples' behalf. "On that day" they will have immediate access to the Father because they love Jesus and believe that he has come from God (16:26b–27).

In the Old Testament, "that day" is a traditional way of referring to "the day of the Lord," when God will intervene finally and decisively in human history (Isa. 2:12; Jer. 46:10; Ezek. 30:2–3; Amos 5:18–20; Zeph. 1:14–18) to judge and to save. It belongs to the language of Old Testament eschatology or teaching about the end time. Johannine eschatology is different. In the Fourth Gospel "that day" refers to a quality of existence (eternal life) in which disciples, after Jesus' death, resurrection, and return as the Paraclete, enter with Jesus into the eternal "now" of God. This relationship with God is a joy even deeper than that of answered prayer, for it is communion with the one who said, "I came from the Father and have come into the world; again, I am leaving the world and am going to the Father" (16:28). This verse states in plain words the key to Jesus' enigmatic announcement in 16:16. In combination with John 3:16 it also expresses the basic message of the Fourth Gospel.

The long response of Jesus to the disciples' confusion (16:19–28) has ended with the plain statement, "I am going to the Father." The disciples speak again, expressing their satisfaction that he is no longer using any figure of speech (*paroimia,* "riddle," 16:29). They reflect on the fact that Jesus did not need them to ask the question they had in mind in order to know what it was (16:19). They conclude that he is omniscient ("You know all things") and therefore affirm, "We believe that you came from God" (v. 30). They think they now understand his words about the woman in labor and they are satisfied.

Jesus, however, replies by asking them a question ("Do you now believe?" v. 31) and adds a postscript consisting of two points. The first alludes to their coming abandonment of him when he is crucified ("You will be scattered . . . and you will leave me alone," 16:32a) and points to the fact that he is never truly alone ("the Father is with me," 16:32b). The second alludes to all that he has said since he first addressed the disciples' troubled hearts (14:1). The blessing of peace that served as an initial bracket (14:27) now brings to a close the entire final discourse with his disciples (16:33). They may not fully know this peace immediately after Jesus' resurrection, for in the world they will face persecution (16:33b) and more trials than they can bear to hear about ahead of time. But the Advocate will be with them through it all, reminding them of Jesus' words and assuring them of his presence in such a way that anguish will turn into joy and peace will permeate even their pain. They can face with courage the world and all that the powers of darkness can muster against them, for Jesus will no more leave them alone than the Father left Jesus alone. Abiding in him, they will share his victory over the world.

Preaching and teaching the Word

"In the world you face persecution. But take courage; I have conquered the world!" (16:33)

Of all the words to live by in the Fourth Gospel, these are perhaps the most triumphant. Yet they do not appear in major lectionaries currently in use in the churches. This is perhaps a good thing, because to preach this text routinely as a given Sunday comes around each year would tend to trivialize it.

The text includes two clues to the occasions when it is appropriate for use in preaching, teaching, or pastoral ministry: the word "persecution" and the plural form of the pronoun "you." These words of Jesus are addressed to his fearful disciples as a community of faith and love that can expect powerful and sometimes deadly opposition after Jesus' own death and resurrection. They ring truest when addressed to Christian minorities living under oppressive regimes or facing social ostracism in any time. Most readers of this commentary, like its writer, have not known and probably never will know such a situation. To preach this text to a comfortable, bourgeois congregation in a tastefully appointed sanctuary would appear to Jesus and his disciples, as well as to the evangelist and his readers, to be utterly out of place. This text foreshadows the death of Jesus by which he conquered the world, and it speaks eloquently to Christians living under the cross throughout the world in every age. Such communities of Christians through the ages have found in it a source of courage to bear what they must and even to do so with good cheer (AV, RSV). Their aim and effect is to bring peace to disciples in the midst of violent storms.

Although the primary addressees in this text are groups of Christians, appropriation of it by individuals is not excluded. The second person plural can be read distributively as well as corporately. Furthermore, the word for "persecution" can also be translated "trouble," "tribulation," "suffering," and "distress," and these deep waters are not limited to situations of martyrdom. Through the years this text has spoken to countless individual Christians passing through many a valley of deep darkness. Preachers and teachers who accompany their sheep regularly will know how to evoke such situations without betraying confidentiality, and the Paraclete who is at their side in such situations will apply the words of Jesus to troubled hearts. There may be better contexts than the church sanctuary in which to bring these words to the remembrance of Jesus' disciples–places like a hospital room, or the bedroom of a dying saint, or the living room of an abandoned spouse, or with the parents of a youth who has made a shipwreck of life.

In such situations it is often by no means evident that Jesus has overcome the world. Neither was it evident in the events reported in John 18 and 19, namely, Jesus' betrayal and arrest (18:1–11), his condemnation by religious and civil authorities (18:12–19:16a), his crucifixion, death, and burial (19:16b–42). Only Jesus' resurrection and return to the Father lends any credence to his claim to have overcome the world, and these are not subject to empirical proof. Are they true? An affirmative answer to that question is always the work of the Spirit of truth, who in ever-new situations leads Jesus' disciples into all the truth (16:13). And it is Jesus' indwelling presence with believers in the person of the Advocate (rightly called the Comforter in situations of distress; see AV at 14:6, 26; 15:26; 16:7) that enables believers not to avoid trouble but to experience peace and joy even in the midst of it.

The promise of seeing Jesus again is open-ended in John 16:16–33 because it is fulfilled again and again in countless ways through every generation. African American slaves in the United States knew that Jesus had gone to the Father, and they knew that he was with them in their troubles. They appropriated the message of John 16:33 by singing, "Soon I will be done with the troubles of the world. . . . I'm going to live with God!" Others find fulfillment even in this world when, buoyed by the Holy Spirit in their hearts, they discover that Jesus is with them and "eternity is now."[2]

In a different vein, interpreters might focus on the analogy of the woman in labor to preach a sermon or teach a lesson on present pain and long-term joy. In a culture whose motto seems to be "Hope deferred makes the heart sick" (Prov. 13:12a), a word from Jesus that helps us to live hopefully before our desire is fulfilled (Prov. 13:12b) can bring joy and peace even when gratification is deferred. "Get a life," they say, and the expression often implies instant gratification. Jesus proposes to his disciples a life of peace and joy during the time when his way seems to be defeated, as well as ultimate fulfillment when all that the Father has given to the Son will be raised up (6:39, 40, 44, 54) and his disciples' joy will be complete.

The Great Prayer

Chapter 17 contains the great prayer that follows Jesus' farewell discourse with his disciples. The setting is still the Last Supper (13:1–4), and Jesus is still speaking, but no longer directly to his disciples as he has done in chapters 13–16. Jesus, as he lifts his eyes to heaven, prays to the Father. As prayer, chapter 17 is like a family conversation in which the Father and the Son, in complete unanimity (17:11), discuss what Jesus has done and is about to do for his disciples and what he wishes the Father to do for and through them after Jesus' return to the Father. Jesus prays aloud, however, so the disciples will hear (see 11:42). It is a revelation to them as well as a prayer to God,[1] and through its inclusion in the Gospel it is instruction for disciples of every time and place. It serves as climax and conclusion of part two of the Gospel (chaps. 13–17) and also as introduction to John's account of the death and resurrection of Jesus (chaps. 18–21).

Exploring the text

The entire chapter is a literary unit that in the penultimate paragraph returns (vv. 22–24) to the opening theme of glory (vv. 1–5) and in the final paragraph affirms (vv. 25–26) that God's essential nature ("name") is love. The structure indicated by the paragraph divisions in the NRSV is clear: Jesus prays for himself (17:1–5), for the disciples with him at table (17:6–19), and for those who will believe in him through the word of the first witnesses (17:20–24); then he adds a closing declaration and promise (17:25–26). The perspective of this text is that of the risen Lord looking back on Jesus' public ministry and looking forward to the next generation of believers.[2]

JESUS PRAYS FOR HIMSELF:
"FATHER, GLORIFY ME" (17:1–5)

"Glory" and **"glorify"** are key terms in the Fourth Gospel.[3] "Glorify" can mean simply to honor someone (8:54; 21:19), but in John it more often means to reveal or show someone's true nature (11:4; 12:28; 14:13; 15:8; 16:14; 17:10). The "someone" is always God, the Father, or the Son, and the manner of revealing the true nature of God is supremely through Jesus' crucifixion, resurrection, and return to the Father viewed as a single act of being lifted up (12:16, 23–24, 32; 13:31–32). The opening paragraph of Jesus' great prayer brings all three of these meanings together in the richest single text on glory/glorify in the Fourth Gospel (17:1–5).

"Father, the hour has come" (17:1) echoes earlier references to the hour deferred (2:4; 7:30; 8:20) or arrived (12:23, 27; 13:1). The reference in each case is to the hour of Jesus' death and resurrection considered as a single act of being lifted up (3:14–15; 12:27–28, 32). This final reference to "the hour" introduces the narrative of the arrest, trial, crucifixion, death, and resurrection, which begins at 18:1. Jesus is here contemplating his immediate future.

"Authority" in verse 2 parallels a major theme of the Gospel of Mark, which shows Jesus' authority over nature, demons, sickness, and sin, and the climactic final words of the Gospel of Matthew (Matt. 28:18b–20), which proclaim Jesus' authority over everything in heaven and earth. The Fourth Gospel emphasizes Jesus' authority to do what the Father does (5:19–30, esp. v. 27), in particular, to raise the dead and give them life, and also to execute judgment. The Son's authority to give eternal life is underscored in 17:2. Jesus is the agent through whom the gift of eternal life that God wills for the whole world becomes available to whoever believes (3:14–16). This is the authority that the Father has given to the Son, and in exercising it Jesus glorifies God, for he reveals God's true nature as the source of life and light (1:1–5).

In the phrase "to all whom you have given him" (17:2), the Johannine theme of election surfaces once again. Jesus has authority over all people, but only those to whom the Father grants the gift of believing (6:37, 44) possess eternal life.

Verse 3 is important because it defines one of the key terms and major themes of the Fourth Gospel. In John eternal **life** is not merely a future hope. It is a present reality that consists essentially of knowing God through Jesus Christ and living in obedient response to God's creative power and love. It begins on earth but does not end when physical life is ended, because the believer, like Jesus, lives in the eternal love of God now and always.

The voice of Jesus and that of the evangelist are frequently blended in the Fourth Gospel,[4] but never more obviously than here. Nowhere else in any of the four Gospels does Jesus refer to himself as "Jesus Christ," though the evangelist does so at Mark 1:1 and John 1:17. This definition of eternal life—"to know you, the only true God, and Jesus Christ whom you have sent" (17:3)—expresses in capsule form the theology of the Fourth Gospel, in which "see," **"believe,"** and **"know"** are virtual synonyms, and in which abundant life is life in union with Jesus, the true vine, through whom believers experience mutual indwelling with God the Father and the Son.

In verse 4 Jesus looks back to the way he has glorified God through finishing the work God gave him to do during his public ministry. In word and in deed throughout this dramatic narrative, Jesus has finished the work the Father gave him to do, and through it all he has glorified God; that is, he has honored God and shown what God is really like.

Now Jesus looks beyond the immediate future of death and resurrection to his return to God (17:5). "The glory that I had in your presence before the world existed" sends the reader back to the prologue, which speaks of the eternal Word sharing the life and light of God in the beginning (1:1–5). It is this Word become flesh whose glory we have seen in Jesus (1:14), and Jesus now prays to be lifted into primordial glory again. John's image of the descent and ascent of the Son of God is a parabolic curve characterized by glory at every point, although the glory during the earthly portion of this trajectory is visible only to eyes of faith. From the perspective of his humanity Jesus prays to be taken back into the presence of God, where the splendor of his true nature will be as fully evident as it was before all creation.

Through Jesus' prayer for himself (17:1–5) the evangelist summarizes the risen Lord's ministry on earth for disciples of all time.

Preaching and teaching the Word

Part two of the Gospel of John is studded with words to live by, and one of them appears in this brief paragraph: "This is eternal life, that they may know you, the only true God, and Jesus Christ whom you have sent" (17:3). This is the Fourth Gospel's answer to the question put to Alfie in the 1960s, "What's it all about?" It's not about the Hokey-Pokey, or getting and spending, or reality TV. It's about intimate communion with our Creator and with Jesus Christ, the one who lived among us as the embodiment of God's love. This text speaks to the universal will to live life to the full. It also affirms that the desire to keep on living corresponds to a profound reality.

Preparation to preach or teach this text could begin by reviewing the uses of a couple of its key terms throughout the Fourth Gospel: "eternal life" and "know." A sermon or lesson on eternal life could then compare how it is used in various contexts in the Fourth Gospel and in common parlance today. Reflection on usage today may reveal how often and glibly we speak of "heaven" and how seldom of "eternal life." A sermon on eternal life might be in order, and not only on the Seventh Sunday in Easter of year A, when the Gospel lesson is John 17:1–11.

Similarly, preachers and teachers might reflect on the ways we use "know" today as possible clues to or distortions of its meaning in this text. For instance, "I thought I knew her, but obviously I didn't really" reflects different levels of knowledge of another person. Those who know Jesus Christ find in him the answer to the universal hunger of the human heart for contact with ultimate reality. The preacher or teacher has an opportunity to suggest ways to nurture a daily walk with Jesus, the natural outcome of which will be a deep and satisfying communion with God that not even death can end. Part of such a communion will be the realization that we are known by God and kept securely in the Good Shepherd's fold.

A fundamental suggestion has to do with the chapter as a whole. Teachers and preachers can use the threefold division of John 17 as a model for their own praying. Read the chapter straight through once or twice, then pray for yourself, for those who look to you as a guide, and for those whom your life may touch in the future. Write your prayer, pray it, and keep it in your Bible or your journal.

Here is one such prayer :

> Lord, may my life be a credit to you.
>
> Lord, may those whom my life seeks to guide (my parishioners, my students, my children, my friends) be led into lives that are a credit to you.
>
> Lord, may those who remember me down the road remember above all my love for you, and may they be a credit to your name. Amen.

JESUS PRAYS FOR HIS FIRST DISCIPLES (17:6–19)

This is the central and longest part of the great prayer of Jesus that concludes part two of the Fourth Gospel. The entire prayer is presented as a window into the heart and mind of God. It lifts the reader out of time and into the presence of eternity, where Jesus is always praying for his disciples.

Although Jesus does not announce that he is praying for his first disciples until verse 9, they are the focus of attention as he looks back at the work God gave him to do on earth (vv. 6–8). These verses are therefore included as an introduction to the prayer in verses 9–19 to constitute a single paragraph in the NRSV (17:6–19). This is the Gospel pericope for the Seventh Sunday of Easter of year B. The unit ends at verse 19 because at verse 20 Jesus turns his attention to future disciples. This distinction is reflected by a paragraph division in many translations, but the following notes recognize that Jesus' prayer for his first disciples applies to succeeding generations as well.

Exploring the text

The text lifts Jesus above time by its unusual shifts in temporal viewpoint. At one point Jesus has already left the world and is on his way to the Father (17:11); two verses later he is still in the world looking forward to his death, resurrection, and return to the Father (17:13), and in verse 18 he has died, risen, and sent his disciples into the world. In the next unit he is already in glory with the Father (see 17:24). These anomalies bear out the claim that "the Jesus of the Last Discourse transcends time and space, for from heaven and beyond the grave he is already speaking to the disciples of all time."[1]

Like the whole of John 17, verses 6–19 presuppose more than one audience. By speaking aloud, Jesus addresses those present with him in time, as well as God. Furthermore, by including this prayer in the Fourth Gospel, the evangelist addresses yet another audience near the end of the first century and serves as intermediary for the risen Christ to continue to address successive audiences of disciples in every place and time.

What Jesus Has Already Done (17:6–8)

Jesus has shown his disciples what God is like. The verb "made known" (17:6a) is also translated as "manifested" (RSV) and "revealed" (NIV). It is the Greek term for what a revealer does, and in the Fourth Gospel Jesus is above all the revealer of God. (The **"I Am" sayings** point us to this.) The direct object, "your name," is weighty with all the significance of the divine name in the Old Testament. "Name" here stands for the essential nature and personhood of God, so its translation as "you" in the NIV is not incorrect. The indirect object, "those whom you gave me from the world," although it refers primarily to Jesus' disciples during his earthly ministry, applies also to all subsequent disciples of Jesus. The following phrase (17:6b) underscores that they already belonged to God, who gave them to Jesus. That they do not belong to the world is spelled out in verses 14–16. That disciples belong both to God and to Jesus is affirmed when Jesus says, in effect, "I have revealed your true nature to my disciples–the ones who belonged to you and whom you gave to me by drawing them to me (6:44)–and they have continued to believe that what I told them is true. They now believe that I have indeed come from you" (17:6–8, author's paraphrase).

What Jesus Asks God to Do (17:9–10)

The petitions in this part of the text are introduced by two verses that limit the scope of Jesus' prayer to "those whom you gave me" (v. 9). The immediate reference is to the disciples who overhear his words, but it is phrased in such a way as to include all disciples. **"World"** in this verse could refer generally to all human beings ("I am not praying for just everybody," 17:9 paraphrased), but in the context of a prayer for protection it probably carries the specifically Johannine sense of those who have rejected Jesus and are under the power of Satan, from whose power Jesus prays God to protect ("guard" or "keep") his disciples (17:11, 15). "World" here is the sphere of enmity to God, as at 1:10–11; 7:7; 12:31; and 15:18–19. From the Johannine perspective, "the world is not to be prayed for but proved wrong (16:8–11) and conquered (1 John 5:4–5). . . . The world must pass away (1 John 2:17)."[2]

Verses 9b–10 reinforce the idea that the disciples belonged first to God and now belong both to God and to Jesus. The affirmation in the past tense that Jesus has been **glorified** in the disciples presupposes the temporal perspective of the evangelist. As his disciples participate in Jesus' mission of glorifying God in the world, Jesus is glorified in them.[3]

First Petition: Protect Them (17:11–16)

There are actually only two petitions in Jesus' prayer for his first disciples, each of which is accompanied by statements that explain its rationale and purpose. The first petition is expressed first as an imperative ("Holy Father, protect them," v. 11) and in conclusion as a statement ("I ask you to protect them from the evil one," v. 15). This petition is accompanied by two reasons and a statement of purpose. The first reason introduces the petition: while he was with them in the world, Jesus protected (literally "kept") them in God's name (v. 12), but now that he is leaving, he asks God to act directly on their behalf. The Greek preposition *en* ("in") can be used in many ways. Here, it can either mean that God's name is the instrument Jesus wields to protect his disciples ("by the power of your name," v. 11, NIV, TEV, NEB) or that Jesus acts as God's agent ("I protected them in your name," v. 12, AV, RSV, NRSV). God's name (essential character), like the disciples themselves, has been given to Jesus by God.

The other reason for Jesus' prayer of protection is the hostility the disciples will face as they carry out their mission of taking Jesus' words (= God's word; compare vv. 8 and 14) to the world. Jesus has warned them about the world's hatred earlier (15:18–16:4); now he asks the Father to protect them when they confront it (17:14–16).

Between these reasons for the first petition, Jesus mentions two purposes or effects that he has in mind, each introduced by "so that." Jesus asks the Father to protect his disciples "so that they may be one, as we are one" (v. 11c), and he speaks these things, including this petition, while he is still in the world "so that they may have my joy made complete in themselves" (v. 13). The goal of Jesus' prayer is the unity and joy of his disciples. The theme of unity is further developed in the final portion of the prayer and will be treated there (vv. 20–23). This mention of joy concludes a theme introduced at 15:11 and developed in 16:15–24. Jesus does not pray God to ease his disciples' pain by taking them out of the world (v. 15a). He does ask the Father to keep them safe while under attack (v. 15b), so that their unity will be preserved (v. 11) and their joy made complete (v. 13).

In using the past tense to speak of the world's hatred (17:14), the text places Jesus at the side of his disciples in moments of crisis that are still future in the setting of the farewell discourse. Jesus is leaving the world to return to the Father, while the calling of the disciples is to remain in the world. He glorified God by his death, resurrection, and ascension; the disciples are to glorify God by their faithful witness to the eternal Word as they confront the evil one (17:15) in the person of those who reject Jesus. Here and in the Lord's Prayer (Matt. 6:13) the AV translates "the evil one" (*ho poneros*) as an abstract noun, "evil," but the expression refers in both cases to the one who elsewhere in John is called the devil (6:70; 8:44; 13:2), Satan (13:27), or the ruler of this world (12:31; 14:30; 16:11).[4]

A parenthetical remark acknowledges that one, but only one, of the first disciples was lost, "so that the scripture might be fulfilled" (v. 12b). The comment is another stroke in the Fourth Gospel's bleak portrait of Judas (6:70; 13:2, 11, 18, 26–30). The Scripture referred to is doubtless Psalm 41:9, cited explicitly at John 13:18. Despite his knowledge of Judas's treachery, Jesus still refers to him as a disciple–one of those whom God gave to Jesus (v. 9), but who was also a "son of perdition" (AV, RSV and Greek, *huios tes apoleias,* a Semitic turn of phrase translated as "the one destined to be lost," NRSV; "bound to be lost," TEV; "doomed to be lost," REB; "doomed to destruction," NIV). The Johannine theme of foreordination surfaces again in the reason given for Judas's apostasy: "so that the scripture might be fulfilled."[5]

Second Petition: Sanctify Them (17:17–19)

The repetition of "They do not belong to the world, just as I do not belong to the world" (v. 16) concludes the prayer for protection and serves as transition to the second petition: "Sanctify them in the truth" (v. 17a).

"To sanctify" means "to make holy," that is, "to set apart for a divinely appointed task." The disciples are to be set apart from the world, to which they no longer belong. Verse 18 specifies the task for which they are set apart: "As you have sent me into the world, so I have sent them into the world." Jesus speaks here as the risen Lord who commissions his disciples on the evening of the first Easter Day (20:21; see notes there).

To sanctify disciples "in the truth" means to set them apart for their mission "by the truth" (NIV, NEB) or "by means of the truth" (TEV), understanding "in" in its instrumental sense, as at verse 11. But "in" here also retains its local sense. The disciples are to be set apart by means of their union with Jesus Christ, who is the truth, in whom they are to abide as branches of the true vine (15:4–8; 17:11, 21–23).

Truth is a key term in the Gospel of John.[6] "Your word is truth" (v. 17b) is a subtle allusion to John 1:14. Although Jesus is never explicitly called "the Word" in the body of the Gospel, this understanding of him underlies the affirmation here. God's Word, incarnate in Jesus, is truth–as well as the way and the life (14:6).

In verse 19 Jesus turns his attention back to himself, as at the beginning of the prayer (17:1), but petition here gives way to revelation: "For their sakes I sanctify myself." Jesus here seems to think of his impending death and sees himself as a priest offering himself as a victim for those whom God has given him, on the analogy of the depiction of Christ as high priest in the letter to the Hebrews (Heb. 9:11–14; 2:10–11; 10:10).[7] In John, the sanctifying of Jesus and that of his disciples are integrally related. "Their holiness, Jesus' and the disciples', is their being set apart from the world for the sake of the world."[8]

Preaching and teaching the Word

This text is appropriate for teaching because it includes words, phrases, and ideas that need explanation in today's world. It merits preaching because it reveals Jesus' prayer for his first disciples and for us as well. His first petition is the climactic verse in the Gospel reading for the Seventh Sunday of Easter in year A (John 17:1–11). Both petitions appear in the Gospel reading for the same Sunday in year B (John 17:6–19).

1. Protect them (v. 11). Jesus prays first that God will protect his disciples. The text is timely in a world that is preoccupied with–even obsessed by– the desire for security, as a result of terrorist acts. Jesus recognizes the legitimacy of his disciples' need for protection then and now. In his unity with the Father he prays that God will provide it.

The means of protection to which Jesus appeals, however, is not that to which nations and individuals usually turn. He appeals to the divine name–God's essential nature–for the protection of the disciples. Jesus is talking not about insertion of the word "God" into a nation's pledge of allegiance but about trust in the providence of God and obedience to the voice of the Good Shepherd.

Jesus knows that his flock will be assailed by external enemies, but the particular danger in view here is that it will be torn apart by dissension and lack of love: "Protect them in your name . . . so that they may be one, as we are one" (17:11b). The theme of unity is developed further in the next pericope (17:20–23), but its inclusion in a prayer for protection shows that Jesus views disruption of the community as a mortal danger. The source of this danger is the evil one (v. 15), who sets disciples at odds with each other so that they are no longer one as the Father and the Son are one (v. 11c). The text about unity is often used to bolster appeals for ecumenism. The context, however, is a prayer for God's protection in the spiritual struggle for survival of a community of love. Let Jesus' disciples in every age hear the Shepherd's voice.

When conflict threatens to divide denominations, congregations, and individual Christians into hostile camps, preaching and teaching this particular petition from the pastoral heart of Jesus might reveal more clearly the source of disruption and the resource for overcoming it.

2. Set them apart (v. 17). Jesus' second petition for his disciples is that God will "Sanctify them in the truth." The preacher or teacher can illuminate "sanctify" by reflecting on how various religious communities, including the church, have understood and practiced sainthood. Few of the common uses of the term "saint" reflect biblical usage. According to Paul, who uses "sanctify" occasionally and "saint" very often, all believers in Jesus are called to be saints (Rom. 1:7; 1 Cor. 1:2), for God's call sets them apart–that is, makes them saints. According to John, Jesus sets a task for his disciples (17:18) and prays that God will set them apart for that task (17:17), just as God had set the Son apart (sanctified him) and sent him into the world (10:36). In John, as in Paul, it is God's setting them apart for a task that makes saints of disciples. Each group of hearers can reflect on what task(s) God sets for them.

Jesus wants God to dedicate his first disciples to the task of standing fast in the truth he has taught them through the words God gave Jesus to say (12:50), but the explanatory affirmation, "your word is truth," suggests another understanding. In the Fourth Gospel, Jesus is the Word, and Jesus is the truth. Jesus here prays the Father to set the disciples apart for their task by means of their union with the one who assigns it. Jesus sets himself apart by his obedience to the task God gave him–to reveal the true nature of God and to take away the sin of the world (1:29). He does this so that we also may be set apart for our tasks by abiding in him (17:19).

3. Joy according to John (v. 13). "But now I am coming to you, and I speak these things in the world so that they may have my joy made complete in themselves" (17:13) is the third and climactic appearance of joy in part two of the Fourth Gospel, following on 15:11 and 16:24. It offers a good occasion to preach or teach the specifically Johannine understanding of joy.[9]

While the focus of the two earlier texts on joy is the disciples, this one focuses on Jesus and the Father. To be sure, Jesus prays that his first disciples will experience joy, even in face of attacks from the evil one, but what he prays for is that *his* joy will be made complete in them. The text is concerned not only with how Jesus can make us happy, but how we can make Jesus happy. (An analogy might be seen in the battle of the bumper stickers: "God bless America," answered by "America bless God.") The joy Jesus wants for his disciples is their joy in him, and his own joy is made complete in that of his disciples. The other distinguishing mark of this third text on joy is that it occurs in the context not of instruction but of prayer. Joy comes from the Lord!

4. In the world but not of it (vv. 14–18). Disciples do not belong to the world, any more than Jesus did (v. 14), but they are called to be in the world (v. 18), which is their field of mission. They are to be sanctified, set apart from the world for their mission in the world (vv. 17–18).

This sounds like double-talk until one remembers that John uses **"world"** in several different ways. When Jesus says that his disciples do not belong to the world, just as he himself does not belong to the world (vv. 14, 16), "world" refers to the realm of unbelief, those who fail to recognize Jesus as the Christ, the Word, the Son and light of God. When Jesus sends his disciples into the world, as he himself was sent into the world (v. 18), "world" refers to the inhabited world and all its inhabitants, the theater of human history, the object of God's saving love (3:16). Jesus once said, "As long as I am in the world, I am the light of the world" (9:5). Now he prays that his disciples, too, will be in the world without becoming contaminated by the world's darkness.

Some Christians have withdrawn from the world, practicing a spirituality that is not of the world but not in it, either: they are neither in the world nor of it. Other Christians are fully engaged in a mission in the world but with nothing to distinguish them from it: they are both in the world and of it. Still others have adopted the world's standards but have no sense of responsibility for the mess those standards have made of the world: they are of the world, but not in it. Teachers can use this paradigm to encourage learners to become interpreters themselves as they identify and discuss the various ways we Christians relate to the world, in light of Jesus' example. Preachers can call us to be in the world but not of it, as revealed in Jesus' heartfelt prayer for his disciples every day.

JESUS PRAYS FOR HIS FUTURE DISCIPLES AND CONCLUDES HIS PRAYER (17:20–26)

Twice in the first half of the twentieth century great nations found themselves locked in mortal combat in world wars. During that same period, when Western civilization appeared to be coming apart at the seams, Christians around the world were coming together in what came to be known as the ecumenical movement, widely hailed as "the great new fact of our time." Its rallying cry was "That they all may be one," words of Jesus that are the center of gravity of the lectionary Gospel for the Seventh Sunday of Easter, year C (John 17:20–26). At the outset of the twenty-first century, the movement greeted with the joy of discovery a century ago arouses little enthusiasm, and the text (17:21) seems tired. Can it be reclaimed?

Exploring the text

This passage is the final section of Jesus' great prayer at the end of the discourses in part two of the Gospel of John (chaps. 13–17). It begins with a shift in focus from the disciples with him to those who would become disciples in the future (17:20). Its conclusion is indicated by the closing formula, "After Jesus had spoken these words" (18:1a; see Matt. 7:28; 11:1; 13:53; 19:1; 26:1). The final verse of the prayer (17:26) leads directly into John's passion narrative, the story of "the hour" in which Jesus is lifted up in glory on the cross and from the grave to return to the presence of the Father.

Prayer for Future Disciples (17:20–24)

In verse 20 Jesus announces that he is no longer praying only for the disciples present with him but for all who will in the future believe in him through the testimony of these first witnesses. The first disciples came to believe through the words and deeds of Jesus, in whom words and the Word are one. Now Jesus looks ahead, beyond the first generation of his disciples, to all who will come to believe only through the words and deeds of subsequent witnesses. That includes us. His prayer consists of two petitions.

First Petition (17:21–23)

The basic petition is "that they all may be one" (v. 21a). The nature of the unity for which Jesus prays is described in verse 21b, and its goal is stated in verse 21c. Jesus says, in effect, "I pray that those who will believe in me in the future may all be one—one in us, as you, Father are in me and I in you. Make them one in us in order that everybody in the world, including those who now reject me, may come to believe that you have sent me" (17:21, author's paraphrase).

This is a prayer, not an exhortation. The unity among Christians for which Jesus prays is spiritual, constituted by their mutual indwelling with the **Father**, the Son, and each other. This kind of unity is a gift from God, not an ecumenical achievement. Jesus, in unity with the Father, prays for God to give it. The entire prayer is a kind of divine internal dialogue that reveals God's nature and will. Only indirectly and in a secondary way can it also be construed as exhortation, since it does let us know what Jesus wants for his disciples.

The spiritual unity Christ seeks is inseparably linked to the glory that the Father gave the Son—glory that Jesus has given and still gives to his disciples (vv. 22–23a). **Glory** is an important but elusive concept in the Fourth Gospel, whose use in various contexts helps to focus our understanding of it. To "give glory" in the present text is not a synonym for "to praise" (as it sometimes is), but rather reflects one of the basic meanings of "glorify": to reveal someone's true nature. Jesus is saying, "I have shared your essential nature with them just as you have shared your essential nature with me, and I have done this so that the relationship that unites you and me will also unite them with each other and with us—I dwelling in them and you dwelling in me, so that they may become completely united with each other in us" (vv. 22–23a, author's paraphrase).

The mutual indwelling of which Jesus speaks here and elsewhere in the farewell discourse (14:10, 15–18; 15:1–7, 9–10) is closely related to the Christ mysticism expressed by Paul through the expression "in Christ." Its importance is underscored by repetition (vv. 21a–b, 23a) as well as by its climactic position in Jesus' great prayer. Mystic union with Christ has often been understood to be the major theme of the Fourth Gospel, from Clement of Alexandria at the dawn of the third century to William Countryman at the end of the twentieth.[1] An interpretive tradition this ancient and persistent is not likely to be wrong, but it is subject to misunderstanding. As a leading Roman Catholic scholar has commented,

> Divine indwelling is an intimate union that expresses itself in a
> way of life lived in love. If we understand this truth, we shall avoid

the mistaken identification of John's concept of indwelling with an exalted mysticism like that of a Teresa or of a John of the Cross. To remain in Jesus, or in the Father . . . is intimately associated with keeping the commandments in a spirit of love (Jn 15:10; 1 Jn 4:12,16), with a struggle against the world (1 Jn 2:16–17), and with bearing fruit (Jn 15:5)–all basic Christian duties. Thus, indwelling is not the exclusive experience of chosen souls within the Christian community; it is the essential constitutive principle of all Christian life.[2]

Inner communion with Christ and loving service to others are all of one piece in the Fourth Gospel.

The purpose and goal of Jesus' prayer for unity is spelled out in the final clause of each statement of this petition: "so that the world may believe that you have sent me" (v. 21c), and "so that the world may know that you have sent me and have loved them even as you have loved me" (v. 23c). These verses express two things that Jesus wants the world to believe and know: "that you have sent me" and "that you have loved them even as you have loved me." These two verses together capture the central message of John's Gospel. They recall the core of the gospel in general (succinctly expressed in 3:16) and the goal of the Fourth Gospel in particular (20:31), stating them as the deep desire of the one who has been sent. He is nearing the end of his assigned mission, which he now entrusts to his disciples to complete–a task that will take more than one generation. The goal of Jesus' prayer is the continuation of his mission to make known God's love for everybody in the world, a love that draws all believers in Jesus into communion with the Father, the Son, and one another.

Second Petition (17:24)

Jesus further desires that "those also, whom you have given me"–that is, all whom God in future generations will draw to Jesus (6:37, 44)–"may be with me where I am, to see my glory" (v. 24a). Here, as in his earlier reference to "my Father's house" (14:2), Jesus is thinking ahead to his return to the Father. He wants his disciples to be so united with him in God's presence that they will see the full splendor of God's nature in Jesus.

The glory of which Jesus speaks is his own, yet it is a derived splendor, for it came from God ("my glory which you have given me," v. 24b). At the same time, it is a glory that the Father shared with the Son as an act of love before all creation (v. 24c). This evident reference to the prologue (1:1–5) deepens our understanding of that rich text. The mutual indwelling of God and the Word in the beginning is a glorious relationship at the heart of which is divine love. Jesus has been emissary, object, and channel of that love while he was on earth. Now he anticipates his return to the Father to be fully reunited with and absorbed into that love, and he wants his disciples to be there and to see him as he truly is.

Jesus here contemplates life beyond death for his disciples as well as for himself. In the Fourth Gospel the traditional futuristic eschatology of the earliest Christian communities has been reinterpreted but not eliminated, as this text demonstrates. Jesus prays for reunion with his disciples after his death, and after theirs as well.

Closing Declaration and Promise (17:25–26)

To conclude his prayer, Jesus takes stock of the results of his earthly ministry. He addresses God as "Righteous Father" (v. 25), referring to God's divine attributes, including justice. The adjective used here is translated as "just" in Latin and languages derived from it. This form of address is functionally synonymous with "Holy Father" (v. 11). Both are titles of respect reserved for God in the Fourth Gospel, derived from the holiness and justice that are basic attributes of God in the Old Testament. Jesus states that he knows the Father, that the world does not, and that his disciples are open to learn, since they know that Jesus is the Father's emissary (v. 25). Looking back, he reports that he has revealed to the disciples God's essential character and power ("I made your name known to them," v. 26a). Looking ahead, he promises to continue to make God's nature known to his disciples (v. 26b). God's essential nature is revealed in the love shown through the Word made flesh in Jesus Christ, and Jesus promises to continue to make that love known to future generations of disciples.

The final words of this prayer and of the farewell discourse point to the goal of all the teaching in these chapters (13–17) and express Jesus' deepest desire for his disciples of all time: "so that the love with which you have loved me may be in them, and I in them" (26c). If, in the preceding paragraph, Jesus prays that his disciples will, after their death, be with him where he is (v. 24), here at the climax of his prayer he expresses his yearning to come and live in them where they are, here on earth. "I in them" fulfills the promise, "I am coming to you" (14:18), and describes the nature of the mutual indwelling of Father, Son, and believers. It is love.

Preaching and teaching the Word

Is it, then, possible to reclaim the power of Jesus' prayer for the unity of his disciples? Perhaps it would help to begin by considering themes that inform the entire passage (17:20–26), rather than particular texts in it.

These themes might suggest occasions on which the unit might be taught or preached.

1. Prayer. The text can be approached not as an exhortation but as a prayer. What if we considered the church not as an institution but as the community of those for whom Christ prays? What if I considered myself not as an ambitious achiever or a failed sinner, not as a thinker or a doer, but as one whom Jesus loves and prays for? What a boost for healthy self-esteem! Approached in this way, the first step for interpreters might be to allow this intimate converse between the Son and the Father to transform their own conception and practice of private prayer. One of the words to live by in this section of the Fourth Gospel is "Father, I desire that those also, whom you have given me, may be with me where I am, to see my glory, which you have given me because you loved me before the foundation of the world" (v. 24). Perhaps we need to remember Jesus' "I in them and you in me" (v. 23), "so that the love with which you have loved me may be in them, and I in them" (v. 26), and spend more time in contemplation of the glory of our risen Lord. Prayer in this mode would lead to "knowledge of him who called us by his own glory and goodness . . . [to] become participants of the divine nature" (2 Pet. 1:3–4). Such an understanding and practice of prayer might inculcate in us his love for the world and transform our teaching and preaching of other themes that emerge in this prayer of Jesus for his disciples.

2. Love. Three moments in the love of God are reflected in this text: the love of the Father for the Son before creation (v. 24c); God's love for the world made known through Jesus' ministry on earth (v. 23b–c); and the love of God in Christ that dwells in believers till the end of time and beyond (v. 26c). No one is too young to learn about the love of God ("Jesus Loves Me") or too old to appreciate the rich baritone of George Beverly Shea singing "The Love of God," for the theme comes from the heart of the gospel and speaks to the hearts of all God's children. In his great prayer Jesus invests the theme with theological depth and personal appeal. Any interpreter who helps people to lay hold on the love of God in their minds and hearts becomes a channel through which Jesus' prayer is answered in the lives of Christians in every generation.

3. Mission. Sermons during mission season often gravitate toward the two major forms of the Great Commission (Matt. 28:9–20; Acts 1:8) or John's statement of the gospel in a nutshell that announces the foundation and motive for Christian mission in the world (John 3:16). John 17:20–26 offers a different approach to mission that may allow the preacher to treat the subject in a fresh way.

Although earlier in the great prayer Jesus seems to show concern only for his disciples and not for the world, in these verses (17:20–26) he underscores the essential role of Christian witness and entrusts to his disciples in every age his own unfinished mission to the world. In this text the motive to be about mission and evangelism is not the fear of hell but the love of God. Those who are already disciples will want to fulfill Jesus' desire to make God's love known to all the world. Those who are not disciples have a God-shaped hole at the heart of their lives that can be filled by the Word Jesus has entrusted to his witnesses.

4. Unity. Jesus knows that the world will not believe the message if it cannot see the love of God in the messengers. The spiritual unity of Jesus' witnesses must find practical expression if it is to be believed. So he prays "that they all may be one," one in God and therefore one with each other.

This petition is underlined by repetition; it appears three times in the great prayer (17:11, 21, 23). These three texts can be fruitfully combined in a sermon or lesson. The first (v. 11) presupposes that conflict among Christians is the work of the evil one, from whose manipulations Jesus prays the Father to protect us. The second (v. 21) prays for unity among believers so that the world may come to believe that Jesus is truly sent from God and really is the eternal Word made flesh, the Son of God and Israel's Messiah. The third (v. 23) prays that the world may come not only to know that God has sent Jesus, but to know that God loves the messengers and everyone who hears the message.

This understanding of the unity Jesus prays for suggests a new way of living with fellow Christians (in love, v. 26) and a new mode of witness to the world. Instead of "How can I prove to the other that I am right?" we might try "Where in the other do I see Christ?" Such an approach may lead to the discovery, above and beyond all human barriers, of a unity God has already given. Mohandas Gandhi, the nonviolent liberator of India and great admirer of Jesus, is reported to have said that he would have become a Christian but for the behavior of Christians.

PART THREE

The Word That Does Not Die

18:1–20:31

Passion Narrative

18:1–19:42

"The hour" toward which the plot of the Fourth Gospel has been moving from the beginning is narrated in John's account of the death of Jesus (chaps. 18–19) and his resurrection (chaps. 20–21). Readers have seen in part one how the eternal, living Word became flesh and encountered all sorts of people, whose various responses included curiosity, acceptance, and rejection. When the opposition of those who rejected him became intense and the scope of those who accepted him expanded to include some Greeks, Jesus knew the time had come for him to be put to death and to return to the Father. In part two he uses the occasion of a Last Supper with his disciples to prepare them for what lies ahead and to give them words to live by after his departure. This done, the plot moves in part three to tell the story of Jesus' death and resurrection, a single drama of exaltation in which the living Word is lifted up on a cross, then out of a tomb, so that even death becomes a triumph.

The basic elements in the passion narrative are the same in all four Gospels. Even a casual effort to identify the common elements, however, reveals how many details distinguish this Gospel from the other three.

John's witness to Jesus differs in its omission of certain elements found in the Synoptic Gospels: the agony in Gethsemane, the kiss of Judas at the arrest, Simon of Cyrene carrying Jesus' cross, the derision and the cry of dereliction from the cross.

Elements added in the Fourth Gospel and found only there are even more significant: the commanding role of Jesus at his arrest in a garden; his challenge to Annas; the extended dialogue with Pilate; his sentencing about noon on the day of preparation of the Passover; carrying his own cross to Golgotha; the three languages of the inscription on the cross; the group at the foot of the cross; Jesus' three last words; the piercing of his side; the role of Nicodemus in Jesus' burial in a garden tomb.

In addition to these major distinguishing features, the Fourth Gospel's account of the passion differs from the others in many details, whose particular significance is considered in the following notes on these chapters. Taken as a whole, these omissions, additions, and variations reveal the evangelist's special interests and serve as clues to substantive and faithful interpretation of the text. They are highlights in John's portrait of Jesus, the Son of God who voluntarily lays down his life to take away the sins of the world and, through his majestic death, reveals the very nature of God.

Teaching and preaching the Word

1. Good Friday services. The Revised Common Lectionary appoints the whole Johannine passion narrative to be read as the Gospel on Good Friday every year (John 18:1–19:42). This takes twelve to thirteen minutes, and the other three readings (O.T., Psalm, and Epistle) in their entirety would require another ten to eleven minutes. It would be difficult to add a sermon to that much Scripture within the confines of the time usually allotted to public worship or the limits of the average worshiper's attention span. Yet there are important reasons to read the entire passion narrative straight through, chief of which is the power of the unadorned story. Interpreters should reflect on how best to let it speak to a community of faith.

One way is through special Good Friday services that last from noon till 3:00 P.M. In this setting the three hours could be divided into six thirty-minute segments with one segment allotted to each of the units in the Johannine narrative (dividing the trial before Pilate into two units, as indicated by the chapter division). This would allow time for silent meditation and expository comments during each of the six time segments.

2. The passion in art. Art can be a powerful exposition of the meaning of Jesus' death. The witness of artists from many centuries and cultures can enrich worship any time the Johannine passion narrative is chosen as the Gospel reading, such as the Sunday before Easter (Passion/Palm Sunday) or on the last Sunday of the liturgical year (Christ the King/Reign of Christ). In such a one-hour context, the use of carefully selected interpretations of the text by poets and hymn writers and works of visual art, interspersed with unhurried periods of silence, could enhance the hearing of John's account without interrupting the flow of the narrative. Hymnals with a Scripture index allow preachers and teachers to identify hymns based on texts from John 18 and 19. Hymns that speak of the glory of the cross all reflect the central emphasis of the Johannine passion narrative. Anthologies of Christian poetry are helpful, as are illustrated books of Christian art. A particularly helpful resource is Hans-Ruedi Weber, *On a Friday Noon,*[1] whose opening meditation combines Scripture (1 Cor. 1:18–24; John 12:23–33), a color plate of "The cross of transfiguration" (a sixth-century mosaic in Ravenna), and the sixth-century passion hymn by Venantius Fortunatus that includes the vivid line "God has reigned from a tree."

The preacher or teacher's role in this approach is to read the text clearly, correctly, and with understanding, making sure that other elements in the service are subordinate to the unadorned power of John's narrative. To plan a service of worship simple enough to accomplish that end is in itself an art.

3. An adult education series. Raymond E. Brown's *Death of the Messiah,* a commentary on the passion narratives in all four Gospels,[2] can serve as a major resource for an adult education series on the passion narrative. His scholarly yet pastoral exposition arranges the successive incidents into four acts, three of which are subdivided into two scenes. An adult study of the four portraitlike accounts in the Gospels lets the particular emphasis of each evangelist stand out sharply, giving a more complete picture of this central event in the New Testament and in human history. This stereophonic treatment of each scene lays great demands on the interpreter as teacher but offers extraordinary rewards to all participants in the class. Observing differences among the four Gospels provides an occasion to discuss questions of historicity in the context of shared faith.

4. Jesus Christ died like a God. A communion sermon preached by an aged, blind Presbyterian minister named James Waddell (d. 1805) captured the essence of the Fourth Gospel's passion narrative. It was preached some twenty years after the American Revolution in a country church in Orange County, Virginia, and described in full by a former British spy named Wirt, who chanced upon the place of worship while revisiting places he had first seen during the war. Wirt portrays the remarkable eloquence of the preacher as he depicted the crucifixion, his blind eyes streaming in tears. "The whole house resounded with the mingled groans, and sobs, and shrieks of the congregation. It was some time before the tumult had subsided, so far as to permit him to proceed. . . . I could not conceive how he would be able to let his audience down from the height to which he had wound them, without impairing the solemnity and dignity of his subject. . . . But—no; the descent was as beautiful and sublime as the elevation had been rapid and enthusiastic. The first sentence with which he broke the awful silence was a quotation from Rousseau: 'Socrates died like a philosopher, but Jesus Christ like a God!' I despair of giving you any idea of the effect produced by this short sentence."[3] It is precisely the effect intended by the Johannine account of Jesus' death.

5. Tragedy or triumph? The Gospels of Mark and Matthew present the crucifixion as a tragedy in which Jesus, in his only word from the cross, cries out, "My God, my God, why have you forsaken me?" (Mark 15:34//Matt. 27:46). The apostle Paul speaks of the cross as "a stumbling block to Jews and foolishness to Gentiles" (1 Cor. 1:23), and the Epistle to the Hebrews says that Jesus "endured the cross, disregarding its shame" (Heb. 12:2). Early apologists had to defend the Christian faith against attacks by those who scorned it because its founder was condemned and executed as a common criminal. Yet the Gospel of John speaks of Jesus' death on the cross as being "lifted up" and glorified, and Christians sing hymns about "the wondrous cross on which the Prince of glory died." Some sing, "In the cross of Christ I glory," while others find morally unacceptable the idea of an innocent person's death somehow taking away the sin of the world. How can the fourth evangelist view the cross as triumph rather than tragedy? Why is Jesus' death not tragic, like the deaths of Lincoln, Gandhi, and King? These questions could be dealt with in a sermon on the Johannine passion narrative or in a teaching situation allowing dialogue among those who wrestle with them.

BETRAYAL AND ARREST (18:1–12)

> One is nearer God's heart in a garden
> than anywhere else on earth.[4]

The fourth evangelist never heard of Dorothy Frances Gurney or her lines about the charm of an English garden, but two significant scenes in the passion narrative of the Fourth Gospel (and in no other) are set in a garden. The familiar expression, "garden of Gethsemane," obscures the fact that the name Gethsemane is found only in Matthew and Mark, while only John calls the place across the Kidron valley a garden. (Luke speaks only of "the Mount of Olives.") Could John have thought there is something special about gardens?

Exploring the text

The time of Jesus' betrayal and arrest is described only as "after Jesus had spoken these words" (18:1a). The main function of this clause is to bring closure to the discourses of the preceding five chapters. The actual time of the arrest is suggested by the mention of lanterns and torches in verse 3.

The Setting (18:1–2)

The place is located "across the Kidron valley," or Cedar Gulch. The word used for the stream that formed the valley refers to a watercourse that flows only after rain–a *wadi* in the Middle East or a dry gulch in the

American West–and its proper name is the Greek word for "cedars." John's text calls this place across the valley "a garden, which [Jesus] and his disciples entered" (18:1b). No name is given; it is just "a garden." It must have offered quietness and privacy, for "Jesus often met there with his disciples" (v. 2).

The Betrayal (18:2–3)

Judas is introduced in verse 2 as the one who betrayed Jesus. His only action is described in verse 3: he served as guide to bring the agents of the authorities to a place where they could arrest Jesus unobtrusively.

The arresting party consisted of a "detachment of soldiers" (the technical term used here refers to a Roman cohort, which usually consisted of six hundred men) and "police from the chief priests and the Pharisees." Obviously the detachment in this case was only part of a cohort. Its significance lies not in the exact number, but in the fact that Jewish and Roman authorities collaborated in the use of disproportionate force to make this arrest. In addition to the lanterns and torches necessary to find their way in the dark, they were armed with unspecified weapons. Judas goes out from the Last Supper into the night (13:30), and later that same night he comes with arms and artificial light to confront the light of the world–a striking example of John's use of the theme of **light** and **darkness** throughout this Gospel.

The Arrest (18:4–9)

Some of the boldest strokes in John's depiction of Jesus appear in these verses. At this point the other three Gospels report a brief interchange between Jesus and Judas, who betrays Jesus with a kiss. John's only note about Judas is that he was standing there with Jesus' adversaries (v. 5). Here the significant dialogue is between Jesus and the arresting party, and the significant action is their being taken aback and literally grounded by the power of Jesus' words, "I am he" (vv. 5, 6, 8).

An editorial note underscores Jesus' divine omniscience. Jesus is not flustered by the approach of his enemies, for he knows "all that [by God's design] was to happen to him" (v. 4). It is as though Jesus, as lead actor and knowing the script, takes control of the scene by stepping forward to interrogate the "extras." He asks, "Whom are you looking for?" (v. 4) and when they answer, "Jesus of Nazareth," he replies as he did to the Samaritan woman (4:26), his adversaries in Jerusalem (8:24, 28), and his disciples at table earlier in the evening: "I am he"(13:19; 18:5, 6, 8). This is the last occasion in the Fourth Gospel on which Jesus uses the absolute form of the expression **"I am"** (the Greek text includes no predicate nominative) to identify himself. The threefold use of it in the present scene "suggests a form of theophany which leaves men prostrate in fear before God."[5]

In a further touch that heightens the commanding stance of Jesus, he says, "If you are looking for me, let these men go" (v. 8). The evangelist adds that he said this "to fulfill the word that he had spoken [to his Father in the great prayer, 17:12], 'I did not lose a single one of those whom you gave me'" (18:9). This comment equates the words of Jesus with the revelatory words of Scripture in the Old Testament.

Peter's Use of the Sword (18:10–11)

The final verses are parallel to an incident reported in the Synoptic Gospels, but with significant variations. All four Gospels report that someone drew a sword and struck off the ear of a slave of the high priest. Who struck the blow? The Synoptic Gospels say it was a bystander or one of those who were with Jesus (Mark 14:47; Matt. 26:51; Luke 22:50); only John identifies the attacker as Simon Peter (John 18:10). Whose ear was it? Only John gives the slave's name: Malchus. And which ear did he lose? Mark and Matthew do not say, but Luke and John specify the right ear (Luke 22:50; John 18:10). This has led to speculation that Peter was left-handed—a reasonable guess, unless Malchus had turned or ducked to avoid the blow. Much more certain and more significant is the fact that once again Peter acts impulsively and Jesus rebukes him (John 13:6–10, 37–38; Mark 8:32–33).

There are also significant variations in the reports of Jesus' reaction to this act. Mark reports no reaction to the attacker (Mark 14:47). According to Luke, Jesus says, "No more of this" and shows his compassion by healing the victim (Luke 22:51). In Matthew and John, Jesus orders the attacker to put away his sword, and John specifies the sword's place, using the correct term for "sheath" (Matt. 26:52; John 18:11). Then, instead of the wisdom saying, "All who take the sword will perish by the sword" (Matt. 26:52), Jesus says to Peter, "Am I not to drink the cup that the Father has given me?" (John 18:11). This is a distinct parallel to the Gethsemane scene in the Synoptic Gospels, in which Jesus prays earnestly that, if possible, God would remove this cup (Mark 14:36//Matt. 26:39//Luke 22:42). In John, however, Jesus willingly accepts his suffering and rebukes Peter for seeking to save him from it. Peter has not understood that Jesus' kingdom is not of this world; he would gladly fight to keep Jesus from being handed over to the religious authorities who wished to kill him (see 18:36). The only clue about why Peter would have been carrying a sheathed sword is found, not in John, but in Luke 22:36.

In the incident about the sword, as throughout the arrest scene, Jesus comports himself regally with the bearing of one whose kingdom is from above. Not even God takes his life from him; as the good shepherd and God's own Son he lays it down (10:11–18).

Transition (18:12)

Although verse 12 appropriately appears as the first verse of the following paragraph in most versions of the text, it would make sense to include it with verses 1–11, since it narrates the actual arrest. It is a transitional verse that concludes one paragraph and begins the next.

Preaching and teaching the Word

1. Differences between the Gospels. A Bible study on the betrayal and arrest of Jesus offers a good opportunity to explore the phenomenon—for many people, the problem—of divergent accounts of the same event in the Gospels. The usual approach to the differences is to harmonize them, as illustrated in the term "the garden of Gethsemane," which does not appear in a single one of the four Gospels. Such an approach gives a richer picture of the setting and a more detailed account of the arrest than does one Gospel alone. However, it obscures the radical difference between the Synoptic Gospels' picture of Jesus on his knees in anguished prayer in Gethsemane and John's picture of his adversaries on the ground before a majestic Jesus in the garden.

Reflection on these differences has led skeptical critics to believe that John invented the detail about the arresting party's reaction to Jesus' thrice-repeated "I am" saying. After all, they say, why would Roman soldiers even recognize the divine claim in those words, much less be knocked to the ground by it? They conclude that the Fourth Gospel, written later than the others, is here reading back into history the higher (more divine) Christology that had developed in the Johannine community. As for the sharper details in the incident about the sword (the names of Peter and of Malchus, the right ear), that would be the growth of history into legend as a result of the universal tendency to embroider stories by filling in details.

Wrestling with these issues can result in growth beyond a literal, historical reading of Gospel texts that misses their theological richness. It can also lead learners to be more critical of the critics when questions are asked from a perspective that lies beyond literalism and rebellion against it. Through discussion the interpreter can bring participants to appreciate the subjective element inherent in the testimony of any witness, while understanding better the truth to which all witnesses point. The Fourth Gospel is the witness of one among the many who have met Jesus and come to know him as Christ the King whose light outshines that of lanterns and torches. One thinks of the Lord's servant in Isaiah "who walks in darkness and has no light, yet trusts in the name of the Lord and relies upon his God," finding the light of God to be better by far than the firebrands that humans kindle (Isa. 50:10–11).

2. *God in the garden.* Commentators ancient and modern have seen a connection between this garden and the garden of Eden in Genesis 1–3.[6] Although the evangelist may not have had such symbolism in mind, preachers today, as in the fourth and fifth centuries, can fruitfully juxtapose John's two garden scenes (18:1–11; 20:11–18) and the one in Genesis 2:8–3:24 to reflect upon God in the garden, God's dealings with humanity in each scene, and how we humans respond. Anyone following this lead should recognize that the word for garden in the Septuagint version of Genesis 2:8 ("paradise," *paradeisos*) is different from John's common word for garden (*kepos,* 18:1; 19:41) and that the garden of the arrest on the east side of Kidron is not the same as the garden of the burial just outside the city wall. These are three different gardens, but each is a place of revelation, and placing them side by side might prove to be revelatory for preachers and hearers alike. Eden is the garden God made for humans to live in, and to which God came in the cool of the day to call them to accountability. The garden of the arrest is where Jesus reveals himself to be the one who was sent to bring humanity back to God through his death as lamb of God. In the resurrection garden God's victory over death makes new life possible for all, and God's risen Son, mistaken this time for the gardener, validates that message to one distraught disciple, calling her by name (20:16). For John there is indeed something special about this garden.

INTERROGATION BY THE HIGH PRIEST
AND DENIAL BY PETER (18:13–27)

After the arrest of Jesus the events of his "hour" are portrayed by the evangelist in rapid succession. They follow the common tradition of all four Gospels, but with some surprises. Jesus is bound and taken to Annas, named only in John, and what follows is not a trial (as in the Synoptics) but an interrogation. The trial reported here turns out to be that of Peter, who is interrogated, not by a Jewish leader, but by three persons of no particular importance other than their appearance with Peter in this scene.

Exploring the text

The report is carefully crafted. By sandwiching Jesus' interview with the high priest between two panels of the interrogation of Peter, John highlights the bold response of Jesus by contrasting it with Peter's cowardly collapse under pressure. The smoothness of the narrative is marred by the fact that Caiaphas, introduced as "high priest that year" (v. 13), is the normal referent of "the high priest" who questions Jesus in verses 19–23, but in verse 24 the questioner is Annas. According to Roman historical sources, Annas was appointed by the Roman legate in Syria in 6 C.E. and deposed by the Roman prefect in Judea in 15 C.E. Caiaphas, Annas's son-in-law, was appointed in 18 C.E. and remained in office for eighteen years, until 36 C.E., the longest tenure in New Testament times. Although the text does not resolve the question of why Annas questions Jesus if Caiaphas is high priest, the continuing influence of Annas is consistent with what is known of him and his family from secular history.[1] John's major interest in introducing Caiaphas at this point is to remind readers that he was the one who, by virtue of his office but unintentionally, had prophesied that Jesus was to die for the people (18:14; 11:50). This reference is to the meeting of the Sanhedrin (council) following the raising of Lazarus when it passed sentence upon Jesus without a trial (11:47–53).

The Setting (18:12–14)

The actual arrest of Jesus is reported in a transitional sentence (v. 12). The arresting party takes him bound to Annas (v. 13). The physical setting is the residence of the high priest. It is still night (v. 3)–a cold night (v. 18). The residence has a courtyard (v. 15) with a gate and a guard (v. 16).

Denial by Peter, Part 1 (18:15–18)

In the Synoptic accounts Peter "followed [Jesus] at a distance right into the courtyard of the high priest" (Mark 14:54//Matt. 26:58; Luke 22:54). John at this point calls him "Simon Peter," a reference to his preapostolic name that subtly downgrades his cognomen, "Rock." The Fourth Gospel also introduces "another disciple" (v. 15) who was known to the high priest and without whose intervention Peter would not have been admitted into the courtyard. "The other disciple" and "the beloved disciple" are identical in 20:2, and "another disciple" in 18:15 probably refers to the same

person. If this is true, then the disciple who brings Peter into the courtyard is also the one who figures prominently in the narrative from the Last
Supper onward (13:23–26; 19:25–27; 20:2–10; 21:1–8, 20–23). According
to the writer, he is also the disciple who is the source of what is written in
the Fourth Gospel (21:24), which is called "the Gospel according to John,"
because of early church tradition that identified the "beloved disciple" as
John the apostle, son of Zebedee. This traditional identification is dubious, but the priority given to "the other/beloved disciple" in the Fourth
Gospel is not. The "beloved disciple" appears only in the Gospel of John,
almost always in the presence of Peter, and always in a role that places
Peter in the beloved disciple's shadow, as in this text.

"Woman who guarded the gate" (v. 16) combines the Greek word for
"gatekeeper" (vv. 16 and 17) with the description of her as a "servant girl"
(*paidiskē*) in verse 17. Her question to Peter, "You are not one of this man's
disciples, are you?" is introduced by a Greek word (*mē*), which, in negative questions, indicates that one expects a negative reply. She posed no
threat, and her way of posing the question made it easy for Peter to deny
that he was a disciple of Jesus. Peter's answer, "I am not," is the reverse
image of Jesus' bold affirmation, "I am" (8:24, 28, 58; 13:19; and three
times in the present context, 18:5, 6, 8).

Verse 18 gives a vivid picture of the scene, allowing readers to visualize and even, with a modicum of imagination, to feel the situation. It gives
details that complete the setting introduced in verses 12–14.

Interrogation by the High Priest (18:19–24)

Although the high priest is not named in verse 19, the closing sentence
of the paragraph (v. 24) leaves no doubt about his identity. It is Annas
who, at the close of the interrogation, sends Jesus bound to Caiaphas.

The dialogue in this indoor portion of the scene includes three people:
the high priest, Jesus, and one of the police. Only Jesus' words are
reported at length. The high priest questions Jesus about his disciples (to
learn who is involved in this incipient Jesus movement) and about his
teaching (to determine how dangerous it is, and whether Jesus can be led
to incriminate himself). His exact questions are not reported. Instead of
answering them, Jesus takes the offensive and says, in effect, "Why do you
ask? My teaching is a matter of public knowledge. Ask those who heard
what I said" (vv. 20–21). Jesus counts on the testimony of his anonymous
witnesses to establish his identity in the face of a hostile world.

One of the guards standing by finds this reply to be impertinent, gives
Jesus a slap, and rebukes him like a naughty child. It is as close as John

gets to the mockery at the Jewish trial described in the Synoptic Gospels (Mark 14:65; Matt. 26:67–68; Luke 22:63–65). Undaunted by this action and rebuke, Jesus challenges the guard to say what was wrong in his remarks and then, in question form, rebukes the guard for striking him. What the authorities intended to be an interrogation of Jesus turns out to be Jesus' interrogation of them. Jesus controls the interview throughout. Annas, reduced to silence, sends Jesus bound to Caiaphas the high priest (v. 24).

At this point the reader expects that Jesus will be questioned by Caiaphas. It is here that Mark 14:53 and Matthew 26:57 report an extraordinary meeting of the Sanhedrin during which Jesus is arraigned and witnesses are called; at the conclusion of the meeting Jesus is condemned to death. None of this appears in the Fourth Gospel, however, for in John the council has already condemned Jesus in absentia and made plans to put him to death (11:47–53). Instead of the appearance before Caiaphas or any trial by the Sanhedrin, John reports the concluding part of the denial of Peter.

Denial by Peter, Part 2 (18:25–27)

Back outside in the courtyard, those standing around the fire with Peter put to him the same question in the same form as that of the woman who guarded the gate. Peter again gives the expected negative answer, "I am not" (vv. 17, 25).

One person standing there, however, a slave or servant of the high priest, has good reason to expect a positive answer. This person is a relative of Malchus, whose ear Peter had cut off. He asks, "Did I not see you in the garden with him?" (v. 26). The question is introduced by a Greek word (*ouk*) that indicates that a positive response is expected. For a third time Peter answers in the negative, contrary to what Malchus's relative knows to be the fact. It may have been easy by now for Peter to lie, but it was not easy to get by with it. He probably did not deceive Malchus's relative, and he surely did not deceive himself. The rooster crowed.

All three Synoptics quote what Jesus had said to Peter at table a few hours earlier and report Peter's bitter tears (Mark 14:72//Matt. 26:75//Luke 22:62). John is more subtle. He simply expects the reader to remember Jesus' saying, "Very truly, I tell you, before the cock crows, you will have denied me three times" (13:38), and to realize the impact of this sound upon Peter.

Although the Gospels differ in details, they are unanimous in their witness that Jesus predicted Peter's denial and that Peter had solemnly declared that he would be faithful unto death (Matt. 26:33–35//Mark

14:29–31//Luke 22:33–34//John 13:37–38). Furthermore, all four emphasize the fact that Jesus' prediction, not Peter's promise, proved to be reliable. The Fourth Gospel's description of the scene, more detailed than the others, contrasts the cowardice of Peter with the boldness of Jesus and of the other disciple more starkly than any other Gospel. Peter's three denials in the courtyard match Jesus' three affirmations at his arrest. The interrogation and denial scene is a powerful proclamation of who Jesus is and a solemn warning to disciples about who they are, despite their best intentions.

Preaching and teaching the Word

1. Courage and cowardice. The contrast between Jesus' courage and Peter's cowardice is evident in all four Gospels. This contrast can be used as an exhortation to try to do better than Peter and also as a proclamation of the good news that our salvation depends not on our own performance but on the power and faithfulness of God shown in Jesus Christ. The vivid scene evoked by this text lends itself to a role play focused on the dramatic elements in the story underlined by the Fourth Gospel. Those preparing to teach such a lesson will find that a synopsis of the four Gospels is essential and that Raymond E. Brown's *The Death of the Messiah*[2] is a rich resource. This text does not appear as a single unit in the Lectionary, but it is appropriate to preach on Good Friday or on Passion/ Palm Sunday when it (or its parallel in the Synoptics) is part of the lengthy readings suggested.

The particularly forceful way in which John weaves together the themes of Jesus' interrogation and Peter's denial draws attention to the inherent majesty of Jesus' nature, at the same time human and divine, as well as the frailty of our human nature. Jesus' bold response to the high priest, set in the context of his crucifixion and death, shows the cost of courage (it comes high), and Peter's cowardly caving in under pressure illustrates the worth of his earlier bravado (it is cheap). What Jesus demonstrates, of course, is not simply human courage; it is the power of one who speaks the truth, a power that comes from God. Disciples of Jesus such as Dietrich Bonhoeffer, Martin Luther King Jr., and many an unsung hero in whom Jesus' Spirit abides exemplify his courage in our own time.

2. Promises. A sermon focusing primarily on the denial of Peter might be called "When Life Puts Us on the Witness Stand." It would reflect upon how hard it is to keep a serious promise, made with the best intentions. There is a scene in *The Wind in the Willows* in which Toad in the smoking room solemnly promises to give up motorcars forever and moments later stoutly refuses to tell his friends what he had admitted and promised. "'What?' cried the Badger, greatly scandalized, 'You backsliding animal, didn't you tell me just now, in there–' 'O, yes, yes, in *there*. . . . But I've been searching my mind since, and going over things in it, and I find that I'm not a bit sorry or repentant really.'"[3] The illustration is not fully apt because Toad's promise was made against his will, but it may point the way to the ease with which we make promises to Jesus in church or in our hearts and the frequency with which we break them in the world.

3. Recognition. "And at that moment the cock crowed" (v. 27) suggests a sermon about defining moments, when some trigger event shocks us into a sudden, clear recognition of the way the world really is and who our nation, our church, or we ourselves really are. Alan Culpepper has analyzed the entire narrative of the Fourth Gospel as a "succession of recognition scenes, partial recognitions, and failed efforts to recognize Jesus,"[4] some of which will leap to the preacher's mind: the Samaritan woman at the well (4:29), Mary Magdalene at the empty tomb (20:16), Thomas in the closed room (20:28). These all recognize who Jesus really is. Peter, thanks to that rooster, realizes who he really is, and it is not good news. Those who choose to preach on this theme will need to relate it to real experiences. Which of us has never had the experience of doing something we knew we would never do? Such a sermon should not ignore the good news of Peter's restoration in chapter 21.

TRIAL BEFORE PILATE (18:28–19:16a)

Certain moments in time are, for those who experience them, also moments in eternity. The trial of Jesus before Pilate is such a moment, and the Fourth Gospel depicts the drama of that moment with such clarity that readers whose minds and hearts are quickened by the Holy Spirit can almost experience it themselves.

The event is clearly a moment in time. That Jesus of Nazareth died on a Roman cross on a Friday noon under sentence by a provincial official named Pontius Pilate is an undeniable fact of ancient history. That it is also an event that placed Pilate and all who ever learn of it in the presence of eternity is the uniform witness of all the writers of the New Testament and of Christians through the ages. Though the basic elements in the story are common to all four Gospels, the Fourth Gospel reports this historic event and bears witness to its eternal significance in language that is distinctly Johannine.

Exploring the text

Of the four accounts of the trial before Pilate, John's is the longest. The narrative is written in dramatic form closely resembling the script for a play in seven scenes. The major roles are three: the leaders of the Jewish religious establishment, the official representative of the Roman Empire, and Jesus, whose identity is to be established in this trial.

Historical narratives, whether plain prose or a novel or a play, are written in order to interpret as well as to report historical events. The fourth evangelist sees in this event the confrontation not just of three protagonists but of two realms of reality: **"above"** and **"below,"** God and the world. In the eyes of the world and in their own self-understanding, the Jewish authorities represent God and Pilate represents Rome, the dominant world power of the time. At the trial of Jesus these two confront each other in a struggle for power, more political than religious, each manipulating the other to their own ends. Both finally reject Jesus and opt for the power of this world. In the evangelist's portrayal of them, both parties show that they are coming from "below." They belong not to the truth but to the world.

Over against these two stands Jesus, who also claims to be a king. He rejects the title "King of the Jews," which Pilate sees as the issue on which the trial turns. He speaks instead of a kingdom that is not "from this world" but from above. He confronts Pilate just as surely as Pilate confronts him, in an encounter that continues and concludes the series of decisive meetings with all sorts of people in the first half of the Fourth Gospel. The fateful nature of Pilate's reaction to Jesus brings to a climax the theme of judgment that runs throughout John's Gospel. For the evangelist, it is not Jesus who is in the dock, but Pilate, the religious authorities, and ultimately the reader of the text.

The function of this dramatic narrative is to lead readers to see that all who find themselves in the presence of Jesus, the living Word, are judged by their reaction to him. Readers are expected not to judge the protagonists in this drama, but rather to see themselves in the narrative and then to choose for Jesus instead of against Jesus in the common tests of daily life.

Scene 1. Jewish Authorities Demand Jesus' Death (18:28–32)

The first scene occurs early in the morning outside the governor's headquarters, which the Jewish leaders "did not enter . . . so as to avoid ritual defilement and to be able to eat the Passover" (v. 28). The scrupulosity of the Jewish leaders about traditional rules concerning defilement, while they are blind to the living revelation of God in their midst, is an example of the irony that abounds in this Gospel. The time and place (Roman headquarters) are identical in all four Gospels, but only John specifies that it was the morning before the Passover was to be eaten.

Jesus' Last Supper with his disciples, eaten just before his arrest, was therefore not the Passover according to John, who has Jesus die at the time the Passover lambs were being slaughtered on 14 Nisan. Scholarly discussion about which date for the Last Supper is historically accurate is endless and inconclusive. It is enough for the interpreter to recognize the importance of this detail for a full understanding of John's theology, which, alone among the Gospels, speaks of Jesus as the Lamb of God who takes away the sin of the world (1:29, 36).

Only John reports that this first scene in the Roman trial took place outside Pilate's headquarters. The evangelist thereby sets up another split stage, as at the Jewish interrogation of Jesus (vv. 13–23), but this time the Jewish authorities are outside (vv. 28–32, 38b–40) while Jesus is inside (vv. 33–38a). Although this scene is played out in the light of morning, in the evangelist's view those outside are in spiritual darkness, while inside is the Light of life. Pilate attempts, by "shuttle diplomacy," to find a way to avoid choosing between the two. The effort fails.

The dialogue consists of two exchanges between Pilate and the Jewish leaders. In accordance with proper legal procedure, Pilate first asks the plaintiffs to specify the accusation against the prisoner (v. 29). They decline to do so but simply affirm that they would not have handed him over to a Roman court if he were not a criminal (literally, "doer of evil," a vague phrase that specifies no crime, v. 30). The verb used for "handed over" has been used thus far in the Fourth Gospel for the betrayal of Judas, who handed Jesus over to the Jewish authorities (6:64, 71; 12:4; 13:2, 11, 21; 18:2, 5; see also 21:20). Here and in a subsequent scene of the trial, it refers to the handing over of Jesus by Jewish authorities to a Roman authority (18:30, 35; 19:11); at the moment of Jesus' death on the cross, he hands over his spirit to God (19:30).

The refusal of Jesus' accusers to specify his crime may reflect impatience with Pilate, who had acquiesced in the arrest of Jesus by providing Roman soldiers on the ground of his alleged claim to be a king (see Luke 23:2). Pilate's impatience with them is obvious when, in the second exchange, he tells them to handle the case themselves according to their own Jewish law (John 18:31a). The accusers respond that they are not permitted to put anyone to death (v. 32b), reflecting the earlier judgment of the Sanhedrin that Jesus must die (11:47, 53). No clear external evidence of this limit on Jewish authority during the Roman occupation has been found, but it is quite clear that any execution under Jewish law would be by stoning and not crucifixion. The evangelist explains that the Jewish authorities sought a death sentence from the Roman governor "to fulfill what Jesus had said when he indicated the kind of death he was to die"

(18:32). Earlier, in speaking of the hour of his death, Jesus said to a crowd in Jerusalem, "I, when I am lifted up from the earth, will draw all people to myself " (12:32), and the evangelist explained, "He said this to indicate the kind of death he was to die" (12:33, wording identical to 18:32). Had Jesus been executed under Jewish law, he would have been stoned and knocked to the earth, not "lifted up from the earth" on a Roman cross. The evangelist's explanatory notes (12:33; 18:32) ground his narrative in a historical fact that is also a fundamental article of the Christian faith: Jesus "suffered under Pontius Pilate [and] was crucified."

Scene 2. Pilate Questions Jesus about His Kingship (18:33–38a)

After this first encounter with Jesus' accusers outside his headquarters, Pilate goes back inside ("back" is a better translation of *palin* than "again" in v. 33a) and summons Jesus, who may have already been taken inside. The question he puts to Jesus, identical in all four Gospels, is the basic issue for Roman law as well as for Johannine theology: "Are you the King of the Jews?" (v. 33b; see Mark 15:2; Matt. 27:11; Luke 23:3). A claim to be king could be construed by Rome as rebellion, and the recognition of Jesus as Messiah (king) and Son of God is the goal of the Fourth Gospel (20:31).

Jesus' answer, "You have said so," follows immediately in all three Synoptics. In John Jesus gives the same answer in different words ("You say that I am a king," v. 37), but only after a substantive interchange with Pilate in verses 34–37a. The accused prisoner first questions the judge. In asking, "Do you ask this on your own, or did others tell you about me?" (v. 34), Jesus is seeking a person-to-person contact with the governor, as he has done with the Samaritan woman by asking her for a drink of water (4:7). He is giving Pilate a chance to encounter the living Word personally, rather than simply as another case to be adjudicated.

In response, Pilate ignores the proffered opening and, like colonial overlords before and since, shows his disdain for the people he governs: "I am not a Jew, am I?" (v. 35a; the Greek negative *me* shows he expected a negative answer). Continuing his interrogation of the prisoner, he acknowledges that the Jewish people and their religious leaders must have some cause for handing him over to the Roman authority, but, as a fair-minded judge, he is more interested in what the accused has done than in what his accusers say about him (v. 35b).

Jesus again takes control of the interview. Instead of telling the governor what he has done, he reverts to the original question about kingship (v. 33), which he had at first seemed to ignore. He speaks first of the nature of his reign: "My kingdom is not from this world" (v. 36a NRSV). The Greek preposition used here can mean "out of," "from," or "of." The AV, RSV, and NIV use "of," the sense of which is stated in the TEV and NEB through the paraphrase, "My kingdom does not belong to this world." The NRSV, by using "from," opts for a more literal translation and draws attention to the theological import of Jesus' origin "from above" in John (3:2–3, 7, 31; 8:23; 19:11). Elaborating on the divine origin of his kingdom, Jesus acknowledges Pilate's legitimate concern for law and order in this Roman province: "If my kingdom were from this world, my followers would be fighting to keep me from being handed over to the Jews" (v. 36b).[1] Readers know that Peter has done exactly that when Jesus is arrested, demonstrating his misunderstanding of the true nature of Jesus' kingship, but hardly inciting the people to revolution, which is Pilate's concern. "But as it is," Jesus continues, "my kingdom is not from here" (v. 36c), hammering the key idea home for a third time in these two verses.

Pilate sees here a possible opening to elicit a confession that might allow him to find Jesus guilty on a charge of insurrection against Rome and thus to placate the chief priests and their people. "So you are a king?" he asks (v. 37a).

The first part of Jesus' reply, "You say . . ." comes from common Gospel tradition (Matt. 27:11; Mark 15:2; Luke 23:3), but the conclusion, ". . . that I am a king," is a Johannine alteration of the initial question (v. 33) that shifts the claim of kingship from the political arena to a more universal realm.

The next two sentences belong to the core revelation of the living Word in the Gospel according to John. Jesus declares, "For this I was born, and for this I came into the world, to testify to the truth" (v. 37c). This claim picks up a theme announced in the prologue (1:9, 14, 17) and associates the coming of truth into the world with the birth of Jesus Christ. The reference to Jesus' birth lies close to the heart of John's message and embodies three of its key terms: coming into the world, testify, and truth.

"Everyone who belongs to the truth listens to my voice" (v. 37d) echoes the metaphor of the sheepfold (10:3, 4, 8, 16). In addressing them to Pilate, Jesus the good shepherd utters words that his own sheep, including those of another fold, would recognize. By his response to them Pilate, the judge, is judged.

His response is as unforgettable as it is enigmatic: "What is truth?" (v. 38a). It is one of the places where tone of voice would be a major aid to interpretation, and some level of interpretation is prerequisite to any audible rendition of the text. Does the question express scorn, contempt, skepticism, cynicism, impatience, wistful yearning, or serious philosophical interest? Commentators have expressed each of these opinions with some justification. By walking away without awaiting Jesus' reply, Pilate shows he is not interested in a philosophical discussion. The question is rhetorical; it expects no answer but serves to break off the conversation. Pilate may have been impatient with the subject (truth), for "the prisoner is talking a language which is not the language of politics."[2]

The question appears only in the Fourth Gospel, which is supremely interested in **truth**. The evangelist expects the reader to reflect on the subject that Pilate walks away from and to remember its importance in John's story of Jesus. This scene is the climactic moment in John's development of the theme. Jesus stands in human form before the local representative of the greatest world power of that time and in his living presence testifies to God's truth because he is the way, the truth, and the life. Jesus opens the door of life to Pilate, but Pilate turns his back and walks away. His interest is in Roman law and in the maintenance of order and his own authority. Jesus poses no threat to public order, nor has he done anything seditious under Roman law, and there's the end of the matter as Pilate sees it. In the presence of God's light he shows himself to be as blind as were the Pharisees who had hounded Jesus for healing a blind beggar on the Sabbath (9:40–41) and whose leaders have now handed Jesus over to Pilate. Pilate does not accept their charges against Jesus, but he, like them, is turning his back on the light and is thereby judged (3:19). He does not recognize the truth when it is right before his eyes.

Scene 3. Pilate Pronounces Jesus Innocent (18:38b–40)

Pilate returns to the Jews outside and disappoints their expectations by reporting his finding that there is no legitimate case against Jesus (v. 38). Eager to resolve the matter without violating his sense of justice, he reminds them of their customary demand for the release of a Jewish prisoner at Passover time as a gesture of Roman clemency. This custom, for which there is no extrabiblical confirmation, is included in Matthew and Mark, but only John refers to it as a Jewish custom (v. 39a; see Mark 15:6; Matt. 27:15). Pilate offers to release for them the King of the Jews (v. 39b). Pilate suggests this title for Jesus, who never uses it of himself.[3] According to John, the Roman soldiers use it to mock Jesus (John 19:3), and Pilate labels Jesus with it on the cross to mock the Jewish people and their leaders. Pilate surely recognizes that the last thing Jesus' accusers want is his release, and calling him "King of the Jews" is simply a way of taunting them. He and they had reached a modus vivendi during the ten years that Pilate and Caiaphas were both in power, but their relationship was anything but cordial. The response of the hostile Jewish authorities (still outside, according to John) and the crowd (according to the Synoptics) is the same in all four Gospels. They shout back (not "again"), "Not this man, but Barabbas!" (v. 40).

Nothing is known of Barabbas outside the Gospel accounts of this incident. Mark says he "was in prison with the rebels who had committed murder during the insurrection" (Mark 15:7). According to Luke, he was "a man who had been put in prison for an insurrection that had taken place in the city, and for murder" (Luke 23:19). Matthew says only that he was "a notorious prisoner" but adds that he was "called Jesus Barabbas" (Matt. 27:16). John concludes the scene by observing, "Now Barabbas was a bandit" (v. 40). The same word is coupled with "thief " in the metaphor of the sheepfold to describe those against whom the good shepherd must protect the sheep (10:1). Nowhere in John is the choice of darkness over light more dramatically portrayed than in the moment when God's own people (1:11) choose the bandit instead of the shepherd.

Preaching and teaching the Word

1. The reign of Christ. The Gospel reading for Christ the King Sunday (the Sunday between Nov. 20 and 26, alternatively designated as Reign of Christ Sunday)[4] in year B is John 18:33–37. The reading for year A is the scene in which the Son of Man sits enthroned as king at the last judgment (Matt. 25:31–46), and for year C it is Jesus' crucifixion as King of the Jews (Luke 23:33–43). Jesus' entry into Jerusalem as Israel's king, lowly and riding on an ass's colt, is reported in all four Gospels (Matt. 21:1–9; Mark 11:1–10; Luke 19:28–40; John 12:12–19), giving evidence of the prominence of the kingship theme in the earliest gospel tradition. The term "king," which in our time has become the title for a constitutional monarch in most countries that continue to use it at all, once meant a hereditary ruler whose word, though capricious, was law. Against the latter background each Gospel presents the paradoxical nature of Christ's reign from its own viewpoint and with its own emphases.

In the Fourth Gospel the whole of Christ's trial before Pilate portrays dramatically two contrasting views of royal power, one incarnate in the Roman Empire and the other in Jesus Christ. Pilate's interrogation of Jesus on the subject of his kingship (18:33–37) offers a fine occasion for interpreters to explore and proclaim the meaning of a reign which does not originate in this world nor reflect the world's values (v. 36).

Many of the liturgical elements likely to be used in worship in an affluent congregation on Christ the King/Reign of Christ Sunday are likely to communicate this world's picture of royalty, reinforced by the Johannine emphasis on the glory of Jesus Christ. There is a tension in the Bible between royal theology and prophetic theology. These strands converge in the New Testament witness to Jesus Christ. The dominant traits in the Synoptic portraits of Jesus are prophetic; Jesus speaks of the kingdom of God. In John the royal aspects of Jesus are more prominent; the Fourth Gospel highlights Christ the King. It is up to the preacher of this Johannine text on kingship to see and to show Christ's reign as John does: in a cross, a crown of thorns, a towel, and a basin, all of which reveal the glory of the divine Ruler above.

2. What is really real? Interpreters who agree with the usual paragraph division in the printed Greek text and modern versions could choose to include verse 38a in the Gospel reading for Christ the King/Reign of Christ Sunday in year B and preach on the memorable question, "What is truth?" Although Pilate's intention in speaking these words was not to initiate a philosophical discussion, the evangelist's intention is another matter, and so is the need of many a hearer in a Christian congregation. The evangelist wants us to ask, "Who is Jesus Christ?" Life often forces us to ask, "What is really real?" The writer of the Fourth Gospel discovered that these are but two ways of asking the same question, for truth is "what is really real" (see notes on 14:6, "I am the truth"). For Pilate, politics was really real. For Jesus' accusers, religion was really real. Preachers might reflect on what is really real for Western civilization in the twenty-first century. The evangelist is an artist. He does not give an answer to Pilate's question but brings us face to face with Jesus and invites us to think about it. The answer of readers and hearers is revealed in the degree to which they walk with Jesus day by day.

3. On choosing Barabbas. John's account of the cry for Barabbas (18:40) is the shortest of the four in the New Testament, but there may be a sermon in pairing it with the account in Matthew that says (in the most reliable manuscripts) that this notorious prisoner was called Jesus Barabbas. The shared name, Jesus, is the Greek form of Joshua, "God saves." According to the Synoptic Gospels, Jesus Barabbas believes that God saves through violence, and he is prepared to fight for that belief. Pilate finds him dangerous. According to John, Jesus of Nazareth believes that God saves through self-sacrificing love and that he himself is the embodiment of that love. The Jewish religious authorities find him dangerous. In reflecting on the two characters named Jesus, preachers could ask how we today believe that God saves. As these words are being written, Western nations are preoccupied by the threat of terrorism. How do we think we shall be saved from it? And whose way do we follow, the way of Jesus Barabbas or the way of Jesus of Nazareth?

Exploring the text (continued)

The story of Jesus' trial continues in four more closely related scenes.

Scene 4. Roman Soldiers Scourge Jesus (19:1–3)

In this central scene of the seven-scene drama, Pilate orders soldiers to flog Jesus, presumably inside the Roman headquarters. Neither Pilate nor "the Jews"[1] appear in this briefest of the seven scenes, yet in John it is the fulcrum for the whole trial, focusing the theme of kingship in a visual way. The crown of thorns, the purple robe, and the derisive obeisance offered to Jesus as to a king create an unforgettable picture. Its dramatic and theological purpose is to underline the counterintuitive and countercultural nature of Jesus' kingship.

In Matthew and Mark, the crown and robe are removed as soon as the soldiers finish making sport of him (Matt. 27:31; Mark 15:20), but in John he still wears them when Pilate brings him out and says, "Here is the man!" (v. 5), and later when Pilate brings him out again and says, "Here is your King!" (v. 14). Alone among the Gospels, John does not use the word "mock" in this scene. In these subtle ways the fourth evangelist transforms the tradition of Jesus' mockery by Roman soldiers into an ironic narrative of Jesus' investiture as king, prefiguring the irony of his exaltation as a king on the cross (v. 19).

Scene 5. Pilate Again Pronounces Jesus Innocent (19:4–8)

Pilate goes outside again to announce to the Jewish authorities for the second time (see 18:38) his opinion that under Roman law they have no case against Jesus. At this announcement, Jesus comes out wearing the crown of thorns and the purple robe (v. 5). European artists who have depicted this moment often entitled their work *Ecce homo,* the Latin phrase ascribed to Pilate at that moment and familiar to users of the Vulgate version for many centuries. The exclamation passed into Western languages, sometimes as an expression of admiration, "What a man!" It can also be seen as an allusion to the Johannine doctrine of the incarnation (1:1–18) or to John's use of the title "Son of Man" in association with Jesus' death (3:14; 8:28; 12:23, 32–34) and the eschatological judgment (5:27–29).

The incongruity of Jesus' situation, the mock insignia of royalty that he still wears in John, and the antagonism between Pilate and the Jewish leaders all point to a continuation of the theme of taunting. The soldiers taunt Jesus by dressing him as a king; Pilate taunts the religious authorities by again alluding to this man—this accused prisoner—as their king.

Each of Pilate's first two declarations of Jesus' innocence is made in a way that mocks his accusers.

Understandably enraged, the chief priests and the police shout, "Crucify! Crucify!" (v. 6). In the Greek text there is no direct object to smooth the abrasiveness of their cry. They know what they want, and they will give the governor no respite till they get it.

Unmoved by their clamor, Pilate replies with an edge of sarcasm, "Take him yourself and crucify him." He and they both know that they are not allowed to administer capital punishment, and if they were, it would not be by the Roman method of crucifixion (18:31). He taunts them as he tries to dismiss them with this suggestion; then for a third time Pilate declares, "I find no case against him" (v. 6).

"The Jews" now disclose the accusation they had declined to bring forward during their first exchange with the governor (18:29–30). Referring to their own law, they report that Jesus has claimed to be the Son of God, a claim they have already judged (dubiously) to be blasphemy (10:33). According to their law, they conclude, "He ought to die" (19:7).

The evangelist concludes this particular episode in the power play between the civil and religious authorities by reporting that Pilate, upon hearing the charge of blasphemy and the appeal to local law, "was more afraid than ever" (v. 8). Since there is no prior mention of Pilate's fear, it would be preferable in this context to translate the expression as an intensive: Pilate became really alarmed.[2] Perhaps Pilate gave some credence to the statement of the Jews that "he has claimed to be the Son of God" and experienced "numinous terror before the divine."[3] However, in introducing their own law into the case, the Jews are referring to the mandate of Roman representatives to respect local laws and authorities insofar as possible. Their motive is political, and Pilate is afraid, because he recognizes that he is being maneuvered into a situation that may place his political future in jeopardy (see v. 12).[4]

Scene 6. Pilate Questions Jesus about His Origin (19:9–12)

Pilate enters his headquarters again and resumes a more serious interrogation of the prisoner. His question, "Where are you from?" is historically plausible, but it is also theologically significant for the fourth evangelist, who has repeatedly made Jesus' heavenly origin the centerpiece of his confrontations with "the Jews" (6:41–42; 7:27–28; 8:14; 9:29). At first Jesus remains silent (v. 9)–a stance reminiscent of the Synoptic accounts (Matt. 27:12–14; Mark 15:3–5; Luke 23:9) and of the Suffering Servant passage in Isaiah (Isa. 53:7).

"How dare you refuse to speak to me?" says Pilate. "Don't you know that I have power to set you free and also power to have you put to death on a cross?" (v. 10, author's paraphrase). Jesus' reply is an example of Johannine double entendre. At one level "You would have no power over me unless it had been given you from above" (v. 11a) points to Caesar as the source of Pilate's political power. But Jesus suggests that the emperor's power, like that of the governor, is derivative. It comes "from above," that is, from God. The comment is that of one who is the Son of God and who knows where he comes from. That is why "the one who handed me over to you is guilty of a greater sin" (v. 11b). The reference could be to Judas, or to Caiaphas, or (more likely) to the delegation of religious authorities standing outside the door. In any case, sin here, as throughout the Fourth Gospel, is failure to recognize that Jesus really is who he says he is–that he really does come from God. Like Jesus' other statements to Pilate reported only in the Fourth Gospel (18:36, 37; 19:11a), this one under- scores an important element in Johannine Christology. It also affirms that ultimate power belongs to Jesus' kingdom "from above" and not the king- dom represented by Pilate, which is "from here" (18:36).

Now the wall that has separated the governor from Jesus' accusers in this drama seems to disappear. The evangelist reports Pilate's inner deci- sion to release Jesus (v. 12a), and those outside respond to his intention by crying out a thinly veiled threat: if he releases Jesus, they will bring against him an accusation of disloyalty to the emperor (v. 12b). Pilate hears their words (v. 13a) and changes his mind. They are threatening his political power, just as Jesus in his ministry had threatened that of the Jewish reli- gious leaders. Jesus dares to claim power greater than theirs–so great that even if he dies at their hands, his death will only verify the sovereign power of God's will.

Scene 7. Pilate Hands Jesus Over for Execution (19:13–16)

John is the only one of the Gospels that states precisely the time and place of Jesus' condemnation to death. On hearing the threat of "the Jews," Pilate brings Jesus outside to the place called The Stone Pavement (*Lithostratos* in Greek or *Gabbatha* in Aramaic) and takes his seat on the judge's bench about noon on the day of preparation for the Passover (vv. 13–14a). Artists and expositors have visualized John's vivid scene, and scholars have debated about every element in it.

With regard to the time, noon on the day of preparation for the Passover (Nisan 14; Exod. 12:6) is the time when regulations for the Passover feast go into effect according to rabbinic sources. These include notably the slaughter of the paschal lambs and the ban against eating leavened bread. In the Synoptic Gospels "day of Preparation" refers explicitly to preparation for the Sabbath (Matt. 27:62; Mark 15:42; Luke 23:54), which means that Jesus was crucified beginning at noon on a Friday. In John "day of Preparation" refers just as explicitly to preparation for Passover (John 19:14), which can fall on any day of the week, and noon is the hour when Pilate handed Jesus over to be crucified. John's report suggests that Passover that year fell on a Sabbath (19:31), so by all accounts Jesus' crucifixion occurred shortly after Friday noon, either the day before Passover (John) or on Passover day itself (Synoptic Gospels).[5]

With regard to the place, there are two possible sites for "The Stone Pavement," one adjacent to Herod's palace on the west side of the Old City, which may well have served as Pilate's headquarters when he was in Jerusalem, and the one shown to tourists that may have been part of the fortress Antonia near the temple on the east side of the Old City.[6] Of greater interest to the interpreter is the fact that there was located the judge's bench on which Pilate sat (intransitive) or on which he seated (transitive) Jesus (19:13). The alternative translation, "seated him," while it is not historically plausible, is grammatically possible and theologically preferable, since for John the true judge is Jesus.[7]

In this final scene of the trial Pilate taunts the Jews again. Jesus presumably is still dressed in the trappings of royalty when Pilate says to them, "Here is your King!" (v. 14). Echoing their response in scene 5 (v. 6), they cry out again, "Away with him! Away with him! Crucify him!" (v. 15a). Pilate's next question taunts Jesus' accusers one last time and sets the stage for the denouement of the drama: "Shall I crucify your King?" (v. 15b).

Exasperated beyond endurance, the chief priests answer, "We have no king but the emperor" (v. 15c). Pilate seems to have won! These fractious subjects have acknowledged their submission to the kingdom he represents. "Then he handed [Jesus] over to them to be crucified" (v. 16). The Jewish authorities seem to have won! They have manipulated the governor into granting what they came for.

In fact, both parties have lost. By acclaiming a king other than Israel's Messiah, the chief priests have lost their credibility as representatives of God, the true king of Israel (Judg. 8:23; 1 Sam. 8:7). By sentencing to death a man he knew to be innocent, Pilate has lost his credibility as representative of the world's finest judicial system, whose symbol of justice was a blindfolded figure weighing evidence without regard to external pressures.

The evangelist, however, sees their loss as far more serious. Standing in the presence of Jesus, they have failed to see in him the Son of God, who is judge of all the earth. In rejecting him, they have judged themselves, for "this is the judgment, that the light has come into the world, and people loved darkness rather than light" (3:19).

Preaching and teaching the Word

1. A dramatic reading. The entire text of the trial before Pilate (18:28–19:16) could be duplicated and used as a script for readers' theater. It might be fruitful to read the entire narrative first, then reread it, stopping for discussion at the end of each scene.

2. Who is to blame? A different approach to teaching would be to focus on a question that has caused endless debate and mutual recrimination between Christians and Jews from the first century until the present day: Who is to blame for the death of Jesus? Throughout most of church history, Christian scholars have blamed the Jews, often in shamefully anti-Semitic terms, and have viewed Pilate as a weak and wishy-washy politician whose repeated declarations of Jesus' innocence have served to advance the gospel. Around Pilate grew up favorable legends that made of him first a Christian, then a martyr, and then, in the Coptic Church, a saint. Jewish scholars, especially since the Holocaust, have proposed that anti-Semitism has been endemic in the Christian faith from its very origins. Some of them hypothesize that since only the Romans executed people by crucifixion, and since Jesus was condemned by a Roman court, his crime was insurrection and the Jews had nothing to do with his death. In their view Gospel accounts that depict Jewish instigation of the case and manipulation of the Roman governor are the result of a biased interpretation of history that reflects the hostility of the earliest Christians toward Jews. The Gospel of John does, in fact, exemplify a writing of history that advances a particular theological viewpoint. Its narration of the sequence of events in the trial before Pilate, however, is plausible. A debate of the question of blame for Jesus' death provides an occasion to explore in depth the power play depicted in the Johannine text and to probe the latent anti-Semitism that is present among us.

3. Ecce homo. Pilate's statement about Jesus, "Here is the man!" (19:5) is as enigmatic as it is memorable—a combination that makes it an apt candidate for a sermon on the person of Jesus Christ, who he was in his ministry on earth, and who he is for each one of us. There is room in the text to interpret the words as an expression of admiration, indecision, or scorn.

4. The locus of ultimate loyalty. What is the true locus of a Christian's ultimate loyalty? This is the question suggested by the closing statement of the chief priests in John's narrative of the trial before Pilate, "We have no king but Caesar" (19:15 AV, RSV, NIV, NEB). Christians have from the beginning affirmed that "Jesus Christ is Lord" (Phil. 2:11), but they have also taught that "whoever resists authority resists what God has appointed" (Rom.

13:2). "No king but the emperor" sent Jesus to the cross, and the clarity Christians feel about the matter in church is sometimes blurred in the pressures and passions of political life. The United States of America is the only major empire on earth in the first part of the twenty-first century. Dare we as Americans explore our reasons for loyalty to our nation with the same objectivity we use in exploring the motives of the chief priests and of Pilate in this text?

DEATH AND BURIAL (19:16b–42)

The literally crucial moment toward which the entire Fourth Gospel has been moving from the wedding scene at Cana (2:4) until now has arrived. The "hour" referred to there and in Jesus' great prayer (17:1) includes Jesus death, resurrection, and return to the **Father**, all considered as his being lifted up and glorified, though many texts pointing to it speak primarily of his death (7:30; 8:20; 12:23–28; 13:1; 16:32).

Jesus' crucifixion is the climactic event in all four Gospels, but each of them adds certain accessory events or details and omits others, in accordance with the sources used and the evangelists' understanding of Jesus. In each case, themes that guide the entire narrative come to a focus in the way the crucifixion story is told.

Exploring the text

The Fourth Gospel underscores Jesus' freely laying down his life, a theme announced in his words to the Pharisees about the good shepherd who lays down his life for the sheep (10:17–18). Jesus, who is in control of the situation at his arrest and throughout the trial before Pilate, remains so on the way to his execution and even upon the cross.

Other Johannine themes, such as the fulfillment of Scripture, emerge as the evangelist recounts the death and burial of Jesus in a dramatic account with seven episodes.

The Crucifixion (19:16b–18)

As in the other Gospels, Jesus is taken away to a place of execution called Golgotha, where he is crucified between two others about whom John says nothing. All the accounts define "Golgotha" as a reference to the skull, but John alone says that the term is in Hebrew (v. 17). What John calls Hebrew was Western Aramaic, the common language on the streets of Jerusalem at that time. "Golgotha" is one of several words of this language preserved in the Gospels.

Only the Fourth Gospel states that Jesus carried the cross–just the horizontal beam if Roman custom was followed–by himself (v. 17). In the other three Gospels, Simon of Cyrene, not mentioned in John, is pressed into service for this task. This difference has theological significance. Of his own will and under his own power, Jesus goes out to die because God wills it. He once said to his disciples, "My food is to do the will of him who sent me and to complete his work" (4:34). On the road to Golgotha, Jesus is nearing the completion of that work.

The Inscription (19:19–22)

All the Gospels report the inscription that was attached to the cross to indicate why Jesus was being crucified. The words common to all four are "the King of the Jews." John's version is the fullest: "Jesus of Nazareth, the King of the Jews" (v. 19). Twice before, the Fourth Gospel has used Nazareth to identify Jesus (1:45–46; 18:5, 7).

John alone reports that the inscription was written by order of Pilate and that it was written in three languages: Hebrew (=Aramaic), Latin (literally, "Roman"), and Greek (the language in which the Gospel is written). This detail is important to the narrative "because the place where Jesus was crucified was near the city" (v. 20, mentioned only in John). Every literate person who might be in Jerusalem for the Passover festival would understand one or more of these languages. That is why the Jewish authorities were upset by its wording.

The inscription also has symbolic importance for Johannine theology. Jesus' hour has come: he is lifted up in a way that judges this world and that will draw all people to him (12:23, 31–32). Jesus is Israel's Messiah, but his kingship is from above and concerns the entire world, to which it is to be announced.

The interchange between the chief priests and Pilate concerning the inscription, found only in John (19:21–22), continues the power struggle observed throughout Jesus' Roman trial (18:28–19:16). The religious authorities never acknowledge Jesus as their king, but they insist that Rome should execute him for claiming to be. Pilate apparently does not care whether or not Jesus claimed to be Messiah, so long as he is not a threat to Roman law and order, but he sees in the inscription another opportunity to needle the local authorities from whom he has extracted a pledge of allegiance to Caesar (v. 15) and to whom he now says imperiously, "What I have written, I have written" (v. 22). So the inscription stands as a witness to the whole world that Jesus is the Messiah, ironically contrary to the intention of Jewish and Roman authorities alike, but contributing significantly to the purpose of the Fourth Gospel (20:30–31).

Soldiers Cast Lots for Jesus' Clothes (19:23–24 [25a NRSV])

This episode is mentioned in the first three Gospels but reported in full only in the Fourth. Four Roman soldiers divide Jesus' clothing into four parts, one for each of them, then decide not to tear his basic, seamless garment but to keep it intact and cast lots for it. The garment, variously translated as "tunic," "robe," or "undergarment," was worn next to the skin but would not resemble any undergarment familiar to readers today. It has inspired great speculation throughout the centuries, most recently in the form of "the shroud of Turin." Its only interest to the evangelist is not historical but theological. He sees here the fulfillment of Scripture (v. 24; see also v. 28 and v. 36). Jesus has already been presented as "the one of whom Moses and the prophets wrote" (1:45) and "the one to whom the scriptures testify" (5:39). In this case the Scripture is, "They divide my clothes among themselves, and for my clothing they cast lots" (Ps. 22:18). It is historically improbable that Jesus went to the cross with enough clothes to divide into four parts (v. 23) in addition to his basic garment. This detail appears to be based on a literalistic misreading of Hebrew parallelism in the text cited, in which the second line repeats the thought of the first.

It is significant that John quotes this particular psalm of lament–referred to some twenty times in the New Testament, including seven direct quotations–but avoids its first verse, "My God, my God, why have you forsaken me?" which Mark and Matthew report as Jesus' only word from the cross (Mark 15:34; Matt. 27:46). The cry of dereliction, as well as the final, wordless "loud cry" (Mark. 15:37; Matt. 27:50), would be incompatible with Johannine theology, according to which Jesus says to his adversaries, "The Father and I are one" (10:30), and to his disciples, "You will leave me alone; yet I am not alone because the Father is with me" (16:32). Psalm 22:18, on the other hand, is appropriate for Jesus, whose experience on the cross fulfills literally this prayer of one who is undergoing intense suffering, humiliation, and the indifference of those who make him suffer.

An evangelist's note (v. 24 in many contemporary translations; v. 25a in the NRSV) underscores that the soldiers did exactly what Psalm 22:18 said. The death of Jesus is part of a divine plan.

The Group Near the Cross (19:25–27)

All four Gospels report a group of women who were witnesses of the crucifixion, but no two agree entirely on their names and identity (Matt. 27:55–56; Mark 15:40–41; Luke 23:49/8:2–3; John 19:25). The Johannine text can be interpreted to refer to two, three, or four women, depending on how one punctuates John 19:25b. One of the gnostic gospels from Nag Hammadi states that there were three Marys,[1] as shown in some artistic representations. Most contemporary translations, however, punctuate the text (19:25) to suggest the presence of four women: Jesus' mother (unnamed), her sister (unnamed), Mary the wife of Clopas, and Mary Magdalene. No formulation of this text in any Gospel refers to "Mary, the mother of Jesus." She is not named here or in the only other scene in which she appears in the Gospel of John (2:1–12).

In the Synoptics the women "stood at a distance" (Luke 23:49; see also Mark 15:40; Matt. 27:55). In John they are "standing near the cross of Jesus" (19:25b). This difference in detail gains significance when in the following verse John speaks only of the mother of Jesus and one other figure, "the disciple whom [Jesus] loved" (19:26), who, like Jesus' mother, is not named.[2] In the first of Jesus' three "words" from the cross reported in the Fourth Gospel, he entrusts his mother and his beloved disciple to each other, saying to his mother, "Woman, here is your son," and to the beloved disciple, "Here is your mother" (vv. 26–27).

The inclusion of a conversation that could be heard only by those very near the cross is plausibly cited to support the traditional hypothesis that this Gospel was written by the apostle John, who is identified as the beloved disciple. Whoever the author may have been, this word is included to show Jesus' filial love for his human family. It also makes of them, together with the other women standing near the cross, the core community that after Jesus' resurrection is to become the church. It is a house church, for "from that hour the disciple took her into his own home" (v. 27b). The Fourth Gospel conceives of the church not as an apostolic institution but as an extended family. It does not narrate the institution of the Lord's Supper or the coming of the Spirit on the day of Pentecost, and instead of the incident in which Jesus keeps his human family standing outside and declares that whoever does the will of God is his brother and sister and mother (Mark 3:35//Matt. 12:50//Luke 8:21), John includes this poignant scene. For him the group near the cross epitomizes the church as the extended family of Jesus, based on his human and divine love. Perhaps the evangelist does not name Jesus' mother or the disciple whom he loved in order to draw attention to their symbolic function.

Jesus' Last Words and Death (19:28–30)

By harmonizing accounts of the crucifixion in all four Gospels, tradition has come up with the "seven last words" of Jesus. Three of them appear only in Luke, three different ones appear only in John, and the remaining one appears in Mark and Matthew as Jesus' only word from the cross. In each case, Jesus' final words give voice to the theology of the evangelist.

The second Johannine word from the cross, "I am thirsty," is introduced by a reference to Jesus' knowing that all was finished (v. 28a). Jesus, knowing what only God can know,[3] is fully aware of what is happening and is in control of the situation, even as he is dying. Jesus' word is further introduced by a parenthetical comment, "in order to fulfill the scripture" (v. 28b). As in all the Gospels and Epistles of the New Testament, the life and ministry of Jesus is seen as the fulfillment of a divine plan made known in the Scriptures of the Hebrew Bible. According to the fourth evangelist, who introduces more explicit citations of Scripture here than anywhere else in the Gospel (vv. 24, 28, 36), this is particularly true of Jesus' death on a cross.

"I am thirsty" is a perfectly understandable remark by a man dying in pain on a Roman cross under the Judean sun. For all his emphasis on Jesus' godlike attributes, John does not lose sight of the humanity of Jesus. He is moved to tears at the tomb of a friend (11:35), and from the cross he calls for something to drink (19:28). For John this word is also the occasion for the offer of sour wine (*oxos*) to drink, a gesture that appears in all four Gospels but is variously interpreted. In John there is no suggestion of delaying Jesus' death long enough to see if Elijah would come to take him down from the cross (as in Mark 15:36 and Matt. 27:49) and no hint of mockery (as in Luke 23:36), but there is an explicit reference to the fulfillment of Scripture. The words "I am thirsty" do not appear verbatim in the Old Testament, but they echo two psalms. As an echo of Psalm 22:15, "My mouth is dried up like a potsherd, and my tongue sticks to my jaws," the reference replaces the use of Psalm 22:1 in Mark and Matthew. More directly, the words and the scene echo Psalm 69, another lament of a righteous sufferer who complains of the enemies who insult, shame, and dishonor him. They show no pity, no comfort, says the psalmist: "They gave me poison for food, and for my thirst they gave me vinegar (*oxos*) to drink" (Ps. 69:21).

The reference to hyssop is problematic (v. 29). It is hard to visualize a branch of hyssop long enough to lift a sponge to the mouth of Jesus, since hyssop is a bushy shrub. The Synoptic parallels say that the sponge was put on a stick (Mark 15:36; Matt. 27:48). The evangelist seems to have written "hyssop" to suggest the Passover texts that would be read on that day, texts that speak of hyssop being used to sprinkle the blood of paschal lambs on the lintel and doorposts of Israelite houses (Exod. 12:22). Here it is used to offer Jesus something to drink at the very time the lambs were being slaughtered for the Passover meal.

Jesus' final word from the cross, "It is finished" (v. 30a), is also rich with overtones of Johannine theology. First, in laying down his own life, Jesus has completed what he was sent to do. He has revealed the true nature of God and on the cross has demonstrated God's love. The work the Father gave him to do in the world is finished (v. 28a). Second, the Scriptures are fulfilled (v. 28b). The Greek word used here, from the same root as the word for "finished" in v. 27a and 30a, also means "accomplished, brought to an end." The death of Jesus has filled with meaning and brought to their intended end the passages of Scripture that speak of him. Third, Jesus' earthly life is now over, as the end of the verse states explicitly.

The actual death of Jesus is reported very briefly: "He bowed his head and gave up his spirit" (v. 30b). Jesus' **life** in the flesh is finished, but not his inner life (in this text, his *pneuma*), which he gives up (literally, "hands over"). Jesus hands over his earthly life just as intentionally as Judas had handed him over to his enemies. This is consistent with the Johannine teaching about eternal life (*zoe*); Jesus' *zoe* is eternal and does not die.

The detail, "he bowed his head," appears only in John. Raymond Brown suggests that this gesture leads the eyes of Jesus and of readers to the group at the foot of the cross (again, only in John) whom Jesus has just constituted as his spiritual family (1:12–13), the community of faith to whom he has promised to send the Holy Spirit (14:15–18).[4]

The Spear Thrust (19:31–37)

Comparison of 19:31 with 18:28 shows that the evangelist understands the day of Jesus' death to be Friday, the day of preparation for the Sabbath, and at the same time the day of preparation for Passover, the "day of great solemnity" (19:31), which coincided with the Sabbath in the year that Jesus died. The Jewish authorities, who would not enter the governor's residence that morning in order to be able to eat the Passover after sundown that night (18:28), now ask Pilate to have the legs of the crucified men broken and their bodies removed before the big day.

The brutal punishment of breaking the bones of crucified criminals was a common enough Roman practice to generate a technical term for it (*crurifragium*). Its role in the death of Jesus is reported only in the Fourth Gospel, where it prepares the way for the piercing of Jesus' side by a Roman soldier's spear (v. 34), also found only in John. Scholars have invested much energy in an inconclusive debate about the historicity of this incident. Of greater interest for interpreters are the ways it functions in the Gospel of John.

First, it demonstrates that Jesus is really dead. This question is raised and answered in Mark 15:44–45. Its theological importance is shown by John's inclusion of this dramatic scene to demonstrate the error of any who might see in Jesus a purely divine being who did not live and die in the flesh (1 John 4:2–3). The Fourth Gospel and the First Epistle of John both insist that Jesus was fully human as well as fully divine. In the language of the Apostles' Creed, "he was crucified, died, and was buried; he descended to the dead" (contemporary ecumenical version). In the Johannine account of this death, the soldiers see that Jesus is already dead and therefore do not break his legs (v. 33). The piercing of his side by one of them offers physical evidence of his death (v. 34).

Second, in reporting this event John points to Scripture. The underlying reference of the quotation, "None of his bones shall be broken" (v. 36) is to the directions given concerning the paschal lamb, "You shall not take any of the animal outside the house, and you shall not break any of its bones" (Exod. 12:46) and "They shall leave none of it until morning, nor break a bone of it: according to all the statute for the passover they shall keep it" (Num. 9:12). The more direct verbal reference is to Psalm 34:19–20, a psalm of praise for God's deliverance of the righteous: "Many are the afflictions of the righteous, but the LORD rescues them from them all. He keeps all their bones; not one of them will be broken." The Roman soldiers' decision not to break Jesus' legs inadvertently fulfills the prescription of the Torah concerning the paschal lamb and also the confidence of a righteous sufferer as expressed in Psalm 34.

Furthermore, the evangelist finds in the piercing of Jesus' side (v. 34) the direct fulfillment of one line from an oracle about events on the day of the Lord: "I will pour out a spirit of compassion and supplication on the house of David and the inhabitants of Jerusalem, so that, *when they look on the one whom they have pierced*, they shall mourn for him, as one mourns for an only child, and weep bitterly over him, as one weeps over a firstborn" (Zech. 12:10, italics added). By a very slight alteration the evangelist reads the italicized words as a prediction: "They will look on the one whom they have pierced" (v. 37). In this reading "they" refers to the Roman soldier and the little group of Jesus' spiritual family standing near the cross. For the evangelist, Jesus is God's only child, whose death causes even those who pierced him to weep.

Third, the piercing of Jesus' side prepares the way for the climactic scene in which Thomas, in response to the risen Lord's invitation to reach out his hand and put it into Jesus' side, makes his dramatic profession of faith (20:27–28). Neither the piercing of Jesus' side nor his postresurrection appearance to Thomas is reported in any other Gospel.

Fourth, the thrust of the lance points ahead to the significance of water and blood in the community of his disciples, for when Jesus' side was pierced, "at once blood and water came out" (v. 34). Debate about the time required for blood to coagulate and the possible composition of the watery substance misses the point of the text. Given the symbolic meaning of "eat the flesh of the Son of Man and drink his blood" (6:53) as a clear reference to the Lord's Supper, interpreters should recognize in the blood that came from Jesus' pierced side a reference to the Eucharist, which lies at the heart of the community of his disciples. The water belongs to the extensive water symbolism noted first at the wedding in Cana (2:1–11) and seen again with reference to new birth from above (3:5), the gift of eternal life (4:10, 13–14), the invitation to come to Jesus and never be thirsty (6:35; 7:37–38), and Jesus' promise of the life-giving Spirit (7:39) who would come to be Jesus' presence with his disciples after his return to the Father (14:16–18). In many of these texts, including the present one, interpreters have seen reference to the sacrament of baptism and to the new life in the Spirit that baptism symbolizes.

The symbolic significance of water and blood was so evident to the Gospel's first readers that the evangelist took care to defend himself against the charge of simply making the story up to fit the community's practice. He appeals to an eyewitness of whom he speaks in the third person and whose veracity the evangelist attests (v. 35). A similar attestation is affixed at the end of the Gospel (21:24) like the seal of a notary public on an important document. In the present instance, the evangelist in effect solemnly affirms that the blood and water really did flow from Jesus' dying body. He does so in order that readers may believe (v. 35) that Jesus is the Messiah, the Son of God (20:31). Seldom is Scripture more clear on the inseparable link between the Jesus of history and the Christ of faith.

The Burial of Jesus (19:38–42)

In all four Gospels, Joseph of Arimathea takes the initiative to ask Pilate's permission to bury the body of Jesus. A composite description gleaned from the Synoptic Gospels depicts him as an honored member of the council (Mark 15:43; Luke 23:50), a rich man (Matt. 27:57), and a disciple of Jesus (Matt. 27:57) who was looking for the kingdom of God (Mark 15:43; Luke 23:51). The Fourth Gospel's description of Joseph is bare by comparison. By omitting all other details, it emphasizes that he "was a disciple of Jesus, though a secret one because of his fear of the Jews" (John 19:38).

In the Synoptic accounts of the burial, Joseph is joined by women who see where he is laid and, in Luke, return to the city to prepare spices and ointments to give Jesus a proper burial after the Sabbath is over (Mark 15:47; Matt. 27:61; Luke 23:55–56). No women are mentioned in John's account. Instead, Nicodemus (found only in John) takes the lead to secure about a hundred pounds of spices (v. 39) and, with Joseph, who had removed the body of Jesus from the cross (v. 38b), wraps the body with the spices in linen cloths (v. 40). Nicodemus was also a member of the council, who, the evangelist is careful to point out, had come to Jesus by night to inquire about the kingdom of God (3:1–10). He had also risked the ire of his peers when he objected to the council's condemnation of Jesus in absentia, reminding them that "our law does not judge people without first giving them a hearing to find out what they are doing" (7:50–52), a role Luke attributes to Joseph of Arimathea (Luke 23:51). Now these two highly placed secret disciples of Jesus are brought together in the Fourth Gospel to bury his body according to traditional Jewish burial custom (vv. 39–40). Both had overcome their earlier fear of their peers, the Jewish leaders, to pay their respects to Jesus in broad daylight, Joseph by boldly asking the Roman governor for his body and Nicodemus by giving him an expensive burial with enough spices for a king. Mary's pound of perfume of pure nard (12:3–5) is dwarfed by Nicodemus's hundred pounds of myrrh and aloes. These two disciples, now no longer secret ones, give Jesus a royal burial in "a new tomb in which no one had ever been laid" (v. 41b). John makes no mention of the tomb's being hewn out of the rock or of their closing it with a stone, though his account is compatible with these details.

John, and only John, does say the tomb was in a garden and that it was close to the place where Jesus was crucified (v. 41a). This detail prepares the way for the scene on Sunday morning, when Mary Magdalene mistakes the risen Jesus for a gardener (20:15). It echoes John's note that the arrest occurred in a garden, though that one was east of the Kidron valley (18:1) while Golgotha and this nearby garden were north of where the city wall then stood.[5] John is more interested in the time than the place. "It was the Jewish day of Preparation" (Friday); so, as good members of the Sanhedrin who did not wish to carry a load on the Sabbath, they laid Jesus in a new tomb in the garden because it was nearby (v. 42).

Preaching and teaching the Word

1. A synoptic study. John 18 and 19 in their entirety are appointed as the Gospel reading for Good Friday all three years in the Lectionary. One way to teach this lengthy block of material would be to do a corporate reading of a portion of the passion narrative in all four Gospels. If participants were divided into three groups with one of the Synoptic Gospels assigned to each group, they could note what John omits and includes relative to the other Gospels, as the teacher reads John aloud episode by episode. John's intention in telling the story of Jesus' death and burial as he did would become apparent.

A study of Jesus' three words from the cross in John could be included in a series of lessons on the seven last words that includes the three in Luke and the one in Matthew and Mark. In each study, attention would be given to major traits in that evangelist's portrait of Jesus: the full humanity of Jesus evident in his cry of abandonment (Mark 15:34; Matt. 27:46); his gentle compassion shown in the prayer of forgiveness for his enemies (Luke 23:34a), his saving grace in the word to the penitent thief (Luke 23:43), and his serene confidence in the face of death in his word to the Father (Luke 23:46). Jesus' regal exaltation on the cross in John is punctuated by words in which he creates a new spiritual family on earth characterized by mutual love and care (John 19:26–27). He expresses a thirst that is both physical and spiritual in his determination to drink the cup of suffering given him by the Father (18:11; 19:28). "It is finished" (19:30) shows his clear sense of obedience to and unity with the God who sent him. In John, Jesus on the cross links heaven and earth and shows himself to be God's Word made flesh, the way to God, God's truth and life.

2. Preaching Jesus' words from the cross. A sermon on John's understanding of the church (ecclesiology) could be based on Jesus' two-part word to his mother and to his beloved disciple (19:26–27) It would point to the church as a community grounded in mutual love. John emphasizes the spiritual essence without which institutional structures and apostolic continuity are empty. Preaching on Jesus' beloved community might help a congregation wounded by church fights and weary of programs and committee meetings to grow into a community of love and service.

"I am thirsty" (19:28) is shocking to hear from one who offered a Samaritan woman living water that will forever slake the thirst of those who drink it (4:10–14) and promised a crowd in Galilee that those who believe in him will never be hungry or thirsty (6:35). Fully human, Jesus experienced every human extremity and in his dying moments suffered thirst. He endured it because his food was to do the will of God who had sent him (4:32).[6] A true thirst for God in disciples today leads to fulfillment of the purpose for which one was born and to moments of obedient service that are like cool water in an arid land.

"It is finished" (19:30) points to Jesus and his completion of the work he was sent to do, but his words can also lead us to reflect on the end of our earthly life. Each of us has "promises to keep, / And miles to go before [we] sleep."[7] Those who live in union with Christ can invest Frost's line with a deeper meaning that grows out of the believer's sense of Christian vocation. "So teach us to count our days" (Ps. 90:12).

3. The inscription. A sermon on the inscription, "Jesus of Nazareth, the King of the Jews" (19:19; see exegetical notes), perhaps on Christ the King Sunday, could compare the meaning of Jesus' kingship in the Fourth Gospel and the meaning of leadership today. Jesus' royalty is humble (12:12–16; 19:2–3, 28); commanding (18:4–8, 23, 33–38; 19:5, 9–11, 14); universal (19:20b); and divine (20:28).

4. Jesus' special garment. The seamless tunic (19:23–24) is a symbol of the unity that characterized Jesus himself, which he wills for the church and for the entire human family. Jesus is one with God (10:30) and in him human and divine attributes are united harmoniously. The thrust of Jesus' death upon the cross is toward the unity of the entire human family. The tunic is described as woven in one piece from the top (19:23, *anothen,* "from above"), the same adverb with a double meaning that is used in Jesus' conversations with Nicodemus (3:3, 7) and with Pilate (19:11). The soldiers say of the tunic, "Let us not tear it" (19:24), the same verb that is used of the net in the next chapter (21:11) which, despite its great catch of fish, is not torn. Through his description of the seamless tunic, John ties the death of Jesus metaphorically to the theme of unity. "When [Jesus] draws all people to himself, he draws them into one body, one community. What God weaves, God weaves whole, from above. There is but one vine, one net, one flock, one shepherd, one Son, and one seamless tunic woven from the top."[8] Readers and hearers today would do well to show at least the sensitivity of those Roman soldiers and try not to tear it.

5. The cross as exaltation. Preachers might draw attention to the crucifixion as exaltation (3:14; 8:28; 12:32–33) and recall Jesus' promise, "And I, when I am lifted up . . ." (12:32). They could ask what is lifted up when Jesus is raised upon the cross and later from the grave. Possible answers to this question include: 1) the cost of obedience to God, for John like Mark depicts a human life that ends in pain; 2) the glory of a whole life lived out in total obedience to God's will and ending with a sense of accomplishment (19:28, 30); and 3) the love of God who gave his only son to take away the sin of the world (1:29; 3:16). Alternatively, the question might be "Who is lifted up?" and the answer proposed by relating Jesus' death to the titles given in chapter 1: the Word that was God, the Lamb of God, the Messiah, the Son of God. The titles might be boring for some, but the message they communicate is not: God is, God has drawn near as one of us, God cares for us with a love that is stronger than death. The cross is a staggering affirmation about God that only faith can grasp.

6. The burial. John's account of the burial (19:38–42) involves the last encounter of three people with Jesus: Pilate, Joseph of Arimathea, and Nicodemus. All three had, at various points in Jesus' ministry, been strongly attracted to him, but none ever publicly declared himself to be a disciple. Their stories afford the occasion for a call to discipleship or an appeal to secret disciples to stand up for Jesus.

In the trial scene (18:28–19:16) Pilate showed that he was favorably inclined toward Jesus, but he was unwilling to entertain the idea of a serious commitment to his truth. Now, when asked by a disciple of Jesus for permission to take away his dead body (19:38b), Pilate grants the permission. This is the last we hear of him in canonical Scripture. Legend has proposed various endings for Pilate's story (some are mentioned in the preaching suggestions for 19:1–16), but for the Fourth Gospel, he stands with another Roman underling (King Agrippa, Acts 26:28) as one who had an opportunity to believe, and was perhaps tempted to do so, but walked away.

All that is known of Joseph of Arimathea (leaving aside the wealth of legend that grew up around him)[9] is what the Gospels report in connection with the burial of Jesus' body. John includes a significant detail found nowhere else: Joseph was a secret disciple of Jesus (19:38a). His fear of disapproval and ostracism by his peers kept him from taking any stand for Jesus during his lifetime, and it is likely that he incurred precisely that as a consequence of coming forward to ask for Jesus' body after his death. The good news is that he did, belatedly, come forward. Preaching about him might move reluctant souls to come forward today.

The three contacts of Nicodemus with Jesus that are reported in the Fourth Gospel are a fruitful case study in reluctant discipleship. A clear pattern of development is seen, from his initial approach to Jesus by night (3:1–2), to the red flag he raised cautiously in the Sanhedrin when the court sought to condemn Jesus without a hearing (7:50–51), to the lavish burial he, with Joseph from Arimathea, gave to Jesus' body after his death (19:39–40). Through this case study preachers can call for bold discipleship while it can still do some good.

With these three actors John presents the last in his series of encounters of various kinds of people with Jesus. Through them the evangelist is making an appeal to secret disciples in his own time, whether Jews, Greeks, or Romans, to come out of the closet and stand up for Jesus. Such an appeal is still appropriate today.

Resurrection Narratives
and First Ending

20:1–31

All four Gospels were written to elicit faith in Jesus Christ, but the specific content and goal of that faith proper to each Gospel is nowhere more apparent than in the way each reports the resurrection of Jesus and the ensuing appearances of the risen Lord. John 20, although it parallels in general the accounts in the Synoptic Gospels, is thoroughly Johannine in its cast of characters and in almost all of its details. Originally the conclusion of the Fourth Gospel, chapter 20 includes four episodes: the empty tomb (vv. 1–10), appearance to Mary Magdalene (vv. 11–18), first appearance to the disciples (vv. 19–23), and appearance to the disciples with Thomas (vv. 24–29). The presence of Mary Magdalene and the continuity of time and place make of the first two episodes a single scene, treated as a whole in the Revised Common Lectionary as the Gospel reading for Easter Sunday every year. Similarly, the appearances to the gathered disciples, though reported as two episodes a week apart in the narrative (20:19, 26), are tied together by the same cast of characters except for the absence of Thomas in the first scene. The chapter closes with an ending (vv. 30–31) that concludes part three and probably once ended the entire Gospel as well.

John's account of the empty tomb and appearances of Jesus returns to a major theme of the prologue: the living Word, who was with God in the beginning, is the source of all life, has life in himself, and cannot be overcome by darkness and death (1:1–5). Other Johannine themes are also carried forward here: Jesus' promise that his disciples would see him again (14:19; 16:16–20); the promise of the Holy Spirit (14:16–18; 15:26; 16:7, 12–14); and the announcement of his return to the Father (6:62; 14:2–3; 16:28).

Exploring the text

The resurrection of Jesus is not described in any of the four canonical Gospels. They are content to present two kinds of evidence that it happened: the discovery of Jesus' empty tomb by women who were his followers and appearances of the risen Lord to various disciples.

THE EMPTY TOMB AND THE APPEARANCE
TO MARY MAGDALENE (20:1–18)

They say that seeing is believing, but sometimes seeing is not enough. Consider what Mary Magdalene and two other disciples of Jesus saw on the first Easter morning.

The Empty Tomb (20:1–10)

In all four Gospels, Mary Magdalene comes to the tomb early on the first day of the week (John 20:1). In the three Synoptics she is just one of a group of women who come to give Jesus' body a decent burial with spices according to Jewish custom. In John, however, she comes alone and not to anoint the body; Nicodemus and Joseph of Arimathea have already done that (19:40). She is drawn only by her love and grief (v. 11). The special emotional tie between Mary Magdalene and Jesus finds strong echo in gnostic writings of the second and third centuries.[1] Seeing that the stone has been removed from the tomb (a detail from the common early tradition; no stone was mentioned in John's account of the burial), Mary Magdalene rushes off to find Simon Peter and "the other disciple, the one whom Jesus loved" (v. 2a). When she finds them, she reports that Jesus' body is gone and "we [another detail reflecting the common tradition of discovery by a group of women] do not know where they have laid him" (v. 2b). An empty tomb does not prove Jesus' resurrection, nor does it at first even suggest it to Mary. She assumes that someone has taken the body away, a hypothesis she repeats a few minutes later to two angels in the tomb (v. 13). It also underlies her request of the man she mistakes for a gardener (v. 15).

At this point the action shifts to Peter and "the other disciple," the only men to show up at the empty tomb in any canonical Gospel. One is the anonymous figure referred to sometimes as "the other disciple" (20:2–4) and sometimes as "the disciple whom Jesus loved" (13:23–24; 20:2; 21:7, 20). The joining of these two expressions in 20:2 shows that they refer to the same person, who appears only in the Fourth Gospel. Although tradition identifies him with the apostle John, son of Zebedee, he is more likely a minor disciple whose name we do not know.[2]

In harmony with Mark's account, in which the women at the tomb are instructed to go tell his disciples and Peter what they have seen (Mark

16:7), Peter is mentioned first in John's account about Mary Magdalene's discovery (John 20:2, 3). It is the other disciple, however, who reaches the tomb first (v. 4) and believes as a result of what he sees (v. 8). It is worthwhile to visualize the race. The two men run together, the beloved disciple reaching the tomb first, bending down, looking in and seeing the burial wrappings, but not entering. Then Peter arrives and rushes right in. Peter sees the wrappings that had been on Jesus' body and the cloth that had been on his head, which are described in some detail but not enough to satisfy all our curiosity about them. They are not a shroud (*sindon*), as in the Synoptics and the apocryphal Gospel of Peter, and they are not linen strips as in Egyptian burials, although the term used (*othonia*) could mean that. They are just "linen cloths," with no indication of what they might have looked like.[3] The other disciple follows Peter into the tomb, sees the same things and believes (v. 8). No direct object states what the other disciple believes, but in other Johannine texts this absolute statement about believing refers to the conviction that Jesus is who he claims to be (3:18; 4:41–42; 16:30–31). In the scene beside the tomb of Lazarus, it refers specifically to belief in the resurrection (11:25–27, 40–42).

Why does one of the two men believe at this point, while the other does not? The editorial note in verse 9 suggests that an understanding of Scripture will later prepare disciples to believe in Jesus' resurrection, but in the early dawn at the empty tomb neither of these disciples has yet achieved such an understanding. The only clue given in the text about the differing reactions of the two men is the special bond of love between Jesus and the other disciple. Throughout the Fourth Gospel, there is a special link between seeing and believing, but the present passage makes clear that seeing at the deepest level is interpreted by love.

The return of the two men to their homes (v. 10) clears the stage for the next episode, in which Mary Magdalene alone is granted the first appearance of the risen Lord.

The Appearance to Mary Magdalene (20:11–18)

In the appearance of the risen Jesus to Mary Magdalene, the evangelist combines effectively two of the prominent literary devices of the Fourth Gospel: misunderstanding and recognition. Misunderstandings in John usually concern Jesus' words and are used to teach a deeper, correct understanding of what Jesus intends. This one concerns Jesus himself, whom Mary mistakes for a gardener. Jesus' correction of that misunderstanding constitutes the first of three climactic recognition scenes in the Fourth Gospel: Mary in the garden (20:16), Thomas in the closed room with the other disciples (20:28), and the beloved disciple at the Sea of Tiberias (21:7). These three are but the last and most powerful of a series of narratives throughout the Gospel in which, during an encounter with Jesus, various kinds of people come to realize in a life-changing way who he is and who they are in relation to him. These last three encounters are with people who already know Jesus, but when he appears to them after the resurrection, it is like "meeting Jesus again for the first time"[4] in a new and dramatic way.

Mary Magdalene (= from Magdala, a town located some seven miles from Capernaum on the northwest shore of the Sea of Galilee) was among the women whom Jesus had cured of evil spirits and infirmities and who accompanied him during his Galilean ministry with the Twelve, providing for them out of their resources (Luke 8:2–3). Mary Magdalene, from whom Jesus had cast out seven demons (Luke 8:2; Mark 16:9), is the first named in every Gospel's list of the women who followed Jesus. She is present at the crucifixion, standing far off according to one account (Mark 15:40; Matt. 27:56), but standing near with Jesus' mother and the beloved disciple according to the Fourth Gospel (19:25). She and another Mary are observers when Jesus is buried (Mark 15:47; Matt. 27:61), a detail that John omits. She comes to Jesus' tomb early Sunday morning, first among a group according to the Synoptic Gospels (Mark 16:1, 9; Matt. 28:1; Luke 24:10) and alone according to John (20:1). She is not mentioned elsewhere in the Gospels.

She is not to be confused with Mary of Bethany, the sister of Lazarus, nor with the unnamed woman in Bethany who poured an alabaster jar of ointment over Jesus' head in the house of Simon the leper (Mark 14:3–9), nor with the anonymous forgiven sinner of Luke 7:36–50 who washed Jesus' feet with her tears, wiped them with her hair, and anointed them with perfume. Though conceivable, the widespread idea that Mary Magdalene was a prostitute is the result of combining elements from all these stories and attributing them to Mary Magdalene. The confusion originated in writings of the church fathers (*sic!*) and was depicted in Christian art such as Matthias Grünewald's *Crucifixion,* in which the sinful woman who anointed Jesus' feet and wiped them with her hair is conflated with Mary Magdalene, given an alabaster box of ointment, and placed at the foot of the cross with Jesus' mother and the beloved disciple. This bit of mistaken identity is even enshrined in the English language, in which the adjective "maudlin," derived from Mary Magdalene, signifies tearful repentance and, by derivation, effusive sentimentality. The suggestion that Mary Magdalene was Jesus' lover[5] and the hypothesis that she was his wife who, as next of kin, was responsible for the proper burial of his body,[6] while not contradicting the biblical evidence, stretch it in sharply different directions. The only extended narrative about Mary Magdalene in the Gospels is the present text (John 20:1–2, 11–18) in which she stands weeping just outside the tomb in the garden early Sunday morning, grieving over Jesus' death and the disappearance of his body. Its drama moves at a deeper level than maudlin sentimentality, and it shows little interest in sexual questions.

The episode includes two parts, one about angels and the other about Jesus. In the first, Mary bends over to look into the tomb, just as the beloved disciple had done shortly before (vv. 5, 11). Instead of the grave-clothes she sees two angels sitting, one at the head and the other at the feet of the place where Jesus' body had been laid. They do not announce his resurrection (as does the young man in Mark 16:6 and Matt. 28:6 and the two men in Luke 24:5), nor do they give any command (as in Mark 16:7 and Matt. 28:7). Instead they simply ask a question that underlines Mary's grief: "Woman, why are you weeping?" Her reply voices her distress and echoes her earlier report to Peter and the other disciple: "They have taken away my Lord, and I [singular this time] do not know where they have laid him" (v. 13; cf. v. 2). The entire first part of the episode (vv. 11–13) prepares the way for her encounter with Jesus in the second part (vv. 14–18), which is punctuated by two acts of turning.

While Mary speaks to the angels, a silent figure appears behind her. She turns and sees Jesus but does not recognize him (v. 14). Jesus speaks, asking her the identical question the angels had put to her, "Woman, why are you weeping?" and adding "Whom are you looking for?" (v. 15a). The first question underscores Mary's grief; the second is a slight adaptation of the one he had put to Andrew and another disciple of John the Baptizer at the very beginning of the story, "What are you looking for?" (John 1:38). Jesus invites those who seek him to reflect on and be ready to expand their understanding of what it is they are looking for.

Mary's reply (v. 15b) specifies her misunderstanding. She thinks Jesus is the gardener who might have removed Jesus' body. It also shows Mary's vigorous activism, in contrast to the more passive Mary of Bethany (Luke 10:39). If the gardener will tell her where to find Jesus' body, she will take it away and give him a proper burial.

Jesus then speaks her name, "Mary."

Turning again (20:16), she also speaks just one word, "Teacher." In her mother tongue it is a term of endearment that expresses the tie between the disciple and her Lord. The risen Jesus has come to make himself known to her, but she does not recognize him until he calls her by name. As Jesus said earlier about the good shepherd, "The sheep hear his voice [when] he calls his own sheep by name" (10:3).

The initial failure to recognize Jesus in the recognition scenes following Jesus' resurrection (John 20:11–18; 21:4–7; Luke 24:13–35) indicates that he has undergone a change from the Jesus they know. The absence of his body from the tomb, however, means that the Jesus who appears to his disciples is the same one they have known in the flesh. Paul's language about a physical body and a spiritual body (1 Cor. 15:42ff.) refers to the continuity and transformation evident in these appearances.

After the moment of recognition, Jesus gives Mary a double command: "Do not hold on to me. . . . But go to my brothers and say to them . . ." (v. 17). Both commands have to do with Jesus' ascension, which, in John, means his return to the Father (see 3:13; 6:62). The older translation of the negative command, "Do not touch me" (*noli me tangere* in the Latin Vulgate), failed to catch the nuance of the Greek tense and mood, which is correctly rendered in most contemporary translations: "Do not hold on to me" or an equivalent expression. Jesus tells Mary not to cling to him "because I have not yet ascended to the **Father**." Then in the positive command he tells her to go say to his disciples (here called "brothers"), "I am ascending to my Father and your Father, to my God and your God" (v. 17).

The main point of the verse is that Jesus is in the process of returning to the Father but that his return is not yet complete. Only after he has returned to the Father will he send the Spirit through whom he will be permanently present in and among his disciples. It is not that holding on to his body could prevent its ascension into heaven. That idea is based on Luke's corporeal, temporal notion of the ascension, so firmly imprinted in our minds today through the vivid picture in Acts 1:3–11.

For John, the ascension is a spatial word used to express the theological idea of exaltation and glorification, and "the hour" is not a chronological period of sixty minutes but a moment in eternity. It is, for John, God's supreme *kairos* (significant time), which embraces the entire process of Jesus' exaltation and glorification. "Jesus is lifted up on the cross; he is raised up from the dead; and he goes up to the Father–all as part of one action and one 'hour.'"[7] That "hour" is not yet complete when the risen Lord encounters Mary Magdalene at the tomb. He is still in the process of "ascending to my Father and your Father, to my God and your God" (v. 17b). Until that process is complete and Jesus has given the Spirit (7:39; 20:22), Mary must not try to hold on to him. This is only a transitional appearance. When the glorification is complete and Jesus gives the Spirit, Mary will abide in him and he in her (14:17; 15:4).

Guided by a temporal understanding of Jesus' hour, interpreters try to place the ascension in John chronologically between Jesus' word to Mary,

"Do not hold on to me, because I have not yet ascended" (20:17a), and his word to Thomas a week later, "Reach out your hand and put it in my side" (20:27). John, however, is not interested in the chronological moment of Jesus' ascension any more than he is in the moment of Jesus' resurrection. His concern is how each is related to the nature of Jesus' presence with his disciples after his return to the Father. We are to hold on to Jesus not through evanescent appearances of his resurrection body but through the indwelling of his Spirit, which makes Jesus' Father our Father, his God our God, and all believers brothers and sisters of Jesus.

Mary obeys Jesus' commands. She goes and announces to the disciples that she has seen the risen Jesus, who is not just her beloved teacher but also the community's Lord (v. 18). Mary's obedience to his command in verse 18 makes of her the very first witness of his resurrection. In bearing testimony to his first disciples, she also becomes "the apostle to the apostles," a title by which she has been honored ever since the ninth century.[8]

The sequence of emptiness, encounter, and obedience portrayed in John's account of Jesus' appearance to Mary Magdalene is a pattern that his disciples in every age can replicate in their own experience. In doing so, we can know Jesus not just as an absent deity, seated at the right hand of God the Father, but as a living presence who in the person of the Holy Spirit may be present in ways we do not at first recognize.

Preaching and teaching the Word

Since John 20:1–8 comes around every Easter Sunday in the Lectionary, it may be hard to find a fresh approach to the text each year. Alternating between the two episodes in this scene, preaching one year on the discovery of the empty tomb (vv. 1–10) and the next on the appearance to Mary Magdalene (vv. 11–18) might help. It would also be helpful to keep on file sermon ideas on these two episodes that come to the preacher throughout the year, particularly during pastoral visits. A commentary cannot measure up to the ideas that come out of life experiences shared with the congregation, but here are a few pump primers.

1. Seeing and loving. The relationship between seeing and believing is a recurrent theme in the Fourth Gospel and an important element in the story of the race to the empty tomb in John 20, dramatically portrayed in a painting by Swiss artist Eugene Burnand (1850–1921).[9] Only the Beloved Disciple, without seeing Jesus himself, believes that Jesus has risen from the dead. Love of Jesus is the key to my seeing and knowing him as my risen Lord. It is also the key to the level at which I see other people. I can really see only those I love.

2. Encounter in the garden. John's location of the tomb in a garden (19:41) and Mary's mistaking Jesus for a gardener (20:15) have suggested to interpreters an allusion to the garden of Eden. This was probably not the intention of the evangelist, since his word for garden is not the one used in the Greek Old Testament. A text, however, has a life of its own beyond the writer's intention, and preachers can draw attention to echoes of Genesis 2 and 3 in the encounter of Mary Magdalene and Jesus in the garden. Some have seen in the story of this man and woman in a garden in the early morning a reference to the creation story and the beginning of a new life in which the resurrection of Jesus has shattered the barrier between life in the flesh and life in the spirit. Some have explored the contrasting parallel of the voice of God "walking in the garden at the time of the evening breeze" (Gen. 3:8) and the voice of Jesus calling Mary by name in the early morning (John 20:16). God found Adam in the garden, and Adam was filled with fear. Mary recognized Jesus in the garden, and she was filled with love and joy. The preacher could explore the reasons for the difference, together with the proximity of God in every human garden.[10]

3. *"Hush, hush; somebody's calling my name."* This African American spiritual captures the sense of reverent awe of Mary's moment of recognition (John 20:16). It also recognizes that the Lord seldom appears to people without giving them something to do: "Oh, my Lord, oh my Lord, what shall I do?" Mary's task is to be a witness. "To witness" means to see something significant. To *be* a witness is to offer reliable testimony about what one has seen. In John, Mary Magdalene is witness to Jesus' death and resurrection in both senses of the term. She saw the death of Jesus; she sees and testifies to his resurrection. The text (John 20:11–18) and the spiritual that interprets it both invite us to listen for Jesus to call our name and then to bear witness to what we hear by our obedient daily walk with him as the living Word.

APPEARANCES TO THE DISCIPLES
AND TO THOMAS (20:19–29)

How can anyone believe that Jesus is alive two thousand years after his death? What makes people think that he is? Is the Christian faith a grand delusion? John 20 is written as if the evangelist anticipated these questions.

Exploring the text

The scene has shifted from the tomb in the garden to a house somewhere in Jerusalem where Jesus' disciples, frightened of the Jewish authorities who had put their Teacher and Lord to death, are gathered behind doors that are closed and locked (v. 19). As in the first half of the chapter, this scene includes two episodes, one involving a group of disciples (vv. 19–23//1–10) and the second focusing on an individual (vv. 24–29// 11–18). In the earlier scene Jesus announced the culmination of his exaltation through his ascension to the Father (v. 17). In this one he gives the Holy Spirit to his disciples (v. 22), indicating that his return to the Father is complete and his coming again to the disciples is a present reality.

First Appearance to the Disciples (20:19–23)

At the tomb in the morning two of the disciples had seen Jesus' graveclothes but not Jesus. On the evening of that same day–Sunday, the first day of the Jewish week–Jesus "came and stood among them," defying the physical fact of locked doors. In referring to the event, Paul uses the verb "appeared" (1 Cor. 15:5), as do these notes. An appearance is something that is seen, and this word suggests the possibility of a vision. John avoids the term; he just says that Jesus stood among them. It was really Jesus, but his body was no ordinary physical body, for he had passed through, or materialized inside of, locked doors.

Jesus is the only speaker in this episode. His communication with his disciples has two parts, each introduced by the everyday greeting, "Peace [*shalom*] be with you" (v. 19), which is at the same time a blessing. This usual greeting has unusual significance under the circumstances, for through it Jesus calms the fear and addresses the uncertainty of his disciples, fulfilling his promise of peace (14:27; 16:33)

He then speaks to them nonverbally by showing them his hands and his side. It is a wordless reply to the unexpressed but urgent question, "Can this really be Jesus?" They get the message. Without a word they see and believe and are filled with joy (v. 20), just as he had promised (16:20–24).

The transition to the second and more important part of Jesus' message is marked by repetition of the greeting, to which he immediately adds a commission: "As the Father has sent me, so I send you" (v. 21). This is a vital turning point in the Fourth Gospel, which has told the story of the one sent by the Father to reveal the true nature of God to the world and to complete God's work (3:16, 34; 4:34; 5:36; 7:28f; 8:26–29; 9:4; 17:3–4). Now, in an action that earlier texts have foreshadowed (4:38; 13:20; 17:18), the risen and glorified Son of God sends his disciples to bear witness to the life and light they have found in him. In the few words of this brief verse the themes of sending and witness come into focus, not to introduce a narrative about the sending of the Twelve but, at the moment in which Jesus breathes his Spirit into his gathered disciples, to make of them a missionary society, a witness for Jesus' way in the world (v. 22).

The parallel with Luke's account of the risen Lord's appearance to his disciples gathered in Jerusalem is striking (Luke 24:36–49). Luke also combines the themes of witness, mission, and empowerment by the Holy Spirit (Luke 24:48–49), but in Luke–Acts the Spirit is not given until the day of Pentecost, and then it comes with great commotion (Acts 2:1–21). In John the Spirit is given directly by the risen Lord on Easter night, and it comes as silently as a breath (John 20:22). The message is the same, but each portrayal undoubtedly reflects the evangelist's understanding and experience.

To the gift of the Spirit, the Fourth Gospel adds an important element in Jesus' commission: the forgiveness of sins (v. 23). The historic argument between Catholics and Protestants over an institutional interpretation of this verse in conjunction with others ("the power of the keys" based on Matt. 16:18–19 and the corollaries of penance, absolution, and indulgences) makes it difficult for Protestants as well as Catholics to hear the Johannine teaching. The context in the Fourth Gospel is the Johannine understanding of the church: a community of believers in Jesus, bound together only by his command to love and serve one another. This word of the risen Lord in the present text can therefore be read as descriptive: if members of the community forgive one another their sins, those sins are forgiven and the community is living from and in the Spirit of Jesus; but if members of the community harbor grudges and resentment toward other members who have sinned against them, then those sins remain to spoil the bond of unity, and the Spirit of Jesus is no longer resident in the community. Unlike the judicial or sacerdotal concept of sin and forgiveness that underlies some parts of the New Testament, the forgiveness of sins in John is an essential component of life in a community whose life breath is the Holy Spirit of Jesus, alive and well in and among its members.

Appearance to the Disciples and Thomas (20:24–29)

In the second episode of Jesus' appearance to the gathered disciples, the scene remains the same except for two important elements: the time is one week later, and Thomas, who was not with the others when Jesus came the first time (v. 24), is present. The evangelist sets the scene by reporting a bit of dialogue among the disciples that has occurred during the intervening week. When the others told him they had seen the Lord, Thomas replied with a vigorous profession of doubt: "Unless I see the mark of the nails in his hands, and put my finger in the mark of the nails and my hand in his side, I will not believe" (v. 25). His skepticism is understandable, and Jesus does not rebuke it.

Instead, he shows his special care for Thomas by coming again to the disciples and Thomas just a week later, under the same circumstances and with the same word of greeting and blessing: "Peace be with you" (v. 26). Then, addressing Thomas directly, he offers him the evidence Thomas said he needed in order to believe. He neither condemns nor commends Thomas's skepticism; he invites him to move beyond it: "Do not doubt but believe" (v. 27).

Jesus invited Thomas to "see" with his finger. Did Thomas in fact reach out and touch Jesus? The text does not say that he did, nor does it say he did not. Given the power of Jesus' words throughout the Fourth Gospel, it seems likely that the presence of the risen Lord and the voice of the living Word was sufficient to elicit from this loyal, realistic disciple (see 11:16) the supreme profession of faith in Jesus Christ: "My Lord and my God" (v. 28). This is the dramatic climax to the series of encounters with Jesus in the Fourth Gospel, one in which disbelief is overcome in a blazing moment of recognition and skepticism is swallowed up by belief, worship, and praise.

Jesus' reply to Thomas (v. 29) seems anticlimactic, but it too marks the climax of another Johannine theme: the relationship between seeing and believing. "Have you believed because you have seen me?" Jesus asks. Then in a final word Jesus addresses Thomas, and the evangelist addresses all who read this Gospel: "Blessed are those who have not seen and yet have come to believe."

Preaching and teaching the Word

1. Teaching the resurrection. The resurrection narratives of John 20 offer a good basis for a comparative study of postresurrection appearances in all four Gospels. The relevant texts are Mark 16:1–8, Matthew 28, Luke 24, and John 20; the longer ending in Mark 16:9–20 and John 21; and Paul's summary of the appearances in 1 Corinthians 15:5–8. The purpose of such a study would be twofold: (1) to deal with questions raised whenever an attempt is made to harmonize all the accounts and (2) to point beyond the problems to the common faith in a risen Lord that has been ratified in the experience of Christians for two millennia. The teacher's preparation should include a careful reading of these texts plus solid studies of them if available.[1] Participants in the study should feel free to propose their solutions to the interpretive problems and to share their experiences of the living Christ.

2. Preaching the birth of the church. The Gospel pericope for the Second

Sunday in Easter ("low Sunday") every year is John 20:19–31. This lection includes the two appearances of the risen Jesus to his disciples gathered in Jerusalem (vv. 19–29) and the first ending of the entire Gospel (vv. 30–31). The Fourth Gospel has no account of Pentecost (fifty days after Passover/Easter), but it does tell how the church was sparked into life on Easter night when Jesus stood among his disciples, gave them the blessing of his peace, commissioned them for service, breathed into them his Holy Spirit, and made the forgiveness of sins constitutive of the community. John 20:19–23 is therefore the Gospel reading for the Day of Pentecost in year A, as well as for the second Sunday of Easter every year. These are good times to preach on the coming of the Holy Spirit into the life of the church and to describe the kind of church the Spirit's breath engenders. For John, the church family and their love for one another is the witness that will draw others to Jesus (13:35). The private prayer of members in such a church might well include a stanza now sometimes omitted from the hymn "Spirit of God, Descend upon My Heart":

> I ask no dream, no prophet ecstasies,
> No sudden rending of the veil of clay,
> No angel visitant, no opening skies;
> But take the dimness of my soul away.[2]

3. The Great Commission in John. Mission season appropriately evokes sermons on Matthew 28:16–20 and Acts 1:6–8. Preaching a mission sermon on John 20:19–23 with emphasis on verses 21–22 might be, for many, a fresh approach. "Mission" comes from the Latin word for "send," and sending is a major theme of the Fourth Gospel. God sent Jesus, and Jesus sends us. In preparation for this sermon, the preacher should review the rather long list of texts in the above notes on verse 21. These are but a selection from the much longer list of Johannine texts in which Jesus refers to himself as sent from God, or to God as the one who sent him (5:23f., 30, 38; 6:29, 38f., 44; 7:16, 18, 33; 8:18, 42; 12:44, 45, 49; 14:24; 15:21; 16:5). Special attention should be paid to earlier references to Jesus sending the disciples (4:38; 13:20; 17:18). The sermon might focus on the privilege, responsibility, and reward of being Jesus' witnesses and messengers in the world and on the inspiration (indwelling) of the Holy Spirit that makes effective witnesses out of reluctant and fearful disciples.

4. Forgiveness and community (20:23). Most fights are unpleasant and disagreeable, but church fights are particularly ugly and distressing. The Fourth Gospel holds out the vision and promise of a community characterized by love and service. When individual Christians and congregations experience periods of dissension, anger, and smoldering resentment, preachers can point their flock to forgiveness as the sine qua non of any resolution of conflict and restoration of harmony. The "If . . . then" statements of verse 23 are conditional sentences, not imperatives. They do not exhort Christian disciples to forgive one another; they simply describe what happens if they do, and if they do not. Examples of each of these options will let hearers draw their own conclusions—that is, preach the sermon to themselves. Let the exhortation from the pulpit imitate that of Jesus: Love one another; wash one another's feet (13:14–15, 34–35). It is not necessary to say which comes first, forgiveness or loving service. The two go hand in hand, even if one starts with the feet.

5. *Thomas the believer.* John 20:24–29 begins with Thomas's doubt (vv. 24–25), and the preacher can begin there too. The point of the text, however, and the goal of the sermon are to move from doubt to faith. Here a little homework on the texts involving Thomas would be in order. Thomas is mentioned in the Fourth Gospel in only a few texts (11:16; 14:5; 20:24–29; 21:2), and his only mention in the Synoptics is in lists of the Twelve. What was the nature of Thomas's doubt? What is the nature of our doubt today? Here the pastoral ministry of the preacher is essential to a sermon that is relevant to the lives of its hearers. A caring pastor may be able to identify the doubts that plague folks who seldom if ever talk about them in church. Jesus was not shocked by Thomas's doubts and does not scold us for ours. Even Martin Luther had doubts. Admiring the childlike faith of his children, he once said, "And I, who would give my body to be burned, find myself asking, 'Is it really so?'" Jesus helped Thomas to see and believe, then added that those who have not seen and yet believe are the blessed or happy ones. Jesus invites each of us to do whatever we need to do in order to take the next step beyond doubt to faith, recognition, adoration, and love.

FIRST ENDING (20:30–31)

Jesus has just pronounced a blessing on those who have not seen him risen from the dead but who have nevertheless come to believe in him (v. 29). Now the evangelist appeals directly to readers to come to the same conclusion Thomas did (vv. 24–28) and to claim that blessing (vv. 30–31). We are invited to believe in Jesus on the basis of the evidence of his defeat of death (the empty tomb, vv. 1–10), of his living presence as the good shepherd who calls his own sheep by name (vv. 11–18), and of the inner witness of the Holy Spirit he has breathed into his disciples (vv. 19–23)– evidence presented through the witness of the fourth evangelist in chapter 20. In this sense, verses 30–31 bring closure to the chapter and to the latter half of the Gospel, in which Jesus seeks to bring his disciples to a mature faith.

Exploring the text

The basis advanced for believing in Jesus is the **signs** that are written in this book. The term "sign(s)" is used sixteen times in the Fourth Gospel to refer to the miracles of Jesus reported in chapters 1–12. Two of these are explicitly labeled "signs" (2:11; 4:54), three more are called signs in the immediate context (6:14; 9:16; 11:47 and 12:17–18), and two other miracle stories in those chapters are generally understood to be signs (5:1–9; 6:15–25). The present text (20:30) is the only time "sign" is used after chapter 12, but the miraculous catch of fish reported in chapter 21 is also a sign, this time combined with a postresurrection appearance. John's use of signs throughout Jesus' public ministry and his reference to other signs that are not written in "this book" (v. 30) are clear indications that the evangelist wants readers to reflect on all the signs recorded in John and their relationship to faith in Jesus.

That relationship is ambiguous. In some texts, faith based on signs is referred to disparagingly (2:23–25; 4:48; 6:30–31; 11:47–48). In his dialogue with the crowd after feeding a multitude with five loaves and two fish, for example, Jesus says emphatically, "Very truly, I tell you, you are looking for me, not because you saw signs, but because you ate your fill of the loaves" (6:26). They did not see what Jesus did as a sign pointing to who he is.

In other texts, signs are reported as a positive influence that opens people to genuine faith: the crowd that followed Jesus in Galilee (6:2, 14); the crowd in Jerusalem (7:31); some of the Pharisees when Jesus healed a man born blind (9:16); many who followed Jesus across the Jordan (10:41–42); the crowd that accompanied Jesus when he entered Jerusalem (12:17–18). In all these cases, signs attracted crowds to Jesus (as they did Nicodemus, 3:2), but they did not always lead them to see beyond a miraculous event to its meaning.

In his dialogue with the Pharisees after the healing of a man born blind, Jesus says, "If you were blind, you would not have sin. But now that you say, 'We see,' your sin remains" (9:41). They had seen the man whom Jesus healed, and they should have seen his healing as a sign pointing to who Jesus really is, but they did not. They think they see but are blind to the meaning of the sign.

In the Fourth Gospel "seeing signs" requires a believing response that is not yet genuine faith but is a step toward it. Several narratives show a development from openness to faith, then to a faith based on signs, and finally to a mature faith.[1] The healing of the royal official's son, for example, leads by stages to genuine faith (4:53–54). As in the Synoptic Gospels, those who demand signs are on the wrong track, for they are preoccupied with the miraculous. But in John, signs get a more positive treatment, for those who see signs and recognize what they signify–namely, that Jesus is the bread of life (6:35, 41, 51), the light of the world (8:12; 9:5), the resurrection and the life (11:25–26)–have been led to the genuine faith that brings life in his name (20:31). This understanding governs the consensus of contemporary scholars who interpret 20:30–31 as the original conclusion of the entire Fourth Gospel.

The question of whether these two verses were intended to conclude the entire Gospel or only chapter 20 (as argued cogently by Paul S. Minear)[2] is closely related to that of the intended purpose and audience of the Gospel. Was the Gospel intended primarily to confirm and deepen the wavering faith of disciples, or was it an evangelistic tract aimed at a wider audience? The statement of purpose in verse 31 says that "these are written so that you may believe that Jesus is the Messiah, the Son of God," but some ancient manuscripts show "believe" as an aorist subjunctive meaning "come to believe" and others show it as a present subjunctive meaning "continue to believe." Translators must decide whether to leave the matter undetermined (AV, RSV, NIV, REB, and TEV text); or to translate the key term as "come to believe" (NRSV), indicating that these verses conclude the entire Gospel; or to translate the verb as "continue to believe" (TEV note), indicating that these verses conclude the chapters that address disciples (13–20, or chap. 20 only).

Whether the Gospel was originally intended for members of the believing community or for prospective members, the true heirs of the blessing in verse 29 and the promise in verse 31 are all readers who are able to see in the text of the Fourth Gospel itself–its dialogues and discourses as well as its miracle stories–signs of who Jesus really is and who, on that basis, come to believe in him. For instance, Jesus is the giver of the Spirit that is living water (4:10, 13–14; 7:37–39; 19:34; 20:22). Even those who have not seen the risen Lord may find in the Gospel of John convincing signs that he can and does offer this gift. Through believing, they receive the gift, and by the indwelling of the Holy Spirit they have life in his name–life that shares the essential nature of Jesus Christ. When that occurs, and only then, the entire Fourth Gospel has come to its intended conclusion and has achieved the end for which it was written.

Preaching and teaching the Word

We sometimes wonder why people say what they do, and why certain sections of the Bible are included. In John 20:30–31 the evangelist tells us exactly why he has told us what he has, and his reason also explains why the Fourth Gospel is in the Bible. This statement of the purpose of the Gospel contains a cluster of words appropriately called key terms because they unlock essential elements in the message of the Fourth Gospel. These terms are discussed elsewhere in the commentary: **sign** (see notes above); **believe** (notes at 1:12); Messiah (notes at 1:41); Son of God (notes at 3:16–18; 5:17–30; 8:14–19; 10:30–39; 11:4, 27; 12:44–45, 49–50; 14:8–11; 19:7); **life** (notes at 1:3b); and **name** (notes at 17:6). They could be studied in a single session or in a series of six lessons.

Most of us know people who have experienced a narrow escape from death and who say, "God must have spared me for a purpose, but I don't know what it is." They have seen a miracle, and they are prepared to interpret it as a sign, but they do not know what it signifies. A series of studies or sermons might be structured on the seven signs in John (20:30a), asking in each case, in addition to what it signifies about Jesus, what believing in Jesus might mean in the life of the person or persons in the text and in our lives as well. Alternatively, a study of signs in John might focus on one or two of them in which a pattern of developing understanding is evident, such as the healing of the royal official's son (4:46–54) or of the blind beggar (9:1–38).

Sermons or studies on signs in the Fourth Gospel, accompanied by the inner working of the Holy Spirit, could lead to moments in which hearers and learners recognize some event in their lives as a sign in which Jesus is present. Mary Magdalene's recognition of Jesus' presence led to his assigning her a task (20:16–18). Perhaps the best suggestion a teacher or preacher can make to someone who recognizes a sign but doesn't know what it means is, "Try asking, 'What do you want me to do?'"

John 20:30–31 articulates a stance that is fundamental to the entire New Testament, all of which was written from faith to faith. Recognition that the Fourth Gospel is the report of a committed witness raises a problem of credibility for those who believe that the only reliable reports are objective reports. John 20:31 states plainly that this Gospel seeks to win readers to faith in Jesus or to confirm them in it. If the Gospel of John is a sales pitch for Jesus, can it therefore not be trusted? When it is time to confront this question directly in a Bible study, here are some points to which the interpreter might call attention:

1. All reports of past events, even those that claim to be objective, involve interpretation and reflect the viewpoint of the reporter. Be grateful for a reporter who makes no pretense of objectivity but announces his or her biases.
2. Although the writer is reporting historical events, the primary

interest in reporting them is in what those happenings meant and mean. The evangelist wants us to know not simply what happened, but what was going on. And what was going on was a struggle for the souls of women and men whom God loves, who are hungry for God, but who have not discovered the right way to find God.

3. When the message concerns the discovery of a life of light, joy, and peace, you would hardly expect the messenger to deliver it with the detachment of an electronic voice announcing the next stop on a subway.

4. The evangelist found truth in a person. Personal truth is every bit as true as objective truth, and is often far more important.

5. The Fourth Gospel was written by a disciple who claimed Christ's promise that after his death the risen Lord would still be with believers in the person of the Holy Spirit, to bring to their remembrance all that Jesus had said and to lead them into all truth. This Gospel as a whole is the voice of the risen Christ, whose Spirit speaks through his beloved disciple. His words are credible when the Holy Spirit whispers in the hearts of hearers and readers, "That's true! It's true!"

Epilogue

21:1–25

Because the Gospel of John finds a natural and satisfactory conclusion in 20:30–31, chapter 21 is appropriately treated as an epilogue that ties up several loose ends. There is no appreciable difference in style or vocabulary between chapter 21 and the rest of the Gospel, nor is there any evidence that the Gospel ever circulated without this concluding chapter. Although many scholars believe that the work was composed in several stages and that its last chapter was added by a member of the Johannine school,[1] others maintain that a single writer–the evangelist–foresaw and produced the Gospel as a coherent whole.[2] Any preacher might suppose that the evangelist wrote an ending to chapter 20 that expressed the purpose of the entire Gospel and then realized that the story was not yet quite complete. Peter and the beloved disciple, whose interaction is a major element in chapters 13–20, were last seen returning to their homes (20:10). It was important for readers to know what became of them and how that might affect the communities that grew from their respective witness, especially after the death of the beloved disciple (21:23). So the evangelist keeps "preaching," even though the "congregation" might have gotten the impression that he has finished. This is poor style in a homiletics class, but it is of little concern to evangelists, apostles, and their readers, who cared more for the message than for literary finesse (consider the multiple endings of Paul's letter to the Romans, 15:13, 33; 16:16, 25–27). However it came to be, this epilogue is an important part of the Fourth Gospel.

The chapter contains the account of a final postresurrection appearance in Galilee (21:1–23), including two distinct but consecutive episodes–the final recognition scene (vv. 1–14) and Jesus' final conversation with Peter (vv. 15–23), plus the formal ending of the entire Gospel (vv. 24–25).

FINAL RECOGNITION SCENE (21:1–14)

Have you ever camped by a lake and, after a restless night in an uncomfortable bed disturbed by unfamiliar sounds, woken up at dawn to watch the sun rise? If you can even imagine such a moment, perhaps you are ready to hear this story told by the disciple Jesus loved.

Exploring the text

Seven disciples have returned to their native Galilee after the death of Jesus. Three of them have prominent roles in the Synoptic Gospels (Simon Peter and the sons of Zebedee, James and John). Thomas appears in all lists of the Twelve but has an active role only in the Fourth Gospel, while Nathanael is mentioned only in this Gospel. Two other disciples are unnamed, leaving open the strong possibility that one of them was "the disciple Jesus loved."

The Setting (21:1–3)

The appearances reported in chapter 20 may have alleviated the disciples' fear, but they are uncertain about what to do next. Peter, always the initiator, suggests that they go fishing, and the others join in. They are back at their old lives as fishermen in the Sea of Tiberias,[3] actually a large lake called also the Sea of Galilee (6:1) or Gennesaret (Luke 5:1). What Peter suggests is night fishing, done with a net (21:3, 6).

Part 1: Jesus' Appearance and the Miraculous Catch (21:4–8)

The disciples are in a boat about a hundred yards off shore (v. 8) when an indistinct figure shows up on the beach in the dim light of morning (v. 4). The stage is set for a recognition scene. They hear a voice asking, "No luck, huh guys?" (v. 5, author's paraphrase).

"No," they shout back, giving the expected negative answer.

Jesus then tells them to cast their net out on the right side of the boat and they will find something. They do so, and the net is so full of fish they can't haul it in (v. 6).

The unnamed disciple whom Jesus loved recognizes who it is and tells Peter, "It is the Lord!" (v. 7a). As at the empty tomb (20:1–9)–though Peter on that occasion initiated the action–the Beloved Disciple first perceives the truth. Only after hearing the Beloved Disciple's witness does Peter, in this account, impetuously throw on some clothes and jump into the lake (v. 7b). That Peter was stripped for work but swam to shore in wet clothes is a detail that adds nothing to the plot but is just the kind of thing an eyewitness would not forget (see 19:35 and 21:24).

Part 2: Breakfast by the Lake (21:9–13)

A charcoal fire with fish on it and bread is what the disciples find when they all get ashore (v. 9). The fire suggests Jesus' preparation for this encounter and the care with which the risen Lord, as master, continues to serve his servants (13:14). The bread and fish point back to Jesus' miraculous feeding of an enormous crowd in an earlier text (6:1–14) and ahead in time to the sacramental meal that, in many an early Hellenistic Jewish and Christian community, consisted of fish, bread, and wine.[4]

Jesus invites his disciples to bring him some of the fish that they have just caught (v. 10). Peter, who had let the others drag the net behind the boat, now hauls the net ashore. It contains 153 fish, and despite its heavy load, it is not torn (v. 11). The unusual number has attracted endless speculation about a symbolic meaning, from Jerome's erroneous zoological argument (that in Greek zoology of the time this was the total number of species of fish, so that in the story it means that the Christian mission will bring in all kinds of humans) to various proposals, ancient and modern, based on the numerical value of letters in the Hebrew or Greek alphabet (gematria). Augustine observed that the figure is the sum of all numbers from one to seventeen, but concluded that its meaning is a great mystery.[5] It still is, and it could simply be a striking detail whose very oddity imprinted it on the memory of an eyewitness and those who subsequently repeated this extraordinary fishing story. In many communities that treasured the story, however, the number was and is interpreted to mean that all kinds of people will be won to Christ by the big fisherman and the other disciples (see Mark 1:17; Matt. 4:19; Luke 5:10). Interpreters are on more solid ground when they point to the fact that the Greek word translated "not torn" here (v. 11) is used in recounting the crucifixion to describe Jesus' seamless robe ("Let us not tear it," 19:24). The tunic and the net can be seen as symbols of the unity among believers for which Christ prayed (17:11, 21–23), a unity that schism (based on the same Greek word for "torn") violates.

The wording of verse 12b is interesting, for it presupposes that the disciples had reason not to be sure who Jesus was, and yet they knew it was the Lord. This is a further example of the continuity and transformation that characterizes the risen one in all the postresurrection appearances (see note on 20:16). As at Emmaus (Luke 24:31), Jesus is recognized by his disciples as they eat a meal with him–a meal at which he acts as host. This time it is not the Lord's Supper but breakfast by the lake, a sort of agape meal at which Jesus "took the bread and gave it to them, and did the same with the fish" (v. 13).

The note that this is the third postresurrection appearance to the disciples (v. 14) overlooks the first appearance to Mary Magdalene (20:11–18), for two appearances to the gathered disciples are narrated in chapter 20 (vv. 19–23, 26–29). The evangelist uses the plural form, "the disciples," to refer to Jesus' followers as a group. It does not necessarily follow that Mary was not considered to be a disciple; she just wasn't considered to be a group.

Preaching and teaching the Word

1. Meeting Jesus in the morning. In the familiar hymn-prayer, "Still, Still with Thee When Purple Morning Breaketh,"[6] Harriet Beecher Stowe captured the magic of meeting Jesus in the morning. The Holy Spirit can use interpreters who have experienced such moments to open the riches of this text to hearers and learners in such a way that starved souls may recognize the risen Lord and be fed. The occasion might be one lesson in a series on spirituality, or a sermon when the preacher discerns that relief from ethical injunction, activist motivation, or theological reasoning might be in order.

The Greek expression translated "showed himself," used twice in verse 1, is based on the verb from which "epiphany" is derived. The NRSV and REB part company with other recent translations, which say "revealed himself" or simply "appeared," to return to the earlier and more literal AV (King James) translation. It is a suggestive expression, reminiscent of the *Showings* Julian of Norwich used to refer to revelations that came to her during twenty years of meditation on a vision she had in 1373. In this final scene in the Fourth Gospel, the risen Lord continues the mission of revelation for which he was sent into the world. In the view of the fourth evangelist, Jesus in revealing himself reveals God, and he continues to show himself after his death, resurrection, and return to the Father. The concept is worth teaching, but its meaning responds better to meditation than to cognition, as the author discovered during the writing of this commentary. About six-thirty one morning, when I was up to make coffee and spend some quiet time with John 21, these words came to me:

> Just after dawn you showed yourself.
> Many heavy days they tried to go on living
> and at last gathered again on that familiar shore
> and went to work at their familiar task at night.
> And then–
>   you showed yourself.
>
> It's after dawn once more and I
> have plodded on for many days at my familiar task–the book.

But all the nets I've cast, it seems to me, come up empty.
And now—
　　you show yourself!

It's you, my Lord, I see there in the dawn.
No form, no face, but you before me in the morning light,
beside me and in me, too.
Lord, tell me where to cast my net.
I've heard your voice. I'll draw the net
and join you on the shore.

Any serious contemplation of this text will lead to reflection on who this is who comes to us as one unknown. It might also lead from reflection to the action of casting a net for Christ so others can enjoy a nourishing encounter with him too.

2. The church as a net. Virtually all the symbolic interpretations of John 21:1–14 understand the net to be an image of the church. Most people would rather be a big fish in a little pond, or even a little fish in a big pond, than to be any sort of fish caught in a net. But who has not looked around at other members of any Christian congregation and reflected, "What a strange assortment of fish"? So understood, the text is, first, about the scope, diversity, and abundant success of the church's evangelistic outreach in the world and, second, about its unity ("the net was not torn"). Unity and diversity are as essential to mission as they are to ecumenism.

Apart from the call stories about four Galilean fishermen (Mark 1:16–20; Matt. 4:18–22; Luke 5:1–11), the only time a net appears in the Gospels is in a parable about the kingdom of heaven and judgment (Matt. 13:47–50). It is an allegory probably intended to apply to the church in the evangelist's time and in all times. It takes in all kinds of fish, including some bad ones. Do not worry, and do not judge before the time; at the end of the age God will sort things out.

John 21:4–14 and Matthew 13:47–50 emerge from two very different visions of the church and breathe two distinct atmospheres: success and unity in John, tensions and judgment in Matthew. Both visions could be included in a single sermon or a pair of sermons or lessons.

3. Table fellowship. Whenever a congregation is at table together, its pastor has an opportunity to reflect on how often Jesus shared meals with his disciples. Breaking bread together is a special kind of fellowship, and recognition of the presence of Jesus can make it very special indeed. On the shore in Galilee soon after the resurrection, Jesus himself fixed breakfast for his disciples. Now he uses the hands of other disciples to prepare food and serve one another. In the service of fellow disciples, the hands of Jesus himself are at work among us and through us. Such an interpretation of this text might transform the most ordinary church breakfast, luncheon, or supper into a recognition scene.

JESUS' FINAL CONVERSATION WITH PETER (21:15–23)

Learning of the death of a friend with whom we have unfinished business leaves us sad. That's the pain Peter was dealing with when he said, "Let's go fishing" (21:3).

When Peter promised that he would follow Jesus to the death (13:36–37), Jesus, instead of accepting Peter's profession of loyalty, predicted that before dawn Peter would deny him three times (13:38). The last word before his death that Jesus addressed directly to Peter was a stern rebuke, "Put your sword back into its sheath" (18:11), and the last words Peter had uttered about Jesus were the three denials spoken in the court of the high priest's residence (18:15–18, 25–27). Their friendship had suffered wounds on both sides. Would things ever be the same again?

Jesus, risen from the dead, has appeared by the sea and fixed breakfast for seven of his disheartened disciples. Impulsive Peter swam to shore to greet Jesus, brought some fish at his command, and shared the meal the Lord prepared (21:1–14). Now, with breakfast over, Peter can talk to Jesus and try to make things all right again between them.

Exploring the text

Jesus initiates the conversation by raising an embarrassing question. In a first movement (vv. 15–19) Jesus reminds Peter forcefully of his earlier failure and gives him a chance for a fresh start. Peter then shifts the conversation to the subject of the Beloved Disciple's future, but Jesus pulls him back to the matter of his own discipleship and mission (vv. 20–23). The conversation focuses first on Peter alone, then on Peter and the Beloved Disciple. It predicts the role of each in the emerging church: Peter, the shepherd, and the Beloved Disciple, the true witness.

Part 1: The Rehabilitation and Recommissioning of Peter (21:15–19)

By his threefold denial of any connection with Jesus, Peter had broken faith with him and disqualified himself as an effective witness and disciple. In this scene the risen Lord does not wait for an apology from Peter, nor does he demand a confession of sin. Instead, he heals the broken relationship with a painful treatment, requiring of Peter a threefold profession of his **love** beside a charcoal fire that must surely have reminded Peter of the fire in the courtyard, beside which his earlier profession of faithful discipleship had proved to be just words. The threefold pattern is important; the variation in the Greek words used for love is not.

It is commonly observed that in Jesus' first two questions to Peter the verb used for love (*agapao*) denotes deep, selfless love, while in Peter's answer the verb for love (*phileo*) denotes the love of a friend, and that in the third exchange Jesus shifts to Peter's terminology, which hurts Peter's feelings. Interpretations based on the premise that two types of love are intended here are attractive but misleading. In the Fourth Gospel these verbs are used interchangeably.[1] The same is true of the alternation of "lambs" and "sheep" in Jesus' command to Peter. There is no clear distinction of meaning in either case; the evangelist is simply reporting the scene in a less monotonous style. Incidentally, Jesus himself would doubtless have been speaking Aramaic, not Greek.

A more interesting exegetical question is the antecedent of "these" in verse 15. It is possible, but not likely, that Jesus asks if Peter loves him more than he loves the accoutrements and life of a fisherman, or whether he loves him more than he loves his fellow disciples. Far more likely is the usual interpretation: "Do you love me more than these other disciples do?" In any case, the comparative element appears only in the first formulation of Jesus' question.

Confronting Peter with his failure and eliciting a new profession of his love are the elements by which Jesus rehabilitates Peter and fits him again for service as a disciple. That done, Jesus assigns the task that is to characterize Peter for the rest of his life: the task of shepherd or pastor. From the very first, Peter was considered to be chief among the apostles and pastor to pastors in the emerging church, a role that in the West evolved into the office of pope. The Fourth Gospel shows no interest in institutional matters, but this scene is a paradigm of the importance of pastoral ministry in the believing community, grounded in the love of Christ. The risen Lord here commissions Peter for that ministry, using the same command, "Follow me" (v. 19), with which, according to Mark and Matthew, he had first called Peter and three others by this lake at the beginning of their ministry together (Mark 1:17; Matt. 4:19). It was Jesus' command to Philip (John 1:43), his statement about all his sheep (John 10:27), and his marching order for anyone who wishes to be his disciple (Mark 8:34; Matt. 16:24; Luke 9:23; John 12:26). In John it is what Jesus had earlier told Peter he was not prepared to do, adding, "but you will follow afterward" (13:36).

This scene by the sea marks the turning point as Jesus points to Peter's future role as shepherd and, in veiled terms, as martyr (vv. 18–19). "The kind of death by which he would glorify God" is parallel to earlier references to Jesus' death on the cross (12:33; 18:32). Jesus spoke of himself as a good shepherd who would lay down his life for the sheep (10:11, 17–18), and by the time John 21 was written, Peter, the fisherman turned shepherd, had probably already died in Rome as a martyr during the persecution under Nero in the 60s, an event that is also hinted at in 2 Peter 1:14. Glorifying God by a martyr's death is a distinctly Johannine way of speaking. The tradition that Peter in fact died in this way is early and well documented. Eusebius quotes Origen (d. 254) as saying, "At the end he [Peter] came to Rome and was crucified head downwards, for so he had demanded to suffer" (*Eccl. Hist.* 3.1.2), a tradition that could scarcely have grown out of John 21:18 but is consistent with it.[2] Jesus has disciples in every time and place who glorify God by the way they die, whether by martyrdom or by the way they accept death.

Having rehabilitated Peter, Jesus recommissions him by saying, "Follow me" (v. 19).

Part 2: Peter and the Beloved Disciple (21:20–23)

Peter's response is not stellar: he immediately takes his eyes off Jesus, looks behind him, and sees the Beloved Disciple doing exactly what Peter has just been commanded to do–following Jesus (v. 20a). The evangelist reminds the reader that this is the anonymous disciple first mentioned as the one that Jesus loved in the account of the farewell supper (v. 20b; see 13:23–25). Peter, like the woman at the well (4:19–20), seeks to change the focus of the conversation when he asks, "Lord, what about him?" (v. 21).

Jesus' reply is underscored by repetition as well as by its position in the story: "If it is my will that he remain until I come, what is that to you?" (vv. 22a, 23b) and is followed by the climactic command, "You follow me!" (v. 22b, author's literal translation), reinforcing the command given without the "you" in verse 19. The emphatic form of the command in verse 22b is expressed by "You must follow me" in the NIV but missed by the NRSV and other translations. Preachers can convey the sense by emphasizing the "you" in the literal translation suggested above.

The historical point of the paragraph is to correct a false rumor. "The rumor spread in the community [literally, among the brothers] that this disciple would not die" (v. 23). This is the only explicit reference in the Gospel of John to a community of faith based on the witness of the disciple Jesus loved. As such, it is a significant clue to the origin and intended readers of the Fourth Gospel. The Beloved Disciple evidently lived longer than any other of Jesus' original disciples, including Peter. So long-lived was he that the rumor spread that he would not die. Verse 23 makes sense if he has just died or is about to do so. This passage reports the basis of the misunderstanding and sets it straight by reporting what Jesus actually said. The phrase, "until I come" (v. 23), is a clue to the interpretation of his earlier promise, "I will come again and will take you to myself (14:3; see notes there) and one of the relatively few texts in which the future eschatology characteristic of Paul's letters and the Synoptic Gospels appears in the Fourth Gospel.[3]

Preaching and teaching the Word

1. On minding one's own business. While the last paragraph functioned historically to correct a false rumor, its abiding significance among the followers of Jesus Christ is found in the emphasized personal pronoun in verse 22, which corrects all who seek to distract attention from their own past failings, present assignment, and future ministry by asking about someone else's discipleship. Every congregation enjoys the dubious blessing of those who feel themselves called to point out the failings of other members. In the Presbyterian Church it is the responsibility of ordained leaders "to further the peace, unity, and purity of the church,"[4] but sometimes zeal in exposing impurities of life or doctrine (always in somebody else) arises out of jealousy or a misguided sense of superiority. This kind of zeal often shatters the peace and unity of the church at every level. The standard prescription for such a problem is a strong dose of Matthew 7:1–5 about logs and specks and hypocrisy. A more positive alternative is this little vignette about Peter and the Beloved Disciple. When Peter turns from his own marching orders to ask about the future reserved for his younger colleague, Jesus says, "What is that to you? [You] follow me!"–in effect, "Mind your own business." Peter, of course, is not criticizing the Beloved Disciple. He is simply distracted from his own discipleship by his uncalled-for interest in that of another. Jesus reminds him whose call he is to answer and whose obedience he is responsible for.

2. The dynamics of reconciliation. The most memorable line from *Love Story,* a best-selling novel and movie of 1970, was "Love means never having to say you're sorry." As questionable as that claim may be, one fascinating aspect of Jesus' final conversation with Peter is that he does not ask Peter for an apology, nor does he wait for one. That does not mean that the restoration of their broken relationship was easy. Those who reflect on the scene from this perspective might find in it a poignant case study in the dynamics of reconciliation, including the restoration of their own relationship with God. We don't make things right; God does.

3. Prayers of confession. The confession of sin is a standard part of the service for the Lord's Day in the Reformed family of churches. Some members use it for genuine self-examination and as an occasion to repent, but others grow tired of it and view it as a ritual that is meaningless at best and hypocritical at worst. The absence of any call for apology in the present text offers the occasion to probe what might be a point of silent—or vocal—resistance to the order of worship in the life of a congregation. While Jesus does not push for a public or even private confession of sin on Peter's part, he does confront Peter with the fact of his failure and invite a new commitment to discipleship. Jesus does not demand apologies from us, but he does require that we forgive those who have wronged us, as we are reminded each time we pray the Lord's Prayer.

In the Broadway musical *My Fair Lady,* Eliza Doolittle grows weary of a young swain's amorous professions of devotion. Exasperated, she sings, "Don't talk of love: Show me!" Jesus' last words to Peter suggest that he is less interested in liturgical correctness and routine confessions of sin than he is in a genuine and perhaps nonverbal repentance that leads to new commitment lived out in the accomplishment of assigned tasks in and beyond the community of faith.

4. Call, restoration, and conversion. The epilogue does more than tie up loose ends in the Fourth Gospel. In its account of the rehabilitation of Peter, it addresses business left unfinished in all three Synoptic Gospels and constitutes a turning point in a story that is finished only in the Book of Acts. The key to the whole drama is in Jesus' final command to Peter, "Follow me" (21:19, 22). Peter's first call comes in exactly those words when Jesus invites him with three other fishermen to leave their nets.[5] They do so immediately, but after a series of failures to understand, Jesus issues a second call to all the disciples, including Peter: "Follow me."[6] Later, Jesus responds to Peter's emphatic declaration of fidelity by predicting Peter's threefold denial[7] and says, "But I have prayed for you that your own faith may not fail; and you, when once you have turned back [= are converted, AV], strengthen your brothers" (Luke 22:32). All four Gospels report Peter's pitiful performance in the courtyard of the chief priest.[8] Only John narrates the restoration of Peter and his third call to discipleship, "Follow me" (John 21:15–19, 22). Once more Peter answers the call, but his conversion is not complete until he is forced to confront his reluctance to include Gentiles in the community of faith, a story whose importance is underlined by its repetition in great detail (Acts 10:1–48; 11:1–18). Only then does Peter show by his action his readiness to follow Jesus.

It is possible to preach the call, rehabilitation, and conversion of Peter in a single sermon, but a series of lessons or sermons would allow the interpreter to do more justice to the riches of his story as a means of calling disciples today to follow Jesus. A familiar hymn conveys the message: "Jesus Calls Us."

5. Following and knowing. Albert Schweitzer (musician, theologian, physician, missionary, 1875–1965) concluded his classic study *The Quest of the Historical Jesus* (1906) with these memorable words:

> He comes to us as One unknown, without a name, as of old, by the lakeside, He came to those men who knew Him not. He speaks to us the same word: "Follow thou me!" and sets us to the tasks which He has to fulfil for our time. He commands. And to those who obey Him, whether they be wise or simple, He will reveal Himself in the toils, the conflicts, the sufferings which they shall pass through in His fellowship, and as an ineffable mystery, they shall learn in their own experience Who He is.[9]

Schweitzer had in mind the first call of Peter and the other three fishermen, but his words apply equally to John 21, in which the recognition of Jesus (vv. 1–8) is tied to a renewed call to discipleship (vv. 15–19, 22). They are particularly appropriate for women and men in our time who are repelled by the Fourth Gospel's insistence on believing that Jesus is who he says he is and who have never had a mystical experience to validate those claims. Schweitzer came to know who Jesus is through his own practical, daily experience of following him. There is more than one way into communion with the ineffable mystery of the living Word.

SECOND ENDING (21:24–25)

Exploring the text

The last verses of chapter 21 contain the only explicit reference to the authorship of the Fourth Gospel within the text itself. Even this reference is inconclusive, because it focuses on the trustworthiness of the message, not on the name of its author. The relevant statements turn upon an "I," a "we," and an unnamed third person, "this disciple." "I" (v. 25b) refers to the writer of this verse at least and perhaps of a little–or a great deal–more. "We" (v. 24b) includes the readers of the Gospel with the writer. "This . . . disciple" (v. 24a) clearly refers to "the disciple whom Jesus loved" (v. 20), whose future role Peter has just asked Jesus about, thus tying verse 24 to verses 20–23. Though not named, the Beloved Disciple is further identified as "the one who had reclined next to Jesus at the supper and had said, 'Lord, who is it that is going to betray you?'" (v. 20; 13:23–25).

Just as the first ending (20:30–31) served as a conclusion to chapter 20 but also referred to earlier material in the Fourth Gospel and stated the purpose of the whole, so this ending, while concluding the paragraph about the role of the beloved disciple by attesting the truthfulness of his testimony, serves to validate the reliability of the Gospel as a whole. The "we" of "we know that his testimony is true" (21:24) echoes the "we" of "we have seen his glory" and "from his fullness we have all received" (1:14, 16), making the entire Gospel the witness of a community of believers for whom the Beloved Disciple was the truthful witness through whom they had come to know Jesus.

The wording of the attestation in 21:24 reflects that of the evangelist regarding the eyewitness at the foot of the cross (19:35). The eyewitness is clearly the Beloved Disciple, who was, according to the Fourth Gospel, the only male disciple who stood near the cross of Jesus (19:25–26). The difference between the two attestations is that 19:35, speaking of the Beloved Disciple, says that "he knows that he tells the truth," while 21:24 affirms, "we know that his testimony is true."

The writer of the conclusion refers to the Beloved Disciple as the one "who is testifying to these things and has written them" (21:24). Putting all these indications together, early Christian tradition from Irenaeus onward (ca. 180 C.E.) held that the writer of this Gospel was John the son of Zebedee, apostle and evangelist, and on the basis of that identification the Fourth Gospel became known as the Gospel according to John. Some scholars who hold to this traditional view of authorship allow that verse 25 may be from another hand, perhaps that of an editor who added it when the Fourth Gospel was included with the other three in the Christian canon of Scripture.

Extensive research by New Testament scholars throughout more than a century of critical study has led to a wide, though by no means unanimous, consensus that the tradition misread the evidence and jumped too quickly to the conclusion of apostolic authorship, in the interest of arriving at an authoritative canon. They point out that the verb form translated literally in 21:24 ("has written them") can also mean that the Beloved Disciple authorizes and authenticates what is written, as at 19:1, where a similar construction is translated in the NRSV as "Pilate took Jesus and had him flogged," though a literal translation would say "Pilate flogged him."[1] Those interested in historical and redaction criticism have posited a process of development from oral tradition to completed Gospel over a period of several decades.[2] Those versed in literary criticism distinguish between the author (evangelist), the implied author (Beloved Disciple), and the narrator (redactor or editor, 21:24).[3] The literature dealing with this question is vast, diverse, and fascinating, but all of it must reckon with the data given in this verse, which links the Fourth Gospel directly to the eyewitness testimony of the Beloved Disciple.

This commentary shares the judgment that all efforts to name the writer of the Fourth Gospel are hypothetical and that the course of wisdom and honesty is to respect the anonymity of the Beloved Disciple. The second ending certifies that this Gospel is the Beloved Disciple's true witness about Jesus to the community of those who believe in him through that testimony. It announces that testimony to the world, with the imprimatur of the community that has found it to be true. This is also the preacher's task today.

In the very last verse, the writer returns to the point mentioned in 20:30, "Now Jesus did many other signs in the presence of his disciples, which are not written in this book," and adds, "if every one of them were written down, I suppose that the world itself could not contain the books that would be written" (21:25). Perhaps no more books are necessary, including this one; but the preaching and teaching of the Fourth Gospel is far from finished.

Preaching and teaching the Word

The evangelist has had his say; now it is the preacher's and teacher's turn. The task is not to comb the archives of apocryphal literature and reports of recent discoveries looking for other things that Jesus did that are not recorded in this or any other canonical Gospel. The task is to witness faithfully to the presence of the living Word today in the world that God loves. The goal is to bear witness in such a way that those who have never known Jesus Christ may meet him, and those whose love has grown cold can meet him again. The interpreter is to become a channel by which the living Christ can give his disciples words to live by, and so to reflect on his death, resurrection, and return to the Father that his glory may be reflected in the life as well as the words of the interpreter. It is a daunting challenge; left alone, no interpreter could measure up to it.

But we are not left alone.

Afterword

A Note from the Author to Readers of This Commentary

Like many of you, I have known and loved the Gospel of John from early childhood, when I committed many of its texts to memory. As I grew older, I discovered troubling elements in it that I could not understand. In seminary I took a course on John that led me to see that the Fourth Gospel is, in the words of generations of interpreters, "a pool in which babies can swim and elephants can wade." That course gave me some answers but a lot more questions. I decided that some day I would take the time to pursue them, and in retirement that time came.

Four of my questions concern the Gospel as a whole, and since they may be your questions too, I want to share my reflections on them.

1. THE PROBLEM OF DISTINGUISHING THE VOICE OF THE EVANGELIST FROM THAT OF JESUS

Did Jesus really say all that is attributed to him in the Fourth Gospel?

The question arises quickly if one glances at a red-letter edition of the Gospels and notes that, in the first three, Jesus usually speaks in short, pithy sayings or in vivid parables, while the fourth, whole chapters are printed in red ink and Jesus' monologues seem wordy and repetitious. Closer study of some of these monologues shows that it is sometimes hard to know when Jesus stops talking and the evangelist begins to comment on what Jesus said. In John 3, for example, the story of Nicodemus's night meeting with Jesus includes only ten verses about their encounter and dialogue. The remaining eleven verses in the story are monologue, and it is hard to tell who is speaking. Translators indicate their decision about this question by their placement of quotation marks to enclose the speech of Jesus that begins at verse 10. The TEV indicates closure at the end of v. 13; the RSV and Goodspeed at the end of verse 15; the five other translations I consulted (including the NRSV and NIV) at the end of verse 21. So if one puts the question, "Did Jesus himself say, 'God so loved the world,' or is this an elaboration by the evangelist?" most translation committees answer, "Jesus," while those that prepared the RSV and the TEV say, "the evangelist." (There are no punctuation marks in the Greek manuscripts, nor any quotation marks in the AV of 1611.)

What I have learned in preparing this commentary is that the question is wrongly put. To try to distinguish between the voice of Jesus and the voice of the evangelist in the Fourth Gospel is a vain effort. There is no appreciable difference between them in vocabulary, grammar, or theology. That does not mean that John includes no authentic sayings of Jesus. It just means that they are much more difficult to identify than in the Synoptic Gospels.

Why, then, does the Fourth Gospel present so much of its teaching as the direct words of Jesus? I think it is because the evangelist believed what he wrote: Jesus did not stay dead. He rose from the tomb, appeared several times to his earliest disciples, and promised to come and stay with his disciples through the presence of the Holy Spirit, who would bring to their remembrance what Jesus had taught them and would lead them into all the truth (14:26; 16:13). What the evangelist attributes to Jesus, then, may not be the very words (ipsissima verba) of the historical Jesus, but they are the lively voice (viva vox) of the living Jesus Christ, preserved through the testimony of the Beloved Disciple and expressed in the language of the evangelist. Reflecting on 21:24, Alan Culpepper writes, "The Gospel is offered as the work of an eyewitness [the Beloved Disciple] who was with Jesus at all the crucial moments of his ministry, one for whom Jesus had a special love, and [as] the product of memory, reflection, study of scripture, and enlightenment by the Holy Spirit."[1] That is why, in the Fourth Gospel, the voice of Jesus and the voice of the evangelist are virtually indistinguishable.[2]

2. THE POLEMIC AGAINST "THE JEWS"

There are more than seventy references to "the Jews" in the Fourth Gospel and fewer than seven in any one of the Synoptics. This is puzzling in a writing about a Jew named Jesus, all of whose first disciples were also Jews. Its major events are located in time by reference to Jewish festivals, and its theology turns upon debates about the interpretation of the Hebrew Bible. Yet Jesus and the evangelist seem to distance themselves from Judaism by constant reference to "the Jews" in the third person. Puzzlement turns to shock when the reader sees how many of these references are pejorative or hostile.

Those who try to understand this phenomenon discover that in the Fourth Gospel the term "Jew" seems to be used in four different senses: "1) its natural sense, meaning simply Jewish people; 2) Judeans, people who live in and near Jerusalem; 3) people hostile to Jesus, and 4) the authorities in Jerusalem."[3] This fluidity in the meaning of "Jew" in the Fourth Gospel helps to explain why, in one text, Jesus can say, "Salvation is from the Jews" (4:22), and in another, speaking to the Jews who had believed in him (8:31), "You are from your father the devil" (8:44). God's salvation has been revealed through the Jewish people (meaning #1), but in John people hostile to Jesus (meaning #2) are of their father the devil.

The problem is more than semantic; it is historical and theological. In the series of confrontations with the Jewish religious leaders (2:13–22; 5:9b–18; 8:12–59, meaning #4) and in the passion narrative (18:1–19:16), the Fourth Gospel depicts the growing hostility of the authorities toward Jesus in language that reveals the evangelist's antipathy for "the Jews." The historical problem is that for two millennia Christian readers of this Gospel have applied to all Jewish people in all succeeding centuries the harsh words of the Fourth Gospel's polemic against "the Jews" (meaning people hostile to Jesus [meaning #3], and particularly the Jerusalem authorities who orchestrated his death [meaning #4]). The result has been a history of nameless horrors largely forgotten by Christians, remembered with pain and bitterness by Jews, and culminating in a tragedy whose name is well known: the Holocaust or *Shoah.* Efforts to trace the roots of modern anti-Semitism have incriminated the anti-Jewish texts of the New Testament, and of the Gospel of John in particular. Careless use of these texts still poisons the relationship between Christians and Jews and violates the spirit of the Christ to whom they bear witness. How is a responsible interpreter to understand them? One way is to seek a historical answer to this historical question.

The landmark study in this regard is J. Louis Martyn's *History and Theology in the Fourth Gospel.*[4] In an effort to understand the vehemence of the way John reports Jesus' conflict with the religious authorities of his time, as well as the fact that in this Gospel the voice of Jesus seems often to be indistinguishable from the voice of the evangelist, Martyn sought clues for the historical situation that may have given rise to the Fourth Gospel. He found such a clue in a word used three times in the Gospel of John (9:22; 12:42; 16:2) and nowhere else in the New Testament: *aposynagogos,* "put out of the synagogue." He also discovered that the twelfth in a list of nineteen benedictions in a Jewish prayer book in use at the end of the first century was actually an invocation against heretics. An early form of this prayer (its exact age is difficult to determine) reads as follows:

For the apostates let there be no hope and let the arrogant government be speedily uprooted in our days. Let the Nazarenes [Christians] and the Minim [heretics] be destroyed in a moment and let them be blotted out of the Book of Life and not be inscribed together with the righteous. Blessed art thou, O Lord, who humblest the proud![5]

According to Martyn, this prayer reflects a formal judgment of excommunication pronounced upon Jewish Christians in about 85 C.E. by the Jamnia Academy, the supreme council or Sanhedrin of Judaism after the destruction of the temple. Before that time, it had been possible for Jews to hold a dual allegiance to Moses and to Jesus as Messiah, and many members of the community of faith centered around the testimony of the Beloved Disciple did just that. But the benediction against heretics, reworded at Jamnia in about 85, was employed in order formally and irretrievably to separate such Jews from the synagogue. Martyn concludes the chapter in which he lays out this hypothesis with these words:

In the two-level drama of John 9, the man born blind plays not only the part of a Jew in Jerusalem healed by Jesus of Nazareth, but also the part of Jews known to John who have become members of the separated church because of their messianic faith and because of the awesome Benediction.[6]

Similarly, Nicodemus becomes representative not only of those Pharisees who were at least open to the possibility of believing in Jesus during his lifetime, but also representative of synagogue authorities who, near the end of the first century, were drawn to the risen Christ, alive and active in the Johannine community, but who were reluctant to break with their past and affiliate openly with the Christian community.

Several points in Martyn's linkage between the Gospel of John and the benediction against heretics have been challenged. The precise words of the benediction were not fixed by the late first century, and the original form of the prayer was probably directed against heretics in general—that is, all Jews who did not adhere to the Pharisaic/rabbinic line—rather than exclusively or explicitly against Christians. Martyn's point-for-point correspondence between John 9:22 and the wording of the benediction against heretics pushes the evidence, and his thesis that the Jamnia Academy effectively expelled all believers in Jesus from all synagogues has been discounted. Nevertheless, Martyn's basic thesis that the Fourth Gospel is a two-level drama, reflecting Jesus and his first disciples at one level and the evangelist and his first readers at another, has created a scholarly consensus that still shapes studies of the Gospel of John.[7]

Martyn's hypothesis does not suggest that the evangelist invented the hostility between the Jewish authorities and Jesus. It does make the Fourth Gospel's vehement polemic against "the Jews" understandable–though not admirable, and surely not an appropriate model for Christian attitudes toward Jewish people throughout all subsequent history.

One challenge to the prevailing consensus about the anti-Jewish texts in John is that of Stephen Motyer, an evangelical Anglican and professor of New Testament and Hermeneutics at London Bible College. In a book entitled *Your Father the Devil? A New Approach to John and "the Jews,"*[8] he argues that *"far from 'demonising' the Jews, this charge is part of a strategy, rooted in the conditions of late first-century Judaism, which is designed to appeal to Jews to see Jesus as the Messiah, and is motivated by a deep commitment to the good of Israel"* (preface, xii). Like Martyn he takes the historical context of the evangelist seriously, but instead of a unified Judaism defined and governed by the academy at Jamnia, he points to the remarkable pluralism within Judaism in the decades after 70 C.E. Motyer thinks that the statement of purpose in 20:30–31 is addressed to Jews, in order to persuade them that Jesus is the Christ who can meet their particular needs after the total loss represented by their defeat by the Romans and the destruction of the temple in 70 C.E.[9] He proposes that Jesus' judgment on "the Jews" in John 8:31–59 does not consign them to the dark side of the Johannine dualism but, in the tradition of prophetic language, "is a judgment out of which restoration may be born."[10] The implied reader is encouraged to react in some way to the violence of "the Jews" who picked up stones to throw at Jesus (8:59). By making murder the work of the devil (8:44), the text suggests that the reader react against that violence and take sides with Jesus.[11]

For Motyer, "'the Jews' is not a global designation of all Abraham's descendants . . . [but] a distinct group within Judaism: the Judea-based, Torah-loyal adherents of the Yavneh ideal, the direct heirs of pre-70 Pharisaism."[12] These are the only ones who would feel directly vilified by 8:44. The implied reader would understand that in the family debate that the Fourth Gospel addresses, all other Jews are being warned and invited to "come on board" and accept the faith of this Christ.

More recently a Jewish scholar, Daniel Boyarin, professor of Talmudic Culture and Rhetoric at the University of California in Berkeley, has dismissed the Martyn hypothesis as thoroughly discredited. He, like most rabbinic scholars, insists that the form of the Twelfth Benediction (against heretics), which Martyn dates to 85 C.E., did not exist at that early date, nor was it directed explicitly against believers in Jesus as Christ. Like Motyer and many others, he affirms a pluralism in the Judaism of that time in which there was no central Jewish institution of dominion that had the power to excommunicate or anathematize individuals or the Johannine community from "the synagogue," understood as the Jewish church or the Jewish people. Boyarin's counterproposal is that "the Jews" are the in-group of the religious elect of Israel, who had maintained their purity during the Babylonian exile and returned to Jerusalem to reestablish the temple. This in-group (including the Pharisees) looked down on those who had stayed behind, to whom they referred as the "People of the Land." Both groups were Israelites, but the Galileans (including Jesus) were "People of the Land." The Johannine distinction between "the Jews" and "Israelites," then, had historic roots, and the debates between Jesus and "the Jews" (*hoi Ioudaioi*) were part of an inner-Jewish tension. In Boyarin's view, the attack on the *Ioudaioi* in the Fourth Gospel is not an attack on Jews or Judaism but on the historical in-group that for generations had excluded the ancestors of the Johannine community from its constituency. In particular, it is an attack on "the members of that in-group who reject the new divine figure who has come to redeem these outcasts from the *Ioudaioi*, together with all Israel."[13]

It is heartening to read a Jewish scholar whose possible reconstruction enables us to understand the Gospel of John as a Jewish, rather than an anti-Jewish, text, even though his basic thesis, that the Fourth Gospel provides no definitive evidence of any parting of the ways between Judaism and Christianity, is debatable.

Motyer's thesis is compatible with that of Boyarin to the extent that he does not understand the polemic language of the Fourth Gospel as an attack on all Jewish people or the Jewish faith as a whole, any more than is Jesus' addressing Peter as "Satan" when Peter suggested that Jesus must not suffer, die, and rise again (Mark 8:33; Matt. 16:23). In both cases the strong, hyperbolic language is designed to correct a misunderstanding of Hebrew Scripture and to call a Jew (Peter) or Jews (those in Jerusalem who had initially believed in Jesus, 8:31) to discipleship and affiliation with the followers of Jesus.

All three positions sketched above are hypothetical, but they have led me to certain conclusions that ring true to me.

- The reports in all four Gospels of Jesus' conflict with the Jewish leaders in Jerusalem is based on eyewitness testimony to certain historical facts.
- The vehemence of those reports in the Gospel of John is a function of conflicts, at the time and place of its writing,

between the Johannine community in which it originated and Jewish authorities who rejected the community's claims for Jesus.[14]

- The Jewish people of Jesus' time and that of the evangelist were divided in their reaction to Jesus. Some accepted him, others rejected him, and some vacillated between these two positions.

- The evangelist's appeal to believe in Jesus applies to everyone, including Jewish leaders who like Nicodemus were attracted to Jesus but reluctant to take a public stand for him.

- Neither Jesus nor the evangelist attacks the Jews as an entire people, though a tendentious interpretation of the Fourth Gospel and other New Testament texts has led people in subsequent centuries to do so.

3. THE EXCLUSIVE CLAIM OF JESUS

The Fourth Gospel insists that the only way to God is in and through Jesus Christ. This exclusive claim is expressed first at the end of chapter 3: "Whoever believes in the Son has eternal life; whoever disobeys the Son will not see life, but must endure God's wrath" (3:36). Its most exclusive formulation is in Jesus' words to his disciples, "No one comes to the Father except through me" (14:6b), but it is implicit in the affirmations of Jesus' unique relationship to God that appear throughout the Gospel. It is also part of the apostolic preaching in the early church: "There is salvation in no one else, for there is no other name under heaven given among mortals by which we must be saved" (Acts 4:12).

Exclusivism is understandable in the context of a messianic sect within the exclusive faith of Judaism, whose fundamental affirmation of faith is that the Lord is one (Deut. 6:4) and whose law (Exod. 20:4–5) and prophets (Amos 2:4; Isa. 2:8–9; 44:9–11; Jer. 2:1–13) insist that the Lord will not tolerate the worship of any other god. Mutual exclusivism is the basic reason for the hostility between the Johannine community and the Jewish authorities, since each community claimed to know the true way to God. This exclusive stance is later shared by Islam, which may be viewed as a third-generation offspring of Israel's monotheistic faith.

Passionate commitment to one religion to the exclusion of others has caused endless bloodshed through the centuries, and its baleful effects are still all too evident. At the same time, in today's shrinking world, increasing numbers of Christians have come to know people of other faiths who demonstrate spiritual insight, ethical integrity, and human compassion that often put Christians to shame. It is hard to believe that they do not know God.

In this situation, we ask, (1) Can we still accept and proclaim Christianity's exclusive claims for Jesus Christ? (2) How are we to interpret those claims as they are so forcefully presented in the Fourth Gospel?

The answer to the first question is, "Yes." Countless millions of thoughtful and responsible people do accept that Jesus is who the Fourth Gospel says he is, and they do so without dismissing the faith of others or presuming to judge the quality of their relationship to God. It is also true that other millions of Christians have assumed the prerogative of God to judge the faith of others and still do so on the basis of the exclusive way Jesus' claims are stated in the New Testament in general and the Gospel of John in particular. That is why the second question is so important: how are we to interpret those claims? Here are some personal reflections on this question.

1. The basic issue is whether or not the claims are true. In company with Christians through the centuries, I believe that they are, as affirmed by the Nicene Creed in language that grows out of the Gospel of John. The interpreter who shares this belief should preach the claims of Jesus with conviction.

2. The claims are such that they require a decision not only at some moment of supreme awareness of Christ's presence and reality, but also— and perhaps more importantly—in the countless decisions one makes daily, surrounded by the clamor of many voices and choices. The decision for or against Jesus is a matter of life and death according to John. We are judged here in this world, as well as in the world to come, by the way we respond now to his light.

This black-and-white language in the Fourth Gospel is grounded in a dualistic view of reality that flies in the face of the relativism which recognizes most of our lives are lived in various shades of gray. I do not like the either-or of dualism; I prefer the both-and of an easy tolerance, especially as it affects my own choices. I think I am not alone in this, for I observe that the theme of judgment has all but disappeared from the hymnals of mainline churches. But the theme of judgment is prominent in the Fourth Gospel, a judgment that is based on the response of individuals and groups to the revelation of God in Jesus Christ. I think the honest interpreter will preach and teach for decision.

3. We, however, are not called to judge. According to John, Jesus says, "The Father judges no one but has given all judgment to the Son" (5:22); "As I hear, I judge; and my judgment is just" (5:30); "I judge no one. Yet

even if I do judge, my judgment is valid; for it is not I alone who judge, but I and the Father who sent me" (8:15–16); "there is one who seeks [my glory] and he is the judge" (8:50); "I came into this world for judgment" (9:39); "I do not judge anyone who hears my words and does not keep them, for I came not to judge the world, but to save the world. The one who rejects me and does not receive my word has a judge; on the last day the word that I have spoken will serve as judge" (12:47–48). These seemingly paradoxical statements have been dealt with in the body of this commentary. The important point here is that at no point does Jesus invite his disciples to judge. *No interpreter is authorized to preach the exclusive claims of Jesus in such a way as to judge the faith of anyone else.* That is the exclusive prerogative of the **Father** and the Son and, on the last day, of the word that Jesus has spoken. I am called to present that word with conviction and urgency but also with humility. I do not know, nor do I need to know, how God deals now or will deal at the end with people of other faiths.

That is why I approached the interpretation of "No one comes to the Father except through me" (14:6b) with great apprehension. On its face, this verse opens the way for me to make a judgment I am not authorized to make. It helps me to avoid the rush to judgment if I remember other parts of the Fourth Gospel's witness to Jesus Christ: "What has come into being in him was life, and the life was the light of all people" (1:3b–4); "The true light, which enlightens everyone, was coming into the world" (1:9); "For God so loved the world that he gave his only Son, so that everyone who believes in him may not perish but may have eternal life. Indeed, God did not send the Son into the world to condemn the world, but in order that the world might be saved through him" (3:16–17); "In my Father's house there are many dwelling places (*monai*)" (14:2)–many places where people may abide (*meno*) in Christ–and they do not all necessarily bear the label of any Christian church. I need also to remember Jesus' reaching out to excluded people like the Samaritan woman (4:1–42) and Pilate, whom he subtly invites to see in him the very embodiment of truth (18:37), as well as Jesus' statement of concern for "other sheep not of this fold" (10:16). The universal love of God and God's desire to include all in the fold of Jesus Christ are evident in all of these texts. A problem arises only when people reject Christ's (or the Johannine community's) invitation to come in.

In the notes on John 14:6, I suggest four avenues of approach that might enable a preacher or teacher to interpret "No one comes to the Father except through me" (14:6b) without feeding the dangerous human tendency to exclude, demean, and even attack people of other faiths. It is perhaps worth repeating them here.

- The text is directed to Jesus' disciples: for Christians, there is no other way to come to God. Other religions are neither affirmed nor rejected here.
- "No one comes to the *Father*," that is, to the intimate relation with God that Jesus enjoyed, except through Jesus. The text does not exclude the possibility of other ways of knowing God, but no other is as full, as deep, and as warm as the knowledge of God in Jesus Christ.
- "No one comes to the Father except through *me*," that is, except through the Father/Son/Holy Spirit reality that Jesus embodied while he was in the flesh and that the Holy Spirit leads believers to recognize in Christlike individuals of other religions or of no religion as "the true light, which enlightens everyone" (1:9).
- Accept what this verse affirms about Jesus as the way, the truth, and the life, but reject what it denies about other approaches to God. Committed to Jesus' way, remain agnostic about other ways, realizing that God is greater than the measure of our minds. Leave to God the acceptance or not of others' credentials.

Christians have espoused each of these ways to interpret John's witness to the claims of Jesus Christ in a way that honors Scripture and heeds the urging of his living Spirit in a pluralistic world. I have been driven toward the fourth approach because of the Fourth Gospel's insistence on the necessity to choose. With regard to Jesus Christ, we must choose. We must choose between believing in him and not believing, and also between the inclusiveness of 3:16 and exclusive interpretations of 14:6b. With regard to other religions, we must love. I am aware that the "new commandment" to love one another (13:34a) is addressed to the in-group of his disciples, but when Jesus adds "just as I have loved you" (13:34b; 15:12), he appeals to a love that is as all-embracing as the true light that enlightens everyone (1:9). A restrictive reading of this commandment might have been possible in the evangelist's world and situation. The living Spirit of Jesus Christ does not lead this interpreter to any such restrictive reading in a world that television and the Internet have made into one neighborhood, particularly when Jesus elsewhere in the Gospels urges us to love all our neighbors (Luke 10:25–37) and even our enemies (Matt. 5:43–48).

It is clear to me that no one has to hate the Jews (or the Muslims or Hindus or Buddhists or animists or those of any other faith or of no faith) in order to love Jesus. On the contrary, all who truly love Jesus will love all those whom God loves and will be eager to share with them the best thing they know: the indwelling Spirit of the living Christ. I therefore accept that Jesus is the way, the truth, and the life (14:6a) but reject the apparent exclusivism of 14:6b that seems to deny any validity to other faiths.

I find it hard to embrace the position to which I have been driven, because it makes me the arbiter of which words in the Bible are words of God and which are the effect of the limited understanding of an earlier interpreter, in this case, the fourth evangelist. This dilemma has led me to a fourth basic question.

4. THE RELATION OF THE FOURTH GOSPEL TO THE WORD OF GOD

This issue is often approached on the basis of prior convictions about the inspiration and authority of Scripture. For a Reformed pastor like me, such convictions are not only relevant; they are inherent in my ordination vows. By all accounts of Jesus' discussions with his religious adversaries, he and his disciples shared with the scribes and the Pharisees the conviction that Israel's Scriptures were inspired and authoritative, but they disagreed profoundly about the interpretation of those Scriptures. The Fourth Gospel gives extensive echoes of that debate, but it also suggests how sterile debates about Scripture are. A more profound series of related questions is posed silently by a significant number of people, including Christians who from time to time find themselves wondering: Is God for real? Is there really an eternal Word prior to all creation and to all our imagining? Did God really come to us in human form, and can I know him today? To this series of questions, the Gospel of John responds with a resounding "Yes!" In doing so, it answers the question of its own relationship to the Word of God.

The question of God's reality is never raised in the Fourth Gospel, because for John God is reality itself, the ultimate reality that lies behind and within all that is real. The evangelist does not use language like this, borrowed from modern philosophy, but in the Fourth Gospel as in life, it is God with whom we have to do. God is a given.

This Gospel begins with words about God in language reflecting the Hellenistic philosophy of its time and echoing the language of Jewish wisdom: "In the beginning was the Word (*logos*), and the Word was with God, and the Word was God" (1:1). "And the Word became flesh and lived among us" (1:14) in the person of Jesus Christ (1:17), "God the only Son" (1:18) whom God gave to the world out of love for the world (3:16). Jesus revealed God's love by his words and his works. He came to reveal the way, the truth, and the life of God to all who would receive and believe in him.

The Fourth Gospel does not present itself as the Word of God. Rather, it bears witness to Jesus, the eternal Word made flesh. Yet it does so in words, and it refers repeatedly to the words of Jesus as words of God (3:34; 8:45, 47; 14:10, 24; 17:8). Similarly, in ancient Israel, Moses and the prophets communicated to the people the words of God, first orally and then through writings that were handed down ("traditioned") to subsequent generations. In time the Scriptures embodying that tradition and known as "Moses and the Prophets" came to be thought of as the word of God, together with a fluid number of other writings that were accepted as holy Scripture by Jews. To these, the emerging Christian movement added the Gospels and other writings that, together with the Jewish Scriptures, are known as the Bible and referred to as "the word of God written."

In the Gospel of John, Jesus voices a stern warning to those who telescoped the process just described and equated the Hebrew Scriptures with the word of God. In John's account of a heated debate between Jesus and those who believed that the books of Moses are the word of God but who did not believe what Jesus was saying about himself, Jesus says, "You have never heard his [the Father's] voice or seen his form, and you do not have his word abiding in you, because you do not believe him [Jesus] whom he has sent. You search the Scriptures because you think that in them you have eternal life; and it is they that testify on my behalf. Yet you refuse to come to me to have life" (John 5:39–40). These were people who knew the Scriptures as the word of God and who looked to them for eternal life. Jesus makes a clear distinction here between Scripture and the word of God when he says that they do not have the word of God in them and that it is wrong to trust the Scriptures as the way to eternal life. The clear implication in Johannine language is that Jesus is the Word of God and that he is the way, the truth, and the life.

The same distinction applies when these very words are read as part of the Christian Bible. The words come from God through a long chain of tradition, as did the words recorded in the Hebrew Scriptures, and in that sense they are the words of God. But they are not life-giving. Eternal life is the gift of the Word of God incarnate in Jesus,[15] who as the Holy Spirit lives in those who receive, believe, and trust in him. The Fourth Gospel is a powerful witness to the Word of God, but trust in the book of John as the word of God can sometimes blind us to Christ himself. This warning is applicable to no one more than to interpreters of the Fourth Gospel, who can study, preach, and teach its words without giving daily evidence that the Spirit of Jesus is living in the interpreter. It is easy to get so entangled in debates over words about the Word as to miss the point of the message, whether it be God's revelation through Moses or God's revelation through Jesus.

The words of the Fourth Gospel teach that God really is, that the eternal Word of God has drawn near to us in Jesus Christ, and that he lives in his disciples as the Holy Spirit. Can I rely on these words as the word of God? Are they words I can live by?

In response to these questions, the Fourth Gospel says repeatedly, "Come and see!" and then depicts Jesus' encounters with all sorts of people, his last hours with and words to his disciples, his final confrontation with those who rejected him, his death and resurrection. The stories themselves raise insistent questions in the minds of many readers: Is God for real? Is there really an eternal Word prior to all creation and to all our imagining? Did God really come to us in human form, and can I know him today?

God's word to me and to all who read this commentary is, "Come and see!"

NOTES

INTRODUCTION

1. *Book of Common Worship* (Louisville, Ky.: Westminster/John Knox Press, 1993), 1035–95.

JOHN 1:1–18

1. Downward: 1:33; 3:13, 31; 6:33, 38, 41–51; 8:23. Upward: 3:14; 8:28; 12:32–33; 14:2, 28; 16:5, 17; 17:5; 20:17.
2. One whom God has sent: 5:38; 6:29; 10:36; 17:3. God as sender: 4:34; 5:23, 24; 6:38, 39, 44, 57; 7:16, 18, 28, 29; 8:16, 18, 26, 29; 9:4; 11:42; 12:49; 13:20; 14:24; 15:21; 16:5; 17:8, 21, 23, 25.
3. Compare Mark 1:1–8//Matt. 3:1–6; Luke 3:1–9, 15–18.
4. This use of "world" is characteristic of the Gospel of John: e.g., 7:7; 14:27; 15:18–19; 16:33; 17:14, 16, 25.
5. Accurate statement: 5:31; 8:40, 45, 46; 16:7. Ultimate reality: 8:31–32; 14:6; 18:37–38.

JOHN 1:19–34

1. See the afterword.
2. Haenchen, *John,* 145–46.
3. Other texts about Christ the lamb: Acts 8:32, 1 Peter 1:19, and thirty times in Revelation, but with a different word for lamb.
4. O'Day, *John,* 528.
5. Isaiah 40:3a and b, conflated in John 1:23 as "Make straight the way of the Lord."

JOHN 1:35–51

1. "On him" is how the Hebrew text is interpreted by Rabbi Yannai in *Bereshith Rabba* 70:12 (cited in Dodd, *Interpretation,* 245–46).
2. Søren Kierkegaard, *Life.*
3. *The Confessions of St. Augustine,* I, 1. Extracts selected and translated by Carolinne White (Grand Rapids and Cambridge, U.K.: Wm. B. Eerdmans Publishing Co., 2001), 14.

JOHN 2:1–12

1. Brown, *John,* cxxxix.
2. See appendix 3 in Brown, *John,* 525–32.
3. Bultmann, *John,* 118–19.
4. See also Matt. 15:28, Luke 13:12, and Brown, *John,* 99.
5. John 3:15; 7:6, 8, 30; 8:20; 12:23, 27; 13:1; 17:1.
6. Barrett, *Gospel,* 159–60.
7. Haenchen, *John,* 173.
8. For examples, see Euripides, *The Bacchae,* 705–7 (New York: Noonday Press/Farrar, Straus and Giroux, 1990), 45; Bultmann, *John,* 119 n. 1; Sloyan, *John,* 36.
9. Bultmann, *John,* 119.
10. Dodd, *Interpretation,* 299.
11. *Theial methel,* Philo, *L. A.* 3, 82, cited in Barrett, *Gospel,* 157; see Acts 2:13.
12. Brown, *John,* 110.
13. Barrett, *Gospel,* 157–58.
14. O'Day, *John,* 538.
15. See afterword, §2.
16. Sloyan, *John,* 37.

JOHN 2:13–25

1. Matt. 21:12–17//Mark 11:15–19//Luke 19:45–48.
2. See afterword, §2.
3. Culpepper, *Anatomy,* 21–22, lists fifteen other examples of the evangelist's omniscience.
4. James L. Mays, *Psalms* (Louisville, Ky.: John Knox Press, 1994), 231.
5. See afterword, §2.

JOHN 3:1–21

1. Haenchen, *John,* 199.
2. Note the use of "we" in 3:2, 11. Culpepper, *Anatomy,* 135–36.
3. Culpepper, *Anatomy,* 152.
4. Ibid., 42.
5. Morton Smith, "Two Ascended to Heaven," in James H. Charlesworth, *Jesus and the Dead Sea Scrolls* (New York: Doubleday, 1992), 294–95; Wayne A. Meeks, "The Man from Heaven in Johannine Sectarianism," *Journal of Biblical Literature* 91 (1972): 52.
6. Culpepper, *Anatomy,* 184.
7. The author is indebted here to a study of this symbol by his student Ann Rutherford, R.N.
8. The familiar phrase "only begotten" (AV), is the result of an erroneous translation in Jerome's Latin version. The Greek term used here means

"unique," as in Heb. 11:17. In John, Jesus' unique relationship with God is based on preexistence, not birth. See Brown, *John,* 13.

9. Matt. 1:21. "Jesus" is the Greek form of the name Joshua; Joshua saved Israel by warfare.

10. Dale Bruner has discerned this Trinitarian pattern that cuts right across the text's literary form of dialogue and monologue (unpublished lectures).

11. J. B. Phillips, *New Testament Christianity* (New York: Macmillan, 1956), 4.

12. "Prayer after a Sermon," in *A Book of Reformed Prayers,* ed. Howard L. Rice and Lamar Williamson Jr. (Louisville, Ky.: Westminster John Knox Press, 1998), 96.

JOHN 3:22–36

1. Rensberger, *Faith,* 54–57; Howard-Brook, *Children of God,* 96.

2. Bultmann, *John,* 49–51; Brown, *John,* lxvii–lxx; Rensberger, *Faith,* 56–57.

3. See afterword, §1.

4. Kysar, *Maverick Gospel,* chap. 4.

5. See afterword, §2.

6. See *apeitheo,* 3, in Arndt, Gingrich, and Danker, *A Greek-English Lexicon of the New Testament.* In John 6:29 Jesus speaks of believing as doing the work of God, and 1 John 3:23 echoes the idea of believing as obedience to the command of Christ.

7. Now in the Unterlinden Museum in Colmar, France (Arthur Burkhard, *Matthias Grünewald: Personality and Accomplishment* [New York: Hacker Art Books, 1976], 25–42).

8. Barth, *Church Dogmatics,* IV/3 (2) (Edinburgh: T. & T. Clark, 1936–77), 554.

9. The Theological Declaration of Barmen was drafted by Karl Barth and signed by leaders of the Confessing Church in Germany who stood firm against Hitler in 1934. It is one of eleven documents in the *Book of Confessions* of the Presbyterian Church (U.S.A.).

JOHN 4:1–45

1. Culpepper, *Anatomy,* 136.

2. Bultmann, *John,* 111–12.

3. *The HarperCollins Bible Dictionary* (1996), 479, sv "Jacob's Well."

4. See afterword, §1.

5. O'Day, *John,* 567.

6. For a careful study of the rise of messianic ideas and movements beginning some fifty years before Jesus' birth, see Michael O. Wise, *The First Messiah* (San Francisco: HarperSanFrancisco, 1999).

JOHN 4:46–54

1. Brown, *John,* appendix 3, 530–31.

JOHN 5:1–18

1. See afterword, §2.
2. Bethzatha ("house of olives") is preferred. Bruce M. Metzger, *A Textual Commentary on the Greek New Testament,* 2d ed. (New York: United Bible Societies, 1994), 178.
3. Brown, *John,* 207.
4. The basis for their objection can be found in the mishnaic tractate *Sabbath* 7:2 and 10:5 (Brown, *John,* 208).

JOHN 5:19–47

1. See afterword, §2.
2. See Klaus Berger, *Die Amen-Worte Jesu* (Berlin: de Gruyter, 1970), 28.
3. The Fourth Gospel as a whole prefers the title Son of God, whether in its full form or simply as the Son. Son of Man is rooted in an eschatological tradition that goes back to Persia (Iran).
4. Lutumba Tukadi-Kuetu, in *A Book of Reformed Prayers,* ed. Howard L. Rice and Lamar Williamson Jr. (Louisville, Ky.: Westminster John Knox Press, 1998), 182.

JOHN 6:1–35

1. See afterword, §2.
2. Culpepper, *Anatomy,* 182–83.
3. John Bunyan, *Pilgrim's Progress,* vol. 15, Harvard Classics (New York: P. F. Collier & Son, 1909), 205.
4. Culpepper, *Anatomy,* 132.
5. Sara Covin Juengst, *Breaking Bread: The Spiritual Significance of Food* (Louisville, Ky.: Westminster/John Knox Press, 1992).
6. Kysar, *Maverick Gospel,* 72.
7. James W. Fowler, *Stages of Faith* (San Francisco: HarperSanFrancisco, 1995); *Becoming Adult, Becoming Christian* (San Francisco: Jossey-Bass, 2000); *Faithful Change* (Nashville: Abingdon, 1996).

JOHN 6:35–51

1. See afterword, §1.
2. Bultmann, *John,* 11.
3. Kysar, *Maverick Gospel,* 86–93.
4. See afterword, §2.
5. *A Book of Reformed Prayers,* ed. Howard L. Rice and Lamar Williamson Jr. (Louisville, Ky.: Westminster John Knox Press, 1998), 7.

JOHN 6:52–59

1. "The First Apology of Justin, the Martyr" and "A Plea regarding Christians

by Athenagoras the Philosopher," in Cyril C. Richardson, *Early Christian Fathers* (New York: Collier, 1970), 258, 293, 303, 338.

2. Brown, *John,* 285.

3. Arndt, Gingrich, Danker, *A Greek-English Lexicon of the New Testament,* 4th rev. and aug. ed. (Chicago: University of Chicago Press, 1957), 836f.

4. Scots Confession, 3.21; Second Helvetic Confession, 5.169, in *The Book of Confessions* (Louisville, Ky.: Presbyterian Church [U.S.A.], 1999).

5. Heidelberg Catechism, 4.066; Westminster Confession of Faith, 6.149; Shorter Catechism, 7.092; and Larger Catechism, 7.272, in *Book of Confessions.*

6. Scots Confession, 3.21, in *Book of Confessions.*

7. Bernard of Clairvaux, "Jesus, Thou Joy of Loving Hearts," stanza 3, *The Presbyterian Hymnal* (Louisville, Ky: Westminster John Knox Press, 1990), 510–11.

8. Doreen Potter and Fred Kaan, "Let Us Talents and Tongues Employ," *The Presbyterian Hymnal,* #514.

9. Thomas à Kempis, *Imitation of Christ* (New York: Pocket Books, 1954), 250.

JOHN 6:60–71

1. See the discussion of excommunication in the afterword, §2.

2. "Believe" and "know" are closely linked in John.

3. O'Day, *John,* 611.

JOHN 7:1–52

1. See afterword, §2.

2. In the Fourth Gospel Jesus refers twenty-five times to God (or the Father) as the one who sent him: 4:34; 5:23, 24, 30, 37; 6:38, 39, 44, 57; 7:16, 18, 28, 29; 8:16, 18, 26, 29; 9:4; 11:42; 12:49; 13:20; 14:24; 15:21; 16:5; 17:8.

3. See afterword, §2.

4. See the extensive discussion in Brown, *John,* 320–21.

5. Ben Jonson, "Drink to me only with thine eyes," *The Forest: To Celia,* stanza 1, *The Complete Poems,* ed. George Parfitt (New Haven, Conn.: Yale University Press, 1975, 1982), 1063.

6. Alexander Pope, *Pastoral Poetry and an Essay on Criticism,* part 2, line 215 (London: Methuen; New Haven, Conn.: Yale University Press), 264.

7. For instance: "Never man spake" (John 7:46, AV)

Who is God?

The one whom Jesus has disclosed to me in his words and in his human life.

The one to whom I say, at his dictation: "Our Father . . ."

Illusion? Frustration? I declare myself incompetent in the matter. I have not studied psychoanalysis, and I have no special

knowledge of the other world. Humanity, on the other hand–
that's my field. But, so far as I can tell, no man ever spoke like
this man. Never was there a man like this man Jesus who tran-
scended all the contradictions in which we flounder. If, therefore,
I recognize in him an unparalleled authority in this field of our
experience, why should I not follow him when he reveals to me
another realm and leads me to the Father? If he had been the
victim of a basic mental illness, how could he have told me the
most authentic things I have heard about myself? And what
would be left of Jesus if I tried to blot out his relationship to God!

All that we can say then about God–his existence or proof of
it, his being dead, his non-existence, or his "return"–fails to grip
us: the matter is decided on other grounds. For me, the question
will be resolved the day I meet another man who will speak to
me a human word more convincing than that of Jesus: a word
more humane and more true, with no reference to God.

I have lived, I have read, I have traveled, I have listened, I
have watched: this man, I have not yet met. (Michel Bouttier,
Quêtes et requêtes [Paris: Éditions du Cerf, 1990], 19, trans. Lamar
Williamson Jr.)

JOHN 7:53–8:11

1. Culpepper, *Gospel and Letters,* 170; Brown, *John,* 335.
2. O'Day, "John 7:53–8:11: A Study in Misreading," *Journal of Biblical Literature* 111, no. 4 (1992): 639–40.

JOHN 8:12–59

1. See 2:13–22; 5:19–47; 7:32–36, 45–52.
2. In addition to 8:26 and 50, see 3:17–19; 5:22–30, 45; 7:24, 51; 9:39; 12:31,
47–48; 16:8, 11.
3. 1:18; 3:34–36; 6:27, 37–40, 46, 57, 65; 12:27–28, 49–50; 14:6–14, 16, 20,
28c; 15:1, 23–26; 16:15; 17:1, 5, 21, 25–26; 20:31.
4. See afterword, §2.
5. 1:9–11; 3:13, 31; 6:33–38; 14:12b; 16:5, 10, 28, 30b; 17:11, 13a; 20:17.
6. It follows the Greek text of Nestle-Aland, *Novum Testamentum Graece,* 27th
rev. ed. (Stuttgart: Deutsche Bibelgesellschaft, 1993) and the interpretive
note in Bruce M. Metzger, ed., *A Textual Commentary on the Greek New Testament,* 2d ed. (New York: United Bible Societies, 1994).
7. See afterword, §2.
8. Barbara Brown Taylor, *Speaking of Sin: The Lost Language of Salvation* (Cambridge, Mass.: Cowley Publications, 2000).
9. See afterword, §1.

10. See afterword, §2.

JOHN 9:1–41

1. See table of contents.
2. See notes on Martyn in the afterword, §2.
3. Rensberger, *Faith,* 44.
4. Brown, *John,* 380–84.
5. Or perhaps only excluded from synagogue leadership, as proposed by Walter Ziffer in a private communication. (See his *Birth of Christianity from the Matrix of Judaism* (Weaverville, N.C.: Or Chadash–New Light, 2000), 162–67.
6. See afterword, §2.
7. Brown, *John,* 374.
8. See afterword, §2.
9. Brown, *John,* 372–73.

JOHN 10:1–21

1. Culpepper, *Gospel and Letters,* 180.
2. See various meanings in afterword, §2.
3. Num. 27:16–17; 2 Sam. 7:7–8; 24:17; 1 Kgs. 22:17; Pss. 23:1–4; 79:13; 80:1; 100:3; Isa. 40:11; Jer. 23:1–4; Ezek. 34:1–10; Zech. 13:7–9; Matt. 10:6; John 21:15–17; Heb. 13:20; 1 Pet. 2:25; 5:1–4.
4. Some readers may recognize an echo of this text in John McCutcheon's song "Calling All the Children Home."

JOHN 10:22–42

1. See various meanings in afterword, §2.
2. Brown, *John,* 402–3; O'Day, *John,* 676.
3. The tension between foreordination and freedom, between election and faith, is dealt with in notes on these earlier passages (pp. 79, 88, 106–7).
4. On these variants, see Bruce M. Metzger, ed., *A Textual Commentary on the Greek New Testament,* 2d ed. (Stuttgart: Deutsche Bibelgesellschaft/United Bible Societies, 1994), 197–98.
5. Smith, *John,* 211.
6. James L. Mays, *Psalms,* Interpretation: A Bible Commentary for Teaching and Preaching (Louisville, Ky.: John Knox Press, 1994), 270.
7. J. S. Bach, *The Birthday Cantata,* no. 208.
8. *Book of Confessions,* 6.097–6.100.
9. Ibid., *Book of Confessions,* 7.190–7.191.
10. Election: 6:37, 44, 65, 70; 8:43–44a; 10:26–28; 12:37–41; 13:2, 21–30; 15:16; 17:2. Free choice: 3:12, 16; 5:39–47; 7:37–38; 11:25–26, 45–46; 12:44–50.

JOHN 11:1–44

1. Brown, *John,* xcv and 423; *Community,* 33–34.
2. Culpepper, *Anatomy,* 54–70.
3. See comments on "glory" at 1:14.
4. See "Jews" in the afterword, §2.
5. Bultmann, *John,* 402.
6. Elizabeth Barrett Browning, *Aurora Leigh,* book 7, line 820, *The Complete Poetical Works of Elizabeth Barrett Browning* (Boston and New York: Houghton Mifflin Co., 1900), 372.
7. Bennett A. Cerf and Donald S. Klopfer, eds., *The Poems and Plays of Robert Browning* (New York: Modern Library, 1934), 201.

JOHN 11:45–57

1. Brown, *John,* 439–40.
2. O'Day, *John,* 698.
3. Num. 9:10–14; 19:11–13; Acts 21:24–26.
4. Mark 13:1–37//Matt. 24:1–44//Luke 21:5–36.

JOHN 12:1–11

1. O'Day, *John,* 701.
2. Culpepper, *Anatomy,* 147.
3. O'Day, *John,* 701, and Kysar, *Maverick Gospel,* 187.
4. For an example of the use of this juxtaposition in teaching, see Frances Taylor Gench and Sarah Covin Juengst, "Anointing and Washing Feet–Expressions of Love," in *Women and the Word: Studies in the Gospel of John,* 2000–2001 *Horizons* Bible Study (Louisville, Ky.: Presbyterian Church [U.S.A.]), 40–45.
5. John Boyle O'Reilly, "In Bohemia" (Boston: The Pilot Publishing Co., 1886), stanza 5.

JOHN 12:12–19

1. 1:7–8, 15, 19–34, 35–51; 4:1–42 and notes.
2. See James L. Mays, *Psalms,* Interpretation: A Bible Commentary for Teaching and Preaching (Louisville, Ky.: John Knox Press, 1994), 379–81.

JOHN 12:20–36

1. "Hellenes" as in John 7:35, not Hellenized Jews ("Hellenists") as in Acts 6:1, 9:29, and 11:20.
2. Parallels in Matt. 16:24–26 and Luke 9:23–25.
3. Sense #4 under "World" in the glossary.

JOHN 12:37–50

1. The analogy is Gail O'Day's, *John,* 718.
2. It is cited seven times in Paul's epistles, sixteen times in the Synoptic Gospels, twice in Acts, extensively in 1 Peter (1:11; 2:22–25), and four times in Revelation.
3. Acts 28:25–28; see also Rom. 11:7–8, quoting freely Deut. 29:4; Isa. 29:10; Isa. 6:9–10.
4. See notes on 6:35–51, 65, 67; 8:31–47; and 10:26.
5. Rev. 22:17; John 15:16.
6. See afterword, §1.
7. See notes on 3:19–21.
8. See notes on 1:4 and 6:40, 47, 51 (pp. 3, 80–81).

JOHN 13:1–30

1. See note at 4:38, another reference to sending that seems out of context.
2. Matt. 26:21–25//Mark 14:18–21//Luke 22:21–23.
3. Brown, *John,* 578.
4. See notes on 6:35–51, 65, 67; 8:31–47; 10:26; and 12:37–43.

JOHN 13:31–38

1. See notes on 1:14.
2. John Randolph Taylor, *God Loves Like That! The Theology of James Denney* (Richmond, Va.: John Knox, 1963), 10, 79.
3. See notes on 17:20–24.
4. "Little children": 1 John 2:1, 12, 28; 3:7, 18; 4:4; 5:21.
5. *The Hymnbook* (Richmond, Philadelphia, and New York: PCUS/UPUSA/RCA, 1955), 307; *The United Methodist Hymnal* (Nashville, Tenn.: United Methodist Publishing House, 1989), 396; *Trinity Hymnal,* rev. (Atlanta and Philadelphia: Great Commission Publications, 1990), 654.

JOHN 14:1–14

1. See afterword, §1; Brown, *John,* 149.
2. See notes on 13:33.
3. Temple, *Readings in St. John's Gospel* (London: Macmillan, 1945), 231. See also "personal truth" in Parker J. Palmer, *To Know As We Are Known* (San Francisco: Harper & Row, 1983); Michael Polanyi, *Personal Knowledge* (New York: Harper & Row, 1958, 1964).
4. See notes on 10:30.
5. Fred Craddock, *John,* John Knox Preaching Guides (Atlanta: John Knox Press, 1982), 98.

6. Roberta Bondi, *Memories of God,* 16; quoted by Kathleen Norris, *Amazing Grace* (New York: Riverhead Books, 1998), 26.

JOHN 14:15–31

1. Brown, *John,* appendix 5, 1139, 1141.
2. See afterword, §1.
3. Brown, *John,* 1143.
4. For further comments on indwelling, see notes on Jesus' image of the true vine in 15:1–11.
5. See Luke 6:16; Acts 1:13.
6. Brown, *John,* 656.

JOHN 15:1–8

1. Culpepper, *Gospel and Letters,* 214.
2. Brown, *John,* 662.
3. Used more than ninety times in the Pauline Epistles. For examples, see Rom. 6:23; 8:39; 1 Cor. 4:15; 2 Cor. 5:17; 12:2; Gal. 3:26.
4. Quickly identifiable in hymnals that have a Scripture index.

JOHN 15:9–17

1. The Greek aorist indicative, normally translated as a past tense, can function like a stative verb in Hebrew, which could refer equally to past or present. Another example of this use of the aorist tense is the heavenly voice at Jesus' baptism, "with you I am well pleased" (*eudokesa,* Mark 1:11//Matt. 3:17//Luke 3:22).
2. As in verse 9, the aorist verb can be translated as either past or present.
3. Rom. 5:8, altered, in *The Book of Common Worship* (Louisville, Ky.: Presbyterian Church [U.S.A.], 1993), 52.
4. Again, the aorist verb can be translated as either past or present: "I call you friends," TEV.
5. Newbigin, *Light,* 204.

JOHN 15:18–16:4a

1. See afterword, §2.
2. See afterword, §1.
3. See notes at 1:10.
4. With regard to the extensive use of this psalm in the New Testament, see James L. Mays, *Psalms,* Interpretation: A Bible Commentary for Teaching and Preaching (Louisville, Ky.: John Knox Press, 1994), 232–33.

JOHN 16:4b–15

1. See notes on 13:31 and 17:4.

2. See notes on 12:44–45/49–50.

3. See the hymn by Carl P. Daw Jr. (1982), "Like the Murmur of the Dove's Song," in *Presbyterian Hymnal* (Louisville, Ky.: Westminster/John Knox Press, 1990), 314, whose second verse asks the Holy Spirit to come to the branches of the vine.

4. Such as these lines from "God's Grandeur" by G. M. Hopkins:

> And though the last lights off the black West went
> > Oh, morning, at the brown brink eastward, springs–
> Because the Holy Ghost over the bent
> > World broods with warm breast and with ah! bright wings.

in *A Hopkins Reader*, Image Books (Garden City, N.Y.: Doubleday, 1966), 48.

5. See afterword, §1.

JOHN 16:16–23

1. See notes on "I will come again" at 14:3.

2. Kysar, *Maverick Gospel*, chap. 4.

JOHN 17:1–5

1. Brown, *John*, 748.

2. Culpepper, *Gospel and Letters*, 219.

3. See the illustration suggested for preachers at 13:31–32.

4. See afterword, §1.

JOHN 17:6–19

1. Brown, *John*, 747; see afterword, §1.

2. Brown, *John*, 763–64.

3. Smith, *John*, 312.

4. On "the evil one," see also 1 John 2:13–14; 3:12; 5:18–19.

5. See notes on 12:37–41; 13:18.

6. See notes on 1:14.

7. Brown, *John*, 766–67.

8. Smith, *John*, 316.

9. See notes at 15:11 and 16:16–24 and the suggestion for preaching and teaching the meaning of Christian joy at 15:9–17.

JOHN 17:20–26

1. Clement called John "the spiritual Gospel"; Countryman titled his commentary *The Mystical Way in the Fourth Gospel: Crossing Over into God*, rev. ed. (Valley Forge, Pa.: Trinity Press, 1994).

2. Brown, *John*, 511–12.

JOHN 18:1–12

1. Hans-Ruedi Weber, *On a Friday Noon* (Grand Rapids: Eerdmans, 1979, jointly published with the World Council of Churches).
2. Raymond E. Brown, *The Death of the Messiah: From Gethsemane to the Grave*, 2 vols. (New York: Doubleday, 1994).
3. William Henry Foote (1794–1869), *Sketches of Virginia; Historical and Biographical, First Series* (New edition, Richmond, Va.: John Knox Press, 1966), 382.
4. Dorothy Frances Gurney (1858–1932), "God's Garden," in *Masterpieces of Religious Verse,* ed. James D. Morrison (New York: Harper & Brothers, 1948), 183.
5. Brown, *John,* 534.
6. Cyril of Jerusalem and Cyril of Alexandria, as well as modern scholars; see Brown, *Death,* 149.

JOHN 18:12–27

1. On the Annas dynasty of priests, see Brown, *Death,* 408, and the chart in O'Day, *John,* 807.
2. See the bibliography.
3. Kenneth Grahame, *The Wind in the Willows* (New York: Bantam Books, 1982), 92.
4. Culpepper, *Gospel and Letters,* 77ff.

JOHN 18:28–40

1. "Jews" here refers to the religious authorities. See afterword, §2.
2. Newbigin, *Light,* 247.
3. Luke refers to it in the charge brought against Jesus by the Jewish authorities (Luke 23:2), and Matthew places it on the lips of magi from the East who came looking for "the child who has been born king of the Jews" (Matt. 2:2).
4. "King" and "kingship" are used in these notes to respect the language of the text; "reign" is used to convey the theological import of these terms and to encourage a less patriarchal and monarchical understanding of the text for our time.

JOHN 19:1–16a

1. "Jews" here refers to the chief priests and the police (v. 6). See afterword, §2.
2. Barrett, *Gospel,* 451, cited by O'Day, *John,* 820.
3. Schnackenburg, *Gospel,* 260, cited by Smith, *John,* 347.
4. O'Day, *John,* 820.
5. Brown, *John,* 882–83.
6. Ibid., 845.

7. O'Day, *John*, 822, with other reputable scholars and some translations, supports "seated him"; Brown, *Death*, 1389–93, holds with the majority understanding, "sat."

JOHN 19:16b–42

1. "There were three who always walked with the lord: Mary his mother and her sister and Magdalene, the one who was called his companion. His sister (*sic!*) and his mother and his companion were each a Mary"—*The Gospel of Philip*, II, 59, 6–11, in *The Nag Hammadi Library in English*, ed. James M. Robinson (San Francisco: Harper & Row, 1988), 145.
2. On the identity of the beloved disciple, see notes at 13:23; 18:15; 20:2; 21:7; and 21:20–24.
3. See also 2:24–25; 5:6; 6:61, 64; 11:42; 13:1, 3, 11; 16:19; 18:4.
4. Brown, *Death*, 1080, 1082.
5. Ibid., 1268–70.
6. This understanding of the physical and spiritual thirst of the Son of God was captured in a prayer by Bénédict Pictet (1655–1724), a Swiss Reformed pastor, theologian, and hymn-writer.

    "*J'ai soif.* What am I hearing, my Savior and my God! You, complaining of thirst? You who have opened the springs from which all peoples drink, who brought water from the very rocks for your ancient Israel? Alas, it is not so much a bodily thirst that presses you as it is the ardent desire you have to finish the work of our salvation. How ineffable is your goodness! Produce in me also a true thirst for your justice, so that I may sense vividly my need for your grace and how unhappy I would be if were deprived of it. Let me seek in you salvation and life, with all the ardor of which I am capable. It seems to me that you have already heard me. I am thirsty. My soul thirsts for you, O living God!" *La tradition calvinienne* (Chambray, France: C.L.D., 1981), 57; author's translation.

7. Robert Frost, "Stopping by Woods on a Snowy Evening," in *The Poetry of Robert Frost*, ed. E. C. Lathem (New York: Holt, Rinehart & Winston, 1969), 225, lines 14–15.
8. Culpepper, *Gospel and Letters*, 232.
9. Brown, *Death*, 1233–34.

JOHN 20:1–18

1. *The Gospel of Mary*, BG, *10*,1–3; *18*,1–15; *The Gospel of Philip* II, *59*,7–10; *63*,33–*64*,9, in Robinson, *Nag Hammadi*, 145, 148, 525–27.
2. See note on "another disciple" at 18:15, Brown, *Introduction*, 191 and *Community*, 31–34.
3. Brown, *John*, 941; *Death*, 1264–65.

4. Marcus J. Borg, *Meeting Jesus Again for the First Time: The Historical Jesus and the Heart of Contemporary Faith* (San Francisco: HarperSanFrancisco, 1994).

5. A suggestion some find in the Broadway musical of the 1970s, *Jesus Christ Superstar.*

6. William E. Phipps, *Was Jesus Married?* (New York: Harper & Row, 1970), 64–70; *The Sexuality of Jesus* (Cleveland: Pilgrim Press, 1996), 136–37.

7. Brown, *John,* 1014.

8. Brown, *Community,* 190.

9. Cynthia Pearl Maus, *Christ and the Fine Arts* (New York: Harper & Bros., 1938), 430–34.

10. ". . . the fool / Contends that God is not / Not God! in Gardens! when the eve is cool? / Nay, but I have a sign, / 'Tis very sure God walks in mine." *My Garden,* Thomas Edward Brown (1830–1897), in *The Oxford Book of English Verse,* ed. Arthur Quillen-Couch (Oxford: Clarendon Press, 1939), 970.

JOHN 20:19–29

1. Raymond E. Brown, *A Risen Christ in Eastertime: Essays on the Gospel Narratives of the Resurrection* (Collegeville, Minn.: The Liturgical Press, 1990); see also Brown, *John,* 966–78.

2. George Croly, 1866; *The Hymnbook* (PCUS / UPUSA / RCA, 1955), #236; *Trinity Hymnal,* rev. ed. (Atlanta: Great Commission Publications, 1990), #338.

JOHN 20:30–31

1. Kysar, *Maverick Gospel,* 85.

2. Minear, "The Original Functions of John 21," *Journal of Biblical Literature* 102, no. 1 (1983): 85–98.

JOHN 21:1–14

1. Brown, *John,* xxxiv–xxxix; *Introduction,* 84.

2. Where Jesus found and called them after John the Baptist was put in prison.

3. Minear, "The Original Functions of John 21," *Journal of Biblical Literature* 102, no. 1 (1983): 85–98; O'Day, *John,* 850f., 854.

4. Erwin R. Goodenough, *Jewish Symbols in the Greco-Roman Period* (Princeton, N.J.: Princeton University Press, 1953), vols. 5–6.

5. Brown, *John,* 1074.

6. *A Book of Reformed Prayers,* ed. Howard L. Rice and Lamar Williamson Jr. (Louisville, Ky.: Westminster John Knox Press, 1998), 86.

JOHN 21:15–23

1. Compare 3:35 *agapao* and 5:20 *phileo*; 14:23 *agapao* and 16:27 *phileo*; 11:3 *phileo* and 11:5 *agapao;* 13:23 *agapao* and 20:2 *phileo.*
2. Culpepper, *Gospel and Letters,* 249.
3. Explicitly in 6:39, 40, 44, 54; 11:24; 12:48 and implicitly in 14:3.
4. *Book of Order* (Louisville, Ky.: Presbyterian Church [U.S.A.], 2003–2004), G-14.0207g and G-14.0405b(7).
5. Mark 1:16–18; Matt. 4:18–20.
6. Mark 8:34; Matt. 16:24; Luke 9:23.
7. Mark 14:29–31; Matt. 26:33–35; Luke 22:33–34; John 13:37–38.
8. Mark 14:66–72; Matt. 26:69–75; Luke 22:56–62; John 18:15–18, 25–27.
9. Albert Schweitzer, *The Quest of the Historical Jesus* (New York: Macmillan, 1964), 403.

JOHN 21:24–25

1. The causative translation in 19:19 is similar; Smith, *John,* 399–400.
2. Brown, *John,* xxxiv–xxxix; Brown, *Introduction,* 62–78.
3. See Culpepper, *Anatomy,* 43–49; Brown, *Introduction,* 79–86.

AFTERWORD

1. Culpepper, *Gospel and Letters,* 250.
2. For this reason *The Five Gospels: The Search for the Authentic Words of Jesus,* a translation and commentary produced by Robert W. Funk, Roy W. Hoover, and the Jesus Seminar (San Francisco: HarperSanFrancisco, 1993), prints no saying of Jesus in the Fourth Gospel in red, and only one (4:1) in pink ("sure sounds like Jesus"). This represents a level of skepticism of which I am skeptical.
3. Robert G. Bratcher, "'The Jews' in the Gospel of John," *The Bible Translator* 26, no. 4 (1975): 409; texts cited for each meaning.
4. J. Louis Martyn, *History and Theology in the Fourth Gospel,* 1968, rev. 1979, 3d ed. (Louisville, Ky.: Westminster John Knox Press, 2003).
5. Ibid., 58. For a careful study setting this prayer, the *birkat ha-minim,* in its historical context, see Ray Pritz, *Nazarene Jewish Christianity: From the End of the New Testament Period until Its Disappearance in the Fourth Century* (Jerusalem: Magnes Press, and Leiden: E. J. Brill, 1988), 102–9.
6. Martyn, *History,* 62.
7. See the review article by D. Moody Smith in the third edition of Martyn, *History.*
8. Stephen Motyer, *Your Father the Devil? A New Approach to John and "the Jews"* (Carlisle, U.K.: Paternoster Press, 1997).
9. Ibid., 73.

10. Ibid., 148.
11. Ibid., 198.
12. Ibid., 212.
13. Daniel Boyarin, "The *Joudaioi* in John and the Pre-history of 'Judaism'," in *Pauline Conversations in Context: Essays in Honor of Calvin J. Roetzel*, ed. J. C. Anderson, P. H. Sellew, and C. Setzer (London: Sheffield Academic Press, 2002), 239.
14. They probably also viewed as treacherous the Jewish-Christians' flight to Pella during the first Jewish war against Rome (66–70 C.E.). I am indebted for this insight to a personal note from Walter A. Ziffer and to Pritz, *Nazarene Jewish Christianity,* 109.
15. "The Confession of 1967," I, C, 2; par. 9.27, in *The Constitution of the Presbyterian Church (U.S.A.), Part I: Book of Confessions* (Louisville, Ky.: The Office of the General Assembly, 1994), 265.

Glossary

Above/below. The contrast of above and below is a visual expression of Johannine dualism. Although "above" (*ano*) appears only seven times in the Gospel (3:3, 7, 31; 8:23; 19:11), usually in the expression "from above," and "below" (*kato*) only once (8:23), these terms express a view of ultimate reality that is fundamental to the Fourth Gospel. Jesus comes down from God or heaven above (3:13, 31; 6:33, 38; 8:42) and then returns from the world below to God above (13:1; 14:2, 12; 16:5, 17, 28; 17:11, 13; 20:17). While a linear view of history based on past, present, and future dominates the letters of Paul and the Synoptic Gospels, John is less concerned with time than with two planes of reality: above (the realm of God, life, light, spirit, and truth) and below (the realm of the world, flesh, the devil, darkness, and death). In the linear view, heaven, the goal and destiny of believers, lies in the future. In the Johannine view, however, heaven is a synonym for the realm above, from which Jesus came, to which he returned, and in which anyone who believes in him enjoys union with God now and forever. In the felicitous phrase of Robert Kysar, for John "eternity is now" (*Maverick Gospel,* 97), and believing in Jesus opens the possibility of belonging to another realm of reality while living in this world–of living the eternal life of communion with God in the spirit while still living in the flesh. Although "above" and "below" are spatial images, the language is not about physics. It is theology or metaphysics: that is, language about God and an ungodly world.

Believe. The stated purpose of the Fourth Gospel is to lead readers to believe in Jesus Christ, the Son of God (20:31). Believe is a major theme of the Gospel, from the prologue (1:12), through the accounts of varied reactions to Jesus (chaps. 1–12), to the climactic scene in which the risen Jesus leads Thomas to believe (20:26–29). "Believe" and "receive" are often used interchangeably in John to refer to a life-giving reaction to the revelation of God in Jesus Christ (1:12; 3:11–12; 12:48; 17:8). Although the verb is followed by "that" and a theological proposition in 20:31, the predominant object of belief in this Gospel is Jesus himself, and the desired response to him is more than intellectual assent to what he says. It is insight into who Jesus really is. In John, believing is often linked to seeing (2:23; 6:26, 30; 9:39–41) and to knowing (4:42; 6:69; 10:38; 16:30; 17:8). True belief means committing one's life to Jesus as Lord (20:28), continuing in his word (8:31), loving him, and keeping his commandments (14:15). John avoids the noun "faith" (*pistis*), which does not appear in the Fourth Gospel, but delights in the verb "believe" (*pisteuo*), which is used ninety-eight times, underscoring the evangelist's understanding of faith/belief as personal commitment to Jesus Christ, an inner movement of the heart expressed in active discipleship.

Father. The Fourth Gospel uses "God" 56 times and "Father" as a reference to God 120 times. All of these references to God as Father are on the lips of Jesus except the two in the prologue, which announce the intimate relationship between Jesus and God (1:14, 18), and one when Philip says to Jesus, "Lord show us the Father" (14:8). This phenomenon, peculiar to John, is not intended to affirm that God is male or to reinforce patterns of male domination, as the prominent role of women in this Gospel demonstrates. "Father" in the Fourth Gospel is not about paternity, which designates a physical relationship, but about fatherhood, which describes an intimate, loving, spiritual relationship (William Barclay, *The Letters of John and Jude* [Philadelphia: Westminster Press, 1960], 87).

Glory/glorify. In the Old Testament, "glory" is the English rendition of a word that can mean weight, substance, and honor or "the dazzling light of the Lord's presence," as the TEV aptly translates it in many Old Testament texts (Exod. 16:7, 10; 24:16–17; 33:18, 22; Ezek. 1:28; 8:4; 9:3). In the first half of John's Gospel, "glory" and "glorify" are often used in their ordinary New Testament sense of honor or praise (5:41, 44; 7:18; 8:50, 54). The specifically Johannine sense of "glory," however, is seen in Jesus' life and ministry (1:14; 2:11), especially in the interpretation of his death and resurrection (3:14; 7:39; 12:16, 23, 28; 13:31–32) and in the resurrection of Lazarus, which prefigures it (11:4, 40). Glory is the hidden but radiant splendor of God's inner nature, and to glorify is to reveal that inner nature in a way that honors God and inspires praise. Jesus' death and resurrection uniquely reveal God's true nature; through them Jesus and God are glorified. Jesus' great prayer brings together the glory he had with the Father before the world existed, the glory of his exaltation on the cross, and the glory he bequeaths to his disciples (17:1–5, 22–24).

"I Am" sayings. In seven texts in the Fourth Gospel, Jesus says, "I am," in a way reminiscent of God's self-revelation in the Old Testament:

1. Jesus said to her, "I am he (Gk.: I am), the one who is speaking to you." (4:26)
2. But he said to them, "It is I (Gk.: I am); do not be afraid." (6:20)
3. "for you will die in your sins unless you believe that I am he (Gk.: I am)." (8:24)
4. "When you have lifted up the Son of Man, then you will realize that I am he (Gk.: I am)." (8:28)
5. "Very truly, I tell you, before Abraham was, I am." (8:58)
6. "I tell you this now, before it occurs, so that when it does occur, you may believe that I am he (Gk.: I am)." (13:19)
7. Jesus replied, "I am he (Gk.: I am)." When Jesus said to them, "I am he (Gk.: I am)," they stepped back and fell to the ground. . . . Jesus answered, "I told you that I am he (Gk.: I am)." (18:5–6, 8)

In seven instances, Jesus' "I am" is followed by a predicate nominative and is a metaphor:

1. "I am the bread of life/the living bread." (6:35, 51)
2. "I am the light of the world." (8:12; 9:5)
3. "I am the gate [for the sheep]." (10:7, 9)
4. "I am the good shepherd." (10:11, 14)
5. "I am the resurrection and the life." (11:25)
6. "I am the way, and the truth, and the life." (14:6)
7. "I am the [true] vine." (15:1, 5)

Know. The Greek word for "know" is used almost fifty times in the Fourth Gospel. It covers a wide range of meanings and can be variously translated in different contexts: "learn," "come to know," "ascertain," "perceive," "recognize," "realize," "understand." Sometimes "know" means to become acquainted with (1:48, where is it used in parallel with "see"), sometimes it means to be inwardly persuaded (7:17, 26), and sometimes it refers to Jesus' clairvoyance or divine omniscience (2:24–25; 16:19; 21:17). More characteristically, however, "know" is used in the sense of intimate personal experience, rooted in Hebrew usage like that in Genesis 4:1 ("Now the man knew his wife Eve, and she conceived") and Matthew 1:25 ("[Joseph] knew her not till she had brought forth her firstborn son," AV). "Know" in the Fourth Gospel does not refer to sexual intercourse, but it does refer to the intimate personal relationship frequently expressed in this Gospel by the verb "abide" (15:4–7). The mutual indwelling of the believer with God and with Jesus Christ in the person of the Paraclete is the most characteristic meaning of "know" in the Fourth Gospel (14:7, 9, 17, 20; 16:3).

For John, to know God is neither intellectual assent to true doctrine nor knowledge of secret truth about God (as in Gnosticism), but a personal relationship of love based on recognizing who God is and what God has done in Jesus Christ. Knowing God in this sense is equated with eternal life (17:3).

Life. The goal of the Fourth Gospel is that through believing in Jesus its readers "may have life in his name" (20:31). Life is introduced as a major theme in the prologue, which affirms that "what has come into being in [the Word] was life, and the life was the light of all people" (1:4). As an essential attribute of God, life is eternal, and eternal life in Jesus Christ is a–if not the–central theme of John's Gospel. Of the three common Greek words for life, the Fourth Gospel uses *bios* not at all, and *psyche* ten times, carefully distinguishing it from *zoe,* which is used thirty-seven times. Eighteen of these usages are in the expression "eternal life" (*zoe aionion*), which is incarnate in Jesus Christ and given to all who believe in him. Many of the uses of "life" by itself in Jesus' dialogues and discourses also refer to "eternal life." In the Nicodemus passage, eternal life is the purpose of Christ's death, the goal of God's love, and a synonym for being saved (3:14–16, 36). "Life" figures prominently in Jesus' dialogue with the Samaritan woman at the well (4:14) and with his disciples on that occasion (4:36). It is central in his controversy with opponents (5:24, 40) and in his offer of himself as the bread of life to the crowd (6:27, 33, 35, 40, 47–48, 50–51, 54–58) and in his words to his disciples (6:63, 68). Two additional "I Am sayings" assert that Jesus is "the life" (11:25; 14:6). As the good shepherd, Jesus says, "I came that they may have life, and have it abundantly" (10:10), thereby pointing to the quality of the eternal life he came to give (10:28). In the summary of his teaching at the close of the first half of the Gospel, Jesus proclaims that the commandment the Father has given him to proclaim "is eternal life" (12:50), and in his great prayer at the end of part two, Jesus claims his authority over all people, "to give eternal life to all whom you have given him" (17:2). What follows is the only definition of eternal life in John: "And this is eternal life, that they may know you, the only true God, and Jesus Christ whom you have sent" (17:3).

What the evangelist means by life is expressed dramatically in two narratives about the victory of life over death: the raising of Lazarus (chap. 11) and the resurrection of Jesus (chap. 20). The life John is interested in is not primarily biological, nor is eternal life only chronological. For John life (*zoe*) is relational and qualitative. It signifies an intimate knowledge of God, available only through knowing Jesus Christ, God's only son, and it issues in abundant living.

Light/darkness. The diametrical opposition between light and darkness is a major theme in the theology of the Fourth Gospel (see **Above/below**). The theme is introduced in the prologue (1:4–9) and developed in the monologue following Jesus' encounter with Nicodemus (3:19–21). It is enunciated most clearly when Jesus says, "I am the light of the world. Whoever follows me will never walk in darkness but will have the light of life" (8:12). Its fullest elaboration is found in the narrative about Jesus healing a man born blind (9:1–39, esp. v. 5). There the affirmations about the Word, made in abstract language in the prologue (1:4–5), become flesh in Jesus and the blind beggar, while the darkness in which the light shines (1:5) becomes evident in the blindness of religious leaders who think they see (9:40–41). These leaders are referred to again as walking in darkness when Jesus speaks of those in Judea who wish to stone him (11:8–10). The theme of light and darkness is prominent in Jesus' summary speeches at 12:35–36a and 12:46.

Love. In the Fourth Gospel, love describes the relationship between God and the world, the Father and the Son, the Son and the Father, Jesus and his disciples, and his disciples and one another. Love is usually expressed as a verb (*agapao* thirty-six times, *phileo* thirteen times) but also as a noun (*agape* seven times, *philia* not at all). These two verbs seem to be used interchangeably in John (3:35/5:20; 11:3/11:5; 13:23/20:2; 14:23/16:27). Jesus' command to his disciples to love one another (13:34–35), linked with the command to "wash one another's feet" (13:14), constitutes the basis for their life together in a beloved community. Their love for one another is grounded in the love of God abiding in them (15:7–11), a teaching that is appropriately expounded and expanded in the First Epistle of John (2:10, 15; 3:10–18, 23; 4:7–21; 5:1–2). First John states that "God is love" (1 John 4:8). One can almost say that in the Fourth Gospel the Word is love.

Name. The Fourth Gospel reflects the Old Testament significance of a name and of the power which resided in it. The term is used once in the much weaker sense of *designation* (1:6; 18:10). More often, however, it indicates *representation*: "in my Father's name" (5:43a; 10:25); "in his own name" (5:43b); "in the name of the Lord" (12:13); "in my name" (14:26; 16:23). Frequently "in my name" is linked with "ask" and means "consistent with my *character*," "relying on my *power*" (14:13, 14; 15:16; 16:24, 26).

In significant verses "name" stands for the whole *person* or *self* (12:28; 17:6, 11, 12, 26), especially when linked with "believe." To believe in Jesus' name is to believe who Jesus is and what he does (1:12; 2:23; 3:18) and in believing to have life (20:31–32).

A characteristically Johannine understanding of "name" is that of *intimate relationship*. "He calls his own sheep by name" (10:3), and Mary Magdalene recognizes Jesus when he calls her by her name (20:16).

Signs. The seven miracle stories in John, all except the fifth accompanied by theological reflection and commonly called "signs," are:

1. Changing water to wine (2:1–11)
2. Healing a royal official's son (4:46–54)
3. Healing a paralytic at the pool of Bethesda (5:1–15)
4. Feeding five thousand people in Galilee (6:1–15)
5. Walking on the sea (6:16–21)
6. Healing a man blind from birth (9:1–41)
7. Raising Lazarus from the dead (11:1–57)

For uses of the term "Sign" in the Fourth Gospel, see notes on 20:30–31.

Truth. The word "truth" appears twenty-four times in the Fourth Gospel. Five times it simply denotes a statement that is accurate or that would hold up in court (5:31–32; 8:40, 45, 46; 16:7), but in key texts "truth" refers to ultimate reality revealed in personal terms (8:31–32; 14:6; 18:37–38). The personal nature of truth and its close connection with Jesus Christ are seen in Jesus' dialogue with the Samaritan woman (4:23–24); in his words about John the witness (5:33) and about the devil (8:44); in his references to the Holy Spirit as "the Spirit of truth" (14:17; 15:26; 16:13), who "will guide you into all the truth" (16:13a); in his prayer for his disciples, "Sanctify them in the truth; your word is truth" (17:17) and "that they also may be sanctified in truth" (17:19); and most vividly in his exchange with Pilate leading to the question, "What is truth?" (18:37–38). "Truth" has different nuances in these various contexts, but the basic note in the chord is sounded in the prologue: "Grace and truth came through Jesus Christ" (1:17).

Word. For the writer and first readers of the Gospel of John, the Word (*logos,* 1:1) had at least four dimensions of meaning, three from the Hebrew Bible and one from the Greek philosophical tradition.

From the Hebrew Bible:

1. *The Word as God's agent of creation.* All things were created by the word of God according to Genesis (1:1–3, 6, 9, 11, 14, 20, 24, 26), Psalms (33:6), and the Fourth Gospel (1:1–5). All of the seven signs by which Jesus reveals his identity in this Gospel turn upon his power over creation, the supreme demonstration of which is his power over death itself.

2. *The Word as revelation of God.* The basic role of prophets in the Hebrew Bible was to speak the words God gave them to say. Their oracles are commonly introduced or concluded by such expressions as "the word of the Lord came to me," "thus says the Lord," or simply "the word of the Lord." In the Fourth Gospel, Jesus is the supreme channel of God's revelation. He is commonly perceived first as a prophet (4:19; 6:14; 7:40; 9:17). He is the one sent by God to speak the words of God. He does only what the Father does (5:19) and says what God tells him to say (12:49). But he is more than a prophet (4:29, 42; 9:35–38). He is the Word that became flesh (1:14).

3. *The Logos as synonymous with the divine Wisdom.* The word of God is parallel to the personified wisdom of God (Prov. 8:22–23; Wis. 7:22, 25–26), so closely parallel that the two are used interchangeably in Solomon's prayer for wisdom in the Wisdom of Solomon (9:1–2), written in Greek by a hellenized Jew of Alexandria in 30 B.C.E. Writing in about 54 C.E., Paul called Jesus Christ "the power of God and the wisdom (*sophia*) of God (1 Cor. 1:24). In John 1:1–18 these understandings of God's word and God's wisdom are brought together by allusion and summed up in Jesus Christ, the incarnate Word of God.

From Greek philosophy and Hellenistic religion:

4. *The Logos as the principle of intelligent order governing the universe.* This idea, prominent in the writings of Philo of Alexandria, finds few if any explicit echoes in the body of the Fourth Gospel, but the coming of the Greeks to see Jesus (12:20–23) marks the opening of the Johannine community to the Hellenistic world, in which Hellenistic Jews already conceived of Wisdom, Word, and Logos as different ways to talk about the same creator God. John's identification of Jesus as the incarnation of the Logos later played a significant role in the theology of the Greek church fathers.

Although the Fourth Gospel opens with a hymn to the divine Logos or Wisdom, neither *sophia* nor *logos* as incarnate Word appears in the body of the Fourth Gospel. For John, the Word became flesh, and it is that incarnate life of the Word, seen and heard in the story of the life and teachings of Jesus, which brings God closer than any philosophical concept.

World. In the New Testament, "world" (*kosmos*) is used in four senses:

1. The universe, or all creation; "the cosmos" (3:17; 10:36; 13:1; 17:5, 11; see "all things" in 1:3).

2. All of humanity, the theater of the drama of redemption (1:9–10; 3:19; 4:42; 9:39; 11:27; 17:18; 18:36–37).

3. Humanity as the object of God's love (3:16–17; 6:33, 51; 8:12; 9:5; 12:46–47)

4. Unredeemed humanity, a metaphor for unbelief (1:10c; 7:7; 8:23; 12:31; 14:17, 27, 30; 15:18–19; 16:33; 17:14, 16, 25).

While the Gospel of John uses world (*kosmos*) in all of these senses, the vast majority of its eighty-one appearances are in the context of the cosmic struggle between light and darkness, belief and unbelief, Jesus and the "ruler of this world."

Select Bibliography

Barrett, C. K. *The Gospel according to St. John: An Introduction with Commentary and Notes on the Greek Text.* London: SPCK, 1956. [Cited in notes as Barrett, *Gospel*]

Brown, Raymond E. *The Community of the Beloved Disciple: The Life, Loves, and Hates of an Individual Church in New Testament Times.* New York: Paulist Press, 1979. [Brown, *Community*]

———. *The Death of the Messiah: From Gethsemane to the Grave: A Commentary on the Passion Narratives in the Four Gospels.* 2 vols. New York: Doubleday, 1994. [Brown, *Death*]

———. *The Gospel according to John.* The Anchor Bible. Garden City, N.Y.: Doubleday & Company, Inc., 1966, 1970. 2 vols. [Brown, *John*]

———. *An Introduction to the Gospel of John.* Edited, updated, introduced, and concluded by Francis J. Moloney. N.Y.: Doubleday, 2003. [Brown, *Introduction*]

Bultmann, Rudolf. *The Gospel of John: A Commentary.* Philadelphia: Westminster Press, 1971. [Bultmann, *John*]

Countryman, L. William. *The Mystical Way in the Fourth Gospel: Crossing Over into God,* rev. ed. Valley Forge, Pa.: Trinity Press, 1994. [Countryman, *Mystical Way*]

Culpepper, R. Alan. *Anatomy of the Fourth Gospel: A Study in Literary Design.* Philadelphia: Fortress Press, 1983. [Culpepper, *Anatomy*]

———. *The Gospel and Letters of John.* Interpreting Biblical Texts. Nashville: Abingdon Press, 1998. [Culpepper, *Gospel and Letters*]

Dodd, C. H. *The Interpretation of the Fourth Gospel.* Cambridge: Cambridge University Press, 1953. [Dodd, *Interpretation*]

Haenchen, Ernst. *John 1: A Commentary on the Gospel of John, Chapters 1–6.* Hermeneia. Philadelphia: Fortress Press, 1984. [Haenchen, *John*]

Howard-Brook, Wes. *Becoming Children of God: John's Gospel and Radical Discipleship.* Maryknoll, N.Y.: Orbis Books, 1994. [Howard-Brook, *Children of God*]

Kysar, Robert. *John, the Maverick Gospel,* rev. ed. Louisville, Ky.: Westminster John Knox Press, 1993. [Kysar, *Maverick Gospel*]

Martyn, J. Louis. *History and Theology in the Fourth Gospel*, 3d ed. Louisville, Ky.: Westminster John Knox Press, 2003. [Martyn, *History*]

Newbigin, Lesslie. *The Light Has Come: An Exposition of the Fourth Gospel.* Grand Rapids: William B. Eerdmans Publishing Co., 1982. [Newbigin, *Light*]

O'Day, Gail R. *The Gospel of John: Introduction, Commentary, and Reflections.* The New Interpreter's Bible, 9: 491–865. Nashville: Abingdon Press, 1995. [O'Day, *John*]

Rensberger, David. *Johannine Faith and Liberating Community.* Philadelphia: Westminster Press, 1988. [Rensberger, *Faith*]

Robinson, James M., ed. *The Nag Hammadi Library in English.* San Francisco: Harper & Row, 1988. [Robinson, *Nag Hammadi*]

Schnackenburg, Rudolf. *The Gospel according to St. John.* New York: Crossroad, 1990. [Schnackenburg, *St. John*]

Sloyan, Gerard S. *John.* Interpretation: A Bible Commentary for Teaching and Preaching. Atlanta: John Knox Press, 1988. [Sloyan, *John*]

Smith, D. Moody, Jr. *John.* Abingdon New Testament Commentaries. Nashville: Abingdon Press, 1999. [Smith, *John*]